A Man Most Driven

Captain John Smith, Pocahontas and the Founding of America

Peter Firstbrook

ONEWORLD

A Oneworld Book

First published by Oneworld Publications 2014

This paperback edition published 2015

A CIP record for this title is available from the British Library

ISBN 978-1-78074-710-1
Ebook ISBN 978-1-78074-107-9

Jacket design by Holly Macdonald
Typesetting and eBook design by Tetragon, London
Map artwork copyright © Peter Firstbrook
Printed and bound in Great Britain by Clays Ltd, St Ives plc

Oneworld Publications
10 Bloomsbury Street, London WC1B 3SR, England

Contents

For the two Georges in my life,

Father and Grandson

Author's Note

Nobody who writes about John Smith could do so without acknowledging two biographers from the past. Bradford Smith, together with his Hungarian colleague, the historian Laura Striker, published *John Smith: His Life & Legend* in 1953. Philip Barbour dedicated much of his later life to writing about Smith, including *The Three Worlds of Captain Smith* (1964) and many papers. Barbour's three-volume set, *The Complete Works of Captain John Smith* (1986), represents a lifetime's passion for the subject, and was published six years after his death.

For simplicity, all quotes from John Smith's writings have been taken from *The Complete Works*. Reading original Jacobean writing in its original form is demanding, so Barbour's typographic changes to Smith's original writings remain here. These include altering "u" to "v" where appropriate, and "v" to "u" where needed. The archaic "vv" has been changed to the modern "w", and I have used the modern "s" to replace "*ſ*". The many italicized words in the first editions have been set in roman.

Quotations from other individuals have been taken from Barbour's two-volume set, *The Jamestown Voyages 1606–1609* (1969), and from Edward Wright Haile's *Jamestown Narratives: Eyewitness Accounts of the Virginia Colony* (1998). The references make these selections clear.

Dates during this period can cause confusion. By the 1600s, the Julian calendar had drifted by ten days from the solar calendar, so some European countries had already adopted the more accurate Gregorian calendar. Italy, France, Portugal and Spain approved this new calendar in 1582, but England retained the Julian calendar until 1750. This biography is predominately about English history, so the old-style Julian calendar has been retained for English dates. Spanish, Italian and eastern European dates have been retained in the new style Gregorian calendar, and are indicted (NS).

However, the calendar is more complicated than this. During the period in question, the New Year also varied. Throughout this book, the modern day for New Year on January 1 is used, rather than the old-style New Year, which began in March. In the old-style, John Smith's baptism day was January 9, 1579, and appears in some modern sources as January 9, 1579/80; here I have used the simpler form, January 9, 1580.

The name of Virginia's first settlement is variously called "James Fort", "James Towne", "Jamestowne" and "James Cittie" in the literature. For consistency, Jamestown has been used throughout. Foreign words are shown in italics.

The correct terminology used to describe the indigenous peoples of the Americas is a topic of ongoing debate. When the English colonists arrived, the region was settled by a confederation of tribes led by a *mamanatowick*, or paramount chief, called Wahunsenacawh. He was known more commonly by the English as Powhatan, after the name of the village where he was most likely born. Each tribe within the Powhatan empire had its own name, and whenever possible I have referred to these peoples by their tribal affiliation. Collectively they are known as Algonquian-speaking peoples, Tidewater people, or most simply the Powhatan.

The term "Indian" results from an historic error made by the Europeans, and where possible I have tried to avoid perpetuating this terminology. Likewise, I have preferred to use the name Wahunsenacawh rather than Powhatan or Chief Powhatan. However, for historical reasons these words do creep into the text occasionally, particularly when referring to the contemporary English or European view of their neighbours (and of course they also appear in the colonists' quotes). When used, no disrespect is intended.

A Man Most Driven

An apocryphal tale? *John Smith Saved by Pocahontas,* painted by Alonzo Chappel, circa 1865.

Prologue

Yet God made Pocahontas the Kings daughter
the meanes to deliver me: and thereby taught me
to know their trecheries to preserve the rest
John Smith, New England Trials (1622)

On December 30, 1607, an Englishman was dragged before the paramount chief of the native Powhatan tribes of Virginia. His abductors brought out two large rocks, and placed him with his head resting on the boulders. He lay prostrate, waiting for a mercifully swift execution. It was dark inside the longhouse, and as the prisoner's eyes adjusted slowly to the gloom he became aware that, around him, about two hundred people were looking on in fascination. For most, it was their first sight of a European.

The prisoner was strong but not tall, standing only as high as his guards' shoulders. His thick beard mainly covered the ruddy complexion of someone who had spent most of his life in the open. The man was a few days short of his twenty-eighth birthday, an anniversary he did not expect to celebrate. As he lay on the ground, the guards raised their war clubs above his head, waiting for the command from their chief to execute the prisoner in their traditional manner – by beating the brains out of his skull.

From the shadows of the smoke-filled longhouse, a young girl of perhaps ten or twelve emerged, naked from the waist up, and with only a wisp of black hair hanging down from the back of her shaved head. She turned to the great man presiding over the ceremony, with a familiarity and self-confidence that suggested she knew the chief well. She did, for he was her father. The girl pleaded for the stranger's life to be spared. The Englishman understood little about what was being said, for his comprehension of the Algonquian language was still rudimentary.

The chief considered his daughter's appeal carefully. He was an old man, perhaps sixty or seventy years, broad-shouldered, fit and powerfully built for his age. He wore a robe of raccoon skins with the tails still attached, and around his neck a chain of pearls. He was clearly held in awe by all those present, and "at the least frowne of his brow, their greatest will tremble with feare".[1] The chief was dispassionate as he considered the young girl's request, his face showing "such a grave and Majesticall countenance".[2]

The Englishman had no option but to await the judgement that would soon enough seal his fate.

The rescue of Captain John Smith, English soldier and adventurer, by the "Indian princess" Pocahontas is one of the oldest and most enduring legends to come out of the colonization of America. Smith wrote that "at the minute of my execution, she hazarded [risked] the beating out of her owne braines to save mine".[3] Since that bitterly cold afternoon in late December 1607, the story has been celebrated worldwide in books, paintings, feature films and animated cartoons.

The only European witness to the event was Smith himself, and his account has been questioned ever since it was first published in 1624. If the only debatable episode in Smith's extraordinary life was this encounter with Pocahontas, then his version of events might not have attracted quite so much attention – or derision. But this was not the case.

Smith's autobiography, *The True Travels, Adventures and Observations of Captain John Smith*, is packed full of the most incredible incidents: that he fought, defeated and beheaded three enemy commanders in duels; that he was sold into slavery, only to murder his master and escape; that he was captured by pirates, survived shipwrecks and marched up to the gallows to be hanged – only to be reprieved at the last moment. All this happened, or so John Smith claimed, even before he met Pocahontas and her father.

Some of Smith's achievements are beyond dispute, most especially his success in saving the Jamestown settlement in Virginia during its first two brutal winters. The surviving settlers recognized that Smith had exercised his skill and experience to help them survive. But he was also a difficult and argumentative man, and he clashed constantly with his fellow colonists. One leader of the colony called Smith "an ambitious, unworthy, and vainglorious fellow".[4]

Centuries later, this reputation lived on. Rather than being universally lauded for saving England's first permanent settlement in the Americas – which ultimately led to North America becoming part of the English-speaking world – Smith was vilified, maligned and pilloried. Was he really such a villain? Or might he be the victim of envy, internal division and misrepresentation, both in his own day and in the historical record?

Indeed, Smith never lost his capacity to stir indignation among his detractors, or to arouse great loyalty in his supporters. He combined admirable strengths with great weaknesses: he was authoritarian and autocratic, yet also vulnerable and insecure. His life was a catalogue of defiance and confrontation, disorder and contradiction. It is these flawed and very human characteristics that make him such a fascinating character.

In his own writings, Smith did little to endear himself to a sceptical reader, or to an assiduous historian. He frequently claimed he was in the right, and that others were grossly incompetent. His spelling was chaotic, his grammar confused, and his dates and timelines an embarrassment to any self-respecting chronicler. In his defence, Smith neither claimed to be an historian, nor would have expected scholars or writers to be poring over his memoirs more than four hundred years after his birth. Nevertheless, given his inflated ego, he would most certainly have taken great satisfaction from knowing that one day this would be the case.

Smith left many diaries and memoirs of his astonishing exploits, but which of his more fanciful claims are the writings of a deceitful self-publicist – and which are anchored in the historical record?

This new evaluation of John Smith combines an appraisal of his life with a detective story, as we follow in his footsteps, constantly challenging and assessing his claims. In doing so, we can test his writings against the local history and geography, about which he wrote so much.

In every sense, Smith was a true Renaissance man: a soldier of fortune, captain of cavalry, colonist, adventurer, diplomat, surveyor and mapmaker; he was also a pirate, a mercenary and a self-confessed murderer. Unravelling the facts from the fiction is complex, but the truth is more revealing and intriguing than you might ever have imagined.

So what can we make of this man? Is he villain or victim? Even making exception for his archaic writing style, it remains to be seen whether Captain John Smith deserves such redemption.

Smith spent his childhood in the village of Willoughby, Lincolnshire, and many of the sights he would have known, including the font in which he was baptized, still stand today (photo by Peter Firstbrook).

I

Apprentice

1580–1600

His minde being even then set upon brave adventures, sould his Satchell, bookes, and all he had, intending secretly to get to Sea

John Smith, *The True Travels (1630)*

On the evening of July 26, 1588,[1] 130 Spanish galleons and armed merchant ships anchored off Calais, a small town on the northwest coast of France. It was the largest fleet ever seen in European waters. The *Armada Invencible* – literally the "Invincible Great Fleet" – had been sent by King Philip II of Spain to rendezvous with a sixteen-thousand-strong army under the command of the Duke of Parma, the governor of the Spanish-occupied Netherlands. Philip's plan was for the invasion fleet to secure a landing zone in the Thames estuary, and then ferry Parma's army across the Channel in barges. Their combined forces of over thirty thousand soldiers would then march on London and claim the English crown for Philip, removing the Protestant English queen from the throne and replacing her with a Catholic monarch. It was an audacious scheme but one that many felt was long in the coming.

For decades, much of the European continent had been torn apart by religious wars fought between the mainly Protestant north and the largely Catholic south. Now Europe's rulers awaited word from the Channel with fascination and fear, as mighty Spain decided to wield its formidable power against its rival.

The English had first sighted Philip's warships off the coast of Cornwall just eight days previously, although the arrival of the fleet had been expected for some time. Beacons were lit across the south to warn the Queen of the impending invasion. This was the moment England had dreaded, for the country was ill prepared for war against Spain, easily the most powerful nation in Europe at the time. Panic spread across the capital. Mobs attacked foreigners at random, and a force of ten thousand men roamed the streets, hunting out papists and spies. Spanish agents were everywhere. One reported back to Philip that the local militia drilled twice a week and were "certainly very good troops considering they are recruits".[2]

When the Spanish fleet arrived off Calais, they found Parma's army was not ready for action – he needed at least another six days of preparations for his forces. Today, Calais is a busy cross-channel ferry port, but in 1588 there was no deep-water harbour where a large fleet might find protection. Instead, the Armada anchored between Calais' sandy beaches and the treacherously shallow banks offshore. The admiral of the fleet, the Duke of Medina Sidonia, understood well enough that his ships were vulnerable at anchor, but there was little else he could do.

As darkness fell, Sidonia did not have to wait long for the English to seize their opportunity. At midnight, his lookouts were horrified to see eight fire-ships bearing down on them in the freshening southwesterly breeze. The vessels lit up the night sky, their decks cracking and buckling as the inferno engulfed the wooden hulls. The Spanish commanders feared the fire-ships were packed with gunpowder, which could obliterate their anchored fleet. In fact gunpowder was in short supply in England, and the fire-ships were filled mostly with pitch, brimstone and tar – all highly combustible but not dangerously explosive. Nevertheless, the tactical effect on the Spanish fleet was immediate.

The well-organized commanders of the principal warships held their positions, but the rest of the fleet – mostly merchant ships with less disciplined crews – cut their anchor cables and took flight. In the panicked confusion, many ships collided, although all managed to avoid the fire-ships. Unable to restore order to the fleet, Sidonia's force was vulnerable. It was time for the English warships to close for action.

The two navies clashed a few miles northeast of Calais, off Gravelines. The English commanders had learned much about the strengths and weaknesses of the Spanish fleet during previous skirmishes in the Channel. They knew, for example, that the large quantities of supplies carried below decks made it difficult for the Spaniards to reload their heavy guns. So the English captains held off at a distance and provoked the enemy gunners into wasting their shot. Then the smaller but more manoeuvrable English ships moved to within one hundred yards of the enemy. After eight hours of close bombardment, the English themselves began to run short of ammunition. Some gunners resorted to using chains in their guns when they ran out of cannon balls. By four in the afternoon, the English sailors' gunpowder was running low, and they withdrew.

Five Spanish ships were lost and several others severely damaged. As the wind veered to the south and strengthened, the "Invincible Great Fleet" was unable to muster a counter-attack, and had no choice but to sail north. Every one of Sidonia's precious warships survived its retreat into the North Sea, but many of the weaker armed merchant vessels were wrecked off the coasts of Scotland and Ireland; nearly half the Armada was lost. King Philip's plan to join forces with Parma's army had been thwarted, and the English gained some breathing space in their undeclared war with Spain.

With the Armada repulsed, England celebrated, and bells rang out from every church in the land. A whole generation of young men and boys grew up, inspired by the heroes of the day: Lord Howard, Sir Francis Drake, Sir Walter Raleigh, Sir John Hawkins. All were renowned for their expertise on the sea, but now the Spanish dreaded them. With men like this commanding the English navy, God must surely be on the side of the Queen. A thanksgiving service was held at St Paul's Cathedral, and a commemorative medal struck, which carried the words: "God blew and they were scattered".[3] The English people genuinely believed the tempest that overwhelmed the Armada was no ordinary storm, but the work of their Protestant God.

Although the Spanish Empire remained dominant for several decades to come, the routing of the Armada marked the beginning of a shift in the balance of naval and global supremacy. England no longer considered itself a second-rate power. The year 1588 was a hinge point in the nation's history, as it opened prospects abroad for a new generation of adventurous young men. Prospects perhaps best displayed in one of the enduring icons of that year: an oil painting of Queen Elizabeth by

Queen Elizabeth after the defeat of the Armada, in a portrait attributed to George Gower (circa 1588); her hand rests on a globe as if to encourage her great naval heroes to broaden their horizons (courtesy of the National Portrait Gallery, London).

George Gower, called the *Armada Portrait*. The window to the left of the seated queen shows English ships bearing down on the Spanish fleet; the window on her right depicts the Armada wrecked on a rocky shore. Most tantalizing of all is Elizabeth's right hand, which rests, relaxed and confident, on a globe. Her fingers point towards the Americas, as if to encourage her loyal and exuberantly joyous subjects to take up the next great challenge of her reign – the English expansion overseas.

One hundred and forty miles north of London, in the county of Lincolnshire, lies the small village of Willoughby. In the year of the Armada, the village comprised a handful of thatched cottages clustered around the church of St Helena, the patron saint of archaeologists. The parish church, built of square-coursed greenstone, has its origins in the early fourteenth century.

A short walk across the fields from the church is a red-brick house called Covells Farm House. The house has been substantially rebuilt from the traditional thatched, "mud and stick" dwelling of 1588, when the bells of St Helena were peeling to announce the defeat of the Armada. In those days, the residents of the house were tenant farmer George Smith and his wife, Alice.

There is no record of the actual birth date of their first-born son, John, but the parish register shows he was baptized on January 9, 1580. In those times, superstitions as well as infant mortality ran high, and parents christened their children on the day of their birth if they possibly could.[4] It was believed a baby was born with original sin, and if the infant died before baptism, it would remain in limbo – on the edge of Hell – for eternity. No God-fearing family would wish such a fate on their newborn. The octagonal stone font baby John was baptized in is still in use, and the remnants of metal hasps once used to secure a wooden lid to prevent witches from stealing the holy water, are still visible on top.

John was followed by a second son, Francis, baptized November 6, 1581. A third son, Richard, and a daughter, Alice, were christened together on July 16, 1586, so they must have been twins; baby Richard only lived for ten days.

The village of Willoughby (or "Wilgebi" or "Willebi", according to the Domesday Book of 1086) lies on the edge of the Lincolnshire Wolds, an area of low, rolling hills and steep valleys. Here, the mix of poor and good land had long been shared fairly between tenant farmers, even before the Domesday Book was written. George Smith's fields were divided into strips, each a furlong long (660 feet), the distance a team of oxen could plough without resting. The fields were a chain wide (66 feet), giving a cultivated area of an acre, which was as much as a man could till in a day. Because the good and poor land was distributed evenly between the farmers, Smith's fields were scattered around the parish. Like most English villages of the period, the pasture grazing was common land, shared by all.

The parish recorder offered a meticulous accounting of the contents of the Smith home in 1596.[5] The family ate from pewter plates, rather than the wooden platters typically used in poorer households. There were at least four feather beds; not the poorer man's straw mattress equivalents. The kitchen contained eight "kittles", five "pannes", three brass pots and "on[e] pot of butte[r] that hath vi [six] cakes". In the farm, the inventory lists three young horses, four mares, two oxen, six cows, and five calves. There were two ploughs plus other farming implements, hay in the yard and corn in the barn. George Smith's chattels were listed as being worth £77 16s 2d (about two years' wages for a craftsman).[6] Such relative wealth meant he could employ a servant girl, and probably a farm labourer or two. George Smith was no impoverished peasant farmer, reliant on the vagaries of storm and drought, or the whims of a capricious landlord. His house was well equipped, and his farm fully stocked with animals, equipment and foodstuffs.

Even so, George claimed to be a "poore tenant" of Peregrine Bertie, the 13th Baron Willoughby de Eresby. Like any typical English tenant farmer, he did not own the land he worked, but instead paid an annual tithe to his landlord. However, George also had his own land, for his will listed seven acres in Great Carlton, Lincolnshire, plus "two tenements" and a house in Louth. Despite these acquisitions, George did not aspire to the title of "gentleman", nor even that of "yeoman". Either title would have brought with it greater social responsibilities – and higher taxes. In the inventory of his estate, he is referred to simply as a "husbandman", a term for a free tenant farmer or small landowner.

Nevertheless, George was for the most part a respected and trusted figure in the community. The court rolls show he was called to be a juror several times between 1584 and 1591.[7] He did run afoul of the law himself on several occasions, appearing before the same court in which he sometimes served as a juror.

We can infer from this information that George Smith was a humble man, content with his position in life and with little ambition to improve it. His father's lack of social ambition probably rankled with John, who spent much of his life fighting the archaic and rigid system of class mobility in England.

Elizabethan society had a well-defined hierarchy: the monarch was God's representative on Earth; the nobility ranked second; the gentry third; then merchants, yeomanry and labourers in descending order. It was believed God had ordained this structure, and each group had specific privileges and responsibilities. Parliament regulated the clothes each class could wear, and it was considered insolent for a member of a lower order to dress in the apparel of the rich. The lords in Parliament claimed these rules helped ensure the maintenance of social order, and they also provided a quick and easy way to identify those of rank and privilege.

It was, however, sometimes possible to move up (or down) the social ladder. The titled nobility recruited from the ranks of wealthy merchants, and bankrupts and defaulters continuously renewed the lowest levels of society. Still, movement between social classes was not straightforward. One route, which no doubt appealed to John Smith, was through profitable ventures. Francis Drake, for example, was the eldest son of a Devonshire farmer; he was knighted by Queen Elizabeth in 1581 for his success as a privateer. The fact that Drake's godfather was Francis Russell, 2nd Earl of Bedford, had, of course, helped matters. Yet despite Drake's strong family connections and his undoubted achievements as a sailor, he was not exempt from derision. As late as 1592, when Drake's triumphs were more than obvious, the Spanish military officer Gonzalo González del Castillo claimed in a letter to King Philip II: "The people of quality dislike him for having risen so high from such a lowely family."[8] Such was the snobbery of late sixteenth-century England.

Despite the shining example of heroes such as Drake, John Smith was reminded regularly of the social ceiling through which a freeman found it all but impossible to rise. Breeding and contacts were everything. No matter how experienced, intelligent, well-informed and competent you might be, if you were not born into the right family, sent to a good school and then a university where you would make valuable contacts, the opportunity to elevate yourself was very limited.

John understood this. He was born into a comfortable but unpretentious household, which held few obligations for the family – but also few opportunities for the son.

In Willoughby, as in every small village across the land, households aimed to be self-sufficient except for an occasional visit to the flour-mill or blacksmith. During the long days of summer, the men were in the fields from daybreak to dusk. During the winter, they spent their time making and mending, repairing implements, tanning leather, carving wooden spoons and bowls, and preparing for the new season. By today's standards, life was tough, tenuous and mind-numbingly tedious.

John's youth was marked by a repetitive annual cycle of hard labour: ploughing, sowing, planting, felling, lambing, shearing, harvesting, slaughtering and then ploughing again. From an early age, John and his brother Francis would have worked in the fields alongside their father. Meanwhile, their sister, Alice, was at their mother's side, helping to cook, preserve, spin and darn. Covells Farm House still has its original vast fireplace, where Alice would have gently stirred a cast-iron stew pot and hung freshly slaughtered legs of pork to preserve in the wood smoke.

However, by 1588, the year that St Helena's bells rang out news of the Armada's defeat, John was already attending a free "petty school" in the market town of Alford, a four-mile walk from home. (The term "petty" probably derived from the French word *petit.*) Schooling might have relieved him of the drudgery of the fields, but life as a schoolboy in sixteenth-century England was no easy option either.

For the next four years, John's day followed the highly structured routine prescribed in the "manner books" of the period. The explosion in printing during the sixteenth century produced manuals on behaviour for every imaginable social situation. As soon as he woke, the young schoolboy would pray, wash, dress, clean his shoes, comb his hair and make his bed; he would then greet his parents and pack his satchel with quill and ink, a penknife, books and paper. There was no breakfast, so his morning walk to school was on an empty stomach. Smith would then have worked until eleven, when the children paused for a midday meal. Lessons resumed at one o'clock and continued until five, when the boys had prayers and were released. John would rarely have been home before early evening.

The petty school in Alford was established in 1566 with a donation of fifty pounds from a local merchant. It was later granted a charter by Queen Elizabeth, "for the Education, Instruction and bringing up of children and Youth for ever to continue".[9] Today, it is a successful grammar school with nearly six hundred students; when John attended, the classroom held barely a dozen pupils.

The school was in a tiny room over the front porch of Alford's parish church, St Wilfrid's. The church is built on a slight rise and has dominated the small market town ever since it was established in the fourteenth century. Remarkably, the schoolroom Smith attended still exists. To reach it involves climbing a narrow, stone spiral staircase before pushing open a heavy oak door to reveal a tiny room with a small fireplace in one corner.

In Elizabethan England, religion was an essential part of a child's education, and so too was Latin – the language of law and the clerics, even after the English Reformation. Every English schoolboy learned from *Lily's Grammar of Latin* – a primer prescribed by Queen Elizabeth since 1559. Lessons at petty school were correspondingly prescriptive, and John's education involved learning to read and write English, to use good manners and behaviour.[10] The Catechism, a critical part of the recent religious reforms, outlined the particulars of the English Protestant faith; children were expected to learn its passages by heart. John read his lessons from a "hornbook", a parchment usually pasted to a wooden board with a handle, and covered with a thin sheet of transparent horn, which made it both durable and inexpensive to produce. The board itself presented the fundamentals of learning: the alphabet in uppercase and lowercase letters, together with the Lord's Prayer (in English) and the sign of the Christian cross.

Notwithstanding these Christian teachings, young John grew into an argumentative and truculent man who regularly questioned those in authority. He is unlikely to have picked up these qualities from his father, who by all accounts was self-effacing and modest. Nor was he likely to have learned them from a close reading of the Bible or the Catechism. However, his schoolmaster, the Reverend Francis Marbury, set a very different example.

The Cambridge-educated Marbury proved to be an irritating thorn in the side of the Anglican Church early in his career as a cleric and teacher. The Reformation was still in its infancy, and many Protestants believed fervently that the reforms had not gone far enough to cleanse the church of Catholic rites. The most vocal of these critics were the Puritans, and Marbury was a member of one of the most radical of their factions – the Presbyterians. The fiery cleric often found himself called upon by God to accuse the bishops of placing badly educated and poorly trained ministers in parish churches.

His bishops took understandable exception to his views, but even more to his outspokenness. On November 5, 1578, Marbury was tried at an ecclesiastical court in St Paul's Cathedral in London. It seems this was a rancorous exchange between the deacon and the Bishop of London, who called him "a very ass, an idiot, and a fool".[11] Marbury was found guilty of heresy and locked up for two years in the notorious Marshalsea Prison, on the south side of the River Thames in Southwark.[12] (The appalling conditions there became widely known after Charles Dickens featured the prison in his novel *Little Dorrit*.)

Marbury was released from Marshalsea in 1580 at the age of twenty-five. Now considered "reformed", he was sent to what was then considered a remote posting: Alford. It was close to his ancestral home, and in that there was a small blessing. He rose to be curate (deputy vicar) of St Wilfrid's parish church, and was then appointed master of the petty school in 1585, not long before John Smith arrived.

Marbury must have been a formidable figure, towering over his impressionable young students as he lectured them. Unfortunately, the schoolmaster could not hold his tongue, and by 1590 he was in trouble again. This time the outspoken curate accused the bishops of being "self-seeking soul murderers" – these blasphemous words articulated from the pulpit of St Wilfred's, no less! In return, the incensed Bishop of Lincoln called Marbury an "impudent Puritan", removed him from preaching and teaching, and put him under house arrest for the next three years.[13]

The Jesuit motto "Give me a child until he is seven and I will give you the man" is allegedly based on the words of Francis Xavier. It is certainly a reminder of the power of early teaching. While there is no direct evidence of how Marbury might have influenced John Smith, Marbury's daughter, Anne Hutchinson – born the year after her father was removed from his teaching post at Alford – may provide some clues. Anne was better educated than most girls of the period, and her father kept a close rein on the direction of her schooling, particularly during her earliest years when he was under house arrest. Like her father, Anne held deep religious convictions that were at odds with the established clergy, and she had the self-belief to challenge the orthodoxy of the time. Later, at her own trial in America, the Reverend Hugh Peter of Salem said Anne had "stepped out of [her] place". He went on to accuse her of being more of "a preacher than a hearer; and a magistrate than a subject".[14] She too was subsequently banished by the court for her outspoken beliefs – not to a rectory garden like her father, but to Rhode Island.

Marbury clearly imparted his contempt for authority on Anne, so it is likely some of his radical beliefs, as well as his temperament, rubbed off on his pupils in Alford. Undoubtedly, ten-year-old schoolboy John Smith would have learned that Marbury had been placed under house arrest for righteously speaking his mind. It was a model of honourable behaviour that Smith would emulate more than once in later life.

In 1592 or 1593, John's father packed his oldest son off to the King Edward VI grammar school. The school was in Louth, a large market town some fifteen miles northwest of Willoughby, and John was a boarder there from around the age of twelve to fifteen. Louth was certainly a step up from Alford, with its Wednesday and Saturday markets and a fair three times a year. The town was larger, louder and rowdier than anything John had experienced, and to his young eye it must have seemed a metropolis. Today, Louth is a refined Georgian market town, but there are buildings still standing there that give a hint to what it was like in Smith's day – thatched houses with wattle and daub walls, small windows, and doors so low you have to stoop to enter. John's father is thought to have owned at least one house in Westgate, and it is possible John lived there when he was at school.

John's classroom in his petty school in Alford (left), over the front porch of the parish church, as it appears today (photo by Peter Firstbrook). Following the dissolution of the religious guilds in 1548, the King Edward VI Grammar School, Louth (the school seal is shown right) was given a royal charter as well as a handsome endowment. By enrolling John in the King Edward VI Grammar School, John's father revealed he had grand ambitions for his son (courtesy of National Education Network).

King Edward VI is one of the oldest schools in England, tracing its origins back to 1276 or earlier. The school regime was strict, with rigid rules governing behaviour: no taunting of masters, no obscene language, no wearing of daggers and no drunkenness. Indeed, the school's seal bore a revealing inscription, translated from the Latin: "He that spareth the rod hateth his son." To ensure the message was not lost, the seal also showed a pupil being thrashed soundly by his schoolmaster.

Apart from the basics of Latin, English grammar and mathematics, the school drummed into Smith strong moral principles: self-discipline, resilience, moderation and a keen sense of justice. George Smith must have held high ambitions for his son, because the costs to keep his son at grammar school were significant, not to mention the loss of the boy's labour on the family farm.

However, John was not a diligent student. When he was thirteen, he claimed to have sold his satchel and books with the intention of running away to sea. On his return to school, his punishment would have been only too predictable.

In 1595, George Smith arranged for his son to be apprenticed to a prominent merchant called Thomas Sendall, of King's Lynn. A young man in John's position would normally be expected to take over the family farm, and this was likely his father's plan. However, a life of hard labour in the Lincolnshire fields seemed not to appeal to John. He wrote in *The True Travels* that as a young boy, "his minde being even then set upon brave adventures"[15]; he wanted more. A merchant's apprenticeship might well have been a compromise acceptable to his father; a livelihood based on trade was safe and comfortable and would make good use of the education George had secured for his son. In time, the job might also allow John to rise to be a member of Sendall's merchant class.

Smith never recorded how he travelled to King's Lynn to pursue his new path towards adulthood. If he walked, he would have taken a sixty-five-mile course that curved around the edges of the low-lying fens which surround the Wash. Attempts to drain the Fenland did not start until the 1630s, so his journey would have been treacherous, traversing wetlands criss-crossed with creeks and ditches, and flooded frequently by the sea. Daniel Defoe described the area as "a flat, level, and often drowned country, like Holland itself; here the very ditches are navigable, and the people pass from town to town in boats, as in Holland".[16] Smith might instead have picked a passage on a coastal ship out of Skegness, Wainfleet or Boston to take him across the Wash to King's Lynn, taking his first chance at sea. If so, it would have been the first of many sea voyages for the young man. In any case, when he got to King's Lynn, he was a world away from the monotony of a life of farming.

As he entered the town John would have been dazzled by the frenetic pace of a busy port. Walking around the harbour, his ears would have been assaulted by the cacophony of half a dozen European languages. The merchant ships were bigger than anything he had seen before, and newcomers strained their necks trying to take them in. An intoxicating perfume of tar and oakum, seaweed and raw sewage hung thickly in the air, and commotion was everywhere. It was a heady mix, and John must have known it signalled more than just his own excitement: here was adventure and opportunity.

King's Lynn had prospered from its position on the country's east coast. The port's merchants had developed a successful trade in wool with the Hanseatic League, a confederation of merchant guilds in the Baltic and North Sea that prospered between the thirteenth and seventeenth centuries. By the 1590s the town's main export was grain. In return, iron, timber and pitch were brought in from the Continent.

The merchant Thomas Sendall became wealthy on this trade – Smith called him "the greatest Merchant of all those parts"[17] – and Sendall was honoured three times with the title of mayor of the town. Appropriate to his standing, Sendall lived in a grand town house on Nicholas Street, close to the harbour and warehouses. (The building is used today as a hotel, which is reputed to be haunted; the huge oak beam over the Elizabethan fireplace still bears the signs of an exorcism.) This was where John Smith unpacked his bags and began his apprenticeship.

John had a binding agreement with Sendall. In return for board and lodging he would sit at a desk all day, poring over the merchant's ledgers. This was not what he had in mind when he left home, dreaming of journeys upon the ocean alongside Sir Francis Drake.

Fate, however, intervened. John had been working for Sendall for less than a year when George Smith died. On April 3, 1596, John returned home to Willoughby to bury his father at St Helena's church. The division of George Smith's earthly possessions followed, John's father having made his will a few days previously, already being "in bodie weake and paynde".[18] Officiating duties were handled outside the family, as George Smith had asked his friend, George Metham, to supervise the division of the estate. To Peregrine Bertie (Lord Willoughby), George left the best of his young colts. George's wife received ten pounds (worth over one thousand pounds today), a bedstead and furnishings, together with the farm at Willoughby, with the proviso that if she remarried, the property went to his eldest son. John got his father's seven acres of pasture in Great Carlton, while Francis was bequeathed the two tenements and the house in Louth; Alice received ten pounds, a bedstead and half the brass and pewter. The poor of Willoughby were also awarded a small donation.

After his father's funeral, John did not return to Sendall's house. Whether Sendall realized the boy's heart was not in the task and decided he was better off without him, or whether John simply chose not return, is not clear. Either way, John was released from following his father's plan, and now, with a modest income from his inheritance, he could take off on his own course. Or so he thought.

In a testy comment in *The True Travels*, Smith complained "the Guardians of his estate more regarding it than him, he had libertie enough, though no meanes, to get beyond the Sea."[19] It appears his father's old friend, George Metham, intervened and blocked his ambitions. Metham would almost certainly have wanted John, as the eldest son and heir, to stay with his mother on the farm. Young John's plans to travel were considered inappropriate.

John's future, however, was not put on hold for long. His mother remarried a few months after George's death, and the farm went to John, according to the terms of the will. The name of her new husband, Martin Johnson, is not found in the Willoughby parish register, which suggests he was from outside the village. The couple moved away, possibly to Boston (more than a day's travel from Willoughby), where Johnson died in 1609.

In the sixteenth century, adults rarely stayed unmarried for long after the death of their partner. Life was too difficult to face alone, especially for a woman. Nevertheless, John considered the speed of his mother's remarriage inappropriate. There is no evidence he ever saw his mother again after the household effects were inventoried in February 1597. A later comment that she had died "when he was about thirteene" – many years earlier than was the fact – may suggest he remained angry about her swift remarriage for the rest of his life.

It's quite possible John felt rejected by his mother, and that once she had a new husband, he considered himself to have no further responsibility for her wellbeing. With his newly acquired income from the farm, he was no longer tied to school, village, apprenticeship or family. He was now a free agent.

Towards the end of 1596, while John was pondering his future prospects, alarming news began to reach England of yet another attempted invasion by the Spanish. Reports varied over exactly where the new Armada intended to strike, but there is historical evidence that the plan was to land fifteen thousand Spanish troops in either Plymouth or Portsmouth, where they could attack key naval dockyards.[20] However, the Spanish plot was defeated by the winds once again. The 1596 Armada left too late in the year, and in mid-October a severe southwesterly gale decimated the fleet. Seven galleons, twenty-five merchant ships, several smaller craft and two thousand men were lost. Nonetheless, it was a timely reminder. Elizabeth's Protestant England was still vulnerable to the might of Philip's Catholic Spain.

There were several options available to an enterprising young man looking to satisfy his appetite for adventure in the late sixteenth century. He could go to sea, perhaps joining the crew of a ship engaged in privateering, in the hopes of relieving the Spanish of their riches on the transatlantic gold run. Alternatively, he could try his hand in Ireland, where the English crown had confiscated land from the clans and was encouraging colonization by English settlers. John Smith eventually did both in later years, but in 1597 he chose a third option: fighting the Spanish Catholics on dry land.

Smith's record of this period in his life is brief, and the chronology is confusing – again adding to earlier biographers' frustrations. A brief line in *The True Travels* mentions a trip to the Continent, where he planned to join Captain Joseph Duxbury's regiment as it prepared to fight in the Spanish Netherlands:

> Peace being concluded in France, he went with Captaine Joseph Duxbury into the Low-countries [the Netherlands], under whose Colours having served three or foure yeeres.[21]

It is a tantalizing hint at Smith's new role as a mercenary, and his references to Duxbury and peace in France have historical credibility. In France, King Henry IV had recently settled his disagreements with Pope Clement VIII, who lifted his excommunication of Henry and declared him to be the "most Christian King of France and Navarre"[22] (despite

Henry's past as a practising Calvinist). This suggests Smith crossed over to the Continent in the spring or summer of 1597.

At the time, the Netherlands and Spain were engaged in a protracted war in the Low Countries – the "Dutch Revolt" or "Eighty Years War". The conflict split the region into an independent northern sector governed by the Calvinist-dominated separatists (an area which would later become the Netherlands) and a southern sector that remained a Catholic stronghold (essentially modern Belgium). In the south, Spain retained a large army to be used against France, if and when necessary. King Philip II had tapped a portion of this army for his invasion of England in 1588, before the Spanish Armada was defeated.

When Smith arrived on the Continent in 1597, Captain Duxbury was serving under Francis Vere, a distinguished military officer who had been fighting in the Low Countries since 1585. After a successful defence of his garrison in 1598, Vere was knighted on the field of battle by none other than Peregrine Bertie, the 13th Baron Willoughby de Eresby, who was then commander of the English forces. (Vere also happened to be the first cousin of Lady Mary, Lord Willoughby's wife.)

From birth, John Smith had been closely associated with Lord Willoughby. His father had left Bertie his finest young colt in his will, and had charged John "to honor and love" his Lordship. Smith would undoubtedly have heard gossip on the quayside in King's Lynn about the latest war against the Catholics, and this must have fired his imagination. It is also possible he used his contacts with Willoughby to secure his position fighting under Duxbury.

As commander of the English forces in the Low Countries, Willoughby was in a difficult position. The Dutch resented the presence of the English and refused to supply Willoughby with money, food or clothing for his troops. Smith's time in Willoughby's army must have taught him as much about the art of scavenging and survival as it did about the art of war, providing him with knowledge that would prove invaluable later in life.

Smith shared very little about his time in the Low Countries, but we can reconstruct his movements from other sources. Duxbury did not gain his commission as a captain until March 30, 1599, and he was killed at Nieuwpoort on June 2 the following year.[23] Therefore, the only likely action Smith would have seen under Duxbury was in the spring of 1599, when the Spanish army laid siege to Bommel, an island in the River Scheldt. Sir Francis Vere arrived with his English army of six thousand men and attacked Spanish positions that had successfully blockaded the Dutch town.[24] So Smith is mistaken about the time he spent under Duxbury; he could only have been with him for a couple of years at most, and not the "three or four years" he claimed. However, there is little doubt Smith saw battle, and he later wrote that he regretted "to have seene so many Christians slaughter one another".[25]

While Smith was in the Low Countries, Willoughby's eldest son, Robert Bertie, saw action in Cadiz, fighting the same enemy. For his "valour" in capturing the Spanish city, Robert was allegedly knighted at the tender age of fourteen.[26] Robert was nearly three years John's junior, and Smith could be forgiven for feeling bitter about being born the son of a farmer, not an aristocrat.

In April 1599, Robert wrote to his father asking if his younger brother, fourteen-year-old Peregrine, could join him "in his voyage", meaning a study tour in France, a popular pursuit of noble young men. Willoughby agreed, and on June 26, 1599, Peregrine was granted permission to travel to France "for 3 years, with his tutor, 2 servants, 2 horses, and £60".[27] This licence to travel was mandatory for all English subjects (except for known merchants), as it helped reduce the spread of plague and other poxes. The licence, granted by a local magistrate, also provided a record of travels to foreign lands at a time when aristocrats and commoners alike could fall under suspicion for supporting the Catholic Church.[28]

By the time young Peregrine had received his licence and was ready to travel, John Smith had returned to Lincolnshire from the Netherlands. Smith offered to accompany Peregrine to France and the Baron most likely did the local tenant farmer's son a favour by agreeing to the request. The group travelled initially to London, giving Smith what was probably his first view of the capital. Then they continued by boat to the Continent:

> At last he found meanes to attend Master Perigrine Barty [Bertie] into France, second sonne to the Right Honourable Perigrine, that generous Lord Willoughby, and famous Souldier.[29]

It would have taken Smith and his charge at least a month to cover the five hundred miles between Willoughby and Orléans, especially as they had the attractions of London and Paris to sample on the way. So they are unlikely to have arrived before August 1599.

Their licence was for a stay of three years, but Smith left almost immediately. He was short on details as to why: "His service being needlesse, within a moneth or six weekes they sent him backe againe to his friends."[30] The Bertie boys gave him ten shillings "out of his owne estate" – in other words, they were kind enough to release his own money to him. Smith went on to say they wanted "to be rid of him", which implies they had a disagreement.

Smith resented the rigid class system, and with two younger aristocratic boys under his wing, he might well have overstepped the line and considered himself their equal, which the boys would have begrudged. It could also be that Smith was simply a difficult, headstrong person to have as a travelling companion. Perhaps having been subjected to harsh discipline at school and in the army, he proved to be too autocratic for the boys, who were now free of any parental control. Smith certainly became a disciplinarian later in his life. His reference to "fatherless children" might be derisive, a judgement on the unruly offspring of Lord Willoughby.

Never missing an opportunity to build his network of connections, Smith stopped in Paris on his way home. He was looking for a friend of Lord Willoughby's, a Scottish nobleman called Lord Alexander Hume. This would have been towards the end of 1599, at the earliest. During his search in Paris, Smith met a relation of his Lordship's, Sir David Hume, a poet and intellectual:

> Growing acquainted with one Master [sic] David Hume, who making some use of his purse, gave him Letters to his friends in Scotland to preferre [present] him to King James.[31]

Smith had to pay handsomely for this introduction to the King of Scotland, but it was an opportunity not to be missed. Smith headed down the River Seine to Le Havre to find a ship for Scotland. He wrote that he was "seeing his money neere spent", so the time was right for him to head home.

It was cheaper, quicker and safer to travel to Scotland by sea, so Smith first sailed to the busy fishing port of Enkhuizen in Holland, before finding a ship for Leith, the harbour serving Edinburgh. It was now late in the year, so the days were short and the sailing conditions unfavourable. His ship for Leith ran onto the rocks on the holy island of Lindisfarne:

> At Ancusan [Enkhuizen] he imbarked himselfe for Lethe, but as much danger, as shipwracke and sicknesse could endure, hee had at the holy Ile in Northumberland neere Barwicke.[32]

Smith's childhood fantasy of a life on the seas was meeting the first of several real-life misfortunes. He was taken ill on Lindisfarne, and it was some time before he could continue on to Scotland.

Now short of funds, Smith most likely walked from Berwick to Edinburgh, a distance of some fifty-seven miles, or relied on the favours of passing carts. He reported that he found the Scots to be hospitable, but his ambitions to be accepted into the Court of King James VI of Scotland never materialized:

> After much kinde usage among those honest Scots at Ripweth and Broxmoth, but neither money nor meanes [sponsorship] to make him a Courtier, he returned to Willoughby in Lincolne-shire; where within a short time being glutted with too much company.[33]

These were the words of a crestfallen man. He had exhausted his funds to get to Scotland and present himself as a potential courtier, but without success. After his shipwreck, illness and rejection at Holyrood Palace, it made sense for Smith to return to Lincolnshire. He was, after all, only the son of a tenant farmer. So he returned to his roots in the spring or early summer of 1600.

But Smith's homecoming did not suit him either. He complained that he was "glutted [overwhelmed] with too much company". This was hardly surprising; apart from the Willoughby family, Smith was the most travelled person ever to leave the parish boundaries, and he was still only twenty. Overcome with his newfound celebrity status, he took off into the woods to be by himself.

The century had turned, and the world was changing; Smith too. He had an income from his father's estate, but he had also witnessed war, seen his comrades butchered on the battlefield and innocent civilians subjected to the utmost depravity. It was time for John Smith to assess his life. His decision to live alone in the woods was unconventional, to say the least, but the seclusion offered more than a break from war; it offered an opportunity for self-improvement.

Over the next few months he read widely, attempting to improve on those parts of his education he thought lacking. He also decided his proficiency in combat and horsemanship needed attention, and he worked hard on developing his skills over the summer months. It was time well spent, as his woodland education saved his life on many occasions to come.

John Smith swimming in the Mediterranean, having been cast overboard by Catholic pilgrims, from Smith's *The True Travels* (1630). The northern coast of Africa is on the left and the southern coast of France is on the right. Smith also appears on an island, praying in gratitude for his salvation.

2
Pirate

1600–1601

They threw him over-board, yet God brought him to that little Isle, where was no inhabitants, but a few kine [cows] and goats
John Smith, The True Travels (1630)

The summer of 1600 was a turning point in John Smith's life, his "coming of age". Having returned disappointed from his abortive attempt to become a sycophant in the court of King James of Scotland, Smith withdrew into himself, and began to think about what he might do next. He had a modest income from his father's farm, but no significant position within society. He had learnt the hard way that opportunity was limited if you were not born into the right family. He was caught between the golden dreams of youth and the harsh realities of Elizabethan manhood.

Smith was brought up at school on a diet of godliness and piety, and every part of his adult life was governed by the strict rules of Elizabethan etiquette. None of this suited his natural temperament, which was prone to challenge the status quo. He decided that it was time to take stock of his existence:

> He retired himselfe into a little wooddie pasture, a good way from any towne, invironed with many hundred Acres of other woods: Here by a faire brook he built a Pavillion of boughes, where only in his cloaths he lay.[1]

Locals in Willoughby believe Smith built his shelter – his "Pavilion of boughes" – in Hoplands Wood, a thirty-seven-acre wood just over half a mile west of the village. According to the Willoughby History Group, deforestation around the village happened long before Smith's time, and the woodland areas today are much as they were during his sojourn.

His intention was to be self-sufficient. Smith had a boy from the village bring him supplies when he needed them, but claimed to have lived mainly on venison that he hunted. Since his father had died, John had been alone and had experienced several turbulent years of travelling and fighting, rejection, and, in some cases, disillusionment. This was the space he needed to make sense of the world, and to refocus his life.

He spent much of his time in the wood practising his horsemanship and his proficiency with a lance, but he also read, expanding his education beyond the Bible and his schoolboy Latin texts. England had recently embraced a fashion for ancient learnedness,[2] and in this respect Smith followed the crowd. We know he read two popular treatises, Machiavelli's *The Art of War* and *The Golden Book of Marcus Aurelius*. Both give an insight into Smith's state of mind during these days.

Niccolò Machiavelli was a politician, philosopher and diplomat based in Florence who had died in 1527. Though *The Art of War* is less well known today than some of his other books, it was the only political work published during Machiavelli's lifetime. By the late sixteenth century it had been translated widely, and adopted across Europe as a guidebook for budding military strategists. The book takes the form of a philosophical dialogue between two characters discussing how an army should be raised, trained, organized and deployed.

Machiavelli used this dialogue to explain his concept of "limited warfare", which, he argued, should be used when channels of diplomacy fail. He believed armies should not be composed of professional soldiers, but should be recruited and trained from among the citizenry as needed. When a war ended, the militia should be disbanded, the men returning to their peacetime occupations.

The Art of War also contained a litany of valuable, practical advice on military matters – from the observation that "knowing how to fight made men more bold, because no one fears doing what it seems to him he has learned to do" to the need "to know in war how to recognize an opportunity and seize it". Smith would draw upon Machiavelli's advice to his advantage on many occasions; indeed, it would even save his life.

His other literary mentor was "Marcus Aurelius", the Roman emperor who wrote the celebrated philosophical tome *Meditations*. However, Aurelius' book was not translated into English from its original Greek until 1634, so Smith must instead have read a book by the Spanish priest, writer and moralist Antonio de Guevara, which Guevara inelegantly called *Marco Aurelio con el Reloj de principes*, or *Marco Aurelius with Dial of Princes*.[3] In English it was often called *The Golden Book of Marcus Aurelius*.

Guevara claimed to have "discovered" an old manuscript by the great emperor, to which he had only bestowed a modern "style". The crude forgery was published in 1529, and despite its doubtful pedigree and verbose style, it became a runaway bestseller in etiquette-obsessed Tudor England. Its truisms were often repeated in the court of Queen Elizabeth by those who aspired to literary taste. By 1600, "Marcus Aurelius" had run to an astonishing fourteen editions. The classical scholar Isaac Casaubon claimed that few books other than the Bible had been translated so much, or printed so frequently.

The first part of the book, correctly called *Marco Aurelio*, was devoted to the life of the emperor and, being filled with counterfeit letters, was mostly fictional. It was the second part, the *Reloj de principes*, that created such a sensation. The title "Dial of Princes" referred to a compass, or direction for leaders. In it, Guevara dispensed trite moral and religious advice to his readers. For example, he intoned, "In the court, it profits little to be wise, forasmuch as good service is soon forgotten, friends soon fail and enemies augment." In another important section he listed eighteen "rules" about how to deal with women.[4] The first guideline warned: "A husband should be patient and tolerant when his wife is angry, for there is no serpent so poisonous as an affronted woman." Other misogynistic advice included "the frail flesh is to blame, but much more is the foolish and light woman in [at] fault", and "you women destroy the goods, honour, and life of the living". Smith felt his mother had betrayed his father by remarrying so quickly after his death, and now the acclaimed emperor – or so John thought – offered some unfettered advice about how he should judge women's behaviour.

Smith was seeking a sense of direction, and these works did not fail him. His chosen writers were didactic and moralistic, happy to offer a set of rules for governing conduct in all aspects of life. He took abundant guidance from both, and followed it for the rest of his life.

His other main occupation, of exercising with a horse and lance, suggests he was drawn towards the pomp and pageantry of the chivalric knight. That iconic figure had all but died out by the late Elizabethan age, supplanted by ships' captains like Drake and merchants like his former master Thomas Sendall. The closest Smith might get to achieving his knightly ideal was professional soldiering, but he could see that he needed further training if he wanted to take to the battlefield to make his living. Foremost, he needed to spar with someone more skilled than a boy from the local village. Some friends agreed, and set out to find him an excellent tutor who might tempt Smith from his self-imposed exile:

> His friends perswaded one Seignior Theadora Polaloga, Rider to Henry Earle of Lincolne, an excellent Horse-man, and a noble Italian Gentleman, to insinuate into his wooddish acquaintances, whose Languages and good discourse, and exercise of riding drew him to stay with him at Tattersall.[5]

Smith does not divulge who "his friends" were. Of course, the only likely aquaintance of Smith's that could have persuaded Henry Clinton, the 2nd Earl of Lincoln, to accommodate him at Tattershall Castle was Lord Willoughby.

Even with this introduction, it is unlikely Smith ever met the castle's owner during his stay. Clinton had a reputation as one of the most unpleasant men in aristocratic circles. His own son-in-law had famously denounced him for his "wickedness, misery, craft, repugnance to all humanity, and perfidious mind".[6] Why would this aristocratic misanthrope want anything to do with John Smith? The fabulously grand apartments at the top of Clinton's castle were likely off-limits to a young man who had only recently emerged from the woods.

The magnificant red-brick castle at Tattershall was one of the finest fortresses in England. Built to a medieval design, the Great Tower stood six storeys tall, with walls over twenty feet thick at the base, turrets at each of its four corners, two moats and a drawbridge. Yet the castle had been built in the fifteenth century by Lord Cromwell, then the King's Treasurer, long after such a defensive structure was needed, and it was nothing more than a huge status symbol – a country mansion.[7] This was the perfect place for Smith to indulge his knightly fantasies.

During his stay, Smith trained under Tattershall's Italian riding master, Theodore Paleologue, who proved to be a practical complement to the philosophical mentorship of Smith's woodland books. In Smith's words, the visit provided a "good discourse". Paleologue taught him the discipline of horsemanship, as well as some Italian, and introduced his pupil to a menace even greater than Catholicism: the "Mahometans", or Muslims. Paleologue knew his enemy well. He was descended from

Tattershall Castle in Lincolnshire, where Smith was tutored in the soldierly arts (photo by Brian Mossemenear, flickr.com/lincolnian).

the family of Constantine XI, the last reigning Byzantine Emperor, who died in 1453 when Constantinople fell to the Ottomans. In front of a roaring wood fire in the vaulted basement of Tattershall, John Smith heard about the power of the Ottoman Empire, the discipline of their Janissary army and the Muslim threat to Europe.

Twenty-year-old Smith was fired up with a clear purpose, and he now possessed a new set of skills to perform it. Machiavelli and Guevara had shown him how to live, but Paleologue had shown him something far more important: how to survive.

It was time to put his new identity into action.

When John Smith left England for the second time, in the latter half of 1600, he decided to travel to familiar territory – the Low Countries. Or so he thought. Upon arriving, he found the situation on the ground to be very different from what he had seen two years previously. The drawn-out war continued between the Independent Netherlands and the Spanish-controlled region (what is now Belgium and Luxembourg), but since the death of Philip II in 1598, the opposing armies seemed to have settled into something of a stalemate. Smith's cavalry commander, Captain Joseph Duxbury, had been killed on June 22, 1600, during an attack on Spanish positions near the town of Niewpoort. Both sides, exhausted from the bloody fighting, withdrew. There was little to be gained by staying, Smith thought, and "he was desirous to see more of the world, and trie his fortune against the Turkes".[8]

Smith met a group of French opportunists in the Netherlands, one of whom claimed to be "a great Lord", and the others, "gentlemen". They too had been fighting in the Low Countries, but now that hostilities between the Dutch and the Spanish were in deadlock, they were heading home to Brittany. There, they maintained, they could gain letters of introduction from the "Dutchesse of Mercury" to her husband, who was fighting the Ottoman Turks in eastern Europe. The Duke of Mercœur commanded the armies of the Holy Roman Emperor, Rudolf II, and was in dire need of troops. The four "Gallants" invited him to come along. It was a proposition Smith could not resist, and his decision to join them revealed his inexperience.

As soon as arrangements could be made, Smith was sailing to France with his new friends. Until this point, his account was thin on facts, and sometimes chronologically inaccurate. But as the group made their way to Saint-Valery-sur-Somme (carefully avoiding Spanish-held Belgium), his story displayed a marked improvement. They travelled in autumn, "with such ill weather as winter affordeth", until "in the dark night they arrived in the broad shallow In-let of Saint Valleries sur Some in Picardie".[9] The commune of Saint-Valery dated back to before the Roman period, and was where William the Conqueror assembled his fleet before invading England in 1066. Smith's description of the harbour was detailed and accurate; Saint-Valery lies six miles inside a wide, shallow bay, accessible only by a long and tortuous channel, just as he said.

However, their adventure was about to take an ill-fated turn. At some point during the voyage, the "Gallants" had plotted with the ship's master to steal Smith's possessions. On arrival, the vessel anchored offshore and the captain ferried the Frenchmen, together with Smith's trunk, ashore in a skiff, promising to return to collect Smith. The captain did not reappear until the following evening, claiming the seas had been too rough to be able to come back sooner. The Frenchmen, he reported, had continued on to Amiens with Smith's possessions, where "they would stay [await] his comming".[10]

Smith immediately grasped that he had been duped, and the rest of the ship's passengers agreed with his assessment. Smith was furious and claimed they would "have slaine the Master, and had they knowne how, would have runne away with the ship".[11]

One of the passengers on the ship, a man Smith calls "Curzianvere", took pity on the naïve Englishman. He told Smith that the leader of the group, one "Lord Depreau", was actually the son of a lawyer, and came from "Mortaigne" [Mortain], a town in southern Brittany. Curzianvere also claimed to know the names of Depreau's three accomplices. They were not gentlemen as they maintained, but ordinary citizens. Curzianvere proposed he travel with Smith to Mortaigne to track down Depreau and his co-conspirators.

It was a generous offer to make to a stranger, all the more so since Smith had lost all his possessions but for the clothes on his back. He had only a single "carralue" in his pocket – a small silver coin of little value, called a quart d'écu, which was in common circulation in France at the time. He was essentially penniless.

Yet Curzianvere's generosity was not limitless, and Smith was forced to sell his cloak to fund his passage to Mortaigne. Smith noted their route across northern France in needless detail, perhaps wishing to convey how relentless he had been in tracking down the men who had swindled him:

> Thus travelling by Deepe [Dieppe], Codebeck, [Caudebec], Humphla [Honfleur], Pount-demer [Pont-Audemer] in Normandie, they came to Cane [Caen] in base Normandie; where both this noble Curzianvere, and the great Prior of the great Abbey of S. Steven (where is the ruinous Tombe of William the Conquerour,) and many other of his friends kindly welcomed him.[12]

At Caen, Curzianvere's associates took Smith to see the tomb of William the Conqueror. William died at the priory of St Gervase in Rouen in 1087, but his body was taken for internment at Caen's Abbaye aux Hommes. The abbey church there is called the Église Saint-Étienne – the church of Saint Stephen. Smith called him S. Steven. Although the abbey is now magnificently restored, Protestant Huguenots had desecrated William's tomb in 1562, and when Smith visited in 1600 the building was in ruins, just as he reported.

After his brief turn as tourist, Smith persevered in his pursuit of Depreau all the way to Mortaigne. But it was "to small purpose": Depreau hid from his accusers, and Smith received no compensation from him for the robbery. The local people were sympathetic to Smith's situation, however, and he was able to muster the funds he thought would be necessary to get to Hungary, where he hoped to test himself against the Turks.

First, Smith had to find passage to eastern Europe. What transpired almost defies belief.

From Mortaigne, he headed west towards the sea, most probably by boat down the River Sélune, wandering from one port to another looking for a vessel to take him to the Mediterranean. He soon ran out of money, and collapsed "neere dead with griefe and cold".[13] A wealthy farmer took pity on the young traveller, fed him, and furnished him with more financial charity. Smith continued, and as he passed "thorow a great grove of trees, betweene Pounterson [Pontorson] and Dina [Dinan] in Britaine [Brittany]", he came across none other than Monsieur "Cursell" (most likely Courcelles), one of the four co-conspirators who had relieved him of his shipping trunk.

Incensed, Smith drew his sword and fell upon the "Gallant". Several farmers were drawn to the fracas and eventually managed to separate the two men, but not before "Cursell fell to the ground". Smith's adversary finally confessed to the theft, and explained that the men had fallen out among themselves and that he too had been cheated. With that explanation, the farmers pronounced themselves satisfied, and let Smith and "Cursell" continue on their separate ways. Smith seemed satisfied with the outcome, for he had defeated his opponent in swordplay.

At some stage in his travels, Smith had been told that the Count Amaury II Goujon, lord of the Château de Plouër, had been brought up in England, and had only recently returned to Brittany. Smith was in need of further assistance as well as sympathy, so he set off by foot for the mansion. Amaury was only a few years older than Smith, and like those strangers before him, he took pity on the Englishman, giving him lodgings and allowing him to rest. Smith must have stayed at the château for a week or more, for the count took his guest on an extensive tour of Brittany. There is still a château on the site in Plouër, although the original building visited by Smith was demolished and re-built in the seventeenth and eighteenth centuries.

Soon after the new year, Smith packed his bags and set off for the Mediterranean. The road south took him by way of Rennes, Nantes, Poitiers, La Rochelle, Bordeaux, Bayonne and then on to Marseilles, where he looked for a ship that would take him to Italy.

Smith's decision to go to Italy by sea was sensible. It was both cheaper and safer than travelling overland. Unfortunately, he seemed jinxed at sea, and he experienced a stroke of very bad luck. The vessel on which he had booked passage sailed no more than fifty miles before putting into Toulon for essential repairs. When it set sail again, it ran into bad weather. According to Smith, the "ill weather so grew upon them, they anchored close aboard the shore, under the little Isle of S. Mary, against Neice [Nice] in Savoy".[14] The master had decided to sit out the gale in the relative safety of a good anchorage.

His fellow passengers were a group of Catholics on a pilgrimage to Rome – he called them "a rable of Pilgrimes of divers Nations", which says much about Smith's opinion of them. The fear of sinking combined with the incessant rolling of the small ship during the bad weather would have unsettled any but the most robust of seamen. The "rable" rounded on Smith, cursing him not only for being a Protestant, but even worse, for being an English Protestant, a nation "they swore were all Pyrats". They "vildly railed on his dread Soveraigne Queene Elizabeth", to Smith's anger.[15]

The consensus among the Catholic passengers was that they would never have good weather for as long as Smith was on board. Their solution was to rid themselves of the troublesome Protestant by throwing him overboard. Fortunately, Smith managed to make it ashore to the "Isle of S. Mary", which he found to be deserted except for "a few kine and goats"[16]. The following morning, after what must have been a wet and miserable night, he came across two other vessels also taking refuge from the gale. He was taken aboard one of the ships, where they "well refreshed him, and so kindly used him, that he was well contented to trie the rest of his fortune with them".[17]

It stretches credibility, but his basic story holds up to the facts: it was winter, and fierce storms are not uncommon in the Mediterranean. Smith reported that the passengers did not like having him in their presence, though we have no way of knowing if he offended some of them, or whether they were simply superstitious and had convinced themselves the situation would improve if he was not on board. In any case, their solution – to throw him over the side – was harsh, but not without precedent when mob rule was dispensed at sea.

There was, however, a fundamental weakness in Smith's tale of distress: on no chart of the Mediterranean does an Isle of St Mary appear. This does not invalidate Smith's description of the incident entirely, as there are several possible explanations for the island's vanishing. One of Smith's earlier biographers, Philip Barbour, speculated that there might have been a small island off Nice that has since been incorporated into the extended breakwaters.[18] Yet any sailing master seeking refuge from a storm would look for a more substantial bolthole than a tiny island so close inshore. Barbour's alternative proposal was that the navigator mistook his position, and the ship anchored behind one of the islands offshore from Cannes, some eighteen miles southwest of Nice.

The truth behind Smith's account could be simpler. To the east of Nice is the long peninsula of Saint-John-Cap-Ferat, with large open bays on each side. These offer easy access for a sailing ship, and excellent protection from gales coming from almost any direction. Unless the wind was blowing from due south, an experienced captain arriving off Nice and looking for refuge from a storm would almost certainly choose one of these bays as an anchorage. While there are no small islands in the area

This retaining sea wall provides a clue as to how a peninsula might have once been an island, proving the plausibility of John Smith's account (photo by Peter Firstbrook).

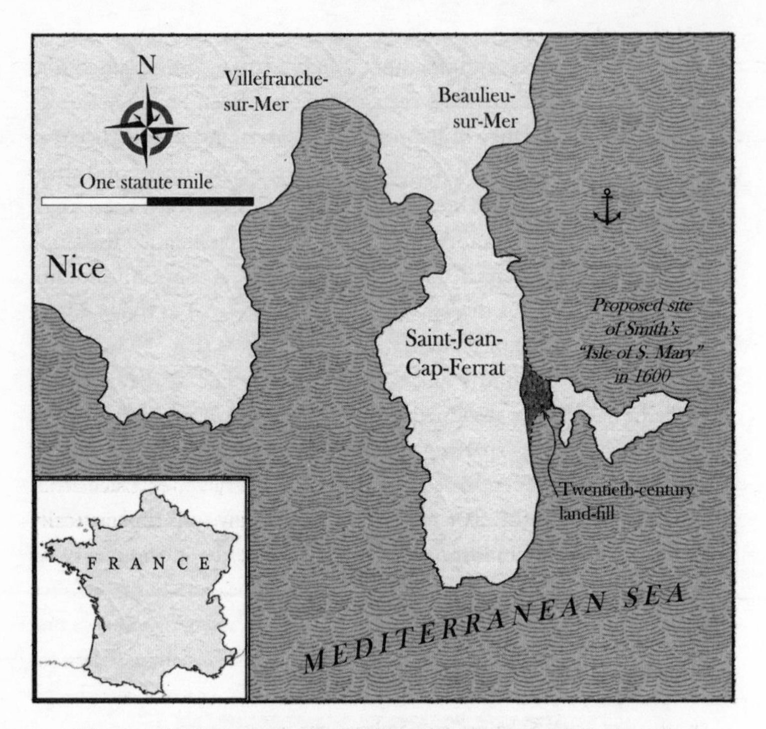

The most likely location of Smith's "Isle of S. Mary" is a peninsula on the eastern side of Saint-Jean-Cap-Ferrat, created by land-fill in the early twentieth century. In 1600, the feature would have been a small island.

which fit Smith's description, on the eastern shore of Cap-Ferat there is a section of land jutting out into the bay – an artificial isthmus built in the twentieth century to give access to the chapel of Saint-Hospice and a cemetery. In 1600, there was no promontory here. Instead, Smith would have seen an island, just big enough for "a few kine [cows] and goats" – presumably the missing Isle of St Mary.

With his new ship, Smith's luck improved. The master was a Frenchman from St Malo called La Roche, and he offered to take Smith to the eastern Mediterranean. It seemed La Roche knew the young Count Amaury of the Château de Plouër, and the captain "regarded and entertained him for his well respected friend".[19]

With fair winds, they sailed south to Corsica and Sardinia, across the Gulf of Tunis "to the Isle of Lampadosa [Lampedusa]", and then, keeping well off the coast of North Africa and away from the risk of pirate attack, on to Alexandria in Egypt. Here they unloaded the ship's cargo. This was far from the battlefields of Hungary, but Smith drank in the sights during this diversion, knowing he was safe in the hands of an experienced sailing master.

Alexandria was Smith's first taste of the East, and exactly the type of place he must have dreamed about when reviewing the ledgers at Sindall's dusty offices in King's Lynn. After centuries of Greek and then Roman rule, the Arabs captured the city in 641, after a siege that lasted fourteen months. The victorious general wrote enthusiastically back to his caliph, 'Umar ibn Al-Khattab, about the glorious city he had taken:

> It is of an immense extent. I cannot describe to you how many wonders it contains. There are in it 4,000 palaces, 4,000 baths, 12,000 dealers in fresh oil, 12,000 gardeners, 40,000 Jews who pay tribute.[20]

Since 1517, Alexandria had been under Turkish rule. This was Smith's first experience of Islam and the rule of the Ottomans – the very people who would soon become his bloody adversaries in war.

From Egypt, Captain La Roche sailed north to "Scanderoon" in southern Turkey, close to the border with modern Syria. Iskenderun was originally founded by Alexander the Great, and was called Alexandretta by the Greeks, but it too had fallen to the Turks two years before they took Egypt, and the new rulers changed its name. During the 1590s, the port became an important stop on the trade route from the Persian Gulf to the Mediterranean. Ships could anchor there on a solid bottom without chafing their cables, but apart from this, Iskenderun seemed to have had little else to offer. Henry Teonge, a seventeenth-century British naval chaplain, had nothing positive to say about it:

> It is, properly speaking, nothing more than a village without walls, in which the tombs are more numerous than the houses...Scanderoon has always been noted as a sickly place, occasioned by the stagnant waters and mephitic exhalations from the marshes which lay around it.[21]

Raising the anchor, La Roche and his crew headed for the western Mediterranean, sailing first to Cyprus, then to Rhodes and on to Cephalonia. They had covered over three thousand miles in a merchant ship, which typically travelled less than a hundred miles a day. With stopovers in various ports, Smith must have arrived in Greece some time in early to mid-March 1601.

It is said that ships and men rot in harbour, and La Roche was keen to return to France for new cargo. As his ship crossed the Strait of Otranto – the part of the southern Adriatic that separates Greece from Italy – the captain spotted a richly laden *argosy*, or Venetian merchant ship, heading south. La Roche tried to make contact with the argosy's captain, but his reply came in the form of a cannon shot, which killed a man on La Roche's ship. A furious exchange of fire followed. It must have made quite an impression on the young sea-goer, as Smith could recount the ensuing battle in detail nearly thirty years after the event.

Smith recalled that La Roche returned fire, first with a broadside, and then with his stern cannon. The argosy turned to escape, but the French ship was smaller and faster, and La Roche constantly harried his foe with shot so "that the Argosies sayles and tackling was so torne",[22] slowing it further. La Roche then positioned his vessel for maximum firepower and "shot her so oft betweene wind and water, shee was readie to sinke, then they yeelded".[23] As the cannonade struck the argosy below the waterline, the Venetians capitulated, but it had been a costly encounter. La Roche lost fifteen men, the argosy twenty, and even more were left injured. Smith's captain sent a boarding party to the stricken ship to try to stop her leaks, and to guard the crew.

The skirmish proved to be lucrative for La Roche's surviving crew. It took a full twenty-four hours to transfer the plunder to the French ship. Smith recalled the manifest: "Silkes, Velvets, Cloth of gold, and Tissue, Pyasters, Chicqueenes and Sultanies, which is gold and silver".[24] The *piaster* was an Italian currency used commonly in the eastern Mediterranean during this period; the *zecchino* (Smith's "chicqueenes") was a Venetian gold coin, weighing 3.5 grams (0.12 ounces), used from the thirteenth to the eighteenth century; and the *sultany* referred to a coin minted in Turkey. The argosy had a substantial amount of coinage on board.

Having unloaded its riches, La Roche cast off the Venetian ship, possibly to a watery end. It was typical of countless small engagements in the lawless waters of the Mediterranean and Atlantic during the period. Smith wrote with enthusiasm about the logistics of the encounter, but makes no comment on its morality; he was a soldier – a mercenary – and this was part of his trade. On this occasion, he did not feel the need to brag about his part in the fighting, but wrote only of the conduct of the crew and of the ship's master. He was still learning, after all.

When La Roche's ship arrived in Antibes in southern France, the crew divided the spoils. Though he was not an official member of the crew, Smith was rewarded generously for supporting the engagement – five hundred zecchini, worth approximately eight or nine shillings each, and a little box "worth neere as much more".[25] Altogether, Smith's share was probably worth close to four hundred pounds – five times the value of his father's household goods when he died, and equivalent to about ten years' wages for a workman.

For the first time in his life, Smith was wealthy, and he was determined to enjoy his good fortune.

Spring was blooming across Europe, and with the season and new riches to distract him, Smith decided his personal crusade against the Turks could be set aside for a while longer. He found passage on another ship crossing the Ligurian Sea, and on disembarking in Leghorn in northwest Italy, continued overland through Tuscany to Siena.

To his surprise, there he ran across Lord Willoughby's sons, Robert and Peregrine Bertie, still on their three-year sojourn on the Continent. The Bertie boys had obviously been in trouble, for Smith noted they were "cruelly wounded, in a desperate fray, to their exceeding great honour".[26] Smith said no more about the matter, perhaps out of deference, but young Peregrine especially had a prickly nature, and disputes like this were not infrequent among headstrong young men. In any case, the Bertie boys did not keep him long in Siena, because Smith travelled south through "many other Cities" and arrived in Rome in time for Easter.

During his stay in the papal capital, Smith took the opportunity to visit the radical Jesuit priest Father Robert Parsons, rector of the English College in Rome. In its day, this was the most important seminary for English Catholic priests taking sanctuary abroad. Parsons had been branded as scheming, dishonest and seditious by English Protestants.[27] He had been involved in several plots to restore Catholic control of England, by either persuasion or force, and had actively encouraged King Philip of Spain to renew attacks on his old adversary. Visiting Parsons would not ingratiate Smith with the Elizabethan establishment, but it was a risk he felt worth taking.

Smith remained enigmatic about his motivation for meeting with Parsons, but the audience was probably the main reason for his trip to Rome. Smith was assiduous in cultivating his contacts, and this would-be crusader needed advice from a well-connected Catholic if he was going to find a way to enrol in the army of the Holy Roman Emperor. His own Protestant beliefs would do him no favours. Smith might even have hoped to secure an introduction to the ardent Catholic general, the Duke of Mercœur, which he had failed to do on his ill-fated trip to Brittany the previous year.

Easter Sunday fell on April 12 in 1601 (April 22 in the new style Gregorian calendar in use in Italy), a date that corresponds with Smith's itinerary of travels since leaving Tattershall the previous summer. He never revealed whether he managed to obtain letters of introduction to the Duke while in Rome, but in any case he seemed to be in no real rush to reach the killing fields of eastern Europe. Smith took a boat down the River Tiber, and then fifty miles up the coast to Civitavecchia, where he embarked on a ship heading south again, this time to Naples. From there he returned to Rome. He next visited several northern cities before arriving in Venice.

Here, he finally looked for a way north to Graz, one of the main recruiting centres for the armies of the Holy Roman Emperor. At some stage in Smith's travels across Italy, someone had given him letters of introduction to contacts in Graz, who could help him find a position in the army of Ferdinand, the Archduke of Austria. Perhaps his audience with Robert Parsons was fruitful after all.

The journey from Venice to Graz should have warned Smith of the wasp's nest of political intrigue and double-dealing that would soon sting him. The overland route via Trieste was less than three hundred miles – perhaps a couple of weeks on horseback – but the journey took him much longer.

The problem was that the direct route via Trieste was closed off to anyone starting from Venice. For most of the previous hundred years, the advancing Ottomans had driven bands of Slavic Christians from their lands in the east. These refugees, called Uskoks, had been pushed westward towards the eastern Adriatic (modern-day Croatia) and survived as best they could as brigands on land and pirates at sea. Fuelled by ideals of honour and vengeance, they channelled their grievances into waging their own holy war against the Turks. The old adage applied – the enemy of my enemy is my friend – and the Holy Roman Empire was happy to support even the unruly Uskoks

The Republic of Venice did not see the situation in quite the same way. Venice was utterly reliant on sea trade, and that meant controlling access to the Adriatic, and thus to the Mediterranean and beyond. The Venetians were even prepared to allow Ottoman ships access to the Adriatic, if it improved trade for themselves. However, the Uskoks were effective pirates, and used their fast rowboats to challenge the Venetians' supremacy in the Adriatic. The headquarters of the Uskoks was Senj in Croatia, but Trieste was one of their main distribution centres. As a rebuke, the Venetian fleet had blockaded the port.[28]

The duplicitous politics of the region meant Smith's route to Austria was anything but direct. He caught a ship from the Venetian port of Malamocco, sailing south through the Adriatic to Ragusa (the Greek name for Dubrovnik, in modern Croatia). He then returned by sea to Capo d'Istria, the modern Slovenian port of Koper, just eight miles south of Trieste. The direct crossing from Venice to Koper is just sixty-five miles, but Smith had sailed more than ten times that to avoid the Venetian naval blockade. It was an important lesson for him in *realpolitik*.

Politics were not the only reason for his slow progress. It is difficult to know how much time elapsed from his audience with Father Parsons to his arrival in Graz, but everything in his account suggests he was content to take his time and see the world. And he had his bounty from Captain La Roche to sustain him. So he probably did not reach Graz until mid-summer 1601.

Still, he was well prepared when he reached the city. Smith was an English Protestant arriving unannounced in a Catholic stronghold, and he knew he needed to work through his fledgling list of contacts and connections. He visited "an English man, and an Irish Jesuite, who acquainted him with many brave Gentlemen of good qualitie".[29] Smith could only have made such contacts through influential intermediaries – most likely the shady Parsons, his new friend in Rome.

Smith's diligence paid off, and through his acquaintances in Graz, he was introduced to noblemen and military commanders who would take him east to wage war against the mighty Ottomans. "To know in war how to recognize an opportunity and seize it is better than anything else," as Machiavelli had taught him.

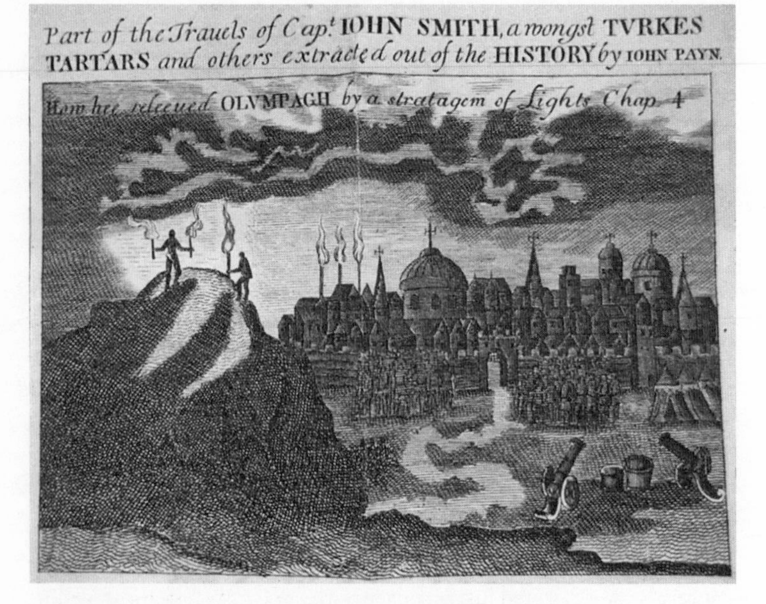

John Smith signalling his commander from a distant ridge during the terrible siege of "Olumpagh", from John Smith's *The True Travels* (1630).

3
Mercenary

1601–1602

Occasioned the Author a good reward and preferment, to be Captaine of two hundred and fiftie Horse-men
John Smith, The True Travels (1630)

John Smith was about to embark on one of the most exciting and dangerous periods of his life. He had been sickened by the destruction wrought in western Europe by the wars between Protestants and Catholics, but he was also only twenty-one, and his enthusiasm for adventure and war was far from satiated. Ever since his summer of introspection in Hoplands Wood near Willoughby, Smith had been dreaming of a career characterized by gallantry and notoriety. All he needed was a just war, in which to demonstrate his newly acquired skills. He could hear his mentor, Machiavelli, urging him on: "Since the handling of arms is a beautiful spectacle, it is delightful to young men."

In *The True Travels*, Smith gave a good indication of his primary concerns. He dedicated just one page to the first fifteen years of his life; another four pages to the next five years travelling in Europe and the Mediterranean; and eighteen pages to the year and a half he spent fighting in eastern Europe. From the day he arrived in Graz in the summer of 1601, Smith had a new purpose in life.

Smith found Graz abuzz with military activity as Rudolf II, the Holy Roman Emperor, organized his forces to defend western Europe. For over a century, the Ottomans had been steadily pressing westwards with the biggest standing army Europe had seen since Roman times. Now the Turks threatened the heart of Christendom, and Rudolf was assembling troops from across Europe to stem their advance.

The Turks had made a steady series of alarming intrusions into Europe.

Sixty-five years after the fall of Constantinople, Egypt had fallen to the Turks – and much of Persia too. Then, in 1521, Suleiman the Magnificent captured Belgrade; twenty years later, he took Buda. He then laid siege to Vienna. The attack was repulsed, but the threat was only deferred.

Under Suleiman, the Ottoman Empire had emerged as the undisputed leader of the Muslim world, and its military might cast a long shadow. The empire's capital, Constantinople (already known also as Istanbul at this time), was five times the size of Paris, and had been renowned as a seat of military and intellectual supremacy since Suleiman's day. By 1600, more than thirty million people, from the coasts of North Africa to the Caspian Sea, lived under the Ottomans. Large swathes of eastern Europe were already under Ottoman control, including all of Greece, Bulgaria, Moldova, most of Hungary, all of Transylvania and parts of southern Ukraine.

By the time Suleiman's great-grandson Mehmed III took the throne (having dispatched nineteen brothers and half-brothers to get there), the Turks commanded the largest army in Europe, and its navy controlled the shipping lanes throughout the eastern Mediterranean. Only a chain of fortresses in western Hungary and the Habsburg army stood in the path of the Turks' relentless expansion. The fear was that Vienna – the seat of the Holy Roman Emperor and the Habsburg family – could be attacked again, and this time the city's defences could falter. It was imperative the Muslims be stopped.

This was the fight John Smith hungered after.

Soon after Smith arrived in Graz, he met two influential men. Both of them were actively involved in the defence of Christian Europe, and in different ways each would shape his life over the next two years. One of Smith's "brave Gentleman of good quality" was "Lord Ebersbaught". Ebersbaught's real identity is still a matter of some speculation, but he was most likely Sigismund von Eibiswald,[1] a veteran of military campaigns in Hungary and Transylvania. Ebersbaught introduced Smith to Lieutenant Colonel Hans Jakob Khissl (Smith's "Baron Kisell"), commander of artillery in Graz.

Smith wanted to join the Holy Roman Emperor's army, but as a Protestant he was not allowed to serve in a frontline regiment. Such units were reserved for Catholic soldiers, so that any victory over the Turks could be claimed as theirs alone. From an early age, John had been brought up to distrust Catholics, and he had spent two years fighting them in the Netherlands. Now he put aside any animosity he might have felt and joined them to fight a common enemy – a pragmatic decision, worthy of Machiavelli himself. The Habsburgs were practical, too. Not wanting to waste a useful soldier, Khissl sent Smith north to Vienna, where Smith's third "brave Gentleman", the Count of Modrusch (Smith's "Earle of Meldrich") was forming a Protestant-Hungarian regiment. Smith was enlisted, and he soon found himself in action.

Smith understood something of the complicated political and

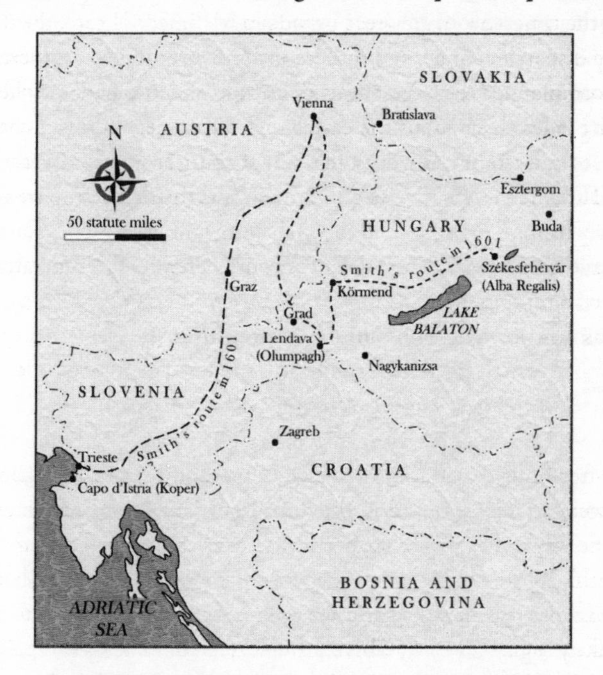

John Smith's travels in Austria and Hungary, 1601. Smith travelled first to Graz and Vienna before being deployed at the siege of "Olumpagh" and the battle at Alba Regalis.

military situation in the region even before he reached the battlefield. The front line between the Habsburg forces and the Ottoman army ran roughly north to south, close to today's border between Austria and Hungary. The previous year, the strategically important fortress of Nagykanizsa in southwest Hungary had fallen to the Ottomans, which was a serious blow. Smith wrote: "After the losse of Caniza [Nagykanizsa], the Turkes with twentie thousand besieged the strong Towne of Olumpagh."[2]

The Habsburgs could not afford to lose another border stronghold, so Modrusch's regiment marched south to reinforce the fort at the town Smith called Olumpagh. But the deployment of the Protestant forces was merely a sideshow. The real assault was planned further to the south, where Archduke Ferdinand II, the cousin of Emperor Rudolf II, was mounting an attack to re-take Nagykanizsa.

Smith's regiment arrived at Olumpagh during the summer of 1601. By then, Ebersbaught was governor of the Imperial forces inside the town's castle, which was surrounded and under siege by twenty thousand Turkish troops. The relief forces had no means of communication with those inside the garrison, and no way of co-ordinating an attack on the Turks.

Smith, however, hatched a plan. When he first met Ebersbaught back in Graz, Smith had made an impression on the commander by explaining a signalling system developed by a fellow Englishman, the mathematician William Bourne.[3] It was essentially an early form of Morse code, using a pattern of lights to convey a message over a distance – in this case, the seven miles between the camp of the relief forces and Olumpagh's castle. Smith proposed Modrusch send a message to Ebersbaught about the timing of a joint attack, in the hope Ebersbaught would remember what Smith had told him about the light code:

> Smith made it so plaine, that forthwith hee gave him guides, who in the darke night brought him to a mountaine, where he shewed three Torches equidistant from other, which plainly appearing to the Towne, the Governour presently apprehended, and answered againe with three other fires in like manner; each knowing the others being and intent;

> Smith, though distant seven miles, signified to him these words: On Thursday at night I will charge on the East, at the Alarum, salley you; Ebersbaught answered he would, and thus it was done.[4]

The message seemed to have been communicated, but there was yet another obstacle to making the attack a success. The commander of the relief forces, Lieutenant Colonel Khissl (who Smith had also met in Graz), was worried he did not have enough men for the assault, and he was hesitant to commit to it. Khissl was an artillery officer, not an infantry commander, so he might have also lacked experience in organizing such a ground offensive.

Fortunately, Smith concocted another subterfuge to give Khissl and his men the upper hand. He suggested "that two or three thousand pieces of match [fuses]" should be fastened to thin lines, six hundred feet long, and stretched between two poles. When the tapers were lit at night, they would resemble the glowing tip of the slow-burning fuses used by the musketeers to ignite their matchlock muskets. He hoped the Turks might mistake the smouldering tapers for a battalion of soldiers approaching the town.

It was a cunning plan, and the enemy fell for it. After spotting the glowing tapers, the Turkish soldiers moved out of their positions to engage the hoax army. Meanwhile, Khissl's forces attacked from the east, and Ebersbaught and his troops routed the remaining enemy troops in a pincer movement:

> A third part of the Turkes, that besieged that side towards Knousbruck, were slaine; many of the rest drowned, but all fled. The other part of the Armie was so busied to resist the false fires, that Kisell before the morning put two thousand good souldiers in the Towne.[5]

The Ottomans were overwhelmed, and drowned as they tried to escape across the river or panicked into retreating south to Nagykanizsa. Khissl reinforced and resupplied the town, then marched his troops thirty-eight miles north to the local headquarters in Körmend (Smith's "Kerment"), where they were received "with much honour". Smith's contribution too was recognized: he was promoted to captain of cavalry and given command of 250 horsemen.

He was only twenty-one years old. If he had not yet attained the status of gentleman, he at least could now call himself an officer.

Captain Smith's enthusiasm for his escapades in Hungary is palpable to anyone reading his accounts. He was keen the reader know of his achievements on the field of battle. When writing about the taking of the Venetian argosy, he had shared nothing of his own role. Maybe because piracy was not a gentleman's profession – and Smith, as a passenger on a French ship, would have known he could not claim to have plundered the enemy in defence of his queen.

Now, however, he was officially enlisted in the Imperial army, and he was free to brag. His account of the relief of Olumpagh is most valuable in trying to reconstruct Smith's movements, but if his details were accurate, they should also help with identifying the location of the fortress town – a subject of much debate. The name Olumpagh (sometimes called Olimpach by other writers) has never appeared on a map.

The place names on the front line offered ample reason for confusion. Eastern Europe had been in conflict for hundreds of years: In succession, Celts, Romans, Magyars, Austrians, Slavs, Poles, Germans and Turks had hacked and slashed their way across this land, each leaving their imprint on the towns and villages they once occupied. Often, the names of the places changed with the names of the conquerors. Smith, of course, was also an idiosyncratic writer and spelled as best he could, usually phonetically, sometimes decades after an event. With "Olumpagh", had Smith fabricated a triumph for himself, or merely misspelt the name of a town?

Over the last century, historians have generally agreed that Smith's Olumpagh was a corruption of Limbach, but that does not settle the question. There are two Limbachs – Oberlimbach (Upper Limbach) and Unterlimbach (Lower Limbach) – in northeast Slovenia. Both towns are strong candidates for Olumpagh, with their castles and their history on the Ottoman front line in the early seventeenth century.

Grad Castle is now part of the Goričko National Park in Slovenia (photo by Peter Firstbrook).

In 1953, historian Bradford Smith claimed Smith had seen action in Oberlimbach[6]; twelve years later, Philip Barbour argued that he was in Unterlimbach.[7] An academic rivalry was born.

In Bradford Smith's view, Upper Limbach held a strategic position on the line of fortresses keeping western Europe safe from the Ottomans. Now called Grad – Slovenian for "castle" – this small village is nestled among alpine hills. Perched on a steep mound, the castle itself enjoys a strong, defensible position; the structure is substantially renovated but looks much as it did in 1601, save for the addition of a bell tower in 1751. During the war with the Ottomans, the trees growing on the hillside would have been felled to give a clear line of sight. Working with Dr Laura Polanyi Striker, a Hungarian historian who pored over the archives in Graz, Bradford Smith was certain there had been military activity at the garrison around 1601. Archduke Ferdinand wrote that after the fall of Nagykanizsa in October 1601, "the enemy raided daily up to Ober-Limbach and Unter-Limbach even to Olsznitz [a German town]".[8] Of course, the whole region was subject to regular incursions by the Turks in those days.

In contrast, Philip Barbour believed Lower Limbach would have been a much more important position for the Habsburgs to hold, and therefore much more likely to have been the scene of Smith's success.

Lendava Castle as it was in 1601 (top; photo by Peter Firstbrook), in a painting on display in the Lendava-Lendva Gallery and Museum; the castle today, looking southwest over the floodplain (bottom; photo by Peter Firstbrook).

Now called Lendava, Lower Limbach lies thirty miles southeast of Grad. There has been a fortress there since the twelfth century, although the present-day Baroque-style castle was built much later, between 1690 and 1707. Beyond the castle, the land opens on the wide, flat valley of the River Mura, which gives an army easy access to the whole region – including Graz and Vienna to the northwest. Strategically, it was essential to hold back any attackers here.

There was regular military activity in the region, and being on the front line, both Limbachs were almost certainly attacked by the Ottomans in 1601. Smith was excited by his first taste of Ottoman blood, and fortunately he wrote in enough detail to test his record of the battle against the lay of the land.

Both Grad and Lendava are overlooked by hills, though none might be called "a mountaine". Grad Castle is at an altitude of 1,127 feet, and overlooked by peaks of up to 1,246 feet. Lendava is lower, at 558 feet, with a ridge behind the castle to the north and east rising to 1,050 feet. Otherwise, the settings of the towns are quite different. Grad is surrounded by rolling, forested hills, and none of the visible peaks are more than a mile from the castle; Lendava is much bigger, perched on the western edge of a hilly region and looking out across a broad, flat floodplain.

It is mainly water that distinguishes the two locations. In Grad, there is nothing more than a rippling mountain stream; in Lendava, the meandering River Mura is two hundred feet wide, bordered on both sides by low-lying wetlands. And though the River Mura is two miles from the castle, it is a critical feature of the area's defences.

The ridge on the opposite side of the valley from Lendava Castle fits perfectly with Smith's description of the site for displaying his flaming torches. The straight-line distance from the ridge to the castle is six miles – Smith wrote it was seven. Although this is a long distance to signal using torches, it is by no means impossible on a clear night and with the aid of a spyglass. It was on this ridge, probably close to the village of Donji Koncovčak (today across the border in northern Croatia) that Smith alerted the besieged Habsburgs of the plan to attack on the Thursday night.

Furthermore, Smith observed that the river divided the Turkish army, and that they could not easily join forces. This suggests the river was wide and deep enough to limit the soldiers' movement on the battlefield. Smith also confided that many of the Turks were drowned during their retreat. The only river in the area wide and deep enough to cause such a problem is the Mura, which flows very swiftly, at three miles per hour or more. This floodplain, overlooked by the castle at Lendava, was Smith's first killing field in his campaign against the Ottomans. The quagmire of water, mud and swamp would have caused havoc among even the most disciplined and well-organized armies.

The skirmish at Olumpagh served as Smith's baptism by fire, and he displayed a remarkable degree of ingenuity there. That ingenuity would be a hallmark of his career for the next decade.

The summer was dwindling, but there was still plenty of military action to be seen. Smith remained part of Modrusch's Protestant regiment, which was now part of Khissl's detachment. The combined forces had travelled north to Körmend.

By a quirk of fate, the general leading the Holy Roman Emperor's forces in Körmend was none other than the Duke of Mercœur, whose wife Smith had tried to meet in Brittany to get himself placed under the ardent Catholic's command. Finally, his prayers were answered. And better yet, he was now an officer, not an upstart volunteer. But Smith had little time to enjoy his new prospects and status before he was ordered to make ready for battle.

Mercœur ordered the troops to move out of Körmend on September 6, 1601 (NS). Their objective was to lay siege to the Ottoman stronghold of Alba Regalis – "Seat of the White Castle", one hundred miles to the east. Now the modern city of Székesfehérvár in Hungary, it had once been the capital of the Magyar kings, and, as such, had been built with an eye to their safety: the city centre was sited on four islands surrounded by marshes and criss-crossed by a labyrinth of streams. The heavily fortified wall that ran around three sides of the city afforded further protection, and beyond the walls were smaller garrisons, giving the Turks a formidable combination of defences.

Strategically, Alba Regalis was significant because it commanded the main route travelling southwest out of Buda, just forty miles away. The Ottomans had first taken Alba Regalis in 1543 after a long siege. Now the Holy Roman Emperor wanted the Magyar fortress back.

To take Alba Regalis, Mercœur employed a clever feigning tactic. He sent one of his most capable generals, Hermann Christof Graf von Russworm, to Esztergom, thirty miles northwest of Buda, to create a diversion. The Ottoman governor of Buda then made a catastrophic mistake: fearing the imminent attack on his city, he sent his valuables to Alba Regalis for safe-keeping and recalled the troops that were there to defend Buda. Mercœur took the opportunity to march east from Körmend and lay siege to Alba Regalis.

The plains to the north of Lake Balaton, like most of western Hungary, were flat and boggy, and heavy going for an army of foot soldiers and horse-drawn wagons. However, it was mid-September, the driest time of year, and by Smith's account Mercœur's forces were able to cover the one hundred miles to Alba Regalis in a little over eighty hours – an impressively quick time for a large army on the move. The first the Ottomans knew of Mercœur's approaching force was when it announced its presence on the outskirts of the fortress-town. The next day, Russworm's diversionary regiments arrived from Esztergom, and the Habsburg army – which Smith noted to be some "thirtie thousand" strong[9] – prepared to attack.

The strike on Alba Regalis was a much bigger military offensive than the relief of Olumpagh. As with the previous assault, Smith described the situation and his exploits with gusto. There were rolling hills to the north, west and east of Alba Regalis, and Mercœur ordered his men to set up their encampment on the high ground to the northeast. From this position they unleashed a relentless bombardment of the city. With the eye of an experienced soldier, Smith said the city was "a place so strong by Art and Nature, that it was thought impregnable".[10]

However, Mercœur had identified a potential weakness in the defences: the southern approach, where there were no fortified walls. In that area, the Ottomans relied on the marshy ground as their defence. With cannon fire maintaining the Habsburgs' offensive, the Duke sent out scouts to find a way through the swamp. Reports from the returning sorties were

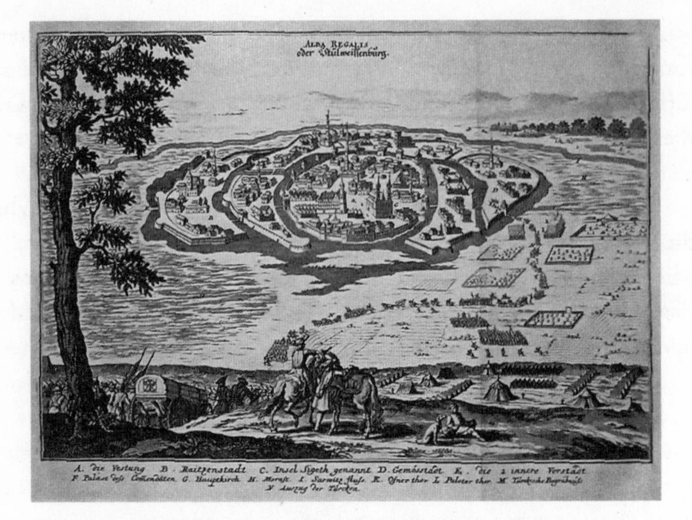

The old city of Alba Regalis, showing the tangle of rivers and marshy ground surrounding it, from Matthäus Merian's *Alba Regalis oder Stuhlweissenburg* (1698).

not optimistic: it would be difficult to attack across this boggy land. Regardless, the general was determined to press on with his scheme.

General Russworm, whom Smith called "Rosworme", offered to lead the assault. As the plans were being finalized, Habsburg and Ottoman regiments clashed on the outskirts of the city. Smith reported high casualties among the German, Hungarian and French troops; this was a truly pan-European Christian army fighting the Muslims. As these skirmishes continued, Mercœur worried his siege would stall and degenerate into a war of attrition, which always gives the advantage to the defender, not the attacker. With winter approaching fast, the general knew he had little choice: he must push his way into the city across the boggy land.

Captain Smith now had the ear of his desperate commander. While they had been resting at Körmend, Smith had demonstrated to his immediate superior, Modrusch, and several other senior officers his ideas for pyrotechnic grenades – Smith called them his "fiery dragons". Essentially, these were crude mortar bombs made by filling "fortie or fiftie round-bellied earthen pots" with an explosive mixture of gunpowder, pitch, brimstone, camphor and linseed. Musket balls were cut into quarters and added to the containers, and a combustible cotton plug pushed on top. Here, Machiavelli's influence over Smith was again evident. Smith was putting one of the great maxims from *The Art of War* into practice, by using "new and sudden thynges, [that] make armies afrayde".

Mercœur decided to try Smith's inventive suggestion. At midnight, the Duke sent a small force of men crawling to the base of the city walls, where they lit the fuses of the "fiery dragons" before lobbing them over the walls using simple slings. The unexpected bombardment had a devastating effect:

> It was a fearfull sight to see the short flaming course of their flight in the aire, but presently after their fall, the lamentable noise of the miserable slaughtered Turkes was most wonderful to heare.[11]

Meanwhile, Russworm and a contingent of one thousand troops stood at the ready; Mercœur pressed home his temporary advantage by ordering the southern attack. The troops moved through the undefended swamp in the early hours of the morning, each soldier carrying a bundle of reeds and wooden sticks, which afforded him some footing in the boggy terrain. Despite this provision, the wretched men would still have had to half wade, half swim through the filthy, stagnant water in the dark. It was a high-risk move, but by daybreak the sappers reached firm ground.

Russworm heralded his arrival at the edge of the city with the sound of trumpets and rolling drums. This may have seemed gratuitous, but it was a signal for Mercœur to start an attack from the east. The Turks were taken by surprise, and withdrew quickly behind the city walls, leaving the ring of outlying forts in Habsburg hands.

Having closed in, Mercœur returned to his bombardment, and on September 20, 1601, the Christians breached the city walls. Now, the combat was hand-to-hand, and the resulting carnage was appalling. Not one to exaggerate suffering, Smith wrote that the city "was so battered, that it was taken perforce, with such mercilesse execution, as was most pitiful to behold".[12] Even the graves of the Magyar kings were plundered. The city was utterly destroyed.

The Turks had occupied Alba Regalis for over half a century, and Mercœur's success was hailed as a great triumph, even though the ruinous siege had rendered the city uninhabitable for the victors. Afterwards, the Habsburg forces, including Count Modrusch's battalion and John Smith, were obliged to camp on a flat plain to the east of the city, most probably the area between the city and Lake Velence.

It took three weeks for the governor of Buda to despatch his troops to reclaim the city after its fall. Smith claimed the Turks "raised an Armie of sixtie thousand men", a huge contingent. In the early seventeenth century, the Turks commandeered the most disciplined and effective army in the world, and this was Smith's first experience of a full Ottoman offensive. For as far as he could see, flags bearing the white star and crescent on a bright red field flapped in the breeze. Janissary foot soldiers armed with matchlock muskets were flanked by cavalry; pike men marched in perfectly ordered squares; more infantry followed to protect the front and rear of the artillery. Behind the main army came the baggage train, protected by still more soldiers.

Smith was used to war camps – the dirty, disorderly, squalid assemblage of hurriedly erected bivouacs and makeshift tents. By contrast, the Ottoman encampment was a transitory city of canvas, silk, brocade and embroidery, laid out to a design pre-ordained by the Imperial Corps of Tent Pitches. Forty years previously, a Habsburg ambassador to Constantinople recorded:

> Any one who knows the conditions which obtain in our own camps, will find difficulty in believing it, but the fact remains that everywhere [among the Ottomans] was complete silence and tranquillity... Moreover, there was the utmost cleanliness, no dungheaps or rubbish, nothing to offend the eye or nose, everything of this kind being either buried by the Turks or else removed from sight...[13]

Such regulations allowed the commanders and their soldiers to find their way around the site easily, because the layout of every camp was the same.

It was an impressive display of strength and discipline. The Habsburg army was heavily outnumbered, and its encampment undefended. The best option for Mercœur was once again to go on the offensive. According to Smith:

> twenty thousand good souldiers, set forward to meet the Turke in the Plaines of Girke. Those two Armies encountred [each other] as they marched, where began a hot and bloudy Skirmish betwixt them, Regiment against Regiment, as they came in order, till the night parted them.[14]

The Christian soldiers had to fight their way out. Smith was in the middle of the mêlée, and recalled:

> that it was a terror to see how horse and man lay sprawling and tumbling, some one away, some another on the ground. The Earle [Smith's commander, the Count of Modrusch] there at that time made his valour shine more bright than his armour, which seemed then painted with Turkish bloud.[15]

Thousands died. Half of Modrusch's regiment were slain. Smith was wounded, and his horse killed under him, "but he was not long unmounted, for there was choice enough of horses, that wanted masters".[16] Only darkness brought the slaughter to a close. The two armies dug in for the night, only to continue skirmishing the next day.

Then, on October 15, it became apparent the Turks were ready to engage in full battle. The armies met at the mouth of Charka Boğazi, "Skirmish Gorge"[17] or Tscharka Gorge.[18] It was another bloody encounter. According to Smith, the Ottomans lost "five or six thousand", and the Habsburg army almost as many, including "divers other great commanders".

With such unsustainable losses on both sides, and the bitter central European winter closing in, the opposing commanders agreed to a truce. On October 25, the Turks withdrew to Buda, and Smith and his fellow soldiers retired to the ruins of Alba Regalis.

Sadly, the modern town of Székesfehérvár, with its sprawling suburbs, electronics factories and hypermarkets, retains very little of its great historic past. This makes it somewhat difficult to identify the key military positions taken by Mercœur and his men in the autumn of 1601. However, to the northeast of the town, comfortable middle-class homes now overlook the city from a low ridge. This would have been a perfect position from which to bombard the Ottomans. Smith's plains of "Girke", where the Habsburg army met its foe, do not appear on any contemporary map. But historical records do confirm that on October 15, 1601, an engagement took place between Christian and Muslim forces at Charka Boğazi, a dozen miles or so north of Székesfehérvár.[19] This seems likely to be close to the modern town of Csákvár.

More problematic is Smith's description of an island lying on the western margin of Alba Regalis, where the city was left virtually without defence because of the natural protection of the river and swamp. The western side of Székesfehérvár is today given over to large apartment blocks looking out on flat marshland and shallow lakes, and on first impression it is impossible to discern anything that might once have been an island. But altitude readings from a simple handheld GPS unit show the builders of the apartments used slight differences in height in their construction. The apartments sit on a low rise, thirty to fifty feet above the surrounding marshland. In 1601, this area would have stood proud of the surrounding floodland – an island in the mire.

As winter began to close on Alba Regalis, the Duke of Mercœur had to decide how best to deploy his troops for the next fighting season. Smith explained how the general divided his army into three parts, a point confirmed in other historic records. The first group was left behind to defend Alba Regalis, although this move failed to prevent the Ottomans from retaking the city the following year. The second group went to support Archduke Ferdinand II in his siege of Nagykanizsa; this engagement was aborted less than a month later, as the Imperial army sustained heavy losses. The third group, which included Captain Smith's cavalry company, was sent east into Transylvania.

Mercœur himself then travelled to Vienna to report to his superiors. By Captain Smith's account:

> having thus worthily behaved himselfe, he arrived at Vienne [Vienna]; where the Arch-dukes and the Nobilitie with as much honour received him, as if he had conquered all Hungaria...[and] preparing himself to returne into France, to raise new Forces against the next yeare.[20]

Smith's portrayal of Mercœur's whereabouts is confirmed by other sources, and Smith also reported accurately that Mercœur died suddenly, before he could return to his native France. Apparently, Mercœur moved on from Vienna to Prague, and then on to Nuremberg, where he died on February 19, 1602 – apparently of "a pestilential spotted fever".[21] This was a captain who was clearly well informed about the movements of his senior officers – or, if Smith gleaned the information at a later date and inserted it into his memoirs, this was a captain who thought Mercœur's status and demise were worth noting.

When Smith left Alba Regalis with Count Modrusch's Protestant forces, at Mercœur's behest, he naturally assumed he was taking the war against the Ottomans further east on behalf of the Holy Roman Empire. In reality, events took a very different turn. What Smith could not have comprehended at the time was that he and his battalion were about to be caught up in a complex web of political intrigue, naked ambition, ruthless suppression and insanity. His year in Transylvania would see his greatest conquests as a soldier, but also his humiliating descent into capture and slavery.

John Smith jousting with an opponent to the death,
in a detail from Smith's *The True Travels* (1630).

4
Knight-Errant

1602

The earth did blush with the bloud of honesty, that the Sunne for shame did hide himself, from so monsterous sight of a cowardly calamity
John Smith, The True Travels (1630)

In the first few weeks of 1602, John Smith and the rest of the Count of Modrusch's battalion spent their time battling deep snow drifts and bitter, icy winds as they headed east through Hungary and into Transylvania. Modrusch's Protestant army stood at six thousand men by Smith's reckoning, and not all of them would make it:

> An extraordinary continuing tempest of haile, wind, frost and snow, in so much that the Christians were forced to leave their Tents and Artillery, and what they had; it being so cold that three or foure hundred of them were frozen to death in a night, and two or three thousand lost in that miserable flight in a snowie tempest.[1]

It is challenging to move an army in mid-winter. The days are short, food is scarce, drinking water freezes, equipment is abandoned, soldiers die by the hundreds, and those who survive are vulnerable to frostbite. As a cavalry man, Smith most likely walked for much of the way, rather than risk riding his horse on rock-hard trails. But this was no ordinary cold spell: tree-ring records show that the winter of 1601–2 was the coldest for six hundred years, and the reason for Captain Smith's misery lay seven thousand miles away in South America.

The previous year, the Huaynaputina volcano in southern Peru had erupted, sending volcanic ash high into the atmosphere. Observers said the mountain looked like a huge fire, with the noise of "cannon-ball explosions". An hour after the eruption, debris began to fall from the sky; within twenty-four hours, ten villages were buried under ten inches of ash,[2] and volcanic mudflows had reached the Pacific Ocean, seventy-five miles away. It was the largest volcanic eruption in historical times, and its effects were felt all around the globe as sunlight was blocked by the large quantities of sulphur particles spewed into the atmosphere.[3] In France, the wine harvest was delayed, and in Germany wine production collapsed completely; the spring blossom arrived late in China, and in Russia the severe winter caused the worst famine in the country's history.

Smith's company of horsemen had to contend with these punishing conditions as they made their way to northern Transylvania and the headquarters of General Giorgio Basta in the city of Bistrița. Apart from simply surviving the winter, the Habsburg army had to avoid enemy patrols seeking to report the position of units and troop movements. So Smith's detachment first skirted Ottoman-held Buda, before looping northeast to Esztergom, and then on to Tokaj, a journey of some four hundred miles. It was a gruelling march, and, as an officer, Smith was now responsible for his men's safety, not just his own.

The captain was heading for a once-isolated principality, a plateau of valleys, ravines and rolling hills, and encircled by the Carpathian Mountains. For the past several centuries, Transylvania had become a strategically important crossroads between eastern and western Europe. Consequently, invading armies had ravished the region at will, leaving the population decimated. They also left a very complicated history in their wake.

The Principality of Transylvania had become a semi-independent state in 1526, under the rule of the Ottomans. Hungarian princes paid tribute to the Turks, and in return their overlords allowed them to enjoy relative autonomy. This put the principality beyond the reach of the Catholic authority of the Holy Roman Emperor, and Protestant doctrine flourished. For a few decades at least, the people of Transylvania had enjoyed relative peace and stability. But it was not to last for long.

Disorder returned to Transylvania in 1588 – the year of the Armada – when Sigismund Báthory (in Hungarian, Báthory Zsigmond) reached the age of majority and took his father's title of *voivode*, or warlord. Báthory came from an eccentric – some would say psychopathic – family, with a history of mental illness. His niece Erzsébet (Elizabeth) is reputed to have killed over six hundred virgins, and bathed in their blood in an attempt to seek eternal youth. Báthory's younger cousin Gabriel was said to be a tyrannical, fickle and sexually debauched maniac, who was betrayed and murdered by his own friends; his naked body thrown unceremoniously into a creek. By comparison, Sigismund Báthory was a paragon of virtue. However, he did suffer from epilepsy and impotence, and some believe he was also homosexual.

Báthory was an ardent Catholic and made no secret of his allegiance to the Church. However, he was also an obedient Ottoman vassal, at least until 1594, when he negotiated an alliance with Rudolf II behind

Sigismund Báthory, Prince of Transylvania, by an unidentified artist (left); Prince Rudolf II, Holy Roman Emperor, by Aegidius Sadeler (right).

the Turks' backs. The emperor recognized Báthory as the Prince of Transylvania, and arranged for him to marry his cousin, the Archduchess Maria Christina. Uniting the Habsburg and Báthory families through marriage was politically expedient for both rulers. Unfortunately, the wedding night was a fiasco, and the marriage never consummated.

The broken-hearted prince sought solace in military glory. Báthory joined forces with Michael the Brave, the Prince of Wallachia, another Turkish-controlled principality to the south of Transylvania. Together, the two princes drove the Ottomans out of the region. The Habsburg–Báthory alliance had its first success.

Back in Transylvania, Báthory's rule faced serious internal unrest, and he returned with his troops to put down an insurgency with appalling cruelty. Those who opposed him faced impalement, hanging and mutilation. Then, in 1597, Báthory decided enough was enough, and abdicated. Alas, one of his many weaknesses was indecision – a contemporary commented wryly that he was as unreliable as April weather. Four months later Báthory's people welcomed him back as their ruler, but within a few months, he tired again of governance. This time, he had his marriage annulled and arranged to take religious orders in the Catholic Church.

By now, Rudolf II was sinking into insanity, and in no position to take control of Transylvania anyway; the principality was descending into ungovernable mayhem in the face of this leadership crisis. Seizing his opportunity, Michael the Brave invaded his northern neighbour. His motivations were not entirely political: Michael was bankrupt from his recent warring, and he levied punitive taxes on his new subjects. His unpaid soldiers followed his lead and looted the Transylvanian countryside, and life for ordinary people again became intolerable.

The state of anarchy in Transylvania now threatened the entire region. Rudolf II had recognized Michael the Brave as Imperial Governor of Transylvania and despatched one of his leading generals, Giorgio Basta, to support Michael against the Ottomans. But Basta decided to join forces with the Transylvanian nobles that opposed the Wallachian interloper. The two armies met in September 1600, and Michael was defeated. Undeterred, he travelled to Prague, where he regained the favour of the capricious Rudolf. The emperor sent Michael back to

Michael the Brave, Prince of Wallachia and the Holy Roman Emperor's governor in Transylvania (left); his sometime foe and sometime ally, General Giorgio Basta (right).

Transylvania with his blessing, and with orders to join forces with his adversary, General Basta.

In this remarkable tale of double-dealing and deception, nothing should come as a surprise. When word of the situation got back to Prince Sigismund early in 1601, he decided to drop his priestly pretensions and raise yet another army. The long-suffering Transylvanian people welcomed him home again. (This was at much the same time that John Smith was being recruited into the Habsburg army in Graz.) On August 3, 1601 (NS), Báthory's army confronted the combined forces of General Basta and Michael the Brave; the Transylvanian army was overwhelmed.

Báthory's defeat left Basta and Michael the Brave in joint control of Transylvania – a partnership that was never going to last. There is some suggestion that Michael tried secretly to re-establish a union with the Turks. Whatever the truth, Basta had Michael assassinated just a few days after their victory against Báthory. It was a cynical move, but Basta assumed it would ensure his unrivalled control. The move failed.

For the third time in four years, Sigismund Báthory returned from exile to reclaim his principality. This time he was supported by a contingent of Turkish troops; apparently, his ardent Catholicism only went so far. The autumn was wet, and heavy flooding prevented Basta from using his full power to stop Báthory establishing a power base. By late 1601 the prince had become the *de facto* ruler of most of the southern half of Transylvania.

Rudolf II was roused from the melancholy clouds of his insanity when he received the startling news back in Prague, and he knew he had to respond. The Transylvanian–Ottoman alliance was in renaissance, and the region was falling back into Turkish hands. Smith and his regiment were despatched to northern Transylvania in late 1601 to meet this new threat.

In January 1602, Rudolf promoted Giorgio Basta to Commander-in-Chief of the Imperial army in Transylvania. He ordered him to unseat Báthory – by persuasion if possible, but by force if necessary. John Smith had no idea how his fortunes were about to change.

Captain Smith, together with the rest of Modrusch's troops, arrived at Basta's headquarters in Bistrița in early March 1602 with orders to support the general. By then, there was intense diplomatic activity between the Basta and Báthory camps, as the general tried to negotiate a peaceful settlement with the ever-vacillating prince. Suddenly, in a surprising reversal of policy, Basta announced he was withdrawing his army from Transylvania. The move took everybody by surprise, but the Habsburg general was being very shrewd.

In his suppression of the region, Basta had relied on roaming bands of mercenaries called Hajdúk, who he had let run amok in the countryside. Some of the Hajdúk were former soldiers of Michael the Brave's army who had been left stranded in Transylvania after Basta had murdered their commander. Smith referred to the Hajdúk as "some Turks, some Tartars, but most Bandittoes, Rennegadoes, and such like"[4] – in other words, they were a semi-autonomous legion of displaced soldiers, robbers and highwaymen of various nationalities, including Turks. As a whole, they were responsible for murders, rapes and arson, and were also blamed for the widespread famine, though Huaynaputina's ash clouds and the terrible winter were also significant factors. Historical reports from the period tell of starving peasants cutting bodies down from the gallows for food, and of children eating the wasted corpses of their parents to survive. Basta had come to realize he could no longer control the Hajdúk. As part of the terms of his departure from Bistriţa, he gave Báthory the authority to rid the principality of these outlaws. In return, Basta made peace and removed his army from Transylvania.

John Smith's travels to Transylvania in 1602. Smith's regiment trekked from Alba Regalis to join General Basta's forces in Bistriţa, before heading south to Braşov in support of Sigismund Báthory's army.

This was the bizarre situation met by Modrusch and his officers when they arrived in Transylvania. They faced a choice: either withdraw to Hungary with Basta and the Imperial army, or stay in Transylvania to fight the Hajdúk alongside Báthory. In a surprising *volte-face,* Modrusch chose the second option. He decided to offer his services to this unstable prince, who only months earlier had been the Habsburgs' enemy. Modrusch took his forces south to Braşov, where he met up with Báthory at his headquarters.

Smith might only have been a relatively unimportant captain, but his understanding of the complex politics involved was accurate and insightful. Most importantly, he understood Modrusch's reasoning for switching his allegiances:

> Hearing of the death of Michael [the Brave] and the brave Duke Mercury [Mercœur], and knowing the policie of Busca [Basta], and the Prince his Roialtie [Báthory], being now beyond all beleefe of men, in possession of the best part of Transylvania, [he] persuaded his troopes, in so honest a cause, to assist the Prince against the Turke [Hajdúk], rather than Busca against the Prince.[5]

Modrusch's switch was also personal. The count's father had been brutally killed by soldiers identified as Hajdúk – who, he believed, were the true enemy of his people.

Modrusch still had to persuade his troops to follow him to Báthory's side. His battalion had spent a hard winter making their way to Transylvania to fight *against* the prince. As Protestants they had not always received the recognition they felt they deserved. Not surprisingly, morale among his troops was low. To make his task a little easier, Modrusch made his men an offer they found difficult to refuse. In Smith's words:

> The souldiers being worne out with those hard payes and travells, upon hope to have free libertie to make bootie upon what they could get possession of from the Turkes, was easily perswaded to follow him [Modrusch] whithersoever.[6]

The offer of plunder did the trick.

When Modrusch sent word to Báthory that his twenty years of military experience, together with his battalion of Protestant troops, were at the prince's service, the offer was keenly accepted. The prince promoted Modrusch to "Camp-master", effectively a colonel. More to the point, the count's soldiers were promised regular pay and the opportunity to pillage. Perhaps Smith recalled Machiavelli's advice as he contemplated what lay ahead: "When they remain in garrison, soldiers are maintained with fear and punishment; when they are then led to war, with hope and reward."

Having committed his regiment to supporting Báthory, the Count of Modrusch wasted no time hunting down the Hajdúk. His first actions in the spring of 1602, according to Smith, were reconnaissance raids from Braşov to the west. "The Earl having made many incursions into the land of Zarkam among those rockie mountains", he wrote. This was where Modrusch's forces first began to flush out the Hajdúk:

> which sometimes hee forces into the Plaines of Regall, where is a Citie not only of men and fortifications, strong of it selfe, but so environed with mountaines, that made the passages so difficult, that in all these warres no attempt had beene made upon it to any purpose.[7]

The siege of the garrison town of Regall became the main focus of their attempts to root out the outlaws. Smith recalled: "The earth no sooner put on her greene habit, than the Earle [Modrusch] overspread her with his armed troopes".[8] The spring offensive in Transylvania had begun in earnest, and it would turn out to be Smith's most fearless year of combat yet.

Modrusch decided to set a trap. According to Smith, his commander sent a Colonel Veltus to lie in ambush with his troops near a small Hajdúk stronghold in "a narrow valley betwixt two high mountains". The next morning, Veltus' force drove all the cattle they could find past the enemy fort. The Hajdúk, seeing a chance to seize some fresh meat, left their defences, and the trap was sprung. Smith said "the Garrison was cut off by the Ambuscado [ambush], and Veltus seized on the Skonces [a small fortification], which was abandoned".[9]

This brief action was typical of the constant skirmishing both sides employed, and the destruction of the sconce gave Modrusch and his men free access through the valley to a much bigger prize: Regall. There was a downside, however, for the enemy now had plenty of warning of their movements. With their new intelligence, the Hajdúk "strengthned the Towne so with men and provision, that they made a scorne of so small a number as Meldritch [Modrusch] brought with him before the Citie".[10]

Smith was in top form as he recalled the military preparations for the siege. He explained that it took Modrusch six days to move his eight thousand troops to the fortress, giving the defenders ample time to prepare for the assault. Almost immediately, the Hajdúk went on the offensive:

> Before they had pitched their Tents, the Turkes sallied in such abundance, as for an houre they had rather a bloudy battell than a skirmish, but with the losse of neere fifteen hundred on both sides.[11]

The next day, much-needed reinforcements arrived under the command of General Mózes Székely (Smith's Prince Moyses), to help Modrusch's forces. The general also assumed overall command of the siege. According to Smith, Székely brought an additional nine thousand foot soldiers and cavalry, together with twenty-six artillery pieces. These reinforcements set up their siege-camp just outside the Hajdúk fortress, which was built on a promontory. Within half a mile to one side, there was a mountain; on the other, "a faire Plaine". Székely's army then spent the next month digging trenches in preparation for a prolonged assault.

By the beginning of the seventeenth century, siege warfare had become sophisticated and specialized. Often, the besiegers themselves had to build elaborate fortifications to defend against a garrison's guns. Preparations for a siege also took time. Smith explained that mounds fifty or sixty feet high were built to raise the twenty-six guns needed for the bombardment. And the logistics of supply added further complications. Apart from feeding seventeen thousand soldiers, Székely had to make sure he had enough gunpowder and ammunition to complete the siege. A single large breach in a castle wall could take fifteen thousand cannon balls, and all this materiel had to be carted long distances along rutted tracks from their supply depots.[12]

Siege armies were often sited close to the walls of the garrison they were attacking, and Székely's force was no exception. His encampment was within hearing distance of the Hajdúk town, inviting the enemy to taunt them. Smith observed the scorn of the Hajdúk at the Transylvanian army's slow work: "the Turkes oft derided, that their Ordnance were at pawne, and how they grew fat for want of exercise".[13] It was classical psychological warfare.

Spring gave way to early summer, and both sides became increasingly bored. During one of their jeering exchanges, the Hajdúk made a proposal for passing the time. They suggested a temporary truce, during which time each side would put forward a champion to fight in single combat to the death:

> That to delight the Ladies, who did long to see some court-like pastime, the Lord Turbashaw [probably a Hajdúk officer] did defie any Captaine, that had the command of a Company, who durst combate with him for his head.[14]

Whether the Hajdúk actually had "ladies" is doubtful, but they certainly had women. Nor was anyone likely to have experienced much "court-like pastime" in a Hajdúk garrison town. But the invitation was accepted all the same.

Smith was carried away with excitement for the knightly combat. Lots were drawn in his camp to select an opponent, and Smith won. Here was his woodland dream come true: all those days practising charging with his lance in the pasture outside Willoughby; his hours studying Machiavelli and Marcus Aurelius; the saddle sores from his tutelage at Tattershall. All, it seemed, had been in preparation for this great day.

However, this was no courtly joust, but a duel to the death, with no outside interference. It wasn't quite what his riding master, Theodore Paleologue, had in mind when he trained his pupil.

Not surprisingly, Smith's account of the contest included every detail imaginable, full of colour and romance, the quintessential medieval knight's tale:

> Truce being made for that time, the Rampiers [ramparts] all beset with faire Dames, and men at Armes, the Christians in Battalio [battle dress]; Turbashaw with a noise of Howboyes entred the field well mounted and armed; on his shoulders were fixed a paire of great wings, compacted of Eagles feathers within a ridge of silver, richly garnished with gold and precious stones.[15]

His rival's appearance was bizarre: mounted on his shoulders the officer had a pair of large wings made from eagle feathers, richly garnished with gold, silver and precious stones. Ahead of him walked a janissary carrying his lance, and two more attendants followed at his side, leading his horse to the field of combat. Turbashaw's supporters created a cacophony from their hautboys, slender double-reeded woodwind instruments rather like a modern oboe. Smith's arrival on the field of battle was altogether more modest: a single "page" led his way before the sound of blaring trumpets.

Both men wore full body armour made from well-tempered steel, which was cleverly articulated to allow the wearer to remain agile. Such lightweight fighting armour typically weighed about forty pounds. Because the overlapping steel plates were spread evenly around the body, the combatants could mount a horse unaided, and move and fight freely on the ground if they were dismounted. Even so, both men must have been sweating profusely under their steel.

As they passed each other on their way to their starting positions, they exchanged a courteous salute. They were handed their lances, which also weighed as much as forty pounds, and a signal was given. Then they charged.

Smith would have been taught by Theodore Paleologue to keep his lance balanced and horizontal and not to allow it to drop as he began his charge towards his opponent. Smith executed his first pass, as he remembered it, without fault. As the two men collided, Smith "passed [pierced] the Turke thorow the sight of his Beaver [the lower part of a helmet], face, head and all, that he fell dead to the ground".[16] Alighting from his horse unscathed, Smith removed his own helmet so he could see better. He then finished off his opponent with a *coup de grâce*, severing the Hajdúk's head, as required by the terms of combat. He then presented his grisly trophy to General Székely, "who kindly accepted it, and with joy to the whole armie he was generally welcomed".[17]

But this was not the end of the matter. Turbashaw had a friend who was "inraged with madnesse" at the outcome, and he issued Smith a new challenge "to regaine his friends head, or lose his owne, with his horse and Armour for advantage".[18]

The second contest was scheduled for the following day, again with lances on horseback. This time the outcome was not as clear-cut: as they clashed, both lances split, rendering them useless; Smith's opponent, however, was nearly unhorsed. Their secondary weapons were pistols, and the Hajdúk took the first shot. It was on target, but it glanced harmlessly off Smith's breastplate. With no chance to reload on horseback, Smith had an uninterrupted aim, and he hit his adversary in the left arm. Unable to control his horse, the Hajdúk fell to the ground, "and so bruised with the fall, that he lost his head, as his friend before him".[19] In addition to decapitating the man, Smith claimed his horse and armour, but sent the headless body and "his rich apparel" back to the Hajdúk castle.

With the gory entertainment over, the two armies continued as before. The enemy made sorties out of their fortress, skirmishing with Székely's forces, but with little effect. The groundworks for the siege continued, but the sappers needed to raise the platforms higher before the bombardment of the fortification could begin. Time, and the summer, dragged on, and the tedium continued. As a captain of cavalry, Smith was likely more bored than most, and with the self-confidence and arrogance of youth, he sought permission from Székely to issue his own challenge to the enemy to fight a third duel.

A man Smith called Bonny Mulgro accepted the offer, and the next day the two men faced each other on the same blood-soaked public killing ground. Smith's account of this duel was longer, more interesting, and certainly more exciting than the two that preceded it. Traditionally, the defendant had the choice of weapon, and Bonny Mulgro wisely avoided the lance and selected pistols and battle-axes instead. On the first pass, they both fired, and both missed. They then fell to their second weapon, "whose piercing bils [hooked blades] made sometime the one, sometime the other to have scarce sense to keepe their saddles".[20] It was a savage, exhausting encounter. Smith came off worse, and received such a resounding blow from his opponent that he dropped his axe. "The Turk prosecuted his advantage to the uttermost of his power."[21] A cheer went up from the ramparts as Bonny Mulgro closed in for the kill. Modest as ever, Smith then explained:

> his judgement and dexterity in such a businesse, beyond all mens expectation, by Gods assistance, not onely avoided the Turkes violence, but having drawne his Faulchion [a small, single-edge sabre], pieced the Turke so under the Cutlets [overlapping plates on his armour] thorow backe and body, that although he alighted from his horse, he stood not long ere hee lost his head, as the rest had done.[22]

Smith was battle-hardened after eighteen months at war, and at twenty-two he was at the peak of his physical fitness. Nevertheless, surviving these three duels was quite an achievement. With three spare horses, and his opponents' heads impaled on spikes, Smith was paraded with a guard of six thousand – or so he claimed – to General Székely's marquee.

The general received him "with as much respect as the occasion deserved", gave him yet another horse (richly furnished with a fine saddle), a jewelled scimitar and a belt worth three hundred ducats. (The ducat was a standard gold coin used throughout Eastern Europe at the time, and Smith's prize was worth about four years' wages for a craftsman.) The Count of Modrusch was equally delighted with Smith's achievement, and promoted him to the rank of sergeant major, which was rated just below lieutenant colonel in Smith's day. Smith never used the title, preferring instead to keep the rank of captain.

Good morale so often helps to win battles, and Smith claimed his success galvanized Székely's army. He was the "one of more life, of more heart, or at least of more authority, who with his spirit, with his words, and with his example keeps the others firm and disposed to fight", as *The Art of War* taught him. It probably also helped that Székely's siege guns were finally ready. Within fifteen days and after thousands of volleys, they made two breaches in the walls of the Hajdúk defences, and the full-scale assault on Regall began.

Smoke from the muskets and cannon was so dense "that day was made a darksome night". The attack was a direct advance up the steeply sloping front of the rocky promontory the castle was built on. The Hajdúk responded by rolling logs, gunpowder barrels and other debris towards them. Székely's troops suffered heavy losses.

Still more reinforcements were called for. Eventually, the Hajdúk were overwhelmed, but Székely refused to accept their surrender. The bombardment from his siege guns continued unabated. The next day, the Transylvanian forces took the citadel. Smith said Modrusch was in the vanguard of the action, set on retribution for his father's death: "all he found [who] could beare Armes he put to the sword, and set their heads upon stakes round about the walles, in the same manner they had used [with] the Christians, when they tooke it".[23] Hundreds, if not thousands of men must have died this way.

General Székely capitalized immediately on his victory. After repairing the ramparts, he moved on and sacked another three Hajdúk strongholds along the Mureş River, which Smith lists as Veratio (Vărădia de Mureş), Solmos (Şoimoş) and Kupronka (Căpruţa) – settlements all dating back to at least the mid-fourteenth century. Smith also reported that two thousand prisoners were taken, but they were mostly women and children, so the men most likely met the same fate as those at Regall.

Eventually, Székely's army "came to Esenberg, not farre from the Princes Palace".[24] This was Alba Iulia (in German, Weissenburg – and in Hungarian, Gyulafehérvár), the capital of the principality. Smith said Prince Báthory came to offer his congratulations and review the troops with his general. Indeed, Báthory was known to be in Alba Iulia between May 24 and June 8 (NS), awarding noble titles.[25]

During his visit, the prince was made aware of the exploits of a certain young English captain of cavalry, and marked him out for a great distinction. Smith wrote, "with great honour hee gave him three Turkes heads in a Shield for his Armes"[26] – an armorial coat of arms. It was a special award, usually bestowed in the midst of battle or in the glow of victory (though it could also be bought by those seeking rank and prestige). The prince also proclaimed Smith to be "an English Gentleman" and granted him an annual pension of three hundred ducats.

These prizes fulfilled Smith's wildest dreams. He was accepted as a gentleman by royalty, albeit Transylvanian royalty, and carried a coat of arms as proof of his military prowess. To top it off, he also had a handsome pension.

With such accolades being heaped upon him, it was little wonder John Smith's writings about this period in his life developed a richly egotistical style. He plainly enjoyed sharing the details of his military triumphs. His observations of the local geography also became more accurate, in part, no doubt, because of their relevance to the fighting. Yet Smith is vague about Regall, the location of the Hajdúk castle. Nor is there any independent account to verify his description of man-to-man combat. So did the three duels really happen? And, if so, where was the site of Regall?

Without any independent corroboration, evidence for Smith's duels has to be circumstantial and anecdotal. His story in *The True Travels* is remarkably similar to one in "The Famous and Pleasant History of Parismus, the Valiant and Renowned Prince of Bohemia", by the Elizabethan romantic writer Emanuel Ford, first published in 1598–99. "Parismus" was the popular tale of the King of Bohemia and Hungary, whose conflict with the Persians was settled by the combat of three knights, and the two opposing armies held daily tournaments "which afforded Pastime to the Ladies of the Court, who took great delight in beholding the Activity and Success of the Black Knight".[27] On the surface, this looks like a case of straightforward plagiarism by Smith, except there is ample evidence these "trials of arms" took place regularly on the battlefields of eastern Europe during Smith's time there. For example, in 1600, General Basta organized several such tournaments at the battle of Mirăslău between the Habsburg army and the Wallachian troops of Michael the

Brave. Stroe Buzescu, an officer in Michael's army, also fought a Tartar leader in hand-to-hand combat during the battle of Ogretin in 1602.[28]

There was a well-established etiquette for such engagements, based on the medieval code of chivalry. The level of violence, and thus the outcome of the duel, was clearly defined. The duel could last until one man was wounded; it could continue to the point of exhaustion, but without taking life; or, in the case with John Smith's purported duels, it finished with the death of one of the combatants. Under the rules of this last option, the victor took the spoils of the loser. In "Parismus", the duel scene ended not with death, but with reunion – the Black Knight identified the armour of a friend, and refused to fight him.

Of course, Smith could have learnt about the rules of single combat during his time in Hungary the previous year, or from veterans of the battle of Mirăslău. He could have fabricated the whole story, and history would be none the wiser. His writing during this complex period of Transylvanian history has otherwise proven to be accurate, but for the moment, his case for winning three duels is "not proven".

There is also the matter of the location of Regall, which has never been identified with any certainty. Fortunately, Smith's detailed descriptions, combined with confirmed historical facts and a little deduction, can help narrow down the options.

Smith's battalion arrived at Bistriţa in early March 1602. Modrush then took his men south to Braşov, and joined forces with Sigismund Báthory, who was about to start his spring offensive against the Hajdúk. Báthory used two armies in his campaign. He sent General István Csáky northwest towards Cluj-Napoca, and his army defeated the Hajdúk at Egerbegy (Agârbiciu), twenty miles west of the city, on March 20 (NS).[29] Fierce fighting continued in the region into June, when Csáky's army took the nearby Hajdúk fortress at Colţeşti (in Hungarian, Toroczko).[30] There is a magnificent ruined castle there, and its location fits Smith's description of Regall quite well. However, the fortress is small, and not "a Citie" as Smith described it. Besides, Smith was fighting not with Csáky's forces, but with Prince Báthory's second army, led by General Mózes Székely.

Székely's force operated against the Hajdúk in the southwest of Transylvania. Therefore, the location of the Hajdúk stronghold can be narrowed down to this part of the principality. Smith wrote that the Hajdúk fortress was "strong of it selfe", suggesting the castle was well defended, and this led some early historians to claim Smith's Regall was actually the Transylvanian capital, Alba Iulia. The topography around Alba Iulia does not fit Smith's description of a city "environed with mountains", however. Furthermore, the history of Alba Iulia is well documented, and there is no mention of a siege during the spring of 1602. This option is best discounted.

According to Smith, Modrusch wasted no time in taking the fight to the Hajdúk among the "rockie mountains" of "Zarkam", and they sometimes pursued the Hajdúk onto the "Plaines of Regall". There is no town on modern maps called Zarkam, but Abraham Ortelius' detailed 1570 map of Hungary shows a Zarkad in the foothills of the western Carpathians;[31] its modern name is Zărand. To the north, west and south of Zărand is flat land, stretching all the way to Budapest, 150 miles away. Perhaps this is the "Plaines of Regall".

After the siege of Regall, Smith said General Székely's forces moved up the Mureş River, sacking three more strongholds before arriving at Alba Iulia (Weissenburg). This indicates Regall was situated on, or close to, the river, but further to the west.

There are still more clues that point to Regall lying close to the Mureş valley. In 1600, the French writer and historian Martin Fumee published his history of Hungary. In it, he wrote about a castle, which he called "Drigal", that was "neerest out of Hungarie into Transilvania".[32] This puts Drigal close to the foothills of the Carpathian Mountains, which in Smith's day formed the boundary between Hungary and Transylvania. Clearly, Drigal was also strategically important, because it was situated "so that they [Hungarians] could not conveniently passe that way", and so that a route close by the castle was "the surest [way] to conduct an armie into the countrie".[33]

One of the easiest routes for an army through the mountains from Hungary into Transylvania was up the valley of the Mureş River. So it is possible Fumee's Drigal was Smith's Regall, as the general location and strategic importance appear similar. However, Transylvania was subjected to many warring factions over the centuries, and the region's

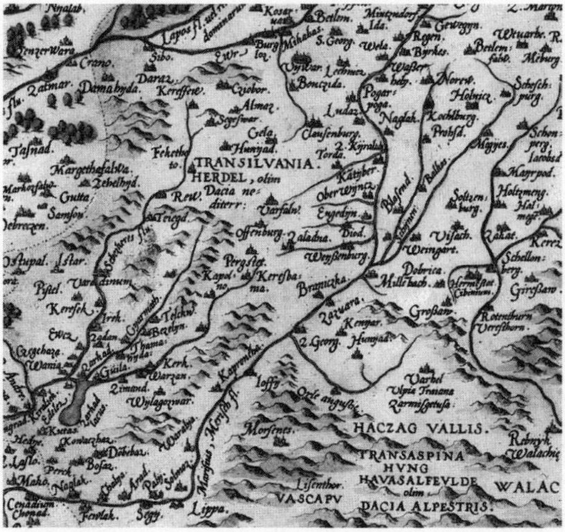

A detail from Abraham Ortelius' *Theatrvm orbis terrarvm: Hungaria* (1570). Zarkad and its lake appear in the lower left; the Mureş River can be traced from the bottom, flowing past Lippa, Solmoz and Kapronika, before turning northeast to Weissenburg (Alba Iulia). The Carpathian Mountains separate Hungary (in the west) from Transylvania (in the east), Siria lies equidistant between Zarkam and Lippa.

various rulers built many hundreds of fortresses of varying size and status. In the environs of the Mureş valley alone, there were several fortresses that could fit Smith's description of a fortress built "upon the point of a faire promontory".

However, there is a final clue in Smith's writing to the location of Regall. Smith was usually very good at identifying any feature that might offer a strategic advantage to his own forces, or to the enemy's. Yet in his description of the fortress, he makes no mention of a river. In the lower reaches of the valley, the Mureş River is more than one hundred feet wide and deep enough to make crossing difficult, and is therefore strategically significant. Smith would not have left out such a feature. This suggests Regall might lie some distance away from the main valley.

There is one castle that fits all these criteria. Almost equidistant between the town of Lippa (now Lipova) on the Mureş River and Zarkad

The remains of the castle overlooking the village of Siria (photo by Dorin Paslaru). Was this Smith's infamous Regall?

(Zărand) is the Romanian village of Șiria. Today, it is an unremarkable agricultural commune at the foot of the Zărandului Mountains, which are part of the Carpathians. Overlooking the town, and perched on a promontory more than 1,200 feet high, is a castle that dates from the thirteenth century. Its position tallies perfectly with Smith's description of Regall as "environed on the one side within halfe a mile with an unusefull mountaine, and on the other side with a faire Plaine".[34]

The evidence is circumstantial, but of all the fortresses in western Transylvania still standing, the castle at Siria fits Smith's description of Regall better than any other.

Later that summer, General Giorgio Basta returned to Transylvania with a new army and an ultimatum from the emperor: Sigismund Báthory was to leave the principality and accept a pension, or suffer the consequences. By the time Báthory learned of the choice facing him, Basta's army had already reached Cluj-Napoca, just sixty miles north of Alba Iulia, where Báthory and his forces were stationed.

Typically, Báthory dithered, but in Smith's view his commander, General Székely, was more decisive:

> [Székely] would doe any thing rather than come in subjection to the Germans, he encouraged his Souldiers, and without any more adoe marched to encounter Busca [Basta], whom he found much better provided than he expected.[35]

Without the authority of his prince, Székely took his forces north to confront the Habsburgs. (Smith did not say if he was involved in the battle, but circumstantial evidence suggests he was not.) The two armies met on July 2, 1602 (NS), at Teiuş (in Hungarian, Tövis), now a sleepy market town eleven miles north of Alba Iulia. Nothing remains as testament to the bloodbath that befell Székely's army there. Basta, who hated all things Transylvanian and Protestant, cut Székely's forces to pieces. Smith said, "that betwixt them in six or seven houres, more than five or six thousand on both sides lay dead in the field".[36] Somehow, the Protestant Székely survived the slaughter and, with the battered remnants of his army, fled west through the mountains to Timişoara (Smith's Temseware). Here, he made a settlement with the Ottomans, preferring an alliance with the Turks rather than the Habsburgs.

Báthory was now forced to make a decision about his own allegiances. He accepted Rudolf II's offer of land and a title in Silesia, in eastern Germany. On July 26, 1602, he left Transylvania, never to return. (He died in Prague eleven years later.)

It was a sorry end to all the fighting. In his writings, Smith rarely wallowed in melancholia, but on this occasion he indulged himself:

> [Transylvania] was now rather a desart, or the very spectacle of desolation; their fruits and fields overgrowne with weeds, their Churches and battered Palaces and best buildings...thus brought to ruine by them.[37]

With Báthory in exile and General Székely defeated, Smith's commanding officer, the Count of Modrusch, had few options. He reaffirmed his allegiance to the Holy Roman Emperor and offered the services of his Protestant battalion to Basta. The Habsburg general also accepted reinforcements from the elements of Székely's Transylvanian army that had surrendered. However, he did not fully trust the Protestant soldiers, so he devised a cynical scheme for deploying them to his advantage.

During the early months of 1602, while the Transylvanians were busy clearing the Hajdúk from their lands, there had been a shift of power to the south, in the neighbouring principality of Wallachia, where Michael the Brave's assassination in August 1601 had left a power vacuum. The Habsburgs had established a new voivode in Wallachia, Radul Şerban, who had ten thousand troops at his disposal. The Ottomans had the same idea, and put their support behind their own man, Simion Movilă.

The Habsburg voivode was nominally in control of Wallachia, but by the summer of 1602, Movilă had apparently raised an army of forty thousand troops. Smith called them a mix of "Turks, Tartars and Moldavians", and Movilă began to gain control of the region, forcing the Habsburg voivode to withdraw his army north into Transylvania. Smith and Basta's worrisome Protestant forces were despatched to reinforce the Habsburg forces and prop up Şerban's push back into Wallachia.

Smith now found himself to be on a fool's errand, rather than pursuing the ambitions of a knight-errant:

> [Basta thought] how good it would be for his owne security to have Wallachia subject to the Emperour, or at least such an employment for the remainders of the old Regiments of Sigismundus, (of whose greatnesse and true affection hee was very suspicious,) sent them with Rodall [Şerban] to recover Wallachia.[38]

By August 1602, they had arrived. The Protestant regiments, Smith said, comprised:

> divers others of great ranke and quality, the greatest friends and alliances the Prince [Báthory] had; who with their thirty thousand, marched along by the river Altus [Olt], to the streights of Rebrinke, where they entered Wallachia, encamping at Raza.[39]

The Olt River flows south out of Transylvania and into Wallachia through the Red Tower Pass, a deep gorge that serves as a strategic link between the two principalities. Today, the busy E81 road and a single-track railway line jostle for position with the river at the bottom of the heavily wooded valley. On each side, mountains climb to over seven thousand feet. In 1602, this route was nothing more than a mud track, making slow progress for an army of thirty thousand troops.

Smith's company marched south to "Rebrinke", where they entered Wallachia, encamping at "Raza". This is generally accepted to be the modern town of Brezoiu, which sits in a side valley off the main Olt River. The position could be defended easily, and here they waited for the attack.

Simion Movilă had set up his camp on the plains of Pitești, thirty-five miles to the southeast, at the town of Curtea de Argeș. Movilă's Ottoman and Cossack force had the assistance of his brother Ieremia's army from Moldavia, and the men were eager for battle. But Movilă preferred to wait for still more forces – the formidable Tartars from Crimea – to arrive. So he bided his time. He restricted his army's activities to sending small parties up into the Olt Valley to reconnoitre and harass the Holy Roman Emperor's forces. Any of these scouts unfortunate enough to be caught, were decapitated, "and in the nights would cause their heads to be throwne up and downe before the trenches", Smith recalled.[40] Not to be outdone for barbarity, when Movilă's soldiers caught seven unfortunate Habsburg porters, they were "commanded to be flayed quicke, and after hung their skinnes upon poles, and their carkasses and heads on stakes by them".[41]

The waiting game did not suit Radul Șerban, who knew that if his Habsburg army was going to defeat Movilă's forces, he had to draw the enemy out before their Tartar reinforcements arrived. Șerban planned a feign attack, marching on Curtea de Argeș in full campaign style, his forces burning and pillaging as they went. Although he met no resistance, the Habsburg commander unexpectedly ordered his forces to withdraw under cover of night. Movilă decided, unwisely, to pursue the Habsburg army. The result was carnage:

> Thus being joined in this bloudy massacre, that there was scarce ground to stand upon, but upon the dead carkasses…leaving five and twenty thousand dead in the field, of both Armies. And thus Rodoll [Radul] was seated againe in his Soveraignty, and Wallachia became subject to the Emperour.[42]

It was a resounding success for the Habsburg side, although Smith noted soberly that his commanding officer, the Count of Modrusch, had his horse killed from under him, and narrowly missed being taken prisoner. Meanwhile, Movilă and his battered army retreated to the northeast, towards Moldavia.

Shortly after the battle, Modrusch – with Smith and a force of eleven thousand men – was sent east to address reports that enemy stragglers were ravaging eastern Wallachia. However, the intelligence was inaccurate, and now they were the ones to stumble into a trap.

The Ottoman forces were lying in wait at Câmpulung, twenty miles east of their old encampment at Curtea de Argeș. On seeing them, Modrusch ordered his forces to withdraw to the safety of the Red Tower Pass, but the Ottoman army delayed the retreat by sending out fast-riding skirmishing parties, which attacked the flanks of Modrusch's formation. By nightfall, the Protestants found themselves trapped in the shelter of an isolated wood. Modrusch ordered his men to fell trees to build a defence, anticipating a ferocious onslaught in the morning.

The next day, the sun rose over a dense autumnal fog. When the Protestant soldiers were finally able to make out their surroundings, they discovered not the expected enemy on the attack, but two thousand scavengers loaded with plunder and driving about three hundred horses and cattle before them. Smith said "most of them were slaine" by Modrusch's men, but a few, held as prisoners, revealed Movilă was still waiting for his Crimea Tartars to arrive, and that they were not far away. This was valuable intelligence.

Modrusch well understood the danger of their position. It was essential his forces withdraw to the relative safety of the Olt Valley. To assist in the retreat, Smith proposed another of his canny "stratagems": he arranged for several hundred casings to be filled with "wilde fire", the flammable mixture he had used so effectively to make his "fiery dragons" during the siege of Alba Regalis. He then fixed these pouches:

> upon the heads of lances, and charging the enemie in the night, gave fire to the truncks, which blazed forth such flames and sparkels, that it so amazed not onely their horses but also their foot [soldiers] too.[43]

As Modrusch's forces charged, Smith's pyrotechnic lances caused many of the enemy's horses to take flight. In the confusion, Modrusch's men were able to break through the Ottoman cordon with few losses. Smith had saved the day once again, or so he claimed.

Alas, their good fortune did not last. Caught at the entrance to the Olt Valley, the enemy again harassed the Protestant forces, and Modrusch was forced to mount a rear-guard action. He ordered rows of sharp stakes to be dug in, pointing towards the approaching troops. He then positioned his own foot soldiers in foxholes between the stakes, with orders to harass the enemy when they approached, and then to retire. Meanwhile, the Crimea Tartars had arrived, and Movilă now stood at the front of a powerful army – altogether forty thousand, according to Smith.

Movilă launched his attack on Modrusch's regiments, "with a general shout, all their Ensignes displaying, Drummes beating, Trumpets and Howboyes sounding".[44] Smith was experienced enough in the field of battle to understand his predicament. The best place to make a defensive stand was: "In the valley of Veristhorne, betwixt the river of Altus [Olt], and the mountaine of Rottenton".[45]

There could be only one outcome. In the face of such terrible odds, Smith could not contain his boiling anger towards the duplicitous Giorgio Basta:

> Here Busca and the Emperour had their desire; for the Sunne no sooner displayed his beames, than the Tartars his colours; where at midday he stayed a while, to see the passage of a tyrannicall and treacherous imposture, till the earth did blush with the bloud of honesty, that the Sunne for shame did hide himself, from so monsterous sight of a cowardly calamity.[46]

Initially, the Protestants hoped they had worked a miracle. Modrusch's plan of using pointed stakes surprised the advancing Tartar cavalry. Their horses were impaled, their riders thrown. Modrusch's foot soldiers did their part, emerging like subterranean spectres from their foxholes, swords in hand, and hacked the dismounted horsemen to pieces. "It was a wonder to see how horse and man came to the ground among the stakes, whose disordered troopes were so mangled", Smith recalled.[47] On the hillside, Modrusch had also mounted five or six field guns, which pounded the enemy below. But their success was short-lived. The Ottoman forces regrouped, and with thousands more soldiers in reserve, they attacked the Protestants again.

It was too late to retreat to the safety of the valley. Two regiments of janissaries, the well-trained Ottoman infantry units that had so greatly impressed Smith in Hungary, overtook Modrusch's men. The Christians were cut to pieces. After nightfall, Modrusch and the remnants of his army crossed the Olt River and escaped into the darkness. Those who had survived were primarily from the cavalry – about thirteen or fourteen hundred horsemen.

A ghastly, grim wreckage of human remains was left behind on the battlefield:

> And thus in this bloudy field, neere 30000. lay, some headlesse, armelesse and leglesse, all cut and mangled; where breathing their last, they gave this knowledge to the world, that for the lives of so few, the Crym-Tartar never paid dearer.[48]

Among the thousands of slaughtered Protestants left prostrate was an officer so badly wounded he was unable to move. Beside him was a shield bearing his coat of arms: three Turks' heads.

The following day, as the sun climbed over the mountain peaks of Rottenton, a group of pillagers began to shuffle among the decaying corpses, claiming their share of the battlefield spoils alongside the carrion crows, vultures, rats and wild dogs. There were rich pickings to be had on the first day after a great fight: armour, weapons, clothing and boots – all had a value. Those who had not breathed their last gasp were usually despatched with a swift slit across the throat.

Among the dead, Smith listed eight fellow Englishmen and one Scotsman, who had also been fighting alongside Modrusch. Smith avoided any mention of his own injuries, except to say they were serious enough to prevent him escaping on horseback with the Count. But he is clear about his own good luck:

> But Smith, among the slaughtered dead bodies, and many a gasping soule, with toile and wounds lay groaning among the rest, till being found by the Pillagers hee was able to live, and perceiving by his armor and habit, his ransome might be better to them, than his death.[49]

It is ironic that, were it not for the coat of arms on his shield, Smith might never have survived the battle at Rottenton. The battlefield plunderers showed Smith no humanity or pity; theirs was purely a decision based on financial gain. His shield and finery marked him out from the other souls, and his potential ransom was worth the trouble of keeping him alive.

In the hands of the very people he had been happy to slaughter the previous day, Smith was nursed back to health. When he could walk, he was taken to the Ottoman slave market in Axiopolis, where he was about to begin the most punishing year of his life.

Sixteenth-century Ottoman slave market by Erhard Schön.

5
Slave

1603–1604

At Axopolis they were all sold for slaves, like
beasts in a market-place, where everie Merchant,
viewing their limbs and wounds, caused other slaves
to struggle with them, to trie their strength

John Smith, The True Travels (1630)

November 19, 1602, dawned dank and chilly, with John Smith left for dead on the battlefield of Rottenton. Though he devoted a mere handful of lines in his memoirs to his capture and enslavement, it is possible, using other sources, to reconstruct his spectacular fall from grace. In just five months, he plunged from the rank of decorated officer with a new coat of arms, to a wretched slave with no rights – and a very bleak future.

Back in the summer of 1602, when Giorgio Basta defeated Mózes Székely's Transylvanian army on July 2, Smith's Protestant regiment joined the Imperial army. Basta then sent the regiment south to Wallachia to support Radul Şerban in his war against Simion Movilă and his overwhelming force of thousands of Ottoman and Tartar troops.

Throughout the year, the Habsburgs and the Ottomans had wrestled for control of Wallachia, and their armies clashed on several occasions. On March 7, Radul Şerban had marched his twelve thousand Habsburg soldiers through the Red Tower pass and into Wallachia, and engaged with Movilă's forces. Şerban's army was defeated and two thousand men in his vanguard were killed.[1] Smith's description of the routing of his own vanguard in November 1602 was eerily similar to the one Şerban's army had experienced in March. However, it is almost certain that Smith's regiment was not involved in that encounter, because they had only just joined Prince Sigismund Báthory's army in Braşov in March 1602.

Then, in mid-September, the two armies met again for a major battle at Ogretin, about fifty miles north of Bucharest. On this occasion, Şerban's Habsburg army was victorious, crushing Movilă's forces.

These two major confrontations preceded Smith's capture at Rottenton. But here is the rub: there is no record of a key battle between the two armies in November of that year. They fought each other several times in Wallachia throughout 1602, and accounts of the skirmishes are scattered across the many archives in the many languages of the region. So it is possible that Smith's battle at Rottenton is buried deep somewhere in those archives. However, if this encounter was as big as Smith claimed, involving many tens of thousands of troops, then it would be very surprising if historians had missed it.

It is therefore difficult to reconcile the differences between Smith's account and the established record, and the battle at Rottenton is probably the biggest inconsistency in the whole of *The True Travels*. Although Smith is unlikely to have been involved in the March battle, he might have spoken with the survivors about what happened that day, when the Habsburg army was defeated and slaughtered so roundly.

Smith was a formidable soldier with an impressive record, and his version of events presented a humiliating end to his Imperial career. Why would he invent such a humbling downfall for himself?

It is quite possible he was at the second battle on September 13 and 14, 1602. Even in victory, many are left injured or dead on the field of battle. Smith wrote about the battle nearly thirty years after the event. Either his memory failed him, and he confused two battles, or he chose to enrich the story of his capture by implying he had been heroic despite a tragic defeat. After all, was this not a more appropriate romantic ending for a knight in shining armour, than to be left for dead while your comrades-in-arms celebrated a great victory?

Smith's captors took good care of him, by his account. Once he had recovered from his injuries, he and the other prisoners were marched two hundred miles east to the Ottoman slave market of Axiopolis, in eastern Romania (today's Cernavodă). Assuming they were able to walk ten miles a day – some still struggling from their wounds, and all of them in chains – it would have taken them nearly a month to get there.

Smith may have learned enough in his travels to know that Islamic law forbade slavery. There were important exceptions, however: prisoners of war and the children of enslaved parents could all be coerced into servitude. As a Christian soldier caught fighting against the Ottoman Empire, Smith was fair game. His description of conditions in the slave market matches those of chroniclers like the Scotsman, William Lithgow, who was travelling around Eastern Europe, Palestine and Egypt around the same time (possibly as a spy). In his book *The Rare Adventures*, Lithgow wrote:

> I have seene men and women as usually sold here in Markets, as Horses and other beasts are with us: The most part of which are Hungarians, Transilvanians, Carindians, Istrians, and Dalmatian Captives, and of other places besides, which they can overcome. Whom, if no compassionable Christian will buy, or relieve; then must they either turne Turke, or be addicted to perpetuall slavery.[2]

On their arrival at Axiopolis, the prisoners became part of a great human bazaar. Smith said they were paraded "like beasts in a market-place, where everie Merchant, viewing their limbs and wounds, caused other slaves to struggle with them, to trie their strength".[3] Setting slave against slave provided light entertainment to passers-by, and gave buyers an opportunity to size up their potential purchases.

Smith presumably performed well enough, because a Turk, a man he called Bashaw Bogall, bought him. Smith's new master acquired him as a gift for "his faire Mistresse". Bogall was probably not Smith's new owner's name, but rather his title, and he may have been a captain in the elite janissaries.[4]

Smith's next trek took him to the south, first to Adrianople (now Edirne), and then on to the very heart of the Ottoman Empire: Constantinople. "By twentie and twentie chained by the neckes," Smith recalled, "they marched in file to this great Citie, where they were delivered to their severall Masters".[5] Inevitably, this human chain only walked at the speed of the slowest, and it was the spring of 1603 before the ragged, half-starved slaves shuffled into the Turkish capital. This was where Smith was destined to serve Bogall's lady.

John Smith must have learnt about Constantinople from Signor Theodore Paleologue, whose ancestor had been the last Byzantine emperor there. Yet nothing could have prepared Smith for the sight of this magnificent city. Built on seven hills overlooking the sea and with a population of some 700,000 people, Constantinople was several times bigger than London or Paris. Sitting at the crossroads of trade between east and west, it was also a meeting place for religious ideologies and intellectual ideas. The Ottoman Turks were relaxed and tolerant of outsiders, and Istanbul – to use the name increasingly preferred by the Turks – had sizeable populations of both Jews and Christians.

Since Mehmed II wrested Constantinople from the last Byzantine emperor in 1453, the city had been completely rebuilt. The sultan's magnificent Topkapi Palace looked out over the harbour to innumerable trading ships jostling for an anchorage alongside Ottoman war galleys and hundreds of smaller galliots and fustas. The domes and minarets of two thousand mosques and three hundred public baths now dominated the skyline. Many grand buildings had been built in the past century, under the guidance of Suleiman's royal architect, Mimar Sinan, the Michelangelo of the Ottomans. Smith would have seen the formidable profile of Sinan's "Suleiman mosque", designed to mirror the old Byzantine Hagia Sophia, on the horizon of Constantinople's "third hill".

But there was little time to gaze upon the sights. Smith and the other slaves were marched through Constantinople's ancient, narrow streets, pressing themselves against walls and doorways to avoid the streams of heavily laden packhorses spilling into the city around them. They were probably taken first to the slave market in the grand bazaar, which remains today one of the largest covered markets in the world. But Smith was not to be resold; instead, he stumbled on to the heavy wooden front door of the house of his mistress, the so-called Charatza Tragabigzanda (also Trabigzanda).

Constantinople, 1580, with European ships and Turkish galleys anchoring between the Bosphorus and the Golden Horn. Turkish horseman and janissaries are pictured along the bottom frame.

Charatza Tragabigzanda was not his new owner's real name, but a description in Greek of who she was: a young woman (*korítsi* in modern Greek) from the Byzantine state of Trebizond (Trapedzoûndos), on the coast of the southern Black Sea. Smith presumably asked the name of his new owner, and was simply told "a girl from Trebizond".

Although officially a slave, Smith would most likely have served Charatza Tragabigzanda as a manservant and gardener. Her comfortable middle-class house was designed in the shape of a square surrounding a courtyard of fountains, ornamental trees and bushes, granting her protection from the glare of the sun and the inquisitive eyes of strangers. Only the house's upper floors had windows, and these mostly looked onto the inner sanctum of the residence itself. She may have lived in one of the many fine houses of the city described by Reinhold Lubenauwas, an apothecary attached to the Austrian embassy in Istanbul between 1587 and 1588. On a boat tour of Istanbul, he saw:

> on both shores of the Bosphorus many exquisite and beautiful gardens built in the Turkish manner with palaces (*palatia*) and pleasure houses (*Lustheuser*), which were planted with extremely beautiful tulips (*Tulipanis*) in a medley of colors and an abundance of Turkish flowers.[6]

Smith understood no Greek, nor did he know much about the care of tulips or Turkish flowers. But Charatza spoke Italian, and she was soon intrigued enough by her new acquisition's other talents, including as a storyteller:

> This Noble Gentlewoman tooke sometime occasion to shew him to some friends, or rather to speake with him, because shee could speake Italian, would feigne her selfe sick when she should goe to the Banians [communal baths], or weepe over the graves, to know how Bogall tooke him prisoner.[7]

Bashaw Bogall had written to her explaining that he had beaten Smith in combat. This lie may have been intended to impress the young woman, and Smith felt compelled to challenge the story, stealing, as it did, what little dignity he had left. He maintained he had never seen Bogall before he was bought as a slave in Axiopolis. Charatza was sceptical of his claim at first, so she invited friends who could speak English, French and Italian to test Smith's account. They found his story plausible, and, according to Smith, they "honestly reported to her, [and] she tooke (as it seemed) much compassion on him".[8] Indeed, after his interrogation, Charatza seemed to be charmed by her new servant, and she made excuses to stay in the house so she could be alone with him. In time, he claimed, she fell in love with him.

The young woman's mother seemed to become suspicious about their blossoming relationship, as Charatza worried that her mother planned to sell Smith off. To avoid this, Charatza decided to despatch Smith to southern Russia, to join her brother, whom Smith called "the Tymor Bashaw of Nalbrits, in the Countrey of Cambia, a Province in Tartaria". The brother was a timariot, a relatively minor Ottoman official who had been granted land (a "timar"), typically as compensation for loyal military or government service. If Charatza was indeed Greek (and therefore an Orthodox Christian), then it is possible her brother had once been a slave of the Ottomans, as Smith now was.

Slaves were an indispensable part of the Ottoman Empire, and served their Turkish masters in many ways – and as a result could achieve high status in Ottoman society. For more than 250 years, young boys were recruited from non-Muslim families under the system of *devşirme*. They were taken to Istanbul, converted to Islam, and then trained for some form of state service. They could become harem guards or government officials, and rise through the ranks to be privy to some of the most sensitive aspects of Ottoman life. Or they could be drafted into the army to become janissaries, the highly disciplined infantrymen that had impressed Smith again and again on the battlefields of eastern Europe. Charatza's brother could therefore have been either a former janissary or an enslaved bureaucrat.

Charatza asked her brother to treat Smith well and give him a chance to "learne the language, and what it was to be a Turke, till time made her Master of her selfe".[9] This is a tantalizing hint from Smith that Charatza might have been looking forward to the day when she was no longer under her mother's scrutiny and could claim control over her own life. Or perhaps she wanted to rid herself of her betrothed Bagshaw when she was older. Regardless, Charatza evidently hoped Smith might be educated in the ways of Ottoman officialdom and eventually return to Istanbul – and to her.

He would have much to learn about Turkish customs. Smith was used to bathing only a few times a year, as in Elizabethan England it was generally believed that people could infect themselves by allowing dirty water to enter the pores of the skin. (Hair was usually washed separately using a solution of lye, with its strong caustic properties.) To counteract the antisocial habit of not washing, Smith would have relied on perfumes, flowers and herbs to disguise his pungent body odour, if he cared to do so at all. By comparison, the Turks were fastidious with their personal hygiene. The prophet Mohammed maintained that "cleanliness is half of faith", and the citizens of Constantinople visited the public baths on most days, and always washed their feet and hands before prayer, or before reading the Qur'an.

Charatza was the first woman Smith wrote about in any detail, but she remains a cipher – a house, an interview, a letter of introduction to her brother. Charatza was a channel through which he could funnel his ambitions – and at this moment in his life, his priority was to escape slavery, even if he was enjoying his current sybaritic life. He liked Charatza and trusted her – that much was clear, as he placed his future in her hands. But did he have any real emotional affection for, or attraction to her? For the most part, Smith kept his motivations to himself, as confused and contradictory as they might have been.

Smith always aspired to be a chivalric knight, and the virtuous nature demanded of such an emblematic figure must surely have given him ample excuse to cultivate close relationships with women like Charatza, though perhaps without the unseemly blemish of sinful fornication. At least as far as the readers of *The True Travels* were concerned.

Smith does not say how long he stayed in Constantinople, but sometime during the early summer of 1603, he found himself on the road again, heading north. His destination was the port of Varna on the Black Sea, in today's Bulgaria. Having been somewhat coy about his relationship with Charatza, Smith returned to a topic he wrote about with far more confidence: his travels across foreign lands. From Varna, he was taken east by boat to the Crimea, with:

> nothing but the Blacke Sea water, till he came to the two Capes of Taur and Pergilos, where hee passed the Straight of Niger, which (as he conjectured) is some ten leagues long, and three broad, betwixt two low lands, the Channell is deepe, but at the entrance to the Sea Dissabacca, there are many great Osie-shoulds [mud banks], and many great blacke rockes, which the Turkes said were trees, weeds, and mud, throwen from the in-land Countryes, by the inundations and violemce of the Current, and cast there by the Eddy.[10]

Smith's ship passed between two capes, which he called Taur and Pergilos – the first being the ancient name for the Crimea – Taurica – and the second probably being Phanagoria (now Taman). They then sailed through the Strait of Ketch (Smith called it Niger, as in the strait of the "Black" Sea), then east into the Sea of Azov (Smith's Sea Dissabacca, from the Italian *delle Sabacche*). They eventually made their way to the entrance of the River "Bruapo", before sailing for six or seven days past a series of stone castles. The only river in the region big enough to sail for such a long time is the River Don, which enters the Sea of Azov at Rostov; the line of castles probably marked the fortified border between the Ottoman Empire and Russia.

Smith's journey in 1603 from Istanbul (Constantinople) to the outlying garrison of Nalbrits in the Russian steppes. The borders of the Ottoman Empire are shown in grey. Smith murdered his slave master and escaped from Nalbrits via Æcopolis and "Corangnaw" to Sibiu in Transylvania. He then travelled to Leipzig, to the court of Prince Báthory.

Smith disembarked at a town he called Cambria, where he recorded that the river was "more than halfe a mile broad" and the "Castle was of a large circumference, [with walls] fourteene or fifteene foot thicke… and then a Ditch of about fortie foot broad full of water".[11] The fortification was probably in the middle reaches of the Don, close to the modern town of Volgodonsk, 125 miles upstream from Rostov. From there he was taken to Nalbrits (which usually appeared as Nalbars or Naubaris on some maps of the day[12]), the garrison of Charatza's brother. Smith observed that his host governed his small fiefdom from "a great vast stonie Castle with many great Courts about it, invironed with high stone wals, where was quartered their Armes".[13] Today, this site is no longer accessible, as the Soviet government built a vast dam in 1952 to create the Tsimlyansk Reservoir. Nalbrits now lies under many feet of water.

If Smith expected a warm reception from his host, he was to be very disappointed. Within an hour of his arrival, Charatza's brother:

> caused his Drub-man to strip him naked, and shave his head and beard so bare as his hand, a great ring of iron, with a long stalke bowed like a sickle, rivetted about his necke, and a coat made of Ulgries haire [horse-hair], guarded about with a peece of an undrest skinne [leather girdle].[14]

Smith was evidently expected at the castle, and the timariot had already decided how to treat his new guest – very cruelly. From what Smith knew, Charatza had written to her brother, asking him to teach Smith the language, and what it was to be a Turk, in preparation for a reunion with her.[15] The brother was therefore unlikely to have abused Smith so badly if Charatza's letter was his only source of information about him. Smith also hinted that Charatza's mother disapproved of their developing relationship, and that she wanted to sell Smith on while he was still in Constantinople. It therefore seems likely that Charatza's mother did not want Smith back in her daughter's life, and it seems she made certain her son knew how she felt. Smith's treatment at the timariot's hand is therefore a clue that Smith had got closer to his mistress than was perhaps appropriate in polite society.

Smith was now thoroughly detached from any life he had known. He was 1,250 miles east of his regiment, which was still fighting the Ottomans in Transylvania, and effectively detained – though his jail was simply a remote outpost on the Russian steppe. However, Smith was not alone. He shared his misfortune with:

> many more Christian slaves, and neere an hundred Forsados [galley slaves] of Turkes and Moores, and he being the last, was slave of slaves to them all. Among these slavish fortunes there was no great choice; for the best was so bad, a dog could hardly have lived to endure, and yet for all their paines and labours no more regarded than a beast.[16]

In the six years Smith had been travelling, he had run into misfortune on several occasions. He had been robbed of all his possessions, cheated, thrown overboard, and left for dead on the battlefield. This was the first and one of very few times he seemed utterly demoralized. The one light in his darkness, he wrote, was "the love of Tragabigzanda", who Smith was certain "was ignorant of his bad usage".[17]

It was inevitable that talk among the slaves would turn to how they might escape from their misery, but "although he had often debated the matter with some Christians, that had beene there a long time slaves, they could not finde how to make an escape, by any reason or possibility".[18] They were marooned in the middle of a wasteland populated primarily by the nomadic descendants of Ghengis Khan's army, who eked out a grim existence by drinking their horses' milk and then eating their flesh.

As harvest time approached, Smith was transferred to a farm "more than a league" (about three miles) from Nalbrits. He was given a simple threshing bat with no flails, with which to separate the grain from the stalk. Several times the timariot visited to check on Smith's work, "and tooke occasion so to beat, spurne, and revile him".[19] These acts of cruelty were to be the brother's downfall. On the timariot's last visit, Smith retaliated. He "beat out the Tymors braines with his threshing bat", took the brother's clothes, hid his bloodied body under a stack of straw, "filled his knapsacke with corne"[20] and escaped into the wilderness on the man's horse.

John Smith kills his slave master and escapes captivity, from Smith's *The True Travels* (1630).

The Russian steppe has a short growing season. Traditionally, rye is harvested in late June, and wheat in July, leaving August and September free for threshing.[21] It must have taken Smith more than a month to cover the thousand miles between Constantinople and Nalbrits, so he was unlikely to have spent more than a couple of months enslaved to the timariot before murdering him and escaping.

By his own admission, Smith had no idea where he was, and spent "two or three dayes thus fearfully wandring he knew not whither, and well it was he met not any to aske the way".[22] Although he had a good horse, and was dressed as a wealthy man, he still had an iron ring riveted around his neck. He knew he had to head west across the featureless steppe if he was ever to succeed in returning to the safety of Europe. Periodically, he came across a signpost. Fortunately, these used pictographs to guide a mostly illiterate population across the territory. A crescent denoted the road to the Crimea, and a sun the road to China, or so he assumed.

A Christian cross pointed the way to "Muscovia" (Muscovy, the predecessor of tsarist Russia), where he found shelter, and a protector:

> Sixteene dayes he travelled in this feare and torment, after the Crosse, till he arrived at Æcopolis, upon the river Don, a garrison of the Muscovites. The governour after due examination of those his hard events, tooke off his irons, and so kindly used him, he thought himselfe new risen from death, and the good Lady Callamata [probably Salamata], largely supplied all his wants.[23]

Again a lady of high standing would rescue John Smith at a time of need. Unfortunately, Smith does not elaborate on what those largely satisfied needs might have been.

The garrison town of Æcopolis is not easy to identify. Smith claimed it was on the main river, but it could be either upstream or downstream from the timariot's Nalbrits. Smith had been on the run for sixteen days, and he could easily have ridden three hundred miles or more in that time. But he was unlikely to have headed downstream for very long, as this would have taken him into the region controlled by the Crimean Khanate, which was allied with the Ottomans. Instead, Smith, keeping his wits about him, would most likely have followed the first sign of the cross he spied, and ridden northeast, upstream along the Don, towards Muscovy.

On one map of the River Don from around this time, a town called Exopolis appears, roughly where the river makes its closest approach to the River Volga,[24] near the modern village of Trëkhostrovskaya, northwest of Volgograd. This area of southern Muscovy, strategically close to two major rivers, would be a logical place to build a garrison town. Exopolis was about two hundred miles from Nalbrits, and therefore an easy distance for Smith to cover since his escape.

Travelling across the lawless Russian steppe was dangerous, so Smith stayed with the kindly governor of Æcopolis "till the Convoy went to Coragnaw" (most likely Chernava). This suggests he travelled to Chernava in the relative safety of a river convoy, rather than continuing by land. The governor also gave him a letter of introduction, which guaranteed him safe passage back to Europe.

The first part of Smith's journey took him through the barren landscape of the upper Don, where "in two dayes travell you shall scarce see six habitations".[25] He covered 1,800 miles, across western Russia and northern Ukraine, cataloguing the towns and cities he passed through along the way, before returning to Transylvania. Of course, his list of place names, although accurate, offers no corroboration of his account of being a slave in Nalbrits, nor of killing his master. It merely shows Captain Smith could trace a route on a map.

However, the Ottomans undoubtedly had a habit of making slaves of Christian captives during the Austro-Hungarian wars, so Smith's tale is not implausible. The clarity with which he observed the lifestyle of the Tartars could be evidence of his having lived among them, though he might equally have read Richard Hakluyt's volume on the "Tartary" in *The Principal Navigations, Voyages, Traffiques and Discoveries of the English Nation,* which had been published between 1598 and 1600. There are some parts of Smith's story that were almost certainly lifted from descriptions written by William of Rubruck, a Franciscan friar from Flanders who visited the Crim-Tartar area in the thirteenth century. Yet neither of these predecessors conveyed the detail Smith shared in *The True Travels,* suggesting that at least some of his reporting was an eyewitness account. None of this proved he had been held as a slave, but it would have been quite a folly, even for Smith, to journey deep into the Russian steppe of his own volition.

The trip from the steppe to central Europe would have taken Smith around three months, putting him back in Transylvania near the end of November 1603. In contrast to his indulgent self-pity when recounting his days in Nalbrits, he turned remarkably upbeat when sharing the tale of his return to freedom. He felt, he said, "glutted with content, and neere drowned with joy".[26]

Smith arrived in Sibiu, Translyvania, towards the end of 1603, having experienced the most traumatic and physically abusive year of his life. Having succeeded in escaping, his next objective was to find Sigismund Báthory. Smith had lost all his papers when he was taken as a slave, and he needed confirmation from the prince of his coat of arms. Smith was told Báthory was in Leipzig, so he took leave of his regiment and headed northwest to Germany.

His route took him through Fiľakovo, Tokaj, Košice, the magnificent Imperial castle at Oravský Podzámok in Slovakia, and then to Prague. For once he did not take a direct course, but doubled back on himself in northern Hungary, choosing to go north into Slovakia, thus increasing his journey time. Smith made no explanation for this diversion, but the simplest reason was that he encountered Ottoman forces as he approached Buda, and chose a detour through territory controlled by the Habsburgs. It was a prudent choice, given his recent history.

In Leipzig, Smith requested an audience with Báthory. The prince "gave him his Passe, intimating the service he had done, and the honours he had received, with fifteene hundred ducats of gold to repaire his losses".[27] This was exactly what Smith needed. He had regained his financial security, together with a *laissez-passer*, a document that combined a passport with a certificate of discharge. On the pass, the prince had called him "an English Gentleman", confirmed his command as a captain of cavalry, and authorized him to carry the emblem of three Turks' heads on his shield. The paper also requested he be given safe passage without hindrance. It was an invaluable document, and Smith was justly proud of it.

With fifteen hundred gold ducats jangling in his saddlebag, Smith surrendered to his love of sightseeing. He covered more than two thousand miles through Germany, France and Spain, and then went to Morocco by sea. The trip took several months, yet in the ten lines he devoted to this sojourn, Smith revealed little more than an inventory of "the faire Cities and Countries" he visited.

Even so, the places on his route do give a hint to the motivations behind his trip: Wittenburg, where Martin Luther first nailed his ninety-five indulgences on the door of the All Saints' Church; Frankfurt, the coronation city for the Holy Roman Emperors; Mainz, the home of Johannes Gutenberg's printing press; Paris, Orléon, Madrid and Seville, all great cities of learning. This was John Smith's educational tour of Europe, perhaps his attempt to improve his understanding of the world, and become a true "English Gentleman".

The last part of his grand tour took him through Spain when the Inquisition was still a very dangerous force. Few Protestants dared to venture into this heartland of fanatical Catholicism. Yet Smith shared nothing of his experience. His *laissez-passer* from the Catholic Báthory may well have given him some protection.

Whatever dangers he might have risked with the "Tribunal of the Holy Office of the Inquisition", it could not compare to his next adventure, this time on the lawless high seas of the Atlantic Ocean.

From Gibraltar, Smith crossed to the African port of Ceuta (also under the governance of Spain), took a passage on a ship going west along the Moroccan coast to Tangiers, and then south down the Atlantic coast to Safi. Today the town is best known for its ceramics industry and magnificent surfing beaches. Its modern, ugly harbour sees the spoils of the country's phosphate mines going out, and the bounty of its sardine fleet coming in. But Safi is also one of the oldest cities in Morocco, and in the early seventeenth century it was one of the most important ports in the country. The town was the closest harbour to Marrakesh, the capital of the sultanate, which had wrested control of Safi from the Portuguese less than seventy years earlier.

Smith was still a tourist, and keen "to see the ancient monuments of that large renowned Citie", although he might also have been on the lookout for opportunities to fight as a mercenary. He made the acquaintance of a man called Merham, the captain of a French man-of-war anchored in the harbour. Together with a dozen other associates, they headed inland across the hot, dry rolling hills of western Morocco to Marrakesh. There, Smith saw "only reliques of lamentable ruines and sad desolution" in much of the city.

To his surprise, he found the *Juderea* (Jewish quarter) was located inside the city. Historically, the Jewish merchants of Marrakesh were given privileged treatment by the sultans and offered safe haven inside the city walls. Even in death, some Jewish advisers were especially favoured, and buried inside the high-status compound that housed the dazzling gilded Saadian Tombs.

Smith went on to report that the quarter's "many pinnacles and towers, with Balls on their tops, hath much appearance of much sumptuousnesse and curiositie".[28] Today, every mosque in the city still displays three brass balls above the main tower. Here, Smith was unlikely to have copied the travelogues of others, as European visitors to Marrakesh were rare at this time.

While in the capital, Smith and his colleagues ran into trouble. One of their party – a man called Henry Archer – was walking to the Juderea, "the way being verie foule", when he had an argument with "a Great priest". The imam expected the Englishman to step aside for him, presumably into the filth of the gutter. Archer took offence and "gave him a box on the eare". This was met with a violent response. Archer was "apprehended, and condemned to have his tongue cut out and his hand cut off".[29] Fortunately, Smith and his group had good contacts within the sultan's palace, and Archer avoided this drastic penalty and was released. It was time to move on.

From Marrakesh, the party headed north to Fez. Although he wrote more favourably about the northern city, Smith did not really enjoy his time in Morocco:

> by reason of the uncertainty, and the perfidious, treacherous, bloudy murthers rather than warre, amongst those perfidious, barbarous Moores, Smith returned with Merham, and the rest to Saffe, and so aboard his Ship, to try some other conclusions at Sea.[30]

Captain Merham was a good host, and once they had returned safely to Safi, he invited Smith aboard his ship. The company must have been relaxed and agreeable, especially after the tensions of Marrakesh, as Merham:

> spared not any thing he had to expresse his kindnesse, to bid them welcome, till it was too late to goe on shore, so that necessitie constrained them to stay aboord.[31]

John Smith was not the first person (nor the last) to find that wind and tide conspire to make it difficult to return ashore after an evening's revelry afloat. A storm began to build and the harbour at Safi in the early seventeenth century offered little protection in such conditions; the consequences of the ship staying at anchor were potentially disastrous. By midnight, Captain Merham made his decision and "they were forced to let slip Cable and Anchor, and put to Sea; spooning before the wind, till they were driven to the Canaries".[32] The storm obviously took them by surprise, for no captain would willingly choose to cut his expensive anchor and chain unless it became impossible to haul it in. Merham had no option but to run ahead of the storm towards the Canary Islands, 350 miles to the southwest.

After the gale had passed, the captain set about making the most of their situation. Although Smith wrote that Merham was "a captaine of a man-of-war", the Frenchman was little more than a pirate. First, the crew boarded a "small Barke" loaded with wine from Tenerife. Then they went in pursuit of "three or foure more" trading ships, and succeeded in taking two of them, but "found little in them, save a few passengers".[33]

The travellers on board one of the ships they had tried to plunder, claimed there were five Dutch men-of-war ships lurking among the Canary Islands. Rather than risk an encounter, Merham laid course for the relative safely of Safi. Before they could reach port, the lookout spotted two ships catching them quickly from astern.

There was little Merham could do against two faster ships, and he hailed them, asking their purpose. In a detailed account that shows Smith was now an experienced seaman, he described how the other ships doused their topsails (to slow down), and invited Merham to come aboard "and take what he would, for they were but two poore distressed Biskiners [Biscayners]".[34] Biscayners were ships from the Bilboa region in northern Spain, and Merham smelled a rat. He ordered more sail to be set, in order to make an escape. One of the "distressed" Spanish ships was quickly in pursuit, Smith said, as "the other tacked after him, and came close up to his nether [downwind] quarter, gave his broad side, and so loufed [luffed] up to windward".[35] Soon, Merham's vessel was under fire from both ships:

> With a noise of Trumpets, and all his Ordnance, murtherers [small deck guns], and muskets, boorded him on his broad side; the other in like

> manner on his ley [lee, or downwind] quarter...after they had battered Merham about an houre, they boorded him againe as before; and threw foure kedgers or grapnalls in iron chaines.[36]

Merham's crew were fighting for their lives. From midday the ship was under a constant barrage, and the battle continued into the night, with only a brief standstill before dawn. But as the sun rose, the Spanish warships revived their attack. An hour later, the Spaniards offered some mercy from the bombardment, calling on Merham to surrender to "the King of Spaine". The French captain would have none of it, and replied with a salvo from a cannon mounted on his stern deck.

At this insult, one of the Spanish vessels came alongside and attempted to board the French ship. Merham's crew desperately fought back, until an explosion set their own ship on fire, killing several of the invaders as a lucky consequence. The Spaniards feared Merham's ship would sink, and quickly abandoned their trophy. Meanwhile, the French captain ordered the fire to be quenched with wet clothes and water, and for the holes in the hull to be covered with old sails to stem the leaks. It was a remarkable display of seamanship under a barrage of deadly fire, and Smith was impressed:

> The angry Spaniard seeing the fire quenched, hung out a flagge of truce to have a parley; but that desperate Merham knew there was but one way with him, and would have none, but the report of his Ordnance, which hee did know well how to use for his best advantage.[37]

The bruising encounter lasted nearly forty-eight hours. Twenty-seven members of Merham's crew were killed, and sixteen wounded; his ship was holed by 140 "great shot". An injured Spanish sailor was taken prisoner, Smith recorded, and the captive claimed that the larger of their two ships had lost one hundred men. The prisoner had abandoned his own ship, fearing the vessel was too badly damaged, and would sink before it could reach port safely.

It was yet another close call for Smith. Although he left a detailed report of the episode, at no time did he mention his own involvement in the fighting, even though he would certainly have been as close to the action as any man. Instead, he closed his account tersely and economically: "Thus reaccommodating [repairing] their sailes, they sailed for Sancta Cruse [Agadir], Cape Goa [Cape Ghir], and Magadore, till they came againe to Saffee, and then he returned into England."[38] Perhaps his modesty came from the fact that this had not been of his own making; he was more a witness to somebody else's misfortune.

John Smith arrived back in London around the close of 1604. Queen Elizabeth had died eighteen months previously, and James VI of Scotland was now King of England and Ireland, thereby unifying the English and Scottish crowns. Smith was nearly twenty-four, and it was time to reassess his life once again.

He had endured privation and slavery, and had faced the very real prospect of his own mortality. He was an experienced traveller and a hardened mercenary. In his pocket he retained a certificate from a prince of Transylvania that confirmed he was not only a man of military rank, but also a gentleman.

If the Old World had shaped the young man, now it was time for the older man to shape the New World. John Smith was ready to seek out a new adventure.

Old London Bridge looking north, from an engraving by Claes Visscher (1616). The heads of executed traitors were dipped in tar and boiled to preserve them, before being impaled above the Southwark gatehouse.

6
Entrepreneur

1605–1606

You may be an alderman there, and never be scavenger;
you may be any other officer and never be a slave
Captain Seagull, from the play Eastward Hoe (1605)

When John Smith arrived in London during the last few weeks of 1604, he ended an absence from his homeland of over four years. He was a changed man. He was certainly older, and by the standards of the day, he was approaching middle age. He was definitely richer, having returned with the remains of his pension of fifteen hundred ducats from Sigismund Báthory,[1] – enough to ensure his financial independence for several years. He had left England a humble Lincolnshire farmer and returned a captain of cavalry with a formidable coat of arms on his shield.

Smith must also have been a good deal wiser, for he had faced a violent death on several occasions, and taken the lives of others on many more. War had hardened him, and made him cynical. Yet the single-minded self-confidence of his youth remained.

England too had changed during his absence. By the time Smith returned, Queen Elizabeth's body had lain cold in its white marble sarcophagus in Westminster Abbey for over a year. The royal chaplain, Dr Henry Parry, claimed she had died serenely: "This morning about three at clocke hir Majestie departed this lyfe, mildly like a lambe, easily like a ripe apple from the tree."[2]

Unfortunately, the country Elizabeth left behind was anything but serene. England had generally prospered under her reign, but she had fought her mortal enemy, Spain, to a stalemate, and the fighting had practically bankrupted the nation. Elizabeth had also died childless, and even on her deathbed she refused to name a successor. As Thomas

Wilson, who wrote an assessment of the state of the nation in 1600, wryly commented, "this Crowne is not like to fall to the ground for want of heads that claime to wear it".[3]

James VI of Scotland was the most obvious heir, but there was no certainty he would go unchallenged. James' father, Lord Darnley, and his mother, Mary Queen of Scots, were grandchildren of Henry VIII's elder sister, which supported his claim to the throne. Not least among James' "qualifications" was that he already had sired two sons, and many hoped this would resolve the quarrels around succession for the foreseeable future. Yet despite his compelling arguments of blood and progeny, James was an unprepossessing figure. He was garrulous and lacking in self-discipline, neither a populist nor a cheerleader as Elizabeth had been, and he never succeeded in winning the devotion of the English people as the Virgin Queen had. He preferred to present himself to his people as a learned scholar, debating the law and the duties of king – subjects about which he wrote several books. He also relied heavily on a very small circle of confidants.

James' tendency towards self-indulgence might be seen as a wisely nurtured instinct for self-preservation, given his family's recent history. His youth had been marked by tragedy. His father had been assassinated before his first birthday – a murder probably committed with the assent of his mother, in a series of intrigues surrounding the news of her pregnancy and the ongoing power struggles between Protestants and Catholics in Scotland. James' mother was next forced to abdicate, and James became a toddler king. Four of his regents died through violence and he was subjected to regular beatings by a sadistic tutor. His mother was found guilty of treason against Elizabeth and executed in 1587, before his twenty-first birthday. As King of Scotland, he became obsessed with the threat of witches, and instigated their wholesale persecution – a turn of events not lost on William Shakespeare when he scripted *Macbeth*.

Elizabeth died on March 24, 1603, and James was named King of England that same day, in an effort to ensure a peaceful succession. Less than a fortnight later, on April 5, he left Edinburgh for London, dispensing royal prerogatives at will on his way. He was so impressed by the wealth south of the border, he claimed he was "swapping a stony couch for a deep feather bed", and promptly knighted any host who ventured to ask the inexperienced monarch for the honour.

In London, one of James' immediate priorities was to sort out England's mounting financial worries. The quickest solution, he decided, was to wind down the war with Spain, and in August 1604 he agreed a peace treaty with Philip III. As part of the accord, England would withdraw support from the Dutch rebellion against the Spanish, which had originally sparked the fighting back in 1581. In doing so, James hoped to safeguard the Protestant Reformation in England.

The Church of England was also very much on James' mind. Early in the year he authorized a new English translation of the Bible, which became known as the King James Version. It was the third official translation into English since the Reformation, following Henry VIII's Great Bible of 1539 and the Bishop's Bible of 1568. The new version, James maintained, would address several concerns raised by Puritan believers, but the instructions given to the translators seemed primarily intended to bolster the Church's ecclesiastical hierarchy and societal influence.

The committee convened by James to re-translate the Bible settled down to their work late in 1604, around the time John Smith was making his way home from Morocco. As Smith's ship sailed up the Thames estuary in early December, the prospect of returning to the capital must have excited him. London could not rival the opulence of Istanbul, but it was a city of hope and opportunity, especially for an opportunist like Captain Smith. He would stay in the capital for two years, pursuing his prospects.

As his ship sailed up the Thames, he could just make out the villages nestled along the Kent and Essex shorelines. At low tide, acres of dark mud were exposed in the lower reaches of the wide estuary, offering a breeding ground for endemic malaria – then called the ague, or marsh fever. Off Greenwich Palace – the late queen's favourite residence – he drifted past Sir Francis Drake's flagship, the *Golden Hind*, at anchor, her oak frames rotting slowly in retirement. Still, she was a testament to the first English circumnavigation of the globe, and deserved this token of royal respect. Closer to London, the pastoral riverbanks gave way to the noise and clutter of shipbuilding yards feeding the booming maritime industry. English trade had expanded greatly in recent decades. Drake, Walter Raleigh, John Hawkins, Humphrey Gilbert and Richard Grenville – all had been knighted by Elizabeth for their contributions to the rise in Her Majesty's power overseas.

Upstream from Greenwich, the Thames flooded over the mud flats to form a vast, natural harbour. One traveller of the period counted over one hundred ships in the short mile between St Catherine's and London Bridge. The river was the artery of the nation's capital, delivering much of the sustenance needed for life in the seventeenth century. As Smith approached the city, he could not miss the Tower of London looming on the north bank. Once the residence of kings, it was now serving as an armoury and a prison for serious offenders – including Sir Walter Raleigh, no longer a favourite of the court.

A soldier, sailor, explorer, courtier and man of letters, Raleigh had been appointed Governor of Jersey by Elizabeth in 1600. After her death, he was caught in a trap set by his enemies at Court, and his fall from grace was swift and severe. On July 19, 1603, he was arrested, accused of being part of the "Main Plot" to remove James from the throne. Raleigh was sentenced to death for treason, but the new king had been lenient, and Raleigh was now in the first year of a thirteen-year residence as the guest of His Majesty. Raleigh's internment most likely came as a shock to John Smith. The news would have given him some inkling that England was now a very different place from the one he had left.

When Smith's ship finally arrived in the Pool of London, swans flocked around it, so tame that passengers aboard some of the smaller boats in the harbour could lean over the side and stroke them. The birds were protected by royal decree and seemed to relish their cosseted status. Later, they would be plucked, so that their down might comfort the monarch in his sleep, and roasted, so that their meat might furnish his dining table.

The swans may have been unruffled, but the river was not. Tilt-boats conveyed the wealthy on well-upholstered embroidered cushions, the passengers' heavy perfume manfully making light of the stench rising from the churning waters. The Thames not only brought life-blood into the city, it was also its sewer, charged with carrying away the waste of many thousands. These days, more often than not, the male passengers on the tilt-boats wielded a clay pipe packed with tobacco – the very latest fashion from the Americas – whose smoke helped mask the river's aroma. The myriad sights and smells of the capital and its river inspired both devotion and disgust. The Elizabethan poet Edmund Spenser rejoiced: "Sweet Thames! Run softly till I end my song". By contrast, a foreign ambassador of the period said the city stank, and was "the filthiest in the world".

It was no wonder. London was experiencing a population explosion, having doubled in size within two generations. By 1604, it was a seething metropolis, housing nearly a quarter of a million people,[4] ten times the size of England's second largest city, Norwich. The capital had long ago spilled out beyond its medieval city walls, and houses were crammed together into the two square miles between the Tower and Westminster. London had overgrown itself not because families were getting bigger – disease still killed more people than were born in the metropolis – but because a tide of immigrants kept arriving to seek their fortune.

To squeeze the newcomers into the city, London's houses had grown taller, with three or four storeys not uncommon. The upper storeys projected out over the alleyways, depriving the narrow streets of sunshine as well as breeze. It was not an easy city to live in, and nor was it healthy. Plague returned regularly – the most recent epidemics had struck in 1593 and 1603 – each time killing up to a fifth of residents.

Nobody would even consider drinking the filthy water of the river, which was said to be rife with pestilence. Ale was the tipple of choice, even for breakfast. Not surprisingly, alehouses became popular places to meet, as the Swiss traveller Thomas Platter found when he visited the city in 1599:

> There are a great many inns, taverns, and beer-gardens scattered about the city, where much amusement may be had with eating, drinking, fiddling, and the rest, as for instance in our hostelry, which was visited by players almost daily.[5]

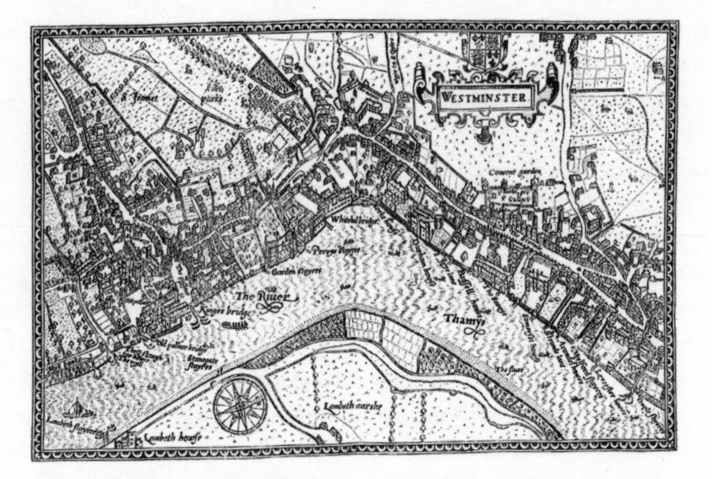

John Norden's map of Westminster from *Speculum Britannia* (1593). The area around the Abbey was a warren of medieval alleys crammed with shops, slums, taverns and tenements that harboured Westminster's notorious thieves, beggars and vagabonds.

The Thames was London's thoroughfare and its natural southern boundary. London Bridge was the only river crossing, and it connected the capital with Southwark, infamous for its salacious playhouses, bear-baiting pits and clap-ridden prostitutes. For any man-about-town, single or otherwise, Southwark offered the most riotous amusements on offer. In the Paris Garden, a show of animal baiting cost 1d. for those in the stand; 2d. if you wanted a seat in the gallery. The main attraction of the evening featured a bull or bear chained to a stake, upon which huge, half-starved mastiffs were unleashed. Over a hundred dogs were kept in kennels at the back of the rings in order to provide this very popular entertainment.

For those with more refined tastes, there were theatres – the Rose, the Swan, the Red Bull and the Globe. All were outside the official city limits of London, because the Lord Mayor had branded plays as "godless". Some of Shakespeare's finest works were being performed for the first time during Smith's sojourn, including *Othello*, *King Lear* and *Macbeth*, which made its debut in 1606.

Norden's map of the City of London. On the north bank of the Thames is the Tower of London (right); on the south bank is Southwark, with its pleasure gardens, playhouses and bear-baiting pits. The coat of arms of the twelve most influential city guilds are shown on the map border.

There was no other place in England quite like it for sheer scale or excitement – or for the chance to make (or lose) a fortune.

Smith found Londoners new and old to be pugnacious, quarrelsome, dirty and very, very noisy. In the narrow streets, overhung by gables and made slippery from the fetid ooze of refuse, horses' hooves and ironclad coach wheels clattered on the cobbles. On the river, boatmen jostled for customers, crying "Westward-ho!" or "Eastward-ho!" depending on whether they were travelling up or downstream.

Smith's own conduct in London is frustratingly obscure, for he wrote little of significance about his couple of years in the city. In many respects this is not surprising, for he was in limbo, suspended between his three exotic years battling the Turks in Europe and his legendary time in North America. In any case, he would have been financially comfortable. He had sufficient funds from Sigismund Báthory to rent decent lodgings in a tavern. Later in life he stayed in the Newgate area, just outside one of the seven historic gates into the city. There was a celebrated coaching inn nearby, next to St Sepulchre's Church, called the Saracen's Head,[6] and he must have enjoyed the irony of the name every time he walked past it.

Smith felt he needed to move on with his life, and soon. He was always a consummate networker, and most likely he reached out to the three families he knew in England who had the power and contacts to help him. He had known them all since his youth. First were the Berties. Peregrine Bertie, 13th Baron Willoughby de Eresby, had died in office as governor of Berwick-upon-Tweed in June 1601, and his two sons now held their own positions of influence in London. Robert, the eldest, had taken up the family's seat in Parliament when he became 14th Baron Willoughby de Eresby (later rising to the more senior ranking of 1st Earl of Lindsey). Peregrine, the younger brother, had entered the service of Henry, Prince of Wales, the heir apparent. (Peregrine would later be knighted in 1610 for his services, two years before the prince's death from typhoid fever.) The "fatherlesse children" from Smith's earliest travels on the Continent would have been his first port of call.

His second useful contact would most likely have been George Metham, the supervisor of his father's will. Metham was now closely linked to the Berties through marriage and business.[7]

Finally, there was Smith's mercantile mentor, the wealthy Thomas Sendall of King's Lynn. While Smith had been away battling the Turks, Sendall's son had married a woman who was cousin to both the Berties and the Methams. After Smith's long absence, a visit to King's Lynn and Willoughby would have provided an opportunity to visit his brother and sister, check on the family farm in Lincolnshire, and restore links with his influential contacts. Although he did not mention going there, it is very likely he made the trip.

Yet Smith's prospects at home may also have taken him further afield. It was common around this time for young men to try their luck in Ireland as soldiers or colonists, and there is evidence Smith might have done this after he got back to England. In 1536, Henry VIII conquered Ireland, and the English had been reinforcing and expanding their rule there brutally ever since. By 1603, the whole country was under James' nominal control. Typically, the Crown would confiscate land from Irish clans, then arrange to settle the resulting "plantations" with English colonists who brought their own language and culture, as well as loyalty to the new king in London. At the time, Ireland was England's only colony, and it would be entirely in keeping with Smith's relentless search for action to test the waters across the Irish Sea.

Smith does not directly mention being in Ireland, but he does refer to Irish clothing, later claiming that cloaks worn by the Native Americans were similar to those worn by the Irish: "The better sort use large mantels of deare skins not much differing from the Irish mantels."[8] The reference does not provide conclusive evidence he had seen the mantles in Ireland, for he might also have seen them in London, on some of the Irish who had moved to the English capital like so many other immigrants.

But there is another intriguing hint at a trip to Ireland in Smith's life. In the autumn of 1607, after he had gone to Virginia, a furious argument broke out between Smith and a fellow colonist, Edward Maria Wingfield. During a harsh exchange of words, Wingfield said of Smith: "It was proved to his face, that he begged in Ireland like a rogue, without lycence".[9]

Wingfield had been garrisoned at Drogheda, north of Dublin, during the 1590s, and he would have retained contact with soldiers who had also served in Ireland. Although Wingfield was no longer in Ireland in 1605, when Smith might have been there, the insult seemed to be based on knowledge of Smith's behaviour that Wingfield could easily have picked up from soldiers who had recently returned to London.

If Smith had indeed spent time in Ireland, it could not have been for very long; nor could it have been very successful, or he would surely have written about it. Regardless, by the middle of 1605, he was certainly in the capital, and ready to pursue the next chapter in his life – making his name in the Americas.

Smith's first plan for adventure was meant to take him not to North America, but to the southern continent. He hoped to join an expedition led by Charles Leigh, who had sailed from Woolwich on March 21, 1604, before Smith's return to London.[10] Leigh was a Puritan and sympathetic towards the Separatists, who wanted to form congregations independent from the established Church of England.[11] Smith wrote:

> Captaine Ley, brother to that noble Knight Sir Oliver Ley, with divers others, planted himselfe in the River Weapoco, wherein I should have beene a partie; but hee dyed, and there lyes buried, and the supply mis-carrying, the rest escaped as they could.[12]

Leigh's ship had arrived at the relatively small Oyapoc River, now the border between French Guiana and northeastern Brazil, on May 22, 1604. His intention was to establish a tobacco plantation. The local native people were friendly, but Leigh soon fell sick and wrote back to his brother, Sir Oliph Leigh, asking that additional supplies be sent out.[13] The relief ship sailed from London on April 14, 1605,[14] and this is likely to be the voyage Smith was referring to. On arrival off the Guiana coast, the ship was swept past the entrance to the river by strong currents and found it impossible to return.[15] The supplies never got to Charles Leigh, and he died the following year. His expedition became the latest in a string of failed English attempts to colonize the Americas.

The English had long watched Spain grow rich and powerful on Aztec gold and Incan silver, but this disappointment in South America seemed to seal their fate on that continent. Spain dominated the south, and the English were apparently unable to maintain a foothold without embarking on a truly massive expedition – and such an undertaking would surely aggravate Philip III so soon after the signing of the peace treaty. This left the English to contemplate North America, which had already proved to be challenging enough.

In 1497, five years after Columbus sailed to the Caribbean and paved the way for the conquistadors' plundering, another Italian, John Cabot (Giovanni Caboto), had sailed from Bristol to claim the half-frozen "New-Found-Land" for his new patron, Henry VII of England. Cabot's landing was the founding block of the British Empire. He returned the following year with three ships to consolidate the claim, and there is circumstantial evidence that during this trip either he or his crew mapped the eastern seaboard of North America as far south as Florida.[16] However, Cabot and his fleet apparently never returned from this second voyage, so the full extent of their exploration is not known for certain.

The Bristol merchants were keen to capitalize on Cabot's discoveries, and it was not long before English fishing boats regularly spent the summer months hunting for cod off Newfoundland's Grand Banks. The word was that the fishing was excellent. The Milanese ambassador to England wrote to his prince in Italy about Cabot's boasts: "the sea is swarming with fish, which can be taken not only with a net, but in baskets let down with a stone".[17]

In 1504, Cabot's son, the English-born Sebastian, sailed for the New World, and returned with a commercially lucrative cargo of salted fish. There is also some suggestion he engaged in exploration, for Henry VII rewarded him for services "doon unto us in and aboute the fyndynge of the new found lands".[18] Sebastian headed west again in 1508, this time in search of the fabled Northwest Passage to the Orient, but without success. He later worked for the Spanish crown, which he found to be more supportive of his wanderings.

Meanwhile, other powers were grabbing their pieces of North America. The Spanish landed in Florida in 1513, and by 1565 they had established St Augustine, the first permanent European settlement in North America. The French were also active in Florida, and tried to found a colony around what is now Jacksonville. The Spanish were having none of that, and within a year they had massacred their rivals. (This was partly why the English later feared aggressive Spanish interference in their own colonies.)

The French were also interested in the far north of the continent. Jacques Cartier sailed from St Malo in 1534 and explored the Gulf of St Lawrence. The following year, he sailed up the St Lawrence River as far as Montreal, opening a safe passage into the interior of North America and staking France's claim there. After Cabot's expedition in Newfoundland, the English had generally kept their explorations to the coastline north of Florida. Now the French were re-entering the fray from the north, and the territory available to the English was being squeezed from both north and south.

This was an age of great English explorers, however, and they were not going to leave the continent to others. In 1576, Martin Frobisher persuaded the Muscovy Company, which held a monopoly on trade between Moscow and London through a royal charter, to fund the first of his three attempts to find the Northwest Passage – as well as gold. He was disappointed on both fronts, but he explored Baffin Bay and the Hudson Strait. Then, between 1577 and 1580, Francis Drake circumnavigated the globe, landing somewhere on the western coast of North America and claiming the area – most likely what is today called Drake's Bay, just north of San Francisco. He called the land "New Albion" and received his knighthood from Queen Elizabeth in honour of his circumnavigation. But neither of these English land claims was followed up with a permanent settlement.

English exploration of the eastern seaboard of North America finally got a boost after Drake's celebrated homecoming. In August 1583 Sir Humphrey Gilbert sailed with a fleet of five ships to Newfoundland and took possession of the island for the English Crown. One of his first actions was to levy a tax on the fishermen operating out of St John's Harbour. On his return voyage, Gilbert's ship was lost with all hands during a storm. His charter from Queen Elizabeth consequently passed to his half-brother, Walter Raleigh.

Raleigh despatched a contingent in April 1584 to explore the territory north of Spanish Florida, a region which he named "Virginia", after the Virgin Queen. (He bestowed this name to the whole of the eastern seaboard of North America as far north as present-day Maine.) His charter gave him seven years to establish a colony, or lose his right to do so. But Raleigh did not merely want to establish a settlement; he expected his venture to be commercially viable, and, in addition, to provide a convenient base from which to send out privateers to raid the treasure fleets of Spain.

Raleigh never visited North America himself. Instead he sent two deputies, Arthur Barlowe and Philip Amadas, to found the Roanoke Colony, in what today is North Carolina. The expedition returned with two Croatoan native people, who described the geography of the area and the tribal politics to Raleigh. Barlowe was enthusiastic about the region and encouraged Raleigh to send over two more groups of colonists, but both attempts ended in disaster. The last 115 or so settlers, including the first English child born in the Americas, a girl called Virginia Dare, disappeared mysteriously, and Roanoke became known as the "Lost Colony".

In 1602, Bartholomew Gosnold, a trained lawyer turned explorer, sailed for Maine. After landing there, he continued south down the coast, naming Cape Cod and Martha's Vineyard on the way. He established a trading post on Cuttyhunk Island off the coast of Massachusetts, and planned to trade with the locals. Unfortunately, he found them to be hostile, and abandoned the settlement after only a few weeks. Despite his short tenure, he managed to return home with a cargo of cedar, sassafras and furs – and a desire to see the Americas again.

Each of these attempts by the English to settle Virginia had failed. Raleigh alone claimed to have spent £40,000[19] (nearly £6 million in today's money[20]) trying to establish the colony on Roanoke Island. Now the former favourite of the Queen was locked in the Tower with a death sentence hanging over him. Clearly he had lost his colonizing rights, and this opened up opportunities for new, intrepid adventurers and investors.

By 1605, London was positively buzzing with news of the various schemes to establish new settlements in the Americas.

Although Bartholomew Gosnold's attempt to establish a colony on Cuttyhunk Island in 1602 had failed, he was still well regarded for his success as a privateer. Gosnold decided to trade on his reputation and began to promote an even more ambitious plan for the Americas.

Many of Raleigh's former associates were petitioning King James to allow new initiatives for colonization – the King had spared Raleigh, after all, and so good favour and good fortune could still be theirs. Among these men were such luminaries as the geographer and writer Richard Hakluyt; Sir Thomas Gates, who later became the governor of Jamestown; Admiral Sir George Somers, an experienced mariner who later founded the English colony in Bermuda; and lawyer and soldier

Edward Maria Wingfield, who had extensive experience fighting in the Low Countries and Ireland.

Smith claimed to be involved in these men's early discussions about new American settlements. It is quite likely Smith made Gosnold's acquaintance through his contact with Robert Bertie, who was related by marriage to Gosnold. In one way or another, all the influential people Smith would have contacted after his return to England had business or familial links with the promoters of what would become the Virginia Company of London. Smith's network was growing, enough so that he could claim Gosnold specifically had asked him to take part in planning his newest undertaking:

> Captaine Bartholomew Gosnoll, one of the first movers of this plantation, having many yeares solicited many of his friends, but found small assistants [assistance]; at last prevailed with some Gentlemen, as Captaine John Smith, Master Edward-Maria Wingfield, Master Robert Hunt [a preacher], and divers others, who depended a yeare upon his projects, but nothing could be effected, till by their great charge and industrie, it came to be apprehended by certaine of the Nobilitie, Gentry, and Marchants, so that his Majestie by his letters patents, gave commission for establishing Councels, to direct here; and to governe, and execute there.[21]

It is worth noting that Smith not only referred to himself here as a "Gentleman", but also self-importantly put himself ahead of Wingfield on the list, despite Wingfield being one of the group's leaders, as well as a cousin-by-marriage of Gosnold. Already, Smith's arrogance and the potential for friction with the colony's top men were evident.

Long gone were the days when a monarch financed an overseas colony, as Henry VII had done with John Cabot. The cost was also too great for just one individual to take on, as Walter Raleigh had discovered with Roanoke. If there was any hope of founding successful settlements in Virginia, money would need raising far and wide. A proposal was made to create an English joint-stock company, supported with the imprimatur of a royal charter from King James. It would follow the model of the

Company of Merchant Adventurers to New Lands of 1553 (whose governor was Sebastian Cabot) and the Muscovy Company of 1555 (which had underwritten Martin Frobisher's explorations). Already the most famous of the joint-stock companies was the East India Company, which had been granted a royal charter by Elizabeth in 1600.

While plans for the new joint-stock company for a Virginia colony were being discussed, an expedition was quietly funded by the Earl of Southampton (Shakespeare's patron) and despatched across the Atlantic. The ship left in March 1605 and returned in July, docking at Dartmouth, Devon, carrying precious information of Virginia – and, most valuable of all, five kidnapped locals. With this thrilling human cargo to exploit, it was time to announce the new company's existence. The publicity coup stoked public interest, breathing life into the royal charter.

A few months later, an assasination attempt on the King threw London into such turmoil it could have derailed the project completely. English Catholics were losing hope that the greater religious tolerance James' ascent to the throne promised would ever become a reality. Plotters hatched an audacious plan to blow up the House of Lords during the opening session of England's Parliament. At least a dozen conspirators were involved, but it was Guy Fawkes, who had fought for ten years with the Spanish in the Low Countries, who was charged with the task of laying and guarding the gunpowder in an undercroft of the Palace of Westminster.

An outbreak of plague in the city delayed the re-opening of Parliament by more than a year, but all the while the plotters stood at the ready. Then, on November 4, the day before the state occasion, an anonymous warning to a member of the House of Lords led Parliamentary officers to search the building. Fawkes was discovered there, together with his barrels of gunpowder hidden under firewood and coal.

At their trial on January 27, 1606, eight of the conspirators, including Fawkes, were convicted of high treason and sentenced to be hanged, drawn and quartered – a particularly unpleasant way to die. The execution required that the condemned first be hanged almost to the point of death, then castrated and disembowelled while still alive, before being beheaded; then each of the limbs was hacked from his body. The severity of the punishment was considered to fit the crime, but it was nothing compared with the agonizing death to later befall some of the Virginia colonists then being recruited on the streets of London. Yet despite the uproar caused by the Gunpowder Plot, plans for the Virginia colony were moving forward.

Four key elements were required for the enterprise to be a success: adequate financial backing through the issue of shares; a sound understanding of the region to be colonized; meticulous planning; and royal assent. The first three conditions were still a work in progress, and the Gunpowder Plot may have been taken as a sign that Catholic Spain was potentially a mortal menace to any new English arrivals in the New World. But King James was undaunted and signed the company's charter on April 10, 1606, giving his full blessing to the venture. In return for a twenty per cent share of any precious metals found in the colony, James granted the patentees permission to:

> make Habitation, Plantation, and to deduce a colony of sundry of our People into that part of America commonly called VIRGINIA, and other parts and Territories in America, either appertaining unto us, or which are not now actually possessed by any Christian Prince or People.[22]

The new plans created two separate companies, known collectively as the Virginia Company. The Virginia Company of London (or "London Company") and the Virginia Company of Plymouth (or "Plymouth Company") were issued identical charters, covering two distinct but overlapping territories. The London Company was granted the right to establish settlements up to one hundred square miles between the 34th and 41st parallels of latitude (roughly between Cape Fear in modern North Carolina, and Long Island in New York); the Plymouth Company had the right to establish similar colonies between the 38th and 45th parallel (from modern Philadelphia, north to the Canada border). Though the territories overlapped, the charter stipulated that the two companies could not establish colonies within one hundred miles of each other.

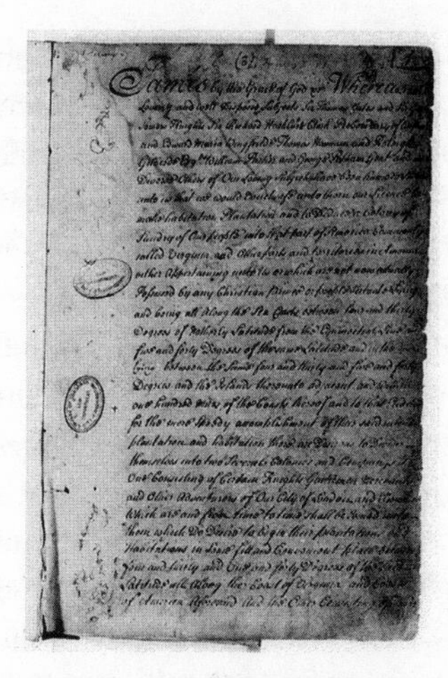

James' royal charter of 1606 creating the London Company of Virginia. It is interesting to note that on the first page the names of Sir Thomas Gates, Sir George Somers, Richard Hackluit [sic], Edward Maria Wingfield and others are all mentioned, but not John Smith (courtesy of the US Library of Congress).

The London Company and the Plymouth Company were managed by the Royal Council for Virginia, based in the capital. To begin, the council comprised fourteen members, with King James in ultimate control. But the company's directors understood they would not be able to govern the daily affairs of the colonies from London. Any expeditionary force would need to be governed on a daily basis by its own members. The charter therefore allowed the company to appoint a governing council of up to thirteen men in each colony.

According to Smith's own account, he was involved in the Virginia project a full year before James signed the company's charter, and by May 1605 he was almost certainly helping Bartholomew Gosnold plan aspects of the expedition; Smith even invested some of his own funds in the fledgling venture.

The royal charter had taken months of painstaking preparation and lobbying – areas that were Gosnold's speciality, as he was trained as a lawyer. It also required the backing of scores of men, the cutting of yards of red tape, and the liberal greasing of many palms. While Smith may have been helpful in considering tactics and providing some of the funds, he was unlikely to have been a leading partner in the resulting company.

Not all the gossip about the new venture was flattering. Several playwrights took to satirizing the scramble for riches in the Americas, most notable being Ben Jonson (Shakespeare's rival), George Chapman and John Marston, who together wrote the play *Eastward Hoe* after the call to potential customers from the Thames boatmen.[23] The play offended the King with its short outburst of anti-Scottish comedy, and landed its three authors in jail. However, its main themes of fraud, ambition, vanity and morality spoke to the zeitgeist.

For the shareholders in the London Company, the scramble for riches trumped all other considerations. The Virginia expedition had two prime objectives: to search for gold, and thereby match Spain's success in accruing New World treasures; and to find a route west to the Orient, thus fending off Dutch and Portuguese pioneers in the Far East. The English were determined they too should get a slice of the huge riches to be found overseas. Furthermore, several leading men saw the potential for turning a profit by obtaining fur pelts, fish and timber from beyond England's shores. The straight pine trees of the Americas were especially coveted by English shipbuilders, who wanted them to make masts for the expanding national fleet.

But there were other benefits to colonizing the Americas that made it politically expedient for James to grant his charter. At this time, England was believed to be overpopulated, and more and more people were finding it difficult to scrape a living, especially in the cities. Overseas colonies could address this problem, as Sir John Popham, the King's chief justice, explained:

> The infinite numbers of cashiered captains and soldiers, or poor artisans that would & cannot work, and of idle vagrants that may & will not work, is affectionately bent to the plantation of Virginia.[24]

Colonizing the Americas would also provide more employment, for sailors and shipbuilders alike. It was a win-win situation.

There were also some who said the Virginia ventures carried a higher religious purpose, "in propagating of Christian Religion to such People, as yet live in Darkness and miserable ignorance of the true Knowledge and Worship of God".[25] However, saving the souls of "heathen savages" was not the only religious motivation. Despite the new peace treaty with Spain, signed in August 1604, anything that limited the spread of Catholicism was also considered beneficial to England.

It is easy to understand why Smith wanted to take his chance in Virginia. At heart he was still a knight-adventurer, still driven to better himself. His experience as a mercenary undoubtedly intrigued, maybe even charmed, some of the colony's early organizers, though his brash pride over his past exploits might also have unsettled others. Perhaps arrogance was easily forgiven in this group. All the men attracted to the Virginia project were seeking to better themselves, through wealth, status or a combination of the two. As Captain Seagull of *Eastward Hoe* quipped, in Virginia you would find:

> gold is more plentiful there than copper is with us...Why, man, all their dripping-pans and their chamber-pots are pure gold...wild boar is as common there as our tamest bacon is here; venison as mutton. And then you shall live freely there, without serjeants, or courtiers, or lawyers, or intelligencers...You may be an alderman there, and never be scavenger; you may be any other officer and never be a slave.[26]

The opportunity to leave behind the suffocating class system must also have appealed to Smith and many others.

It was now time to appoint the sailing captains and settlement leaders. The captain of choice to "command" the fleet was Christopher Newport, one of the most experienced and reliable mariners of the age, and he accepted the position readily. He was given full responsibility for the success or failure of the expedition, until a site for the new colony was found.

Newport had sailed to South America at the age of twenty-one, and for twenty years harrassed the Spanish as a privateer. In September 1582, he made his name by bringing the celebrated Spanish warship the *Madre de Dios* into Dartmouth harbour with five hundred tons of spices, silks and gems on board – the richest prize ever taken by one of Elizabeth's Sea Dogs. In September 1605, Newport had returned from Santo Domingo with two young crocodiles and a wild boar as gifts for James, thereby winning the King's favour.

Second-in-command was Bartholomew Gosnold. Gosnold was not as experienced as Newport, but he had his own credentials. He had developed useful contacts in London, and called the well-respected geographer Richard Hakluyt a friend. He had also sailed with Walter Raleigh before his fall from grace, and four years previously he had commanded his own voyage to the Americas.

The third captain of the fleet, John Ratcliffe, left little trace in history, except that he also used a second name, Sicklemore. Ratcliffe and John Smith became fast friends, but this would prove to be short-lived.

The next matter to consider was the selection of the ships. Following the peace treaty with Spain, there were plenty of vessels to choose from – England no longer needed to protect its coasts from the Catholic invasion. However, the London Company was out to make a profit, so one of the greatest considerations was cost. Newport's flagship would be the *Susan Constant*. She was leased from the firm Colthurst, Dapper, Wheatley and Co of London, and it appears that one of the firm's partners, Wheatley, was associated with a business that sold timber for ships. This would have made him extremely interested in what lumber the London Company might snatch from Virginia, and he may have been eager to strike a good deal.

The *Susan Constant* was registered in London, and was about a year old when she left for Virginia. A month before her departure for the Americas, she had collided with a smaller ship, the *Philip and Francis*, in the River Thames. Although the accident caused only minor damage, it was sufficient to provoke a day in court. From the statements and depositions presented during the lawsuit we know something of the vessel.[27] She was a typical medium-sized ship of the period, with a carrying capacity of about 120 tons, a little over a hundred feet long on deck and a beam, or width, of just twenty-five feet. Even so, the *Susan Constant* was twice the size of the fleet's other two ships combined.

The *Godspeed,* under Gosnold's command, was leased from the Muscovy Company. The ship was forty tons, a little over sixty feet on deck and with a beam of about fifteen feet. The *Discovery,* captained by John Ratcliffe, was tiny, not much bigger than a modern yacht at just twenty tons and little more than thirty-five feet long with a beam of about twelve feet. She was small to face the fury of the Atlantic's winter storms, but she had been chosen for a reason: the captains knew the shallow draft of the *Discovery* would help in the exploration of the rivers and creeks of Virginia. Also to this end, Newport loaded a small boat, called a shallop, in kit form on the deck of the *Susan Constant.*

The fleet was loaded with crew, colonizers, equipment and stores. No passenger lists have survived, if any ever existed. In his work *Purchas his Pilgrimes,* published in 1625, Samuel Purchas gave some numbers in a marginal note: 71 on the *Susan Constant,* 52 on the *Godspeed,* and 21 on the tiny *Discovery,* making a total of 144.[28] Other reports put the total number of settlers at 104, 105 and 108 men, which suggests Purchas' figure of 144 included the crew. Smith would have been classified as a passenger, and he is thought to have sailed on the *Susan Constant.*

Although Newport was responsible for getting the settlers safely to the American mainland, his duties ended once the site for the colony was chosen. Then, under the terms of the London Company's charter, the governing council took over, electing a president from among themselves. The charter authorized a council of up to thirteen members, but the managers in London opted to select only seven men. For the moment, no one on the ships knew who these men were. The names of the council members were locked in a box, with strict instructions it was not be opened until the day of their landing in Virginia.

There were a couple of good reasons for the secrecy. Foremost, if the governing council was known during the voyage, it could undermine Newport's authority. For the moment, he needed all the power he could muster to ensure the fleet's safe arrival. Secondly, if the membership of the council was published even in limited form, the information would inevitably find its way to one of the many Spanish spies in the capital. The London Company obviously wanted to avoid that.

Regardless, there must have been considerable speculation during the voyage about the names in the box. Almost certainly, Edward Maria Wingfield and Captain John Martin would be members of the council, for they had both paid considerable sums to invest in the company – far more than someone like Captain Smith had at his disposal. Both men were also experienced leaders. Most likely, George Percy's name was there too, for he was the son of the 8th Earl of Northumberland, one of the great English families of the time, and to leave him off the list would be seen as a terrible rebuke. The three sailing masters were all experienced leaders in different ways, and they too could expect to be named. That was six – less than half of the possible seats on the council.

Who among the remaining settlers might find their names in the box? Nearly half of the colonists were gentlemen – not members of the nobility, but men with a higher social status than a tradesman, craftsman or yeoman. Many of these gentlemen had good family names and some experience of management of estates or trade enterprises, and many would have considered themselves suitable candidates for a seat around the proverbial council table. The one exception was the Reverend Master Robert Hunt, who as chaplain to the colonists was barred by his profession from joining the council.

In addition to these gentlemen, there were numerous artisans and craftsmen who possessed the day-to-day skills needed to establish a permanent colony: two surgeons, a blacksmith, a barber, a tailor and a mason, as well as carpenters, bricklayers and lowly labourers. None of these men would expect to be named to the council. In total, 108 men had signed up to establish the first permanent English colony in the New World, but few of them were making the journey with the expectation of being their leader.

The expedition was the seventeenth-century equivalent of a Mars landing. These adventurers were travelling to a land they knew very little about, and few of the original contingent would ever return to English shores. In fact, by the end of their first year, only thirty-eight of the men would still be alive – just over a third.

Everything had to be taken by ship to ensure the men could establish a functioning settlement. They needed supplies to plant crops, protect against illness and injury, survive attacks, and cope with the bitter American winter. They carried food, clothing, tools, water, wine and ale, even livestock to provide fresh meat and milk on the voyage, and animals to work and breed in the colony they established at its end. Just as important, they took with them a multitude of trinkets for trade with the locals – glass beads (blue was especially valued) and copper beads and ornaments, for the indigenous peoples prized copper as the English did gold.

It was the custom of the day for an expedition's leading men to dine aboard Drake's *Golden Hind*, still at anchor at Greenwich Palace, not far from Blackwall. Once that formality was complete, it was time to leave. On December 20, 1606, the London Company's three ships cast off their moorings and sailed downriver on the ebb tide.

The winters were bitter in England then, and the wind blew damp and cold off the low, grey Kentish marshland. As the vessels slipped down the Thames, bystanders on the shore paid little attention. It was a most inauspicious departure for the three ships, which were now on course to change history.

Unknown to the settlers on board, the wily Spanish ambassador in London, Don Pedro de Zúñiga, was fully aware of their movements. Even though King James had recently agreed the terms of peace with Philip III, de Zúñiga would soon recommend to his king that he put a swift end to this little English enterprise in far-off Virginia.

1607.

A true report of certaine wonderfull ouerflowings of Waters, now lately in Summerset-shire, Norfolke, and other places of England: destroying many thousands of men, women, and children, ouerthrowing and bearing downe whole townes and villages, and drowning infinite numbers of sheepe and other Cattle.

Bad weather plagued John Smith's departure for America, with the effects of storms captured in this woodprint entitled "A true report of certaine wonderfull Ouerflowings of Waters, now lately in Summerset-shire, Norfolke" (1607).

7
Colonist

1606–1607

We set sayle from Blackwall, but by unprosperous winds, were kept six weeks in sight of England; all which time, Master Hunt our Preacher, was so weake and sick, that few expected his recovery
John Smith, The Generall Historie (1624)

January 1607 was neither a good month for English farmers, nor for English sailors. As the Virginia fleet sailed down the Thames estuary and into the North Sea, England was about to experience one of the most serious natural catastrophes in its recent history. On January 20, violent storms swept across the south, bringing torrential rain and causing widespread flooding. As many as three thousand people reportedly died.[1] Newspapers were unknown at the time, but printed pamphlets were often used to spread word of major events. One such booklet led with a story that would have done justice to any modern tabloid newspaper:

> A true report of certaine wonderfull ouerflowings of Waters, now lately in Summersetshire, Norfolke, and other places of England: destroying many thousands of men, women, and children, ouerthrowing and bearing down whole townes and villages and drowning infinite numbers of sheepe and other cattle.[2]

The west of England and the Severn estuary were particularly badly hit, but London and eastern England also suffered the effects of the severe storm.

Just days after leaving the protection of the Thames estuary, the London Company's fleet, under the command of Captain Newport, was caught in these treacherous conditions. The three ships had sailed down the River Thames with a westerly wind behind them, but when they rounded the northeast coast of Kent, called the Downs, fierce headwinds brought them to a halt. One of the colonists, George Percy, wrote in his journal:

> the fleet fell from London, and the fift of January [1607] we anchored in the [Kent] Downes: but the winds continued contrarie so long, that we were forced to stay there some time, where wee suffered great stormes.[3]

The Kent coast and the southern portion of the North Sea are notorious for their shallow offshore sand banks, and the area is particularly treacherous in strong winds. This is where the Spanish Armada finally admitted defeat nearly thirty years previously. Now, similar conditions threatened the Virginia expedition, and there was nothing they could do about it, for it was impossible for the ships to sail down the English Channel against a fierce westerly wind. Newport's only option was to order his ships to anchor and wait for a more favourable wind. But during the first half of January, a series of deep depressions marched across southern England, and there was no escaping the squalls.

The three ships were packed to the gunwales with men, equipment and stores. Overloaded and top-heavy, the vessels rolled relentlessly at anchor, making cooking, eating and sleeping all but impossible. Inevitably, the driving rain found its way down through the leaky decks and hatches, giving those huddled below no respite from the appalling weather. John Smith's account of this start to the voyage was typically short and pithy:

> On the 19 of December, 1606, we set sayle from Blackwall, but by unprosperous winds, were kept for six weeks in the sight of England; all which time, Master Hunt our Preacher, was so weake and sicke, that few expected his recovery.[4]

The Reverend Hunt was only twenty miles from his home in Reculver, Kent, but he had already arrived in another world – hell and high water. Before long, the drinking water began to go stale, food ran low, and an unremitting stench rose from the bilges, testing even the strongest of stomachs. The unscheduled delay forced the ships' captains to order short rations, thereby increasing the misery of everyone on board. Not for the first time, Smith passed his birthday in acute discomfort.

On the evening of Tuesday, January 20, the tail of the big storm struck Newport's fleet, still at anchor off the Downs. The situation on board grew abysmal. Smith recalled that only the intervention of the sickly reverend settled the passengers' frayed nerves, because:

> so many discontents did then arise, had he [Hunt] not had the water of patience, and his godly exhortations (but chiefly by his true devoted examples) quenched those flames of envie, and dissention.[5]

Although George Percy made no mention of the restlessness on board, Smith seemed to be aware of seeds of discontent already sown among the colonists, even though they were still in sight of England's shores. The "flames of envie" would smoulder on the outward journey, waiting to flare up in the years to come.

Smith said the fleet was delayed "for six weeks in sight of England". Near the end of the month, the storm finally passed, and the wind changed direction. This is exactly what Captain Newport had been waiting for, and without delay he ordered his ships to haul in their anchors and head down the English Channel. Even with a following wind, it would have taken them most of a week to sail through the Channel and out into the Atlantic.

Once into the Western Approaches, Newport signalled his fleet to alter course south for the Canary Islands. He chose the traditional route across the Atlantic to the Americas, giving the rocks around Ushant a wide berth, and sailing across the Bay of Biscay, before heading south-southwest.

The fleet was finally free of the constraints of the Channel, but their problems were not over. February is not a favourable month to be heading into the North Atlantic, and Percy recorded: "The twelfth day

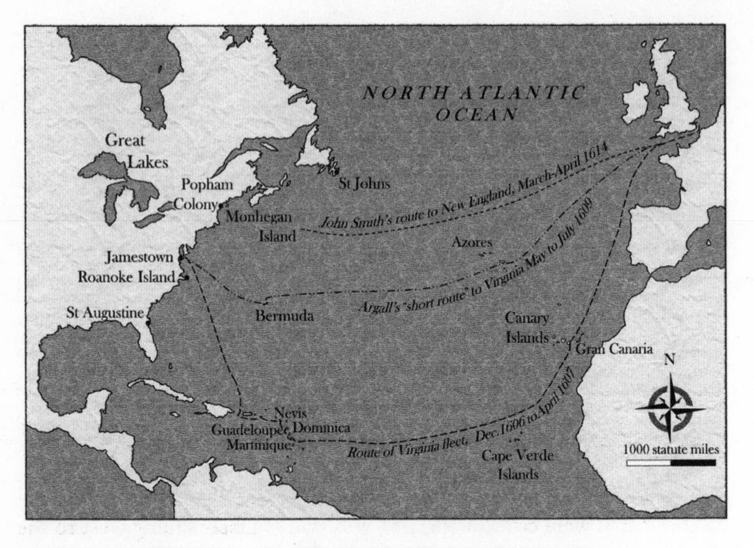

The route to Virginia taken by the fleet of the London Company in late 1606 and early 1607. Samuel Argall's "short route" via and the Azores and Bermuda is also shown, together with John Smith's crossing in 1614 to New England.

of February at night, we saw a blazing Starre, and presently a storme [blew up]".[6] Percy's "blazing Starre" was not Haley's Comet (which did not appear in the colonists' sky until later that year), but it was unnerving nonetheless. The people of the seventeenth century clung to superstitions, and the appearance of anything unusual in the heavens was considered a bad omen.

By the third week of February, the fleet reached Gran Canaria in the Canary Islands.[7] They were sailing at an average speed of 100 miles a day, and had traversed some 2,100 miles in about three weeks. Since Columbus' historic voyage to the Caribbean in 1492, the Canaries had been used as a stopover by ships heading west for the Americas. Here, the fleet took on fresh water and provisions and made last-minute repairs. Once clear of the islands, the ships hoped to pick up the Trade Winds, a prevailing northeasterly wind that blows fairly constantly throughout the year. With the wind behind them, it was a straightforward run of less than 3,000 miles before they expected landfall on one of the islands of the West Indies.

Ships of the period rarely sailed more than 100 miles in twenty-four hours, so Newport knew the voyage would take at least four weeks – assuming he could keep track of the fleet's position. It was a long time to be out of sight of land with only the most basic navigational techniques. His navigators could determine the ships' latitude (the distance north or south of the equator) reasonably accurately using a cross-staff or an astrolabe to measure the angle of the sun. Indeed, in 1989 the British sailor Sir Robin Knox-Johnston experimented with an astrolabe to measure latitude, and found that his average error was only about fifteen miles.[8] To measure longitude (position in an east–west direction) reliably was impossible until accurate marine clocks, known as chronometers, were developed in the mid-eighteenth century. All the navigators had in these days were crude estimates, and every master sailing west to the Americas worried about his longitude, because making an error could mean running aground on arrival.

There was really only one technique that could help minimize the risk: "dead reckoning". Ships leaving the Canary Islands often paused at the westernmost island, El Hierro (Ferro), which had been used to establish zero degrees longitude since the second century AD. (Ptolemy defined this zero meridian as the "westernmost" position of the known world; only in 1884 was the Greenwich Meridian adopted as the world's Prime Meridian.) With that confirmed position at the start of his journey, a navigator would meticulously record his ship's direction at regular intervals, using the time of the sun's position at midday. The ship's speed was calculated by throwing over the side a weighted wooden board to which was attached a light line running out from a reel on the deck. Knots were tied along the line at intervals of forty-seven feet, three inches, and the number of knots that slipped through the navigator's hand in twenty-eight-seconds – measured by sandglass – was directly proportional to the speed of the ship. Hence the term "knots" became the standard measure of nautical speed.

Each of the three ships in Newport's fleet came equipped with a crude compass mounted inside a wooden box. The box was held together with wooden pegs, because the magnetism from iron nails would distort the compass reading. The compass itself was simple: a circular card over which a magnetized iron needle rotated freely on a brass pin, allowing the needle to point to magnetic north, thus showing the ship's heading.

From his many voyages over the previous ten years, John Smith had extensive experience of ocean navigation, and he was familiar with the instruments at the navigators' disposal. He was also well acquainted with the waters around the Canary Islands from his time travelling with Captain Merham and his French privateers. No doubt he would have needed little encouragement to remind his fellow passengers of his adventures around the islands.

Whether his boasting about his maritime feats tipped the balance is not clear, but shortly after leaving the Canaries, Smith was accused of mutiny and imprisoned:

> Now Captaine Smith, who all this time from their departure from the Canaries was restrained as a prisoner upon the scandalous suggestions of some of the chiefe (envying his repute) who fained he intended to usurpe the government, murther the Councell, and make himselfe King.[9]

It was a preposterous accusation, but it is easy to understand how tempers might begin to overheat as the men remained cooped up in tiny, stinking, rolling ships for ten weeks without adequate food and water. Samuel Purchas, who chronicled many of the English voyages of the period, did not think much of the trumped-up charges against Smith: "The next day Cap. Smith was suspected for a Mutinie, though never no such matter."[10] Nevertheless, to be charged with mutiny was a very serious offence, punishable by death. Not for the first time, nor the last, did Smith's argumentative temperament get him into serious trouble. Somehow, he had made enemies of some very powerful people.

There are enough reports from the voyage to establish the basic facts. As we have seen, even before the fleet left the Kent Downs there had been some serious unrest on board, and the Reverend Hunt had been instrumental in easing tensions. The settlers broadly fell into three distinct groups: firstly, the crew, who were under the direct command of the ships' masters, and therefore reasonably disciplined; secondly, members of the aristocracy and gentleman, who were well educated and often with some military experience in the Low Countries and Ireland, and who consequently often held and expressed strong opinions; and finally, the tradesmen and labourers, men with skills but little education, who generally accepted their lower social status in life without complaint. There were, however, a few outliers. The Reverend Hunt, the only religious man on board, was one, and he quickly adopted the role of diplomat and peacemaker. The other main exception was John Smith.

Smith did not fit comfortably into any of the social categories of the late Elizabethan and early Jacobean age. He could not shake the simple fact that he had been born to a tenant farmer, a relatively lowly status within the prevailing social hierarchy. In the eyes of the aristocrats and gentlemen on board, it made little difference that he had been awarded a coat of arms from a Transylvanian prince – a man most had never heard of and cared little about. Smith was a hardened soldier and adventurer, who, by the age of twenty-seven, had probably seen more bloody combat than anyone else in the fleet. Undoubtedly he had travelled further afield than anyone else, and had witnessed customs and practices that most could scarcely imagine.

Yet these experiences also meant nothing when it came to life on ship – and Smith's pugnacious nature and irrepressible pride made for a combustible mix in those confined quarters. The craftsmen and tradesmen on board were most likely awed by the exploits of this farmer's son from Lincolnshire; the aristocrats and gentlemen much less so, and they would take exception to Smith's arrogant assumption of a higher status than he was born to.

Among the class-conscious gentlemen on board was George Percy, the eighth son of Henry, the 8th Earl of Northumberland, who traced his ancestry back to the Norman Conquest. It was said at the time that "the Percys are almost without a peer even in the peerage of Great Britain…the family banner bears a galaxy of heraldic honors altogether unparalleled".[11] Just eight months Smith's junior, Percy himself boasted impeccable credentials: he was a graduate from Oxford, a lawyer at the Middle Temple, and had served in the army in the Low Countries and Ireland. He had the highest social rank of all the colonists, and could well assume he was on the secret list to form the governing council when the settlers arrived in Virginia. Yet Percy was also ill-suited for the demands of the expedition. He suffered from a variety of ailments for much of his life, possibly including chronic diseases such as severe asthma and epilepsy. Given these complaints, he was an unlikely fellow to earn the respect of a man like Smith, who bragged of despatching far stronger foes with brute force.

But Smith's true *bête noire* was Edward Maria Wingfield, whose family seat was Kimbolton Castle in Huntingdonshire; here Catherine of Aragon had been sent to live out her last days after she refused to accept an annulment of her marriage to Henry VIII. Wingfield followed family tradition and became a soldier, also serving in the Low Countries and Ireland. He was more experienced than Percy, and he was the only senior civilian of the London Company of Virginia to be on the expedition. Wingfield was also a cousin of Bartholomew Gosnold, the master of the *Godspeed*, and the two men had worked closely together to recruit about a third of the colonists. Wingfield was also thirty years older than Smith and could reasonably have expected Smith's deference. But it was not to be.

From the outset, it seems Winfield and Smith despised each other, and it was almost certainly Wingfield who called for Smith's arrest. It is thus likely they were trapped on the same ship in the fleet, which given Wingfield's status, would have been the *Susan Constant*. Wingfield was a founding member of the London Company, so Newport would have been obliged to take his accusations against Smith seriously.

However, Smith had his supporters, too. There is some evidence that a young gentleman called Stephen Calthorp (or Halthrop) was involved in Smith's attempted "mutiny". Calthorp was treated less harshly, being a gentleman. He might also have been related to Edward Maria Wingfield, which would have afforded him some leniency.[12] (Calthorp is believed to have died in Jamestown on August 15, 1607, just three months after arriving in Virginia.)

Smith was confined for the duration of the voyage, making his passage even more uncomfortable in the overcrowded ships. Given the circumstances of his arrest, it is likely he had very limited contact with the rest of the passengers, and would have been kept well away from them below decks, in his own secluded hell.

Only the captains, and possibly Wingfield himself, would have had the luxury of a private cabin and free roam of the ship. All the others lived and slept on top of the cargo, crawling around their quarters with only a few feet of headroom. There was little light or fresh air below, and rarely an opportunity to go up on deck, which the masters and their crews preferred to be kept clear of passengers. Water would seep through the hull and decks, whether from rain or from crashing waves, saturating the men and their belongings on a regular basis. Sanitation was almost non-existent, and if a man wanted to wash (and most declined the opportunity), it was in a bucket of saltwater.

Food was basic, unappetizing, and frequently mouldy or infested with weevils. Beef, pork and fish were preserved by salting, supplemented with hardtack (a hard, dry biscuit), cheese, butter, dried peas and beans. If weather permitted, the food was cooked over charcoal fires in metal boxes called braziers. Often, conditions at sea made these fires too hazardous, and food was eaten cold. Fresh drinking water was always taken on board whenever possible, but it soon developed an unpleasant aftertaste, and before long became unsafe to drink. Instead, as in London, people usually drank weak beer; the hops act as a preservative, making it safer (and more palatable) than stale water.

Yet despite these privations, passengers of the period frequently claimed that the biggest problem on the long, transatlantic voyages was not poor food or foul water, but boredom. The days were grindingly monotonous. The men spent most of their time squeezed below decks with only the creaking of the hull, the slop of waves, the whistling of the wind in the rigging, and the irritating foibles of their fellow passengers to break the tedium. And Smith no longer had the bad habits of others to distract him. The days were even worse for him.

According to George Percy's diary, the fleet sighted the island of Martinique in the West Indies on March 23, 1607, and then made their landing on Dominica the next day to obtain fresh water and other essentials. They had been at sea for more than three months.

For Captain Newport, it was a return to a region he knew well. He had first sailed to the West Indies in 1590, on what was his first command. On that trip, he had lost his right hand while leading an attack against a Spanish ship off Cuba. He later became notorious for his raids on enemy ships and settlements – seizing more than any other English privateer. Some portraits of Newport painted after his death show him with a hook in place of his right arm, but other reports suggest he had a prosthetic. Whatever the reality, some claim Newport was the inspiration for J.M. Barrie's Captain Hook.

For the next two weeks, Newport's fleet worked its way north and west through the islands of the West Indies. It is interesting to compare Smith's account twenty-three years afterwards with that of George Percy's contemporaneous diary. Even with the distance of time, Smith was obviously still smarting from his incarceration, and said little about life on the islands. By comparison, Percy wrote little about the Atlantic passage but was impressed with the exotic sights and smells of the new land. On March 24, he reported that they had anchored off Dominica:

> a very faire Iland, the Trees full of sweet and good smels inhabited by many Savage Indians, they were at first very scrupulous to come aboord us. Wee learned of them afterwards that the Spaniards had given them a great overthrow on this Ile, but when they knew what we were, there came many to our ships with their Canoas, bringing us many kinds of sundry fruits, Pines, Potatoes, Plantons, Tobacco, and other fruits...[13]

Except for a few of the more experienced sailors in the crew, this was the colonists' first glimpse of the New World, and their first introduction to the local peoples. Immediately, Percy said, the islanders began to trade goods, and the colonists came well prepared:

> We gave them Knives, Hatchets for exchange which they esteeme much, wee also gave them Beades, Copper Jewels which they hang through their nosthrils, eares, and lips, very strange to behold, their bodies are all painted red to keepe away the biting of Muscetos, they goe all naked without covering:...they are continually in warres, and will eate their enemies when they kill them, or any stranger if they take them.[14]

Percy was fascinated by these encounters, as well as the wonders of the natural world, most especially "a Whale chased by a Thresher and a Sword-fish: they fought for the space of two houres...in the end these two fishes brought the Whale to her end".[15]

The ships next sailed for Guadeloupe, where they discovered the volcano of Grande Soufrière was active and "a Bath which was so hot, that no man was able to stand long by it".[16] This was no safe harbour, and Newport ordered the fleet to move on.

They found an anchorage off Nevis. Here, the captain decided to give his men six days ashore to recover from their long weeks at sea.

The accusation of mutiny was still hanging over Smith, and with the whole crew now on land, it was time to decide his fate. Smith remembered the moment with typical bravado:

> Such factions here we had, as commonly attend such voyages, that a paire of gallowes was made, but Captaine Smith, for whom they were intended, could not be perswaded to use them.[17]

He was marched to the gallows, based on this account, but no one else on the journey reported him coming so close to being executed. Why would he fabricate such a story?

The planned execution is plausible. The death sentence was frequently passed in cases of mutiny, and Wingfield (and possibly other influential gentlemen on the *Susan Constant*) had little time for Smith; many would have been happy to see him gone from their company. Their six-day stay on Nevis was the first time in many weeks that the whole company could assemble and discuss the matter of his alleged treason; it was also the first chance they would have had to build a gallows on dry land. Smith's "confederats were dispersed in all the three ships", but this suggests he had only a handful of supporters across the entire expedition.

So why, then, was Smith reprieved? Any explanation has to be conjecture, but the instructions from the London Company were plain: until the ships arrived at their chosen place of settlement, Captain Newport retained absolute authority over the group. There is no evidence Smith had fallen foul of Newport while they were at sea, although this state of affairs would not continue forever. Newport was also an experienced leader and understood fully the challenges ahead – not only to establish a colony, but to protect the expedition against attack from the native peoples. He could ill afford to lose a man of Smith's background and experience, and he had the legal right to reprieve him. However, Newport refrained from granting him a full pardon, and Smith remained under arrest for the rest of the voyage, up to and including the landing at Jamestown.

Still, after his brush with death on Nevis, Smith began to document the details of the island. He was especially attuned to the lay of the land, inventorying local features that might be important for future settlement or defence. He took special note that "it is all woddy, but by the Sea side Southward there are sands like downes, where a thousand men may quarter themselves conveniently".[18]

But Nevis was no Eden. The men were ignorant of the strange plants around them, some of which, Smith claimed, were poisonous to the touch, and that:

> in some places so thicke of a soft spungy wood like a wilde figge tree, you cannot get through it, but by making your way with hatchets, or fauchions: whether it was the dew of those trees, or of some others, I am not certaine, but many of our men became so tormented with a burning swelling all over their bodies, they seemed like scalded men, and neere mad with paine.[19]

This must have been the manchineel tree, *Hippomane mancinella,* which is native to the Caribbean. Growing upwards of fifty feet tall, the tree bears fruit and leaves and otherwise resembles a small apple or wild fig.

Its milky white sap, which Smith described as "dew", contains phorbol and other skin irritants, which cause a strong allergic reaction – a single drop of rainwater containing the sap can blister the skin. Indeed, the sap was so noxious that the Carib Indians used it to poison their arrows, and also tainted enemies' water supplies with the tree's leaves.

The Englishmen soon realized they might need to protect themselves from attack by the local peoples. Newport took several precautions, according to Percy:

> There the Captaine landed all his men being well fitted with Muskets and other convenient Armes, marched a mile into the Woods; being commanded to stand upon their guard, fearing the treacherie of the Indians.[20]

After their eventful stopover on Nevis, Newport laid a course for the "Ile of Virgines" – the Virgin Islands. They passed the smaller islands of Sint Eustatius and Saba on their way, then anchored "in an excellent Bay able to harbour a hundred Ships", which may have been Road Harbour in Tortola, but was perhaps more likely to be Round Bay and Coral Bay on the island of St John. Here, the fleet found no fresh water, but Percy said they managed a coup nonetheless: they collected enough fresh fish and "Sea Tortoises" (turtles) to supply the men with fresh meat for three days.

Next, the ships sailed west and made a landing on the island of Mona, in the straits between the islands of Hispaniola and Puerto Rico. The water they had taken on at Nevis was already foul, so they emptied and refilled their casks. Newport despatched a hunting party, which killed two wild boars and several iguanas. These large, plant-eating lizards, which Percy described as "in fashion of a Serpent, and speckled like a Toade under the belly", were five or six feet long and supplied many meals.

The men were overdressed, as was the fashion of the period, with heavy woollen doublets and breeches; some may also have worn armour as protection against attack. It was now the middle of April, and daytime temperatures were climbing to over eighty degrees Fahrenheit (twenty-seven degrees Celsius). Percy observed that they were struggling in the heat, and that:

> many of our men fainted in the march, but by good fortune wee lost none but one Edward Brookes Gentleman, whose fat melted within him by the great heate and drought of the Countrey: we were not able to relieve him nor our selves, so he died in that great extreamitie.[21]

Most were lucky. The heat of the tropics, combined with their low supplies of fresh water, were a perfect combination for severe dehydration. The symptoms were predictable. The men would first have felt thirsty; within a short time, severe muscle cramps would begin, and they would grow faint. The body would try to compensate by drawing fluid from the blood and other tissues, but this could only afford a short reprieve unless water was taken. If not, the body would soon go into shock – dizziness, confusion, loss of consciousness, low blood pressure and a high heart rate would overcome the body as it desperately worked to get blood to the vital organs. Without immediate care, shock led to death. This is exactly what would have happened to the unfortunate Edward Brookes. Thankfully, after their latest port, the ships were again well stocked with fresh food and water, but dehydration would return.

The fleet left the island on April 10, laying a course roughly northwest for Virginia, a distance of some 1,400 miles. The passage was expected to take about two weeks, and Percy said on the fourth day, they crossed the Tropic of Cancer, about 390 miles along their route. This put them on schedule for a landfall in Virginia towards the end of the month.

Regardless of all the miles they had sailed, and despite how close they were to their destination, Smith noted that "the company was not a little discomforted" by their progress. His friend John Ratcliffe, master of the tiny *Discovery*, at this point even argued for giving up the voyage and returning to England. It is impossible to know whether the discontent was a revival of old feuding, or simply growing impatience at being cooped up in close quarters for so long. Whatever the reason, Newport must have been looking forward to relinquishing his command on arrival.

Late in the afternoon of April 21, a storm struck the fleet. According to Percy:

> about five a clocke at night there began a vehement tempest, which lasted all the night, with winds, raine, and thunders in a terrible manner. Wee were forced to lie at Hull that night, because we thought wee had beene nearer land then wee were.[22]

As the thunder rolled and lightning flashed across the boiling seas, Newport ordered his crew to take in all sail and allow the ships to "lie a-hull", bobbing around at the mercy of the elements. The storms off the Kentish Downs and now off the coast of Virginia, together with the sighting of the cursed star, might have convinced some that the expedition did not have the blessing of the Protestant God who had so visibly shown His hand against the Armada in 1588.

The storm abated in the morning, and the ship's crew spent the following three days trying to get a sounding to determine if they were close to land. These attempts were frustrated. Assuming they made constant progress from Mona, they would still have been about 150 miles off the coast of the Carolinas, with very deep water beneath them, probably more than 6,500 feet. Their hundred-fathom lead line would therefore have been far short of reaching the bottom.

At four in the morning on April 26, 1607, just as the sun began its climb over the eastern horizon, a lookout sighted land. From their latitude of thirty-seven degrees north, Newport knew they had reached Virginia. The watch had spotted the headland to the south of the entrance to the Chesapeake Bay, *chesupioc* being a local term meaning "great water". Their navigators had been spot-on.

The fleet had now been away from England for eighteen weeks, and the men were utterly spent from the constant rolling, the endless bickering, and the incessant stench rising from the bilges. It must have been a great relief to everyone when the fleet rounded the southern headland they later called Cape Henry, and dropped anchor inside the protection of the bay. George Percy was glad the voyage was over, but somewhat disappointed that outcrops of gold and silver were not immediately obvious on the shore:

> The same day wee entred into the Bay of Chesupioc directly, without any let or hindrance; there wee landed and discovered a little way, but

> wee could find nothing worth the speaking of, but faire meddowes and goodly tall Trees, with such Fresh-waters running through the woods, as I was almost ravished at the first sight thereof.[23]

For his part, Smith, still in the captain's custody at this time, described eloquently what could be seen from the ship:

> There is but one entraunce by sea into this country, and that is as the mouth of a very goodly Bay...The shew of the land there is a white hilly sand like unto the [Kentish] Downes...Within is a country that may have the prerogative [superiority] over the most pleasant places of Europe, Asia, Africa, or America, for large and pleasant navigable rivers never agreed better to frame a place for mans habitation...here are mountains, hils, plaines, valleyes, rivers, and brookes, all running most pleasantly into a faire Bay compassed but for the mouth with fruitfull and delightsome land.[24]

Of course, the London Company's vanguard was not the first landing of Europeans in the area. Spanish ships had sailed up the coast as early as the 1520s, though there were no reports they had entered the Chesapeake Bay in those early days of exploration. But in 1561, a Spanish galleon had most definitely landed in the region, for the crew had kidnapped the teenage son of a local chief during their visit.

In captivity, the boy converted to Christianity and was baptized with the name Don Luis. He spent several years in the Spanish colonies of Mexico and Cuba before travelling to Spain, where he received a Jesuit education. In 1570, he had returned to the Americas when the Jesuits attempted to establish a viable Catholic mission in the Chesapeake Bay region.

Home after so many years, Don Luis took his chance and escaped, leaving the Spanish missionaries to their own fate; they were massacred the following year in a raid led by Don Luis himself. King Philip II sent an expedition to extract retribution, and many of the local people were killed – either shot or hanged efficiently from the rigging of the Spanish galleons. For decades afterwards, the local peoples had dreaded the return of these vengeful strangers.[25]

Then in July 1603, just four years before the London Company settlers arrived, an explorer called Bartholomew Gilbert brought his ship into the Delaware Bay. Gilbert had sailed previously with Bartholomew Gosnold, now captain of the *Godspeed*, on their failed attempt to settle Cuttyhunk Island. Gilbert and four of his crewmen were killed when they ran across a group of warriors. Later, a second ship, under the command of Samuel Mace, sailed into the Chesapeake Bay, kidnapped some locals, and took them back to England – and this only confirmed local peoples' apprehensions about any newcomers. There is also some suggestion that the redoubtable Captain Newport might have visited the area on one of his earlier voyages, which would also explain why he was the top choice to lead the London Company's fleet.[26]

The Algonquian tribes of the area passed on their greatest tales and lessons through a tradition of oral history, and incidents such as the massacre of Gilbert and his men, or the kidnapping of locals, were not quickly forgotten. Newport would certainly have been aware of Gilbert's fate and taken sensible precautions for the fleet's landing. When Newport and a party of twenty or thirty men went ashore, they were well armed. Captain Gosnold, Edward Wingfield and the self-appointed recorder of the expedition, Gabriel Archer, were among the scouting party. The discredited John Smith remained detained on board, although they could well have used his help, particularly the skills he had gained during his two summers on the battlefields of eastern Europe.

The first encounter between the London Company and the local peoples was a classic opportunistic ambush. Newport's men went ashore, but found little "worthy of speaking about". There was no moon, so it became very dark not long after sunset. The landing party dallied, and when they finally decided to make their way back to the ships, they were attacked from the undergrowth. According to George Percy, who was also in the reconnaissance party:

> At night, when wee were going aboard, there came the Savages creeping upon all foure, from the Hills like Beares, with their Bowes in their mouthes, charged us very desperately in the faces, hurt Captaine Gabrill Archer in both his hands, and a sayler [sailor] in two places of the body

very dangerous. After they spent their Arrowes, and felt the sharpness of our shot, they retired into the Woods with a great noise, and so left us.[27]

The fleet had landed in the mouth of the Chesapeake Bay, in a region controlled by a paramount chief the English called Powhatan. However, Powhatan was his title,[28] after the village where he had been a subservient chief. Only later did the English learn that his given name was Wahunsenacawh.[29]

Wahunsenacawh became a local chief sometime between the 1550s and the 1580s, when he inherited the leadership of six tribes from his parents. Through a combination of intimidation and military conquest, he expanded his sphere of influence, and by 1607 he had become the undisputed *mamanatowick*, or paramount chief, of an "empire" of more than thirty Algonquian-speaking tribes known collectively as the Powhatan. This alliance had a combined population of between fourteen thousand and twenty thousand people, scattered across two hundred or more settlements.

The Powhatan lived in the Tidewater region of Virginia, which they called *Tsenacommacah*, the Algonquian term for "densely inhabited land". This land stretched from the Potomac River in the north to what would soon be called the James River, in the south – and included parts of the eastern shoreline of Chesapeake Bay. Each of the tribes had its own chief, or *weroance* (*weroansqua* if female), who gained his or her status through marriage, alliance or coercion. However, these *weroance* – literally "commanders" – were all subservient to the paramount chief, and they paid taxes to him in the form of tributes.

From the outset, the English underestimated the Powhatan, who were masters at living off the land and rivers in an environment that could be plush in one season and punishing in the next. The local tribes were primarily farming people, but they also fished and hunted in order to survive the harsh winters. Their settlements were typically sited on high ground close to a river, and were sometimes surrounded by palisades of tall, sharp-ended timbers for protection. Canoes were their main form

The Chesapeake Bay, showing the location of Jamestown, selected tribes of the Powhatan empire and the Powhatan capital, Werowocomoco.

of transport, and the centre of rivers frequently marked the borders between the territories of the different tribes. When their crops, mostly maize, had used up the nutrients in the soil, they picked up and moved to another spot, slashing and burning the forest as they went.

The English also underestimated the cunning of Powhatan, who was a consummate politician, diplomat and warrior. The paramount chief had originally governed from his village of Powhatan, just below the falls in the river at modern Richmond. This territory was on the western margins of the Tidewater region, and Powhatan had to use all his guile

A native village protected by a palisade of sharp timbers, from an engraving by Theodor DeBry, after a painting by Roanoke colonist John White, in de Bry's *America* (1590). De Bry's illustrated work was commissioned by Richard Hakluyt, and incorporated text from Thomas Hariot's forty-eight-page *A Briefe and True Report of the New Found Land,* which was printed in London in 1588.

when dealing with neighbouring tribes. By 1607, he had ruled over his people for two generations, expanding his power and reach ceaselessly throughout his tenure. He used negotiation, power play, intimidation and, when necessary, brutal suppression to maintain the cohesion of his growing empire. He was a formidable foe for anyone who dared cross his path.

The peoples living beyond the Powhatan empire had learned as much, over the years. At best, they were considered unpredictable rivals for resources; at worst, mortal enemies. To the west, Siouan-speaking tribes were actively hostile to the Powhatan, and annually attempted raids on their settlements; the Massawomecks and Pocoughtaonacks, who arrived in canoes from somewhere in the north, also terrorized Powhatan villages regularly. To the south, the Algonquian-speaking Chowanocs and the Iroquoian-speaking Nottoways and Meherrins maintained an uneasy truce with the Powhatan. Only the Algonquian-speaking tribes living north of the Potomac River were on friendly terms with the Powhatan empire. Between themselves, the Powhatan peoples generally lived peaceably, but disputes could also break out between tribes within the empire at any time.

However, when the English landed in 1607, the Powhatan understood that their main threat came from across the great sea. They had learned from the Jesuit mission of 1570, and the bloody reprisals of 1572, that these interlopers were a vengeful people.[30] It was circumspect to greet any encroaching shore party with a show of force. There were only a handful of Powhatan warriors involved in the ambush of Newport's shore party, and they did little harm to the English. Nevertheless, the act of hostility should have alarmed the colonists, and John Smith claimed that he, for one, understood the serious implications of this first encounter.

There is some debate as to which of the local tribes attacked the settlers. Some historians have argued it was the Nansemond, a small group of about one thousand people that lived along a tributary of the James River in an area they called *Chuckatuck*; others claim it was the Chesapeake tribe. But by 1607 the Chesapeake had been all but exterminated by Wahunsenacawh when they resisted his policy of expansionism. Within a few years, the Chesapeake had ceased to exist.[31] (Today, around two hundred people are affiliated with the Nansemond tribe.)

What the English colonists did not understand at this point, but would soon learn to their cost, was the complexity of the politics of the Powhatan empire. Just as the English, Spanish, French and other European nations all had their own priorities and penchants, so too did each of the individual tribes under Wahunsenacawh.

Aboard the *Susan Constant* there was a pressing formality to be completed: the opening of the small, sealed wooden box containing the

instructions for the new colony's governance.[32] The secrecy was theatrical, admittedly, but the company's directors in England were worried their plans might fall into the hands of Spanish spies, which would have put the settlers and their investment in jeopardy.

Inside the box, a document listed the names of seven men who had been selected to form the colony's council, with their duties defined in some detail. Each councillor would have a single vote on day-to-day decisions. After the councillors were sworn in and the colonists had found a suitable site for settlement, the council then had to elect their president, who would wield two votes on all matters.

It was undoubtedly a solemn affair as the names of the seven men were read out to the assembled group. Not surprisingly, Edward Maria Wingfield was on the list, together with the three captains, Newport, Gosnold and Radcliffe. There was also John Martin, who had sailed under Sir Francis Drake in his New World expeditions in 1585, and with Gosnold to New England in 1602; he may also have been the son of the Master of the Mint and previous Lord Mayor of the City of London. The sixth name was George Kendall, who was supposedly related to a wealthy sponsor of the voyage and had some experience as a leader and privateer.

The seventh name on the list came as more of a surprise, and must have caused some considerable consternation – if not blind panic – among certain members of the group. It was John Smith, that country-born upstart from Lincolnshire, who had the treasonous audacity to talk to the "gentlemen" and Oxford graduates as if he was their equal. In the circumstances, Smith could have allowed himself a wry smile, but it was unlikely. The leadership of the colony was a matter of life and death, as the ambush by the Powhatan had already made clear. Every member of the group would have treated the occasion with appropriate gravity.

Nevertheless, there was uproar over the revelation. The other six members of the council refused to accept Smith's nomination. They argued that his charge of mutiny on the voyage disqualified him, unequivocally. Clearly, Smith had made an enemy of more than just Wingfield on the trip; instead of claiming his role as councillor, he was returned to confinement on board the ship.

Next came the reading of the London Company's detailed instructions for founding the settlement. The colonists were advised to take their time selecting a site, and to choose somewhere that would not take too many men to clear, since they should not "be over burthened with Woods near your town for all the men You have Shall not be able to Cleanse twenty acres in a Year".[33] They were also advised to "have Great Care not to Offend the naturals if You Can Eschew it and imploy Some few of your Company to trade with them for Corn and all Other lasting Victuals". This was wise advice, as the settlers were vastly outnumbered by the Powhatan, and would need their neighbours' help to learn about the area and find sustenance in the early months.

The company's directors also expressed their concerns about the threat the Spanish might pose. As it happened, their paranoia was justified. The Spanish ambassador in London had kept his king well informed about the Virginia expedition. Between December 1606 and December 1609, Pedro de Zúñiga wrote to Philip III about the colony on more than sixteen occasions, and had collected many reports from his secret agents. The English were wise to assume that the main menace to their new venture in the Americas could come from the sea rather than the land.

Native Virginians dancing round a circle of wooden posts; most are wearing apron-skins and their bodies are decorated with body paint. An engraving by Theodor de Bry, after a watercolour by Roanoke colonist John White, in de Bry's *America* (1590).

8
Survivor

1607

When we came over to the other side, there was a many of other Savages which directed us to their Towne, where we were entertained by them very kindly
George Percy, Discourse (1608)

From the moment the London Company's instructions were unsealed, a sense of urgency troubled the colonists. The main reason for leaving England in the middle of that terrible, stormy winter had been to ensure the fleet would arrive in Virginia in good time to prepare land to sow their first crop. This should have carried them through their first winter. However, the winds off the Kentish Downs had delayed their landing by at least six weeks, and it was already late April. Once the governing council was seated (albeit with six members, not its full seven), there was no time to lose. They needed to find a suitable site for settlement and unload the ships so they could start planting.

The most comprehensive observations of the early weeks in Virginia came from the quill of George Percy. As the most senior aristocrat in the expedition, Percy could reasonably have expected to be a member of the council, and it would have been understandable if he resented John Smith's inclusion. Percy's older brother Henry, now the 9th Earl of Northumberland, had served on the Privy Council, the sovereign's formal body of advisers, making him one of the most highly placed men in England. Unfortunately, Henry Percy had fallen under suspicion following the discovery of Guy Fawkes' Gunpowder Plot, and was locked up in the Tower of London in November 1605. Henry was a rich man, and he made himself at home in the Tower by entertaining friends; he even had a bowling alley installed for his personal use. He remained in this comfortable confinement until 1621. Nevertheless, his imprisonment was a significant blow to the family's fortunes, and it is likely that George Percy lost his seat at the colony's top table as a result of the scandal.

The disappointment did not stop Percy from paying close attention to the colony's affairs. The day after their first landing, he reported, Captain Newport ordered the shallop be assembled. This lightweight boat was about thirty feet long; with a shallow draft, it could be either rowed or sailed, and was ideally suited to river exploration. It was large enough to carry a couple dozen of men along with victuals and weapons – the sort of party that could handle itself if it met resistance.

With her masts erected and her sails hoisted, the shallop was soon under way. Percy reported:

> the Captaine and some Gentlemen went in her, and discovered up the Bay, we found a River on the Southside running into the Maine; we entered it and found it very shoald [shallow] water, not for any Boats to swim.[1]

And so the Englishmen began to take their measure of the Chesapeake Bay.

For the next several days, Percy and several other colonists investigated their immediate surroundings. They collected mussels and oysters "which lay on the ground as thicke as stones".[2] Percy's first impressions of the area were generally very positive, and his records are detailed. Perhaps he hoped his survey would show his value to the expedition and earn him the empty seventh seat on the council.

The colonists knew from earlier explorations that the Chesapeake Bay offered a variety of places to make their settlement. Newport moved his ships to a more protected position inside the bay, anchoring the fleet off a headland they called Cape Comfort (now known as Old Point Comfort, south of today's city of Hampton). Then on April 29, the men raised a cross at the entrance to the bay and officially named the headland Cape Henry after the King's eldest son and heir apparent. Erecting such a structure at the entrance to the bay was not an entirely sensible move, as it could attract the attention of any passing Spanish galleon, and the London Company was very concerned about the threat of such intrusions on their patch. The colonists, no doubt, were feeling very pleased with themselves, and they cast caution to the wind.

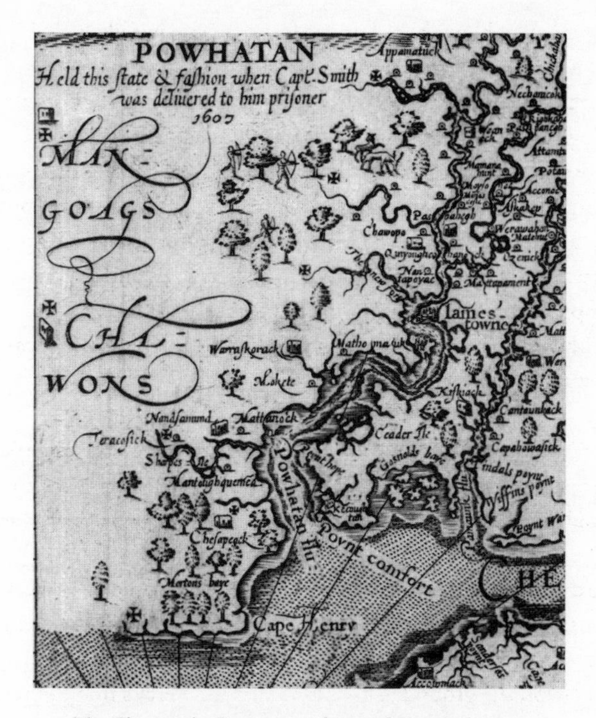

The Chesapeake Bay area, with west facing at the top, indicating the position of Kecoughtan and Point Comfort (lower centre left). The Powhatan "flu" is the James River. A detail from a map drawn by John Smith in 1612 (courtesy of the Huntingfield Collection, Maryland State Archives).

Later that same day, five warriors were spied on the nearby shore. Captain Newport approached them, placing his hand over his heart in a display meant to indicate conciliation. The Powhatan laid down their bows and arrows and "came very boldly to us, making signes to come a shoare to their Towne, which is called by the Savages Kecoughtan",[3] according to Percy. Today, pretty suburban houses are clustered around a network of creeks in the modern community of Kecoughtan, part of greater Hampton. Back in 1607, this was the location of a village under the authority of Wahunsenacawh, paramount chief of the mighty Powhatan empire; Newport and his men decided to visit.

Their invitation was an encouraging sign; perhaps the locals might be friendly, after all. And, at last, the Englishmen were getting a close look at the people they had chosen as their neighbours – and the Powhatan were certainly an impressive sight.

The men shaved the right side of the head so that their hair would not tangle with the drawstring of their bows; in summer they went almost naked, wearing nothing more than a small leather apron. At this time of year the women too were bare-breasted, and simply covered their groin with furs or grasses. The women tattooed their bodies with abstract designs, or with images of fruits, flowers, or snakes and lizards. Some of the women wore necklaces, bracelets and earrings of freshwater pearls, copper or animal bones; these seemed to indicate higher status within the village. Both sexes painted their faces with a mixture of red paint and nut oil, and they smeared themselves with bear fat – a tactic to ward off insects, whose bites were maddening. John Smith was still confined to the ship at this stage, so he was not part of these earliest meetings, but he later wrote that the Powhatan were:

> generally tall and straight, of a comely proportion, and of a colour browne… Their haire is generally black, but few have any beards. The men weare halfe their heads shaven, the other halfe long; for Barbers they use their women, who with 2 shels will grate away the haire, of any fashion they please.[4]

When the colonists entered the Kecoughtan village, they found the residents making "a dolefull noise, laying their faces to the ground, scratching the earth with their nailes".[5] The visitors had arrived in the midst of a religious ceremony. Once it was completed, they were invited to eat, but they rudely grabbed at the food even before sitting down. Thomas Harriot, who had been part of the first expedition to Roanoke in 1584, had written an Algonquian phrase book, but if any copies had found their way to members of the London Company's mission, they were not to hand that day. Despite the lack of a common language, the Kecoughtan made it clear that this was inappropriate behaviour, and the Englishmen promptly settled down and waited patiently for their food to be served.

After the meal, the colonists were treated to an exuberant display of dancing and singing, and then were offered a pipe of tobacco. Smoking tobacco was becoming increasingly fashionable with Englishmen. Sir Walter Raleigh's ships brought the first "Virginia" tobacco to England in the 1570s, but other strains of tobacco had been imported earlier from the Continent, since the Spanish and their allies had been using the plant since the late 1520s. By 1604, tobacco was common enough in England to have drawn the ire of King James, who denounced it in his treatise "A Counter-Blaste to Tobacco" and slapped a mighty tariff on its importation. When the colonists set out from England, only the wealthiest among them would have been frequent smokers.

Tobacco had acquired a very different status among the peoples of the Americas. It was an important trade good among the eastern tribes; sharing a pipe was also a welcoming gesture, since this was primarily done during sacred rites or diplomatic negotiations. According to Percy:

> After we were well satisfied they gave us of their Tabacco, which they tooke in a pipe made artificially of earthe [clay] as ours are, but far bigger, with the bowle fashioned together with a fine of fine copper.[6]

Clearly, the Kecoughtan intended to treat their visitors well, despite the Englishmen's initial disrespect. But the Englishmen saw this first contact in a very different light. They considered the natives of Virginia to be coarse, childish, heathen savages. What other words could describe a people who, for the most part, painted their bodies and walked around naked?

It was the beginning of a clash of cultures.

Cautiously, Newport continued the colonists' forays into the area around the James River. On May 4, the group reached another settlement, Paspahegh (Percy called it Paspihe), about six miles upstream from the bay – a location only identified by archaeologists in 1983.[7]

Again, the colonists were welcomed. In his detailed account of the early days, Percy observed that when the *weroance* of a neighbouring tribe arrived during their visit, the mood changed and that:

> he seemed to take displeasure of our being with the Paspihes: he would faine have had us come to his Towne, the Captaine was unwilling; seeing that the day was so far spent he returned backe to his ships for that night.[8]

It was not clear if the local chief's "displeasure" originated from jealousy or some other emotion. Regardless, Newport was not willing to risk the chance of another nighttime ambush, and they withdrew early.

Word was getting out about the foreigners. The following day, a man appeared bearing a message from Rapahanna, the *weroance* of the Quiyoughcohanock: he also wanted a visit from the Englishmen. The Quiyoughcohanock were members of the Powhatan empire living on the south bank of the James River, now Surry County. Newport despatched Percy with a party to contact this new tribe:

> Wee passed through the Woods in fine paths, having most pleasant Springs which issued from the Mountaines: Wee also went through the goodliest Corne fieldes that ever was seene in any Countrey. When wee came to Rapahannos Towne, hee entertained us in good humanitie.[9]

Apart from the ambush on the colonists' very first day, the Powhatan people had been hospitable. Yet the Englishmen had learned nothing of the complexities of the local culture, and so failed to realize they were now enmeshed in the byzantine rivalries of the many different Powhatan tribes. *Weroance* after *weroance* was positioning himself to improve his tribe's position with the settlers, and therefore with their paramount chief.

Fortunately, by May 12, Percy's party had returned to the fleet's anchorage without incident. The group had been away for a week, and the colonists now urgently needed to find a site for their settlement. Newport took the opportunity of Percy's return to move on. The fleet dropped ten miles downriver, where they saw a location that seemed to have all the qualities they were looking for. Gabriel Archer, one of the Englishmen ambushed by the Powhatan on the first day, apparently spotted it, and it became known as Archer's Hope. George Percy was enthusiastic about Archer's find:

> The twelfth day we went backe to our ships, and discovered a point of Land, called Archers Hope, which was sufficient with a little labour to defend our selves against any Enemy. The soile was good and fruitfull, with excellent good Timber. There are also great store of Vines in bignesse of a mans thigh, running up to the tops of the Trees in great abundance. We also did see many Squirels, Conies, Black Birds with crimson wings, and divers other Fowles and Birds.[10]

Captain Bartholomew Gosnold, along with some other "gentlemen", approved of the situation and urged that a decision be made. However, the London Company had been very prescriptive about the need for the colony to be easily defended from the sea, and here there was no close anchorage for the fleet. It would be impractical for them to board their ships quickly, should a Spanish galleon appear on the horizon. Newport ordered the fleet to sail a couple of miles back upstream to inspect another option more closely.

The new position was a low-lying, marshy peninsula, roughly two miles long by one mile wide, joined to the mainland by a narrow isthmus. Indeed, the isthmus was so narrow the peninsula was virtually an island. At the western end, the river had carved a channel close to the shore, so that the colonists' ships could lie in thirty-five feet of water yet still be tied to trees on land. This feature alone would make unloading the stores from the ships easier; it also made it easy to defend from an attack by land. More importantly, following the directives set by the London Company, it would be easy to defend from an attack by sea. Any Spanish ships sailing upstream would have to turn broadside as they rounded the bend in the river downstream, thus making themselves vulnerable to English guns, which could be mounted on the northern shore.

In any case, time was running out. Newport had to return to England and the men he left behind had to build a settlement and plant crops as soon as possible. Newport and Wingfield – exercising their respective prerogatives as a member of the governing council and the only shareholder of the London Company on the expedition – overruled Archer and Gosnold's suggestion, and picked the marshy peninsula.

Interestingly, John Smith supported the choice as well. By now, his history as a mutineer was fading in the face of the challenges already confronting the settlers, and he was allowed at least to voice an opinion, if not a vote:

> [There was] a verie fit place for the erecting of a great cittie, about which some contention passed betwixt Captaine Wingfield and Captaine Gosnold. Notwithstanding all our provision was brought a shore, and with as much speede as might bee wee went about our fortification.[11]

Smith may have been especially satisfied by the narrow neck of the isthmus and the natural defence it would provide. Here, one could gauge if the Powhatan were mostly cautious or reckless in their interactions with the colonists. For he had learned from Machiavelli that:

> You must never believe that the enemy does not know how to conduct his own affairs. Indeed, if you want to be deceived less and want to bear less danger, the more the enemy is weak or the less the enemy is cautious, so much more must you esteem him.

It was the colonists who were being somewhat reckless, however, and the choice of the swampy land has been widely criticized by subsequent generations. The lack of fresh water and the low-lying, fetid, insect-infested wetland was far from ideal. The locals must have been puzzled when they saw the Europeans begin to unload their ships there, for if the spot had been any good, they would have used it themselves. But the colonists were several weeks behind schedule, and they knew winter was coming. They needed to build a fort, and quickly.

Sure enough, Jamestown was neither a paradise to live in, nor a gold mine to work. In the heat of their first summer, the Englishmen paid a heavy price for choosing such a low-lying place. Malaria was unknown in the New World before European colonization,[12] so the settlers most likely brought the disease with them from England. The mosquitoes of the Kentish wetlands had now found a home in the marshlands of Virginia. The James River swamp proved to be an ideal breeding ground for the insects, and men soon fell ill with malaria. The water was also unsuitable for drinking, and the ravages of severe dehydration put many lives in jeopardy; at the very least, it slowed the colonists' progress in building their housing and defences.

Yet the peninsula also had real and important merits as a site easy to defend from attack. The Spanish never did sail up the James to raid the fort, but at the time this was considered to be a *bona fide* threat, and defence weighed heavily on their minds. Some modern historians have suggested Hampton would have been more suitable, but that location did not fulfil the London Company's directive that the settlement should be "Such A place you may perchance find a hundred miles from the Rivers mouth and the farther up the better."[13]

The colonists knew they had to obey the instructions from London. The peninsula certainly had its limitations, but it is difficult to think of a better site on either the James or the York that would have satisfied all the London Company's requirements, and that was not already occupied by the Powhatan; evicting the local peoples would surely start a war, and the London Company had been very lucid in their directive to maintain good relations with the locals.

The day after the settlers committed to the site, Newport moored his ships to the trees on the shoreline. It was Wednesday, May 14, 1607, (May 24 in the new style Gregorian calendar) and the Englishmen immediately began the laborious task of unloading their cargo. After some discussion, the new settlement was christened Jamestown, after the King, and the actual governance of the expedition changed hands. According to the instructions from the London Company, it was time for Captain Newport to relinquish his role as commander and for the members of the council to take their oath of office and elect their president. To John Smith's chagrin, Edward Maria Wingfield won the vote.

Throughout the proceedings, Smith was barred from taking his seat on the council. Smith recorded that "Master Wingfeild [sic] was chosen Precident, and an oration made, whie Captaine Smith was not admitted of the Councell as the rest".[14] There is no record of what Wingfield, or perhaps Percy said, to swing the vote against Smith. Nor is there any record of Smith's reaction to the assembled colonists when he was prevented from presuming office, although we can reasonably assume he offered his opinion freely.

With what must have been a remarkable effort, the colonists managed to unload the ships and occupy the site in just two days. Smith, still bridling under his nominal confinement, was probably expected to lend a hand, too – and he would have done so without complaint. As they unpacked the cargo, they discovered the tents were in a sorry state and unsuitable for living. Either they were in poor condition when they were loaded in London, or they had deteriorated on the journey. It must have been a huge disappointment, but they soldiered on.

The high expectations of the shareholders back in London were also weighing on the settlers' minds. Before Newport could set sail for England, the colonists had to fill his hold with a return cargo, something of a first instalment towards paying their way to this new life in the New World:

> Now falleth every man to worke, the Councell contrive the Fort, the rest cut downe trees to make place to pitch their Tents; some provide clapbord to relade the ships, some make gardens, some nets, etc.[15]

Not only were the men ordered to cut clapboard timbers from the forests to send back with Newport, they were also required to make their own fishing nets, which ought really to have been supplied by the company.

In this respect, Jamestown was very different from the Plymouth Colony, settled thirteen years later. Plymouth was the work of religious separatists, the so-called Pilgrims, who from the start planned to set up a permanent, self-sufficient community in the Americas. And from the beginning, Plymouth was peopled by families with children, and inspired by a long-term mission. Jamestown, on the other hand, was entirely male for the first couple of years. It was funded by speculators back in London looking primarily for a return on their investment – and the faster the return, the better. The London Company's preoccupation with profit would, for years to come, undermine the Jamestown settlers' ability to function properly as a colony.

Amid the bustle of activity, the locals could be forgiven for at first imagining the English were temporary summer visitors, mostly to be avoided until their departure. Now that the strangers were clearing land for crops and erecting tents and other structures, their stay was unsettling, to say the least. The Englishmen could not have known the peninsula was a long-standing Powhatan hunting ground, where a temporary campsite was set up when necessary; indeed, this fact was only discovered very recently, from archaeological excavations. The area was probably the domain of the Paspahegh tribe, whose main village was only a few miles upstream at the mouth of the Chickahominy River.

Despite warmly welcoming the colonists at first, the Paspahegh now regarded these men as intruders. As Percy wrote:

> The first night of our landing, about midnight, there came some Savages sayling close to our quarter: presently there was an alarum given; upon that the Savages ran away, and we not troubled any more by them that night.[16]

A couple of days later, the Paspahegh *weroance* returned with over a hundred armed warriors, and they were patently not in a friendly state of mind. The lack of a common language was a problem, and misunderstandings arose: a scuffle broke out when a warrior tried to steal an axe, only to have its English owner grab it back. The colonists fired their muskets, which panicked the Paspahegh. The *weroance* and his party left "in great anger".

Forty Paspahegh returned two days later asking to spend the night at Jamestown. The Englishmen were suspicious and refused the request. Before the visitors went on their way, a colonist set up a target a pistol shot could not penetrate. Seeing it, a Paspahegh warrior withdrew an arrow from his quiver and put the arrow squarely through it. The English were astonished, but they also recognized that they could not let this demonstration pass without a response. They set up a second target as a ploy – this time one made of steel. When the archer took a second shot, his arrowhead splintered. The Paspahegh left humiliated.

Relations between the Paspahegh and the settlers had not started smoothly, and the instructions from the London Company had been clear: "In all Your Passages you must have Great Care not to Offend the naturals if You Can Eschew it and imploy Some few of your Company to trade with them for Corn and all Other lasting Victuals."[17]

Despite the increasing tension with the local Powhatan tribe, Wingfield did not order the construction of a defensive palisade around the English compound. He instead relied on a policy of conciliation, taking his cue from the company's instructions. This was too much for John Smith. His antipathy towards Wingfield had only grown since his release from confinement, and now he openly criticized the colony's president. How would they survive if they did not construct proper defences against native attack? Worse, Smith said: "The Presidents overweening jealousie [concern] would admit no exercise at armes, or fortification".[18] The two stubborn men were well on their way to a standoff.

However, Wingfield was not just following instructions about relations with the locals; he actually had little discretion over the day-to-day work of the colony. The company's instructions were very specific about the tasks the settlers were to pursue in the first few weeks. Once the ships were unloaded, they were to be divided into three equal groups, each comprising forty men. The first group was to build a storehouse; the second was to prepare the ground and plant corn and vegetables (although, by mid-May, it was quite late to do so); and the third was to form a scouting party and go upstream "for two Months in Discovery of the River above you".[19]

The directors in London did not leave their specifications at that. The scouting party was to be divided into two units: one party was directed to "Cross Over the Lands and Carrying half a Dozen pickaxes to try if they Can find any mineral"[20] while the other half, under the leadership of Captain Newport, was to search for a route over the mountains to the west and look for a lucrative source of timber. There was profit to be made from a short route to the South Seas, or from a rich lode of gold, or from shipbuilding. These were the company's priorities – coherent, well defined and worthy of any modern micromanager. But also hopelessly ambitious.

With three thousand miles separating the colony from the investors in London, not every instruction could be followed to the letter. Newport was short of men, so he made a pragmatic decision to take just twenty-three men in a single group upriver. He included John Smith in his party, even though Smith was still officially in custody.

Smith could have remained in detention in the Jamestown camp, put to work tilling the ground and planting – after all, he was the son of a farmer. Perhaps Newport thought it prudent not to leave Smith and Wingfield together in his absence, but it is equally likely that Newport recognized Smith's talents and experience, and wanted him at his side. This mission upriver was Smith's introduction to the peoples of the Powhatan empire.

Newport's party left Jamestown at noon on Thursday, May 21. The expedition took the shallop a safe distance beyond the Chickahominy River and the Paspahegh village, anchoring eighteen miles upstream. Here, they found another tribe, the Weyanock, who appeared to be friendly, and the Englishmen were again entertained "with Daunces and much rejoicing". In Captain Archer's view, the Weyanock were "at odds" with their neighbours, the Paspahegh. It was one of the colonists' first insights that the Powhatan empire was not a single entity but a collection of many tribes, each with its own *weroance*, and each with its own agenda.

The next day, the Englishmen were met on the river by eight Powhatan in a canoe. One of them, a warrior called Navirans (Nauriraus), soon learned some English words. When Archer gave him a sheet of paper and a pen, and showed him how to use them, Navirans "layd out the whole River from the Chesseian bay to the end of it so farr as passadg was for boates".[21] It was a remarkable piece of draughtsmanship from somebody whose culture had no written language, and who, they were sure, had no previous experience of any writing. Archer went on to explain that Navirons:

> tolde us of two Ilettes in the Ryver we should passe by, meaning that one whereon we were, and then come to an overfall of water, beyond that of two kyngdomes which the Ryver Runes by then a greate Distance of[f], the mountaines Quirank as he named them.[22]

This assistance was exactly what the scouting party needed. In addition to providing these directions, Navirons promised grain and dried oysters for barter from his tribe upstream. Just as important, the settlers were encouraged that they might have found the coveted route through the mountains to the west. Navirons continued to help the colonists over the next week, and offered them a valuable education in the region.

The English party continued upstream, reaching the territory of the Arrohattoc, in what is now Henrico County, on the eastern edges of modern-day Richmond. The Arrohattoc *weroance* was expecting them. They feasted well that night, enjoying venison, corn, beans, mulberries and bread. They also gained a vital piece of information: they were told of the existence of a chief of the chiefs (the *mamanatowick,* in Algonquian). What the Englishmen had not yet understood was that the *weroances* they had met were all subservient to Wahunsenacawh. It would take them several more weeks to grasp fully the extent of the Powhatan chief's control over the peoples of the area.

As the colonists enjoyed the hospitality of the Arrohattoc, they received word that another chief was about to make a visit. However, the language barrier had reached its limit, and the Englishmen thought they were about to meet the paramount chief of the Powhatan himself. In fact, it was one of Wahunsenacawh's sons, called Parahunt – the *weroance* of a nearby village called Powhatan. It was a logical misunderstanding.

Newport greeted Parahunt with a profusion of gifts, including small knives, bells and glass baubles – all that should be bestowed on what was in effect the emperor of the Powhatan, as far as the Englishmen were concerned. The *weroance* was delighted with these gifts, especially with the supply of cheap knives, for the Powhatan people had no iron.

Newport and Parahunt parted on good terms, and the colonists proceeded upstream, as far as a series of falls, which made further navigation of the James River difficult without moving onto land. (These falls are where the modern city of Richmond is centred.) Smith said that when they arrived at Parahunt's village, they were surprised by how small it was. Powhatan village was "some twelve houses, pleasantly seated on a hill; before it three fertile Isles, about it many of their cornefields, the

The falls in the James River at modern Richmond prevented any further exploration upstream by boat (photo by Morgan Riley).

place is very pleasant, and strong by nature".[23] The visitors must now have had their doubts whether Parahunt was really the paramount chief.

At this point in the river, the Englishmen could take their shallop no further. Newport brought his team back downriver to the Arrohattoc village, where again the *weroance* offered his brother-in-law, Navirons, as a guide. Over the next few days, Newport spent time with the Arrohattoc, and made contact with other local tribes, before returning to the falls.

He knew he would soon have to begin his journey home to England and report to the London Company's directors. Yet still he had not found a route west through the mountains, nor any precious metals. He noted the abundant high-quality timber, which would be worth something back in England, but certainly not enough to offset the money laid out for the expedition. They needed something of much greater value.

The affiliated tribes of the Powhatan empire were the best chance the colonists had to satisfy the shareholders, and the longer the Englishmen spent with the Powhatan, the better they understood their culture and territory. Villages varied in size, with the local *weroance* usually living in one of the larger settlements. Families lived in longhouses called *yehakins,* constructed by bending supple wooden branches over a structural hoop, then covering the framework with woven matting for insulation from the heat of the summer and the cold of the winter. Inside, the family would keep a fire, over which they would cook. It was obvious, entering a Powhatan village, where the *weroance* would be found – he (or she) lived in the biggest *yehakin* around. Each village often had a temple; there were also storage buildings, and sometimes a defensive palisade.

During the spring and summer months, the women took the children to the fields, where they grew corn, beans, squash and sunflowers. In late summer, the crops were harvested and smoked or dried if possible, for use later. During winter, everyone relied on this stored food, supplemented with edible wild plants, roots, nuts and berries. The women also made clothing from deer hides, which were scraped and tanned to soften them.

The men spent their days hunting with spears and arrows. Their main quarry was geese, swan, wild turkey, rabbit and squirrel; occasionally they killed larger mammals, such as deer and bear. They also laid fishing traps and nets, for the rivers were teeming with a wide variety of freshwater and saltwater fish. Smith recorded nearly thirty species in his comprehensive account of the region:

> Of fish we were best acquainted with Sturgeon, Grampus [Orca], Porpus, Seales, Stingraies, whose tailes are very dangerous. Brettes, Mullets, white Salmonds, Trowts, Soles, Plaice, Herrings, Conyfish, Rockfish, Eeles, Lampreys, Catfish, Shades, Pearch of 3 sorts, Crabs, Shrimps, Crevises, [crayfish] Oysters, Cocles, and Muscles.[24]

The men also made and repaired all the tools and weapons they used, the most important being the bow and arrow. The Powhatan appeared to have no source of metal, a disappointment to the Englishmen hoping to find gold. Wood was used for bows and arrows; local and traded stone for arrowheads and axes; sinew and cordage for fastening tools and weapons; oyster and scallop shells for scrapers and jewellery.

Canoes were essential for transport and fishing, and building them was a painstaking process. It began with felling a large tree by burning around the base to weaken it, then chopping it down. Next, the men hollowed and cured the inside of the trunk with a controlled fire, and carved out

"The Manner of Making Their Boates", an engraving by Theodor de Bry, after a John White watercolour, in de Bry's *America* (1590).

the excess burnt wood painstakingly with their shell scrapers. Despite the rudimentary technology, if they worked together as a team, they could complete a large canoe in about a week.

From the age of around six, young Powhatan boys were given training in archery. The greatest advantage of a firearm over a bow and arrow was that a musketeer could become competent with only a couple of weeks' instruction. To achieve a similar level of proficiency with a bow and arrow required a decade of training and immense upper body strength. The loud retort from firing a musket was also a powerful deterrent against unwelcome Powhatan visits, especially in the colonists' early months. However, the accuracy of a skilled archer put sloppy musket fire to shame. The best among the Powhatan could shoot a bird in flight. They could also let fly five or six arrows for every shot taken from a musket. The arrow was also silent when it delivered its deadly blow, which meant that many men could be killed without a general alarm being sounded. A bow and arrow was also just as effective in the rain as it was in the sun – whereas wet gunpowder was no use to anybody.

On Wednesday, May 27, the Englishmen were housed with the Arrohattocs' neighbours, the Weyanocks. Smith's natural instincts for survival were at their most acute, for while many of his colleagues in the party thought the Weyanocks "seemed our good friends", Smith sensed something was wrong. Navirons made limp excuses for why he could not continue downstream with them, and the Weyanocks' behaviour seemed to change. Smith remembered: "till being returned [before we were] within twentie myles of Jamestowne, they gave us just cause of jealousie [concern]".[25]

Newport too sensed danger. He ordered the party to return quickly to Jamestown, only to find the settlement had been attacked the previous day by hundreds of armed warriors. The colonists were completely unprepared, because Wingfield had followed strictly the orders from the London Company "to have Great Care not to Offend the naturals".[26]

Not only was there no defensive palisade around the settlement, but the colonists' main armaments were still packed in boxes. Somewhere between eleven and seventeen men were wounded in the attack (one of whom later died); a young boy who had taken shelter in the *Discovery* was also killed. The Englishmen defended themselves as best they could, and killed at least one of the assailants.

To his credit, Wingfield led from the front, and reported feeling an arrow pass harmlessly through his beard. That did not counter the basic fact that the colonists were outnumbered and overwhelmed. It took fire from the ship's cannon to bring the attack to an end. A cannon ball struck a tree, causing a large branch to splinter and fall; the warriors panicked and fled in disarray. Smith was convinced that, were it not for the shattered branch, "our men had [would have] all beene slaine, being securely all at worke, and their armes in dry fats [casks]".[27]

It was a close call for the colonists, and it was essential they reappraise their position immediately with the locals. The attack was no impulsive action. It had been orchestrated carefully. Ever since Newport and his scouting party had headed upstream in the shallop, Powhatan warriors had been visiting Jamestown one or two at a time. It seemed in retrospect that they had been assessing the settlers' defences and deciding the best time to strike. Even the Weyanocks – whose village was more than twenty miles upstream – had known of the plan. No longer could the Englishmen rely on the locals for relaxed, good-natured feasting. If the colonists were going to survive in Virginia, their tactics had to change.

Smith had been critical of Wingfield's casual attitude towards defence. They had been lucky the ships were still at anchor, and able to direct fire towards the attackers. However, the two larger ships would soon return to England, and the colony would then be left to its own devices. To Smith's relief, Wingfield had a change of heart:

> Hereupon the President was contented the Fort should be pallisadoed, the Ordnance mounted, his men armed and exercised, for many were the assaults, and ambuscadoes of the Salvages, and our men by their disorderly stragling were often hurt, when the Salvages by the nimblenesse of their heeles well escaped.[28]

Smith was back on familiar ground, able to use his knowledge and experience of fighting in Hungary and Transylvania to establish proper defences for the fledgling colony. He asked for a huge effort. Trees were cut and split, then the logs erected vertically to create a palisade twice the height of a man. The shape of the new fort was triangular, with cannons mounted on turret-like circular structures at each corner. Gabriel Archer, who had been appointed as the colony's official recorder, noted Newport's seamen did "the best thereof", which suggests the "gentlemen" did rather less.

Despite these efforts, the colonists knew they remained extremely vulnerable. They ventured out of the fort only at great personal risk: any scuffle in the leaves of the forest floor, or the sharp snap of twig underfoot, could signal a coming assault and near-certain death. They lived in constant peril. All in all, it made the backbreaking work of their first few weeks seem like an idyll.

Over the course of the next week, the Powhatan tested the new defences. On Friday, May 29, Gabriel Archer recorded that the warriors approached to within musket shot, but dared not come closer. From there, they shot forty arrows into the fort, and used one of the dogs in

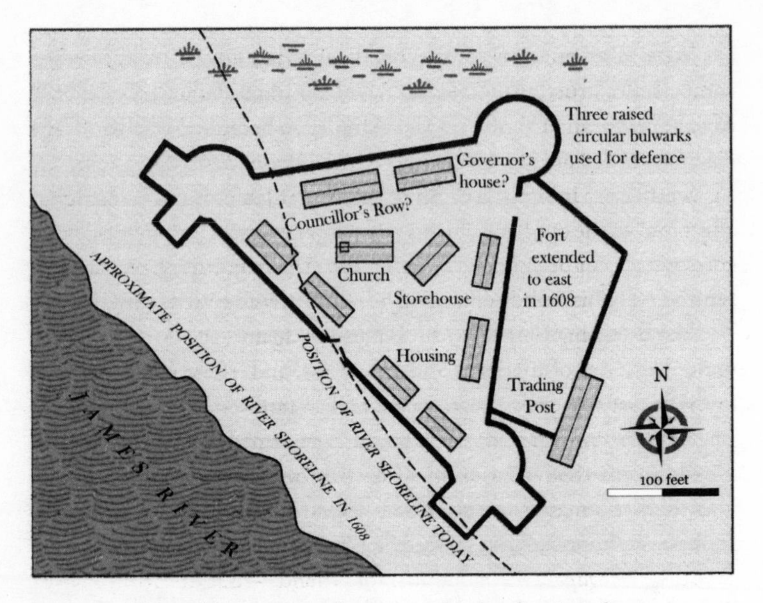

Plan of the Jamestown fort c. 1608 showing the triangular palisaded defences together with the buildings.

the colony for target practice. On the Sunday, they crept up through the tall reeds surrounding Jamestown and fired six arrows at one of the colonists, Eustace Clovell, who had been foolish enough to leave the fort unarmed. Clovell survived another eight days before dying in agony, possibly from septicaemia. The following Thursday brought a similar encounter: warriors hiding in the long grass spotted a colonist outside the fort, "going out to doe the natural necessity", and shot him in the head.

The bloodshed vindicated Smith's criticism of Wingfield's policy of appeasement. The public reproaches were not to the president's liking, as they made him look even weaker. Wingfield ordered Smith be sent back to London on the *Susan Constant* when Newport left, but Smith would have none of it. This time, others came to Smith's side. The Reverend Hunt appealed for unity among the group, as he had done six months previously when the fleet was anchored off the Kent coast. Smith had also won the regard of Newport, who respected the firebrand's skills and experience, if not necessarily the man himself.

When the council next met, on Wednesday, June 10, to review the company's instructions, Newport "shewing himselfe no lesse Carefull of our Amitye and Combyned frendship, then became him in the deepe Desire he had of our good".[29] Gabriel Archer reported that Newport made a powerful case in support of Smith staying at Jamestown, "with ardent affectyon wonne our hartes by his fervent perswasyon".[30] Wingfield's two votes would not be enough to get his way. The majority agreed to allow Smith to take his oath of office, and he was finally admitted to the council.

The following Saturday, the Powhatan again approached the fort under the cover of the reeds and long grass, and "shott Mathew Fytch in the breast somwhat Dangerously, and so rann away this Morning".[31] The next day, two warriors came forward, unarmed, and Wingfield and Newport met them at the gates. Newport recognized one of them as Navirons, the mapmaker who had helped his scouting party during their sojourn upriver. The two men had tried to visit the previous week, shouting *Wingapoh!* – Algonquian for "friend" – but the jittery guards had misunderstood their intentions and fired on them.

Navirons and his companion made a fateful decision that day. They enlightened Wingfield and Newport about the divisions among the various tribes of the Powhatan, and explained which tribes wanted to make peace with the colonists, and those that preferred to be their enemies. Those close to Jamestown, such as the Paspahegh and the Weyanock, feared the English presence; those more distant, such as the Mattaponi, the Pamunkey and the Arrohattoc, wanted peace. It was a fraught situation, for the colonists found it difficult to tell one tribe from another. As Navirons and the other man left, they suggested that the long grass around the fort be cut down, as it gave cover to anyone who wished to creep up on the fort in an attack. They must have wondered why the English had not thought to clear the undergrowth already, as it was an obvious precaution.

Wingfield's planning and strategy clearly left much to be desired, but it is surprising too that Smith had not identified the grasses as an issue. The settlers seemed to have lost all semblances of organization and forethought. The fate of the doomed Roanoke Colony must have weighed heavily on their minds.

As the month wore on, Newport and his crew made preparations for their voyage home. Following the instructions from the London Company, the council wrote a report on their progress. They were decidedly frugal with the truth, however:

> Within lesse then seaven weekes, wee are fortified well against the Indians, we have sent sowen good store of wheate. We have sent yow a taste of Clapboord, we have built some houses, wee have spared some hands to a discoverie and still as god shall enhable us with strength wee will better and better our proceedings…The land would Flowe with milke and honey if so seconded by your carefull wisedomes and bountifull hands.[32]

All six remaining members of the council signed off the report, John Smith included.

Their account was comprehensive but unbalanced, leaving out mention of any problems: there was nothing about their delay in arrival, nothing about the arguments between the colonists, nor anything about the attacks from the natives. It was, however, exactly what the shareholders of the London Company wanted to hear. Newport also carried with him letters from several of the settlers. These would have been checked and censored for any negative comments, but it is unlikely any such action was needed. Everybody remaining in Jamestown was aware of their predicament, and how desperately they needed more supplies and manpower from England. If any of the colonists harboured worries about their future in Virginia, this was not the time to share them with their paymasters in London.

On June 22, Captain Newport ordered his deck crews to cast off their mooring lines,[33] and the *Susan Constant* and the *Godspeed* drifted out into the James River, taking the ebb tide downstream towards the Atlantic. Newport was expected back in Jamestown with reinforcements by early November.

The ships left behind an embryonic settlement that was ill prepared to face the hostile natives or the coming winter. The fort was finished and the fortifications were in place, but the colony was still losing men to covert attacks. This slowed their exploration of the surrounding area, and thus far nothing of significance had been discovered. Wheat had been planted, but too late in the year, and it would remain to be seen if the colonists could even venture beyond their defences to harvest it. There was plenty of game and fish for the taking, if only they could move outside the confines of the fort. Even within the garrison's palisades, things were not as they should be. Though the council's report claimed they had built houses, most of the settlers were still living in the disintegrating tents.

There was, however, some encouraging news from the Powhatan. On June 25, three days after the ships cast away from Jamestown, Wingfield reported that:

> an Indian Came to us from the great Poughwaton with the worde of peace, that he desired greatly our freindshipp that the wyroaunces, Paspaheigh and Tapahanagh should be our freindes; that wee should sowe and reape in peace, or els he would make warrs upon them with us.[34]

Wahunsenacawh was making friendly overtures towards the settlers, yet only two weeks previously the colonists had been warned about the hostility of both the Paspahegh and the Weyanock. Was this a genuine overture of reconciliation, or a deadly deception? Even if the paramount chief's approach was genuine, could he control his tribes, and prevent them from attacking Jamestown? It was a dilemma for the council to consider.

For now, they had to focus on survival. Newport's departure relieved Jamestown of many of the settlement's hardest workers – the ship's crew. As midsummer's day passed, the heat became unbearable, and the colonists grew lethargic. The limitations of the site sapped the men's energy and, at times, their resolve. They had little in the way of crops, and Smith claimed their daily rations were restricted to half a pint of wheat, and the same of barley, which "contained as many wormes as graines".[35] The food was very simply prepared – boiled in water. Smith also recalled, with a wry sense of humour: "Had we beene as free from all sinnes as gluttony, and drunkennesse, we might have been canonized for Saints".[36]

Drinking water was also a problem. Nobody had thought to dig a well, and there was no spring on the mainland nearby. Instead, the men drank from the river. This was less of a problem in the springtime, when the river was swollen with fresh water from rainfall; but in the heat of summer, the river grew increasingly brackish and tainted with human waste. George Percy complained: "at a floud [flood] verie salt, at a low tide full of slime and filth, which was the destruction of many of our men. Thus we lived for the space of five moneths in this miserable distresse, not having five able men to man our Bulwarkes upon any occasion."[37] Their undoing came from the sea after all – not in the shape of a Spanish galleon, but in the form of bad water.

Throughout the summer, the colonists regularly came under attack from breakaway factions of the Powhatan empire, but they were ravaged more by other onslaughts. An outbreak of fatal illnesses was among their greatest enemies. "Flixes", or dysentery, was rampant, most likely caused by amoebic parasites. The men were suffering from body swellings and burning fevers, probably the result of typhoid. But, as Percy explained, "for the most part they died of mere famine". Even Captain Smith, who had the constitution of an ox, became ill. At times, there were only five able-bodied men with the stamina to stand guard, or with the strength to drag out the dead for burial.

It was the end of June 1607, and England's latest attempt to establish a settlement in Virginia was scarcely six weeks old. Newport had departed for England with the two largest ships, leaving the settlers to fend for themselves. Already, a couple of dozen men had died. The survivors were riven with sickness. The group was splintered; dissent was the rule. Everywhere, men were whispering that their president, Edward Maria Wingfield, was not up to the task of leading them. Outside the confines of the fort, the mood of the Powhatan was shifting increasingly from curious and welcoming, to wary, if not hostile.

As summer progressed, Percy stopped recording discoveries about their new life, but instead drew up a roster of the deceased:

> The sixt of August there died John Asbie of the bloudie Flixe. The ninth day died George Flowre of the swelling. The tenth day died William

> Bruster Gentleman, of a wound given by the Savages, and was buried the eleventh day.
>
> The fourteenth day, Jerome Alikock Ancient, died of a wound, the same day Francis Midwinter, Edward Moris Corporall died suddenly.[38]

Percy's roll call of the dead and dying went on and on: August 15, Edward Browne and Stephen Galthrope; August 16, Thomas Gower; August 17, Thomas Mounslic; August 18, Robert Pennington and John Martin; August 19, Drue Piggase.

On August 22, there came the most serious loss of all: Bartholomew Gosnold, master of the *Godspeed* and member of the governing council, was dead. He was given a high-status burial outside the confines of the fort, the sort of privilege that could not be afforded to most of the departed. After the coffin was laid in the ground, a volley of musket shot was fired in his honour; it echoed across the James River, scattering wildfowl to the horizon.

In 2002, archaeologists at Jamestown unearthed what they believed was Gosnold's grave. It was an exciting find, because most skeletal remains decay very quickly in the acidic groundwater. Tests on bone samples showed the man had a diet rich in wheat, rather than American corn, indicating the remains were most likely those of one of the original settlers. Forensic analysis on the well-preserved pelvis suggested the man was in his mid to late thirties; Gosnold was thirty-six when he died.[39] Perhaps the most compelling piece of evidence in the grave was a decorative leading staff of a captain, which appeared to have been placed ceremoniously along one edge of the coffin lid.[40]

Smith credited Gosnold with being the mastermind behind the colonization of Virginia. Wingfield described Gosnold as "the Worthy and Religious gent Captayn Bartholomew Gosnold, upon whose lief stood a great part of the good succes, and fortune of our government and Collony".[41] Gosnold's death was a blow to the settlement.

There was no question now: the colonists were in very serious trouble.

John Smith taken prisoner by the Pamunkey tribe,
December 1607, from Smith's *The True Travels* (1630).

9
Prisoner

1607

They tyed him to a tree, and as many as could
stand about him prepared to shoot him
John Smith, The Generall Historie (1624)

John Smith reported that forty-six colonists died of fever, starvation or native arrows by mid-September. Smith recovered fully from his illness, but many around him did not. The colonists knew the Powhatan were watching their every movement, and they tried to conceal their dwindling numbers by burying their dead at night, under cover of darkness. George Percy wrote that:

> it would make their harts to bleed to heare the pitiful murmerings & out-cries of our sick men without reliefe every night and day for the space of sixe weekes, some departing out of the World, many times three or foure in a night.[1]

One man in the settlement seemed to be impervious to sickness: Edward Maria Wingfield.

Smith thought he knew why President Wingfield and a few of his chosen friends retained their rude health: he had found evidence that Wingfield was hoarding private stores for their own use. While the other settlers were surviving on a bowl of weevil-infested barley-and-wheat gruel, Wingfield and his cohorts were feasting on meat, eggs, oatmeal, liquor and white wine. This was political dynamite. Smith knew that if he played his hand well, the revelation would mark the end of Wingfield's rule.

Smith made a pact with two other members of the governing council, the captains John Ratcliffe and John Martin. Together, they agreed to depose Wingfield and appoint Ratcliffe in his place. Smith considered Martin to be "verie honest" and "wishing the best for the colony", but did not think he had the makings of a strong leader, especially on account of his poor health. Smith barely knew Ratcliffe, for they had crossed the Atlantic on separate vessels, and Smith had been away on the scouting trip with Newport for much of his time at Jamestown. But Smith reasoned that anybody would be better than the incumbent, and Ratcliffe was willing and seemed able. Orchestrating Wingfield's downfall, preferably in disgrace, would doubtless bring huge satisfaction to the Lincolnshire farmer's son. But he had to be sure they could get at least one other vote on the council to avoid a humiliating defeat. With their overarching plan in hand, the three plotters bided their time.

In late August, George Kendall, one of the remaining members of the council, was arrested for a "heinous" crime. In his diaries, Percy shared no detail about the charge, and Smith merely said that Kendall was deposed "for divers reasons". For his part, Wingfield was not shy about Kendall's offences: "Master Kendall was put of[f] from beeing of the Councell, and committed to prison, for that it did manyfestly appeere he did practize to sowe discord betwene the President and Councell."[2] Kendall's military experience and social position had persuaded the London Company's directors he was a good choice for the government, but many in Virginia believed him to be a shadowy figure with doubtful allegiances. Later that summer, there would be claims he was a covert Catholic and Spanish informer. Whatever his crimes against Wingfield, Kendall was imprisoned in the *Discovery* and stripped of his council seat.

With Newport en route to England, Gosnold dead and Kendall in detention, there were only four councillors left – Wingfield, Ratcliffe, Martin and Smith. For now, at least, Wingfield's two presidential votes were outnumbered. On September 10, Ratcliffe, Martin and Smith went to Wingfield's tent and unseated him from the presidency and from the council itself. They immediately named Ratcliffe as Wingfield's successor. Wingfield answered, with feigned indifference "that they had eased him of a great deale of Care, and trouble."[3]

The next day, the deposed president was brought before the whole colony, where Ratcliffe accused him of withholding food. Smith reminded everyone that Wingfield had accused him unfairly of treason, which further riled the ex-president. Martin demanded more food for the men, and especially for the sick among them. Wingfield would not yield, claiming he needed instructions from his fellow shareholders in London. Finally, Ratcliffe explained to the colonists why Wingfield had been removed from office, and Martin and Smith spoke up in Ratcliffe's support.

The only account of the meeting is Wingfield's, which is distorted and defensive. He denied any misconduct, yet his writings about the day come across as arrogant and insensitive. The settlers were very angry, and Wingfield wrote that one Richard Crofts threatened to "pull me out of my seate, and out of my skynn too".[4] An unnamed member of the council, most likely the gentle John Martin, recommended Wingfield should have a personal guard. Wingfield replied, rather piously, "I would [need] no guard but gods love, and my owne innocencie".[5] Wingfield was taken to the *Discovery* to join George Kendall in confinement.

On several occasions, Wingfield was brought back from the ship to answer further accusations to the assembled men of Jamestown. Smith could not resist the temptation to prod the high-and-mighty former leader. He continued to challenge Wingfield about the slanderous accusations made against him – that he had organized a mutiny on the voyage from England. Smith had spent thirteen long weeks in confinement on board the *Susan Constant*, and he was determined to clear his name and receive an apology.

Wingfield had been a lawyer in Lincoln's Inn, and he saw the weakness in Smith's argument immediately. Wingfield maintained that Smith's line of questioning was outside the jurisdiction of the council; they had no standing to hear a legal case. In his new position as colony president, Ratcliffe overruled Wingfield's objection and convened a jury of twelve men to determine whether Wingfield had wronged Captain Smith.

Wingfield now became the scapegoat for everything that was wrong with Jamestown, and Smith secured an easy victory from his peers. The jury agreed that Smith was innocent, and awarded him the sum of two hundred pounds in compensation for the miscarriage of justice. To pay the fine, Wingfield handed over his hidden stash of food, which Smith donated to the colony's general inventory.

Wingfield had very nearly presided over the extinction of the settlement. Half the men had died and most of the survivors were still living in rotting tents. Martin was too weak from disease to be an effective leader, and Smith and Ratcliffe were both recovering from their own bouts of illness. The colonists were now at their most pitiful, and, to a man, they expected the native peoples would soon come and finish the job. Smith was realistic about their predicament:

> But now was all our provision spent, the Sturgeon gone, all helps abandoned, each houre expecting the fury of the Salvages; when God the patron of all good indevours, in that desperate extremitie so changed the hearts of the Salvages, that they brought such plenty of their fruits, and provision, as no man wanted.[6]

Wahunsenacawh stayed true to his word, sending corn and other provisions to the English from the recent harvest. The paramount chief of the Powhatan knew the colonists were all but defenceless, and he could easily have finished them off with one quick attack. Instead, he chose to barter with the Englishmen, accumulating many beads, hatchets and other coveted goods. Wahunsenacawh had proved himself to be a consummate tactician, so he must have had good reason to spare the English. His decision should be considered as part of his long-term strategy.

The Powhatan already feared the Spanish, and by now they would have realized that this settlement on the James River was not linked to them. Wahunsenacawh hoped the English could offer his people some protection from other European intruders. The Powhatan were also threatened by the aggressive tribes who lived to the north and took great pleasure in raiding their villages every year. If the paramount chief could form an alliance with the English, then he might get not just metal hatchets, but perhaps even guns. This would give his people a considerable advantage over their hostile neighbours. Whatever the reason, in September 1607, Wahunsenacawh chose to spare Jamestown.

The Jamestown settlement was not the only English attempt that year at colonizing the eastern seaboard of America. The other joint-stock company formed in 1606, the Virginia Company of Plymouth, was also busy. Their first ship, the *Richard*, had sailed from England in August 1606, four months before the ships bound for Jamestown left Blackwall. Unfortunately, the sole Plymouth vessel was captured by the Spanish off the coast of Florida, the crew taken back to Spain as prisoners. Only a few ever made their way home to England.

Their next effort, called the Popham Colony after its leader George Popham, was more successful. Two ships carrying about 120 settlers left Plymouth, England, on May 31, 1607, and both arrived safely in the Americas in mid-August, landing some five hundred miles north of Jamestown. The Popham colonists established themselves on a rocky peninsula at the mouth of the Kennebec River (about ten miles south of Bath, Maine) and named their settlement Fort George. They planned to trade for precious metals and furs with the native peoples. They also wanted to demonstrate that the region's timber could be used to build ships.

Fort George was a failure. The locals were suspicious of the Englishmen and refused to cooperate with them. The colonists' August arrival meant there was no time to plant crops to sustain them through the winter, and half of the colony returned to England that December. The winters in this part of North America are bitterly cold, and that year the Kennebec River froze over. They must have been desperate to keep warm. There is archaeological evidence of several fires at the colony, including one that destroyed the storehouse and its provisions.

The settlement was abandoned in the summer of 1608, less than a year after they had arrived. Before they left, they built a ship from the local timber – a thirty-ton, twin-masted pinnace called the *Victoria of Sagadahoc*. She was the first ship built in America to sail to England and return, which she did in 1609 and again in 1610 (with supplies for Jamestown). She was built to demonstrate that a shipbuilding industry was to be had in the Americas, for anyone willing to try his hand at it.

As the ships of the Popham Colony made their way west across the Atlantic during the summer of 1607, Captain Newport was returning to England on the more direct, northerly route. On board the *Susan Constant* and the *Godspeed* was the cargo of clapboard the colonists' had harvested for the London Company's investors, as well as a load of glittering minerals.

Alas, the English had a long history of failing to find gold in America. In 1577, and again the following year, when Martin Frobisher sailed to Canada to search for the precious metal, he had returned with huge quantities of ore on both occasions. A smelting plant was specially built in Dartford to handle the aggregate, but it all proved to be worthless iron pyrite – otherwise known as "fools' gold". The waste was eventually used for road surfacing. But the Jamestown colonists had not learned from that humiliation. Newport's holds contained nothing of value beside the timber.

Newport arrived in London around August 8, 1607. Soon the capital was buzzing with news of the "success" of the settlement, gleaned from the letters and reports sent from Jamestown. However, the shareholders in the London Company were not the only ones anxiously awaiting news of the colony. The Spanish ambassador, Don Pedro de Zúñiga, was also keen to hear the latest updates.

Ever since Columbus reached the West Indies in 1492, the Spanish had laid claim to the Americas, north and south, and de Zúñiga maintained the Virginia expedition was a violation of Spanish territory. He had frequently warned King Philip III of the risks if the English succeeded in securing a permanent settlement there. The redoubtable ambassador had spies, or at least informers, inside the London Company, so he could stay well informed about Jamestown's progress. On September 12 (September 22 NS), de Zúñiga wrote to tell his king that Newport had returned:

> They are hurrying to send these ships back with some people, and merchants have invested in the business along with other persons who want to establish themselves there, since that seems the most useful way they have found to play pirate and make assaults on Your Majesty's fleets... It would be very advisable for Your Majesty to root out this noxious plant while it is so easy.[7]

It was time for the ambassador to call on the King of England to express Spain's official concerns. On the afternoon of Sunday, October 7, 1607, de Zúñiga gained an audience with James. The King had kept the emissary waiting two weeks for the appointment, most probably because of the recent death of his two-year-old daughter. James received de Zúñiga courteously, and the ambassador offered his nation's condolences over the death of Princess Mary. The ambassador then moved on to the main purpose of his visit. Philip III requested that he:

> point out how much against good friendship and brotherliness it was for his vassals to dare to want to people Virginia, since it is a part of the Indies belonging to Castile [Spain], and that this boldness could have 'inconvenient' results.[8]

The term "inconvenient" was a common euphemism for the ruinous consequences of war. The veiled threat was not lost on James. However, the King knew it was all a game, and that he had to play his part in the ensuing diplomatic charade. James replied that he was not well acquainted with the specifics of the Virginia venture, nor was he aware that Spain had any right to the territory. De Zúñiga warned James of the dire consequences if England claimed title to those parts of North America. In return, James again denied having any detailed knowledge of the enterprise. The ambassador knew he was being stalled. The next day he wrote to Philip III, adopting his usual forthright manner:

> I said to him again that it was important that a remedy be found for the Virginia affair, for it was necessary to act with some urgency, before it got worse...I think it would be a good idea if the few who are there should be finished outright, because that would cut the root, so that it would not sprout again.[9]

The colonists in Jamestown, of course, were unaware of the political games being played back in Europe, and knew nothing about the advice Philip III was getting from his ambassador. From the many communications sent to the Spanish king, it is clear there was a very real risk that the struggling English settlement could be wiped out by a single Spanish attack.

In Virginia, the situation was shifting rapidly. After John Smith was admitted to the governing council on June 10, he began to exert his influence. Within three months of their arrival, Wingfield had been deposed and Smith's choice, Ratcliffe, had taken the presidency along with the seat's two votes. In some ways, those two votes were more powerful than ever, for by now there were only two other people on the council: Smith and John Martin. John Smith probably saw his opportunity and asked for a position of real power.

Ratcliffe knew he owed his presidency in large part to Smith. He took the pragmatic decision to make Smith the colony's "cape merchant", or supply officer, a crucially important position. (The encumbant, Thomas Studley, had died in August.) It was a good choice. Smith was now responsible for organizing the work in Jamestown, and for all trading with the Powhatan. Both tasks needed urgent attention if the colony was to survive the year, and Smith was not shy about taking them on.

As October rolled into November, chill winds began to cut through the threadbare clothing of the colonists. Migrating wildfowl filled the skies, and the fish too were leaving the rivers for the open ocean. The bountiful conditions of summer were over. The Powhatans' harvest was in, and they had food available for barter. Yet a strange apathy was infecting the colony. Most of Smith's fellow settlers were not working, and they were not interested in making preparations for the winter. Smith knew from his experience in Hungary the price they would pay if they faced a severe winter without proper accommodation: "As yet we had no houses to cover us, our Tents were rotten, and our Cabbins worse than nought".[10] Already their numbers had halved since their arrival; the rest of them could be gone before the spring thaw.

Smith was troubled by their lassitude. The men seemed indifferent to their conditions, even to their future. They seemed content simply to wait for Newport's supply ship to appear on the horizon – and, worse, they were happy to assume it would actually show up.

Smith was a strategist, one of the few people in Jamestown who really understood the need to think more than a few days ahead:

> As at this time were most of our chiefest men either sicke or discontented, the rest being in such dispaire, as they would rather starve and rot with idlenes, then [than] be persuaded to do anything for their owne reliefe without constraint: ...our victualles being now within eighteene days spent, and the Indians trade decreasing.[11]

There are many theories as to why the colonists lacked the motivation to haul themselves out of this listlessness. Of course, many were "gentlemen" and unused to hard labour, and some would have resented being assigned menial tasks, such as cutting clapboard and building houses – perhaps all the more so if the orders were coming from Smith. Newport's crew, now long departed, had built most of the existing structures. However, it is likely the remaining colonists' lethargy resulted from psychological and physiological issues, as well.

The men had endured a longer sea passage than expected, and had arrived in Virginia exhausted. The new country was strange to their eyes and they were in culture shock. The constant threat of attack undermined their confidence; inadequate food and reoccurring illness sapped their energy. They had watched as man after man – often their friends – had succumbed to sickness or a well-placed arrow.

The colonists were also disillusioned. They felt let down by their original president and by their London paymasters. It was now obvious they would never become rich in America, which offered swampy, pestilent dirt rather than land criss-crossed with opulent veins of gold and silver; few now believed they would ever again see the shores of England. They no longer lived by the well-defined rules of Elizabethan and Jacobean society they had followed since birth. This only added to their sense of vulnerability, and contributed to their despondency and hopelessness.

Worse still, the men had been drinking brackish river water for more than six months. Dehydration had always been an issue, but most if not all of the men were probably suffering from chronic salt poisoning by this stage. Brackish water is not as saline as pure seawater, but it still contains more salt than the human body can tolerate for long. The kidneys respond by ridding the body of the excessive salt, which results in further dehydration. Muscle cramps, nausea, weakness and delirium follow. In extreme circumstances, excessive salt can lead to coma, organ failure and eventually death.

The colonists' heavy clothing compounded the problem of dehydration. The men had suffered badly in the heat of the West Indies, where Edward Brookes died from heat exhaustion. During a Virginian summer, daytime temperatures frequently exceed 90 degrees Fahrenheit (thirty-two degrees Celsius), often with very high levels of humidity. Yet the men still wore their woollen tunics, and sometimes their metal breastplates as protection from arrows. The oppressive conditions and the effects of dehydration might also explain the men's cantankerous and irritable attitudes, as well as their leaders' poor decision-making.

Smith knew he could not rely on Newport's ship returning in mid-November as scheduled. Supply ships were notorious for arriving late, or not at all. If the colony was going to survive, it had to be through its own efforts. It was the third week of September, and Smith saw they had food to last for only another eighteen days. Embracing his new position as cape merchant, he set about securing provisions for the winter, launching a series of excursions to neighbouring villages in the hopes of bartering for food.

On his first trip, he took a handful of men in the shallop down the James River to the Kecoughtan village. However, as soon as Smith began to negotiate with the villagers, he realized they had already gleaned how desperate the English were: "The Indians thinking us neare famished, with carelesse kindnes offred us little pieces of bread and small handfulls of beanes or wheat, for a hatchet or a piece of copper."[12] This put Smith in a very poor bargaining position. The Kecoughtan offered him so little in return for a hatchet, it was an insult. He refused to trade like this. Instead, he gave the children small beads and trinkets, hoping to create an impression of largesse. If the colonists were so desperate, he hoped to show, how could he afford to make such a gesture?

Smith's tactic worked. The next morning, the villagers were ready to trade. They were now, he claimed, "no lesse desirous of our commodities than we of their Corne…With fish, oysters, bread and deere, they kindly traded with me and my men."[13]

Smith had been in confinement when Newport visited the village shortly after the fleet's arrival, so this was the cape merchant's first experience of the Kecoughtan. Smith made a close surveillance of what he found – the number of houses, the acreage of the site, its location relative to the peninsula, and so on, all through the eyes of a veteran soldier and explorer.

He returned to Jamestown with sixteen bushels of corn (equivalent to about 128 gallons), but he was stopped on the way by two canoes from another village. These men too were keen to trade their corn, and he loaded up another fourteen bushels – at least, this was the version Smith recalled in 1608. A later version of the same event, written in 1624, presented a hair-raising story of how the shallop was attacked as he made his way back to the fort. With only a small group of men on board, they were vastly outnumbered. Smith ordered the muskets to be fired, ran the boat ashore, and chased the attackers into the woods. The Powhatan

A *weroance* and his weapons, depicted front and back, from an engraving by Theodor de Bry, *America* (1590).

then made a counter-attack, which the Englishmen repulsed. Eventually they made peace, and Smith bestowed the locals with beads and copper in return for more venison, turkey, wildfowl and bread.

It was not uncommon for Smith to write different versions of the same event, and this has led some historians to question the veracity of some of his exploits.[14] Usually, Smith's more adventurous, dangerous and exciting account was published at a later date. The accusation has been made that as he grew older Smith elaborated upon his youthful exploits. This could well be true, but there are other factors that ought to be considered.

Smith's earliest accounts of his time in Virginia, *A True Relation of Such Occurrences and Accidents of Noate as Hath Hapned in Virginia* (1608) and *A Map of Virginia, With a Description of the Country, the Commodities, People, Government and Religion* (1612) were factual records of his sojourn at Jamestown. They were penned during the colony's formative years, when the enterprise was still susceptible to failure. Every report the various colonists sent back to London with Newport in June 1607 was very positive, even though the reality was quite different.

The same rule of self-censorship applied to Smith's early accounts from 1608 and 1612. He was a passionate supporter of colonizing Virginia, and *A True Relation* and *A Map of Virginia* were less of a memoir than a promotional brochure for the London Company. Not one of these early accounts was a balanced and honest appraisal of the problems the colonists were facing, least of all when it came to fighting with the locals. Smith's later accounts usually include a franker assessment of the many horrors that plagued the settlers during their first few years.

As Smith went on more trading missions, he began to learn about the subtle differences between the various Powhatan tribes. When they visited the Paspahegh, whom he called "that churlish and trecherous nation",[15] warriors crept up on the shallop at night and tried to steal the Englishmen's guns and swords. Smith became very wary of the Paspahegh, and feared they were always looking for a chance to catch him off guard.

On November 9, Smith took the shallop up the Chickahominy River, a tributary of the James, and arranged for the *Discovery* to follow on the next tide. Past its narrow mouth, the river widened briefly before tapering, meandering north and then west. On each side of the river, tall marsh grasses and reeds blurred the boundary between water and land. This was the realm of the Chickahominy tribe (the "Coarse Ground Corn People"), who were not affiliated with the Powhatan empire. Smith was keen to develop a fruitful trading relationship with them.

On the first day of the shallop's expedition, Smith and his men visited several Chickahominy villages, showing off the copper, beads and hatchets they had for barter. Smith was conscious of not wanting to devalue his "currency", so rather than trade everything with one village, he brokered small quantities of food from many different settlements. The shallop was soon fully laden, so they dropped downriver, only to find the *Discovery* had run aground there.

The next day, the shallop's cargo was transferred to the larger boat, and then Smith returned upriver to a village called Mamanahunt, where he found the Chickahominy waiting for him with three or four hundred baskets of corn. Smith reported that "so desirous of trade wer they, that they would follow me with their canowes, and for any thing give it me, rather then returne it back, so I unladed again 7 or 8. hogsheads at our fort".[16]

The trading had been relatively easy, and Smith used his excursions to pick up a few words of the Algonquian language and to survey the area. His map can still be used today to navigate the Chickahominy River.

On his return to Jamestown, Smith found the colonists restless and argumentative. Ratcliffe was not an effective leader, and plots and counter-plots were rife. Ratcliffe had rebuked the blacksmith, a man called James Read, over a minor issue, which blew up out of proportion. Curses were exchanged and, in a fury, Read picked up his tools and assaulted Ratcliffe. A jury was convened, and Read was found guilty and condemned to hang. He was on the point of being tilted off a ladder, noose around his neck, when he declared he had knowledge of a conspiracy. The execution was stayed for a moment, so that the council might investigate. Read readily confessed: George Kendall was the ringleader.

The backwaters of the Chickahominy River in winter (photo by Peter Firstbrook).

Kendall had already come under scrutiny when he and Wingfield had crossed each other some weeks previously. Rumours had begun to circulate that he was not to be trusted; now he was accused of being a spy. Dispensing justice was speedy in Jamestown: Read was pardoned and Kendall was shot.

Kendall's death sentence did little to calm the colonists. Wingfield argued in favour of abandoning Jamestown and making haste to England in the *Discovery*. It was an unrealistic proposal, for the boat would not accommodate even the depleted number of Jamestown residents. Even so, Ratcliffe threw his support behind the idea. The other two councillors, Martin and Smith, were adamantly against it. With the council stuck in a stalemate, Smith became aggressive and ordered warning shots to be fired. There was a brief discussion, and it was agreed the colonists would hold out for a little longer. The standoff was over, at least for the time being.

November passed into December, and there was still no sign of Newport's supply ships. Temperatures were falling close to freezing, and the long nights and short days offered little time for hunting and trading. The Powhatan too were beginning to settle in for the long winter and had less food for barter.

In early December, the council again despatched Smith up the Chickahominy River to find its source, and perhaps a continental passage to the South Seas. As president, Ratcliffe was keen to fulfil at least one of the London Company's main objectives. This time, Smith took nine men and the party rowed and sailed the shallop up the snaking river until they reached the village of Apokant, forty miles upstream from the confluence with the James. Beyond the village, all they could see was wilderness. They continued another ten miles up the waterway, and Smith felt sure they were getting close to the river's headwaters. Alas, a tree blocked any further progress. He seemed to be cursed at every turn.

Smith knew he could not return empty-handed from the expedition, for if he did, there were many "malicious tungs [tongues]" who would rejoice in his failure. So he and his men returned to Apokant under a pretext – they told the villagers they wanted to hunt. Smith recruited two of the villagers to take him upstream in a canoe on this bogus quest. He chose two colonists to accompany him, the carpenter Thomas Emry and a gentleman called Jehu (or John) Robinson. The party of three Englishmen and two Chickahominy men got a couple of miles beyond the fallen tree, at which point they pulled ashore to rest and eat.

The seven other colonists had been left in the shallop anchored in the river, "with expresse charge not any to go ashore til my returne".[17] Smith's instincts when it came to military matters were sound, as usual. However, the men on the shallop noticed some women on the riverbank who seemed to return their admiring glances. Disregarding Smith's orders, the men went ashore to see where things might lead. But the women were a trap, and they were ambushed by a group of warriors.

Once the set-up was revealed, the colonists turned heel and ran back to their shallop. One man, a labourer called George Casson, did not make it to the boat, and he was taken prisoner. Immediately, the warriors stripped Casson naked and tied him to a stake. They lit a fire behind him and then, joint by joint, cut off his fingers with mussel shells and threw them onto the fire. They then used shells and reeds to strip the skin from his face, before disembowelling him, again with shells, casting his intestines on the fire, too. Finally, they left Casson's remains to burn to the bones. It is unclear whether this was a ritual sacrifice to placate their gods, or a punishment for the party having trespassed onto their territory. Regardless, it was a horrific execution.

Meanwhile, Smith and the canoe party upstream had finished their meal. Smith and one of the Chickahominy guides walked inland, looking to shoot some wildfowl. Smith left Emry and Robinson with the second guide by the canoe, again with clear instructions to keep their muskets at the ready and to let fly a salvo if there was a problem. Within fifteen minutes of leaving the river, Smith heard hollering in the distance, but no warning shot. He put his pistol to the head of his guide, but immediately realized the man was as confused as he was about the noise. Then, out of nowhere, Smith was struck in the right thigh by an arrow. He turned to see two Powhatan warriors pulling back their drawstrings and taking aim. He fired his gun – but missed. As he reloaded, three or four new attackers appeared. They shot at him several times, but mercifully all their arrows fell short.

Smith and his Chickahominy companion were now surrounded by as many as two hundred Powhatan warriors, by Smith's estimation, and every one of them was armed. Smith tried to make his way through the forest back to the canoe, using his guide as a human shield. Communication must have been frustrating for Smith, as he only had a few words of Algonquian. Perhaps not surprisingly, the two men got into difficulties; they stumbled into a quagmire, and were unable to free themselves from the freezing, glutinous mud. With attackers now bearing down on him, Captain Smith realized his luck had run out. He threw his gun to one side as an act of surrender and was "resolved to trie their mercies". It was the only option he had left.

The warriors took Smith back to the canoe, where the body of Jehu Robinson lay "with 20 or 30 arrowes in him". There was no sign of Thomas

Emry, however. Smith was then taken to the men's leader, a warrior called Opechancanough, who he later learned was one of three younger brothers of the paramount chief, Wahunsenacawh. Opechancanough was a *weroance* of the Pamunkey, who were his captors. Smith recalled the *weroance* was about sixty years old, "a Man of large Stature, noble Presence, and extraordinary Parts".[18]

Smith always endeavoured to understand the culture and beliefs of the Powhatan, and he had seen how much stock they put on rank and status. He needed to inspire some veneration and esteem if he was going to get out of this dire situation alive. From his jacket, he produced a pocket compass and showed it to Opechancanough. In his trips to barter for food, Smith had learned that anything the Powhatan did not understand, they considered supernatural – and therefore powerful. Smith moved the compass around, but the needle inside kept pointing in the same direction. Opechancanough was fascinated. "I presented him with a compasse dial, describing by my best meanes the use therof, whereat he so amazedly admired".[19]

Smith sensed he had captured the *weroance*'s interest, so he launched into an oration about, of all things, the solar system: "he suffered [allowed] me to proceed in a discourse on the roundness of the earth, the course of the sunne, moone, starres and plannets".[20] Smith's knowledge of the Algonquian language was better than most of the other colonists, but he was still limited to asking basic questions such as "*Ka ka torawincs*" – "What do you call this?" – and answering in simple words and phrases. Quite how much of the functioning of the celestial heavens he was able to disclose to the *weroance* is a matter of some conjecture, but it seems his speech did not impress.

Soon enough, "they tyed him to a tree, and as many as could stand about him prepared to shoot him."[21] For all Smith knew, "their mercies" were about to inflict on him a wretched death. But Opechancanough must have had a change of mind, because within an hour, "the King holding up the Compass in his hand, they all laid downe their Bowes and Arrowes, and in a triumphant manner led him to Orapaks [a temporary hunting lodge], where he was after their manner kindly feasted, and well used [treated]".[22]

The Powhatan left no written record of the encounter, so it is difficult to understand what was going through Opechancanough's mind. He assumed Smith was an important leader in the colony, based on his bartering and the deference the other Englishmen paid him. Perhaps the *weroance* also had gathered a general understanding of the newcomers' plans for Virginia – word of the Roanoke Colony, or the Spanish mission, were most likely part of Powhatan oral history.

On the one hand, the Englishmen had metal hatchets, and were willing to trade them for food. Building relations with them could be an asset. On the other hand, the Englishmen also had guns, and had used them not in trade, but to kill brave Powhatan warriors. Was there any question that they were a threat to their people? All this reasoning still left the decision to be made: Was this Englishman better dead or alive? A common man, someone like poor George Casson, could be tortured and killed with impunity; but a leader like Smith, who carried magic in his pocket, was a different matter altogether. This day, Opechancanough decided to play it safe, and kept John Smith alive.

There is some evidence of divisions within the Powhatan empire over what to do about the colonists. The paramount chief, Wahunsenacawh, apparently favoured appeasement of the English, but his younger brother Opechancanough and some other *weroances* thought the settlement at Jamestown should be eliminated. It is possible that Opechancanough's intuition was to kill Smith, but he feared his older brother would disapprove. If he defied his brother's wishes, the consequences for him would be severe. Opechancanough prevaricated and Smith's execution was stayed.

Smith could not have understood fully what was going on, but he might have picked up on some hesitancy as the Pamunkey *weroance* deliberated over what to do with him. He knew the security around him was tight; unlike in Russia, there was little chance of him escaping: "the King well guarded [me] with 20 bowmen 5 flanck and rear".[23] So Smith played for time and charmed the credulous Pamunkey as best he could.

Over the next several days, Smith was alternately bound, then released, then transported on to a new village or hunting camp. "At each place I expected when they would execute me, yet they used me with what kindnes they could", he wrote.[24] Even under this duress, he was able to recall his experiences lucidly. At one of the hunting lodges, the Pamunkey performed a dance before him, similar to the one witnessed by Captain Newport on his visit to the Kecoughtan:

> [They] then cast themselves in a ring, dauncing in such severall Postures, and singing and yelling out such hellish notes and screeches; being strangely painted, every one his quiver of Arrowes, and at his backe a club; on his arme a Fox or an Otters skinne, or some such matter for his vambrace [a tubular covering worn on the forearm]; their heads and shoulders painted red, with Oyle [oil] and Pocones [a vegetable dye] mingled together, which Scarlet-like colour made an exceeding handsome shew.[25]

Whether this was a rite of shamans or warriors, it must have been an intimidating experience, as Smith's memory of the "hellish notes and screeches" testifies. And while he sometimes changed his account of events over the years, Smith was remarkably consistent throughout his life in describing his days as Opechancanough's prisoner.

After the ceremonial dance, Smith was served a meal of venison and bread, and taken to another lodge, where he stayed for several days. Each morning, some women brought him platters of meat and bread; each day, Opechancanough visited his captive and quizzed him. "The King tooke great delight in understanding the manner of our ships, and sayling the seas, the earth and skies and of our God", Smith reported.[26] Smith knew he was being interrogated, if gently, and he drip-fed inaccurate information about the defences around Jamestown, disclosing the position of explosive mines and cannon that surrounded the fort – all of them non-existent. In return, the chief told Smith of a village called Ocanahonan – a distant place where men wore European clothing. Was this, perhaps, the remains of the lost colony of Roanoke? Or was Opechancanough also feeding Smith misinformation?

While Opechancanough continued to probe his prisoner for intelligence, Smith decided to play a new game. He asked the *weroance* if he could send a man to Jamestown with a letter, so that his people "shold understand, how kindly they used me, and that I was well, least they should revenge my death".[27] Opechancanough agreed to send not one messenger but three.

The Pamunkey, of course, could not read the message, so Smith was able to warn the colony of the possibility of an attack. He told the settlers to give Opechancanough's men a fearsome display of cannon fire and asked them to send back items that he had promised to the chief.

On their arrival at Jamestown, the Pamunkey messengers were treated to a spectacular display of firepower and given the items Smith had requested. The three men returned to their chief awestricken and enthralled. Either the paper could speak or the Englishman could divine a message. However it happened, Captain Smith's magic only grew stronger in the eyes of the Pamunkey.

Smith was marched from village to village for the next week. At Menapacant (Smith's Menapacute, located on the big bend in the Pamunkey River north of West Point), another of Wahunsenacawh's brothers, Kekataugh, invited Smith to feast with him. Kekataugh asked Smith to demonstrate the use of his pistol, pointing to a target that Smith estimated was about 120 feet away – about the limit of range of the Powhatans' arrows. Kekataugh must surely have wanted to see if the Englishman's weapon was as accurate as his own. Smith had to think quickly, because he knew he could not hit a target at this distance with a pistol, and this information had to be kept from the Powhatan at all costs. Smith surreptitiously snapped off the cock of his expensive French gun, then showed it to Kekataugh with a face filled with false remorse: his pistol was broken and he could not fire at the target. The "Indians", he said, "were much discontented".

Smith spent his Christmas in a village somewhere in the desolate, low-lying marshland of the upper Pamunkey River. Even if his fellow colonists back in Jamestown could have raised themselves from their torpor, they never would have found him in such remote territory.

Eventually, he was taken to the capital of the Pamunkey tribe, where he was subjected to another ordeal:

> With most strange gestures and passions he began his invocation, and environed the fire with a circle of meale; which done, three more such like devils came rushing in with the like antique tricks, painted halfe blacke, halfe red: but all their eyes were painted white, and some red stroakes like Mutchato's [moustaches], along their cheeks.[28]

Smith assumed the first man was a high priest, who carefully arranged an inner circle of ground corn around the fire. This, he explained to Smith, represented his people's country. Outside the circle, he laid two concentric rings of corn kernels, representing the ocean, and between every few kernels he placed a small twig, which he said signified Smith's country. Smith was told the ritual would tell the Powhatan if he was a friend or a foe. (All this was in Algonquian, of course, and presumably some sign language.) Smith fully understood the consequences if the kernels and twigs said he was not a friend, but he was told nothing more. The ordeal lasted a full three days, after which the priests left without telling him their verdict.

Opechancanough then had Smith removed from the long house to sit down to a feast with Opitchapam, the oldest of Wahunsenacawh's three brothers and the next in line of succession to rule the Powhatan. Smith could only hope that his next host would be the paramount chief himself, given the overtures that Wahunsenacawh had made to the colonists back in the more hospitable days of September. He still did not know what the kernels and twigs had revealed.

On December 30, he was moved again, this time by canoe down the Pamunkey River and into the much wider York River. His destination was Werowocomoco, the capital of the Powhatan empire. As Opechancanough's canoe approached the town, Smith's soldier's eye would have recognized immediately the site's strategic importance.

Werowocomoco was built on a small peninsula set inside a bay on the northern shore of the York River. On each side of the settlement were small tributary streams, effectively protecting the town on three sides by water. As Smith clambered ashore from the canoe, he became the first European to set foot on this revered ground, the first white man the native peoples of Werowocomoco had ever seen.

He was about to face the paramount chief's inquisition. What happened on that winter's day has muddied Smith's reputation for more than four hundred years, and generated one of the most enduring legends in the history of America.

It was the day John Smith met Pocahontas.

Smith awaits execution in Wahunsenacawh's longhouse,
from Smith's *The Generall Historie* (1624).

10
Trader

1608

Then as many [warriors] as could layd hands on him, dragged him to them, and thereon laid his head, and being ready with their clubs, to beate out his braines

John Smith, The Generall Historie (1624)

Smith arrived at the Powhatan capital, Werowocomoco, on December 30, 1607. The town was bigger than anything he had seen in Virginia, and archaeological excavations have since revealed a Powhatan settlement covering more than fifty acres. After easing himself over the side of the canoe into the ice-cold waters of the York River, Smith was escorted up the beach by Opechancanough's guards. As he was marched through the town, many of the inhabitants stared on in fascination. For those who had not yet seen the pale-faced Englishmen, he was a curious sight. Short and stocky, with a reddish-brown beard and wearing strange clothing, John Smith was not what they had expected when they had heard stories of the strangers living on the James River.

About a thousand feet from the river, the town opened up to reveal a large, open area surrounded by a double ring of earthworks. These ramparts separated the compound from the rest of the town, and offered some defence in the event of an attack. This was the heart of the Powhatan universe: a citadel, living quarters and bank vault rolled into one. The centre of the complex was dominated by a large *yehakin*, more than sixty feet long and the size of a Lincolnshire barn. The longhouse was built in the traditional style, with saplings and branches bent to form an arch, which was then braced firmly and covered in reed matting and bark. There was a low doorway at each end, and smoke from the wood fire inside drifted up through vents in the roof. It was by far the biggest building Smith had seen since leaving London.

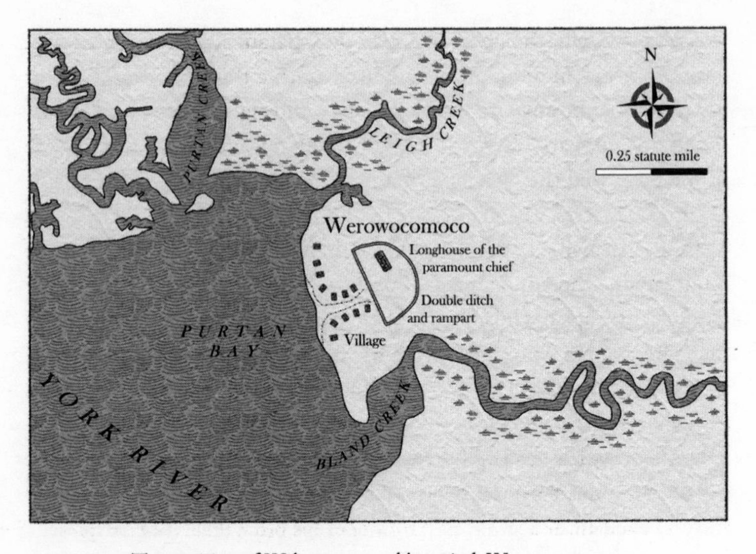

The position of Wahunsenacawh's capital, Werowocomoco, based on initial archaeological discoveries and historical references. The chief's longhouse was situated in a D-shaped area surrounded by a double-ditch to give protection. The town was surround on three sides by water and marsh.

As he was led to the building, Smith carefully marked the distance from the river to the longhouse – thirty score paces. It was always useful to know how far to run if you ever needed to escape. He ducked under the doorway and gave his eyes time to adjust to the dim light. Slowly, he realized his arrival had been expected:

> Here more then two hundred of those grim Courtiers stood wondering at him, as if he had beene a monster; till Powhatan and his trayne had put themselves in their greatest braveries [finest clothing]. Before a fire upon a seat like a bedsted, he sat covered with a great robe, made of Rarowcun [raccoon] skinnes, and all the tayles hanging by. On either hand did sit a young wench of 16 or 18 yeares, and along on each side of the house, two rowes of men, and behind them as many women, with all their heads and shoulders painted red.[1]

Wahunsenacawh, the chief of all the Powhatan, struck an impressive figure. He was an old man, grey-haired, with a thinning beard. Smith judged him to be anywhere between sixty and eighty years old. Despite his advancing years, he was powerfully built, tall and obviously still very fit; he possessed the physique of a much younger man. On either side of him sat priests, various *weroances* and other advisers. In many ways, Wahunsenacawh's assembly was not that different from the court of King James, who surrounded himself with the members of the Privy Council, bishops of the Church of England, and an assembly of pretty men and woman who might serve the monarch in some way. As in any king's court, the people of Werowocomoco stood in awe of their leader:

> It is strange to see with what great feare and adoration, all these people doe obey this Powhatan. For at his feet they present whatsoever he commandeth, and at the least frowne of his brow, their greatest spirits will tremble with feare: and no marvell, for he is very terrible and tyrannous in punishing such as offend him. For example, he caused certaine malefactors to be bound hand and foot, then having of many fires gathered great store of burning coales, they rake these coales round in the forme of a cockpit, and in the midst they cast the offenders to broyle to death. Sometimes he causeth the heads of them that offend him, to be laid upon the altar or sacrificing stone, and one with clubbes beats out their braines.[2]

A woman came forward from the shadows and offered Smith water to wash his hands. She was Opossunoquonuske, the wife of the *weroance* of the Appamattoc tribe. Another woman brought him feathers to dry his hands. Still more brought him food. They "feasted him after their best barbarous manner", in Smith's estimation.

With these formalities over, Wahunsenacawh moved on to pressing business. The chief's brothers had quizzed Smith for over a week, but he wanted to hear from Smith directly. Why, asked Wahunsenacawh, had the English come to his country? Smith knew better than to divulge the plan for a permanent settlement. Machiavelli offered words of advice: "No enterprise is more likely to succeed than one concealed from the enemy until it is ripe for execution". So he lied. Smith told the paramount chief that their ships had been attacked by the Spanish, and that they did not want the fight and had retreated; bad weather had forced them into the Chesapeake Bay, where they stayed to make repairs. They now had to wait for Smith's great father, Captain Newport, to return and take them away. The story had a convincing ring to it, but more importantly Wahunsenacawh could not prove that Smith was lying.

So why, asked the chief of the Powhatan, was Smith captured so far from his camp? What was he searching for? Now Smith was evasive. He explained that he was looking for the sea to the west (true), because the people there had slain one of Newport's men (a lie that was also impossible for Wahunsenacawh to disprove). It was useful, Smith thought, to remind the Powhatan that the English were a vengeful people – for, as Machiavelli said, "It is more secure to be feared than to be loved." Smith hoped his implicit message would be obvious: if he did not return to Jamestown unscathed, then others would come seeking retribution.

Wahunsenacawh was more than a match for Smith and proved to be just as accomplished in deception. He told the Englishman that there was saltwater five or eight days beyond the falls; that the inhabitants there were man-eaters; that there were people living in the lands beyond who wore "short Coates, and Sleeves to the Elbowes, that passed that way in Shippes like ours".[3] This last claim might have referred to French explorers in what is now Canada, but the rest was meant to mislead the English, and perhaps to scare them away.

Wahunsenacawh then turned to his advisers to discuss what to do with their captive. Were these people temporary; or were they here to stay? Was Newport their *weroance* and Smith his underling; or was Smith a *weroance* and Newport a paramount chief? Were they a threat or a blessing? Smith's life would hang on their deliberations.

Elsewhere in the longhouse, the warriors fingered their war clubs. If the chief so decided, they were at hand to deliver a mercifully swift execution. If, however, Wahunsenacawh decided Smith was an English *weroance*, it was against their custom to kill him. As with a woman or child captured in war, a chief was spared, spending the rest of his days in servitude to the conquering chief.

Yet Wahunsenacawh's dilemma was not only about custom; it was also about politics and diplomacy. The confederacy had many enemies, and the English, with their firearms, gunpowder and metal weapons, could be useful allies – if not to the Powhatan, then perhaps to others.

A long consultation ensued. Smith did not elaborate on the discussion, so either he could not understand what Wahunsenacawh and his advisers were discussing, or they talked out of his earshot. Eventually, the chief declared his judgement, and, according to Smith, it was not good news.

Two large rocks were dragged before Wahunsenacawh, "then as many [warriors] as could layd hands on him, dragged him to them, and thereon laid his head, and being ready with their clubs, to beate out his braines".[4] Smith had been in tricky situations before, but he must have felt sure this was his last. Suddenly, a young girl of ten or twelve appeared. She rushed towards Smith and "got his head in her armes, and laid her owne upon his to save him from death". She challenged the executioners to take her own life instead of Smith's. The unwavering devotion of her plea moved Wahunsenacawh to spare this man. As Smith put it, "the Emperour was contented he should live".[5]

The girl was Pocahontas, Wahunsenacawh's favourite daughter. Quite why she should intervene on behalf of a man she had never met before is difficult to explain. Smith attributed her action to concern for a man in distress, "whose compassionate pitiful heart, of my desperate estate, gave me much cause to respect her".[6] Over the centuries, some writers have hinted at a romantic attraction, suggesting the girl had become infatuated with the Englishman. Yet Smith had only just arrived in Werowocomoco that day, and Pocahontas could not have seen him before now.

Pocahontas, whose name meant "mischievous one", might have been fooling around in her father's court, perhaps out of boredom. Alternatively, Wahunsenacawh could have enlisted his daughter in a charade, asking her to plead for Smith's life as a way of giving the chief a convenient excuse to overrule the hawks in his alliance that wanted Smith killed.

But regardless of the motivations behind such an action – was the story itself true? This was one of several encounters when Smith was alone with the Powhatan, and therefore none of the other witnesses were in a position to support or challenge his account in a written record. As with his exploits in Hungary and Transylvania, the only way to get close to the real truth is to test Smith's version of events against circumstantial evidence. Of all the stories surrounding Captain Smith's life, his rescue by Pocahontas is not only the most sensational, but also the most difficult to believe.

Sceptics of Smith's explanation point to one unsettling fact: Smith wrote three versions of this first meeting with Wahunsenacawh, yet only one of them – the last of the three – actually mentions Pocahontas. If she really did intervene to save his life, it was an act fundamental to his survival, and to the survival of Jamestown. So why would Smith omit her from his earlier versions?

For one, Smith was certainly vulnerable in December 1607. He was deeply disliked by some of the senior men in the colony, and many would have liked to see him fail. If he had come back from Werowocomoco with a story of how a young Powhatan girl had saved his life, he would have expected to be met with ridicule. Smith had a huge chip on his shoulder, and would not have found such mockery easy to stomach.

Another good reason for Smith to have kept quiet about the incident was Wingfield's charge of mutiny against him during the voyage from England; that "he intended to usurpe the governement, murder the Councell, and make himselfe king".[7] Had Smith been honest about a close relationship with the "emperor's" favourite daughter, it might have fuelled the old rumours about his ambitions.

Smith's first account of his meeting with the chief of the Powhatan was published in *A True Relation* in 1608. This included a detailed description of how he made his canoeing expedition up the Chickahominy River; and how he was surrounded by warriors, fell into a bog, and was captured. He explained that his two English companions were killed, but added few embellishments. He mentioned how he had impressed Opechancanough with his compass, and his impromptu lecture about the solar system (though neither had done much to affect Smith's fate). Notably, Smith made no mention of the horrible death of George Casson, which he had not witnessed.

In *A True Relation,* Smith said that when he was taken to Werowocomoco, he found Wahunsenacawh "proudly lying uppon a Bedstead a foote high upon tenne or twelve Mattes, richly hung with manie Chaynes of great Pearles about his neck".[8] Around Wahunsenacawh were lesser chiefs, sitting "tenne in a ranke, and behinde them many yong women". Smith claimed the paramount chief was friendly: "hee kindly welcomed me with good wordes, and great Platters of sundrie Victuals, assuring mee his friendship, and my libertie within foure days".[9] This was very much in keeping with the London Company line – that, despite everything, Virginia was a safe place to establish a colony, and worthy of investment. There was no mention of Smith's brush with death in the longhouse – and thus no mention of Pocahontas.

Smith's second version of these events was made public in 1612, in *The Proceedings of the English Colony in Virginia.* Smith reprised his story of the journey up the Chickahominy River, this time including the capture of George Casson (but not his death). Smith went into more detail about his own capture, and how he had taken his guide as a hostage. Again, Smith sidestepped the events of his interrogation by Wahunsenacawh, although he said he had prevented the Powhatan from making a surprise attack on Jamestown by sending a letter to the colony. The climax of the story came when he noted "that those Salvages admired him as a demi-God".[10]

Finally, in 1624, Pocahontas made her debut as Smith's saviour, in *The Generall History of Virginia, New-England, and the Summer Isles,* a comprehensive chronicle of Smith's tenure in America. For the first time, he mentioned that his life was in jeopardy and he had been rescued by the paramount chief's daughter. This was not the only new addition to his storytelling. He also revealed, for the first time, how George Casson had been brutally killed.

The sceptics argue that Smith's 1624 version magnified his role in the colony, that it was nothing but a blatant piece of self-promotion by an old man whose glory days were long gone.[11] By the time *The Generall*

Historie was published, all of those involved in the event who might have contradicted him – Wahunsenacawh and Pocahontas included – were dead. Smith came out looking like a brave man and a hero, and he was canny enough to know there was nobody left to challenge his reputation.

However, Smith had written another, private account of the Pocahontas episode in 1616. This was in a letter to Queen Anne on the occasion of Pocahontas' nine-month-long visit to England, which started in June of that year.[12] As a way of familiarizing the Queen with her new guest, the letter shared some information about Smith's experiences in Virginia, and in it he revealed that Pocahontas had saved him:

> After some six weeks fatting amongst those Salvage Courtiers, at the minute of my execution, she hazarded [risked] the beating out of her owne braines to save mine, and not onely that, but so prevailed with her father, that I was safely conducted to James towne.[13]

The letter to Queen Anne is Smith's first known attempt to commit the story of Pocahontas to paper. Unfortunately, the original is now lost. Smith included a précis of the letter in *The Generall Historie*, and some historians have said that the timing of Smith's book – not long after a Powhatan attack that had killed 347 people at Jamestown – meant Smith was inclined to provide his countrymen "with excuses to root out the 'savages' from Virginia".[14]

Yet Smith's letter did not condone treating the Powhatan as "savages". Instead he suggested to his "Most admired Queen" that she welcome "this Lady Pocahontas" as a royal peer, worthy of respect even though her present circumstances did not "make her fit to attend your Majesty". Smith's letter was essentially a briefing document for the Queen, written after hostilities with the Powhatan had become common knowledge, but before the English had decided to go to war with them. No doubt it was also an attempt to raise Smith's profile and ingratiate himself with the King's wife – and presumably with James himself.

Pocahontas met the Queen when she was in London, probably on more than one occasion. It is difficult to imagine that Smith would have lied to Queen Anne about his close shave with death, knowing that a question to Pocahontas or her English husband, John Rolfe, offered every chance to expose such a fabrication. If his account to the Queen turned out to be a lie, the consequences for Smith would have been very serious indeed.

In his varying accounts, Smith broadly told much the same story, relying on many of the same facts and following the same chronology. It is true that each of them differed in detail and emphasis, but that was because each was intended for a different audience. He had never even intended for *A True Relation*, a brief account of his first year in Virginia, to be published.

His 1612 report was even shorter, and was actually written with other former colonists, for dissemination in England at a time when Jamestown's fortunes were improving, and the London Company was looking to attract more settlers and make the place profitable. Indeed, if *The Proceedings* failed to inspire confidence and funding dried up, Smith could find himself making enemies in both London and Virginia. In those early years, nobody was entirely honest about the full extent of the conflict with the Powhatan, nor did anybody want to highlight failures or embarrassments.

The Generall Historie presented a more reflective version of the events in Wahunsenacawh's longhouse. Opechancanough had already tested Smith's bravery, and he had passed with flying colours. The Pamunkey priests had spent three days evaluating Smith's status. By the time Smith arrived in Werowocomoco, the paramount chief had probably already decided how he would deal with his prisoner.

It was not customary for the Powhatan to honour a guest with a feast and then deliberate over whether or not to kill him. For visitors who were known enemies, the feast would end with an ambush; it was a swift act with no prevarication, resulting in a quick and sudden death. Yet Wahunsenacawh could not have controlled an empire of thirty or more tribes through violence alone. He was the consummate politician, and he already had a plan for handling the colonists long before Smith arrived in his capital.

Smith also misunderstood the type of death he might expect at the hands of his captors. The Powhatan only beat out the brains of their own people, and then only those who had committed a serious crime. As

George Casson found to his cost, foreign enemies were tortured slowly and painfully to death.

It therefore seems likely Pocahontas never "saved" John Smith's life at all, because he was never at risk of being executed. This is not to say that Smith was lying. These were the early days of contact between the English and the indigenous Virginians, and neither understood the other's customs.

It is more likely that Wahunsenacawh decided he wanted the English as allies rather than enemies, and that this process of assimilation started by incorporating Smith into the Powhatan empire. The ceremony Smith experienced may have been his initiation into the tribe, during which he was ritually killed, then reborn. It was pure political theatre.

Two days after the ceremony, Smith was taken to another longhouse, this one in the woods, and left there alone, in front of a fire. A horrifying shriek brought Smith to his senses: "[Chief] Powhatan more like a devill then a man with some two hundred more as blacke as himselfe, came unto him, and told him now they were friends".[15] This was probably the final stage of Smith's induction into the tribe, granting Smith the status of a *weroance*. He was given the Algonquian name Nantaquoud, and offered a village on the York River, a couple of miles downstream from Werowocomoco. Wahunsenacawh most likely assumed he could employ his new recruit in helping to control the English "tribe". He told Smith they were friends, brothers. If he understood anything, Smith did not understand the most important thing: being a *weroance* brought with it innumerable duties and obligations towards the paramount chief.

These duties and obligations would continue to haunt him.

In early January 1608, Wahunsenacawh sent John Smith back to Jamestown with a dozen guides and a request for two small cannon and a grindstone. The chief of the Powhatan was already expecting tribute from his English *weroance*. It was not a long journey to Jamestown; once they crossed the York River, it was about a twelve-mile hike through the woods. Smith was nervous that the Powhatan guides might yet kill him, and he wanted to get to Jamestown before nightfall. His escorts insisted they spend the night in an old Paspahegh hunting lodge: "That night they quarterd in the woods, he still expecting (as he had done all this long time of his imprisonment) every houre to be put to death or other."[16]

The next morning they were up before dawn, arriving at Jamestown soon after sunrise. The sentry at the fort was astonished when Smith, accompanied by a group of Powhatan warriors, appeared as if an apparition from the leafless forest. The colonists had all but given up their cape merchant for lost.

Smith's immediate task was to answer Wahunsenacawh's request for cannon without raising any suspicions that he was not in fact a close ally. Rather than giving the Powhatan a gun they could carry, he offered them a pair of demi-culverins – medium-sized cannon about eleven feet long – each weighing a ton and a half. As he dryly commented: "they found them somewhat heavie."[17]

To demonstrate the guns' effectiveness, he primed a cannon, loaded it with stones, and fired it at the trees. Branches and icicles shattered on impact, terrifying the warriors, who, he guessed, had never heard anything louder than thunder. Once the Powhatan had regained their composure, they realized they could not carry the cannon back to Werowocomoco. In compensation, Smith "gave them such toyes, and sent to Powhatan, his women, and children such presents, as gave them in general full content".[18] Smith might have considered them contented, the Powhatan warriors much less so.

In Smith's absence, Ratcliffe had appointed John Archer to the colony's governing council. John Martin had protested that this was in direct contravention of the London Company's instructions, and against the agreement forged between Ratcliffe, Martin and Smith. However, Ratcliffe, as president, overruled him – in Smith's absence, it was Ratcliffe's two votes against Martin's sole one. Once the winter had arrived with a vengeance, Archer had declared he was ready to go home. Several other gentlemen had cheered him on. Smith had returned right in the middle of the squabbling. After the Powhatan left with Smith's trinkets, he found "some ten or twelve of them, who were called the better sort" prepared to commandeer the *Discovery* for a return to England.[19]

Smith ordered muskets and cannon to be trained on the ship and gave an ultimatum that if anyone cast off, he would instruct the men to fire. Smith won the day, but few friends, and if he thought his welcome at Jamestown was to persist, he was mistaken. Ratcliffe and Archer knew Smith was the main obstacle to their leaving the settlement. Both men were lawyers, and both now detested the jumped-up Lincolnshire farmer. Smith must have known he was in a weak position, as there was no doubt Ratcliffe and Archer could outvote him and Martin.

That same day, the two demoralized councillors mounted their challenge. Archer held Smith responsible for the death of Jehu Robinson, and the presumed death of Thomas Emry, arguing the men had been in Smith's care when they were ambushed by the Pamunkey. It was a damning case, all the more so since only four men were allowed to vote on the verdict. The next morning they announced their judgement: Smith was to be taken out and hanged. After that, the whole of the colony could board the *Discovery* and sail for home.

For the second time in nine months, John Smith faced the prospect of feeling the hangman's noose tighten around his neck.

Smith had been thrown overboard in France, risked his life in battle at sea, faced three Hajdúk knights in single combat to the death, bowed before the hands of a sadist on the Russian steppe, and, just days before, had received a last-minute reprieve from the battering of warriors' clubs against his skull. Each of these trials were plausible in their own right, but we only have Smith's written testimony that they actually happened. For any one person to experience so many heart-stopping dramas in one life is difficult to imagine, and this is one of the main reasons so many historians have doubted Smith's veracity. Yet on this occasion, there was another report of Smith's escape from the gallows, and it came from none other than Smith's archenemy, the colony's deposed and incarcerated president, Edward Maria Wingfield.

As Smith sat that evening pondering the few hours he had left on this earth, a remarkable coincidence saved his life: two months late, Captain

Newport sailed up the James River on his relief ship, the *John and Francis*. Wingfield wrote about the moment in his usual, sanctimonious style:

> hee had hadd his tryall the same daie of his retorne, and I believe his hanging [was to have been] the same, or the next daie, so speedie is our lawe thear, but it pleased god to send Captayn Newport unto us the same eevening, to our unspeakable comfortes; whose arryval saved Master Smyths leif, and myne, because hee tooke me out of the Pynnasse, an[d] gave me leave to lye in the Towne.[20]

Wingfield's account of the miraculous amnesty was confirmed by Smith's own version:

> great blame and imputation was laide upon mee by them for the losse of our men which the Indians slew, insomuch that they purposed to depose me; but in the midst of my miseries, it pleased God to send Captaine Nuport, who arriving there the same night, so tripled our joy, as for a while these plots against me were deferred, though with much malice against me, which captain Newport in short time did plainly see.[21]

In the colony, Smith had frequently been accused of arrogance and self-importance (a charge he would also receive at the hand of later interpreters). Yet here, when he could justifiably be indignant and self-righteous, he portrayed himself as a quite modest fellow – a bit smug perhaps, but restrained and grateful to the heavens for his deliverance.

On his return to Virginia on January 2, 1608, Newport found Jamestown in chaos, and he took immediate control. Archer was removed from the council and returned to his position as recorder; a new arrival called Matthew Scrivener replaced him as councillor. Wingfield was released from confinement on board the *Discovery*, though he was not re-enstated to the council, let alone the presidency. Smith was freed and resumed his seat on the council, too. Had Newport been delayed just a few hours more, Smith's fate would have been sealed. Or if Wahunsenacawh had released Smith a day earlier, or if the Powhatan warriors had not stopped the night en route to

Jamestown, then Newport would have been standing over Smith's freshly covered grave.

The *John and Francis* had arrived carrying about eighty new colonists, including some from Germany and Poland, together with fresh supplies. The new arrivals were essential to Jamestown's survival, for by January 1608, only 40 of the original 104 settlers were still alive.

The newcomers stayed on board for a few days until suitable accomodation could be provided in the fort, but, as it turned out, it would have been safer for them to have remained on the ship for longer. On January 7, one of the new recruits accidently set fire to his lodgings. One Francis Perkins, also newly arrived, wrote back to a friend in London that:

> there was a fire that spread so that all the houses in the fort were burned down, including the storehouse for munition and supplies, leaving three [unburned]. Everything my son and I had was burned, except a mattress which had not yet been taken off the ship.[22]

It was yet another major setback for the colony. Fortunately, Wahunsenacawh sent regular provisions of venison, raccoon and bread, which helped the men to survive despite losing some of Newport's first supply.

As president, Ratcliffe tried to curry favour with the Powhatan, and rewarded them generously for these gifts of food. He hoped this might prove his own "greatness and authority" to them. From his excursions as cape merchant, Smith had gained a clear grasp of how best to deal with the locals. He worried that Ratcliffe and the other colonists were being overly generous, and inflating the prices they could receive with barter:

> We gave them libertie to trucke or trade at their pleasures. But in a short time it followed, that could not be had for a pound of Copper, which before was sould us for an ounce: thus ambition, and sufferance, cut the throat of our trade, but confirmed their opinion of the greatnesse of Captaine Newport.[23]

That winter in Virginia was bitter, for the expedition occurred during what scientists call the "Little Ice Age", which lasted from around 1300 to 1750. During this period, worldwide temperatures cooled, leading to extreme weather conditions: wet springs with flooding, hot summers and long droughts, and, most especially, sub-zero winters. The storm that had delayed the Virginia fleet from leaving England the previous winter was probably part of this same pattern, and back in London the Thames had frozen, producing the first recorded "Frost Fair", or winter festival, held on the solid river. The Little Ice Age was a global phenomenon, and the winters on the eastern seaboard of America would have been markedly colder than they are today.

With no shelter, and short of food and supplies, the colonists once again found themselves in distress. Hunger, sickness and the bitter cold brought still more deaths to Jamestown. The James River also froze in the harsh conditions, as newcomer Francis Perkins recalled:

> The cold was so intense that one night the river at our fort froze almost all the way across, although at that point it is as wide again as the one in London. The ice in the river froze some fish which, when we took them out after the ice was melted, were very good, and so plump that they could be fried in their own fat, without anything added.[24]

Newport told his sailors and the able-bodied settlers to erect crude shelters to give them some protection from the extreme elements. Somehow, they even mustered the energy and will to rebuild the burnt-out church. While the men worked, Smith de-briefed Newport on his newfound knowledge of the Powhatan and the region.

Newport's paymasters in London, the venture capitalists of the day, had given him express orders to find gold. This was the one guarenteed way of getting that sought-after quick return on their investment. Newport was therefore particularly interested in Smith's new friendship with Wahunsenacawh, for if anybody knew where gold might be found, it was the paramount chief of the Powhatan.

Smith must have been delighted that the Powhatan had begun to build bridges with the colonists while Newport was away. Half the food the Powhatan brought to the colony each week was specified for Smith; the rest for "his father", Captain Newport. These supplies from Werowocomoco were often accompanied by a young, impish girl – Wahunsenacawh's daughter, Pocahontas. The two gestures seemed intended to reinforce the message that Smith was a man of high standing in Wahunsenacawh's eyes, somebody to be trusted.

From the spring of 1608, Pocahontas became a frequent visitor to Jamestown, and from Smith's later writings, it was evident he enjoyed these visits. But what sort of friendship could develop between a young Powhatan girl and a grizzled twenty-eight-year-old Englishman? Did Pocahontas come to the colony simply out of curiosity? Or was she there to report back to her father about activities in the colony, independently of his warriors, who might have had their own agendas in mind?

Wahunsenacawh had scores of wives from different tribes, and several hundred children with them. Such "royal" marriages and offspring served an important political purpose: binding the many tribes to the paramount chief through kinship.

There is no written record of Pocahontas' mother's life, but Mattaponi oral history claimed she was Wahunsenacawh's first wife, and the marriage was one of love, not alliance.[25] The Mattaponi maintain his young wife was also called Pocahontas, and had several children by Wahunsenacawh, including Parahunt, who became the *weroance* of the Powhatan tribe, and Pochins, chief of the Kecoughtan. It is impossible to verify this oral history, but according to the Mattaponi, Pocahontas' mother died during labour, and her baby girl was originally bestowed with the name Matoaka, which translates as "flower between two streams"; the site of her birth, probably around 1595, was claimed to be on the southern bank of the Mattaponi River (close to where US Route 360 crosses the tributary). Only later was the baby given the name Pocahontas. Immediately after her birth, oral tradition maintains, Pocahontas was taken to her mother's village, where relatives cared for her. She was later sent to Werowocomoco, where she lived with an older (half) sister, Matachanna. Pocahontas spent most of her time with the other women and girls in Werowocomoco, for the daily lives of men and women were kept mostly separate.

According to Smith, the Powhatan lived in extended families of relatives and step-relatives, usually between six and twenty to a house. So Pocahontas' upbringing was no different from that of any other young girl among her people. Like all Powhatan girls up to the age of puberty, her head was shaved, bar a lock at the back, and she walked around naked, except for shell jewellery and mulberry-red face dye. From an early age, she was accustomed to making her way through the forests, and she learned how to paddle a canoe, skin a deer and tan the hide to make clothing. She collected firewood, fashioned pots from clay, helped to build houses and other buildings, and looked after younger children in the household. Even the daughter of a paramount chief was expected to work hard from first light to dusk.

Her status was due partly to the matrilineal succession the Powhatan peoples adopted. In this system, the chief's immediate heirs were his brothers in order of age, then his sisters in order of age, then his eldest sister's progeny – first the sons and then the daughters. This meant that Pocahontas had no claim to the leadership of the Powhatan. When her father died, Pocahontas would slip down the hierarchy, becoming first the niece, and then the cousin, of the reigning chiefs. Nevertheless, the

Native peoples of Virginia meeting over foodstuffs and tools,
from an engraving by Theodor de Bry, *America* (1590).

English considered Pocahontas a "princess". And in some sense this was true – as a favoured daughter, she was close to the current seat of power.

Wahunsenacawh had secured immense power through his control of the tribes in his empire – power that made him wealthy from the tributes brought by his *weroances*. Every day, canoes ran up on the beach carrying meat, corn, hides, pottery and native copper from throughout the alliance, thus sustaining the chief's power base. When she came to live in the capital, Pocahontas would have been astonished by her crowded and busy new home, for her father was surrounded by wives, priests, councillors, body guards, siblings and half-siblings. Yet, among this ménage, the little girl somehow caught her father's eye.

On the late December day when John Smith was brought to Werowocomoco, the town was full of the news of the pale stranger who had a magic dial in his pocket and carried sticks that could kill a man with their explosion. Whether Pocahontas was officially allowed inside Wahunsenacawh's longhouse to witness Smith's inquisition is impossible to know. There were many people in the chief's retinue whose presence would have been expected, though not a young girl's. Yet would anyone have stopped the chief's favourite squirming her way to the front of the assembly for the best view of this unusual encounter?

Smith's entrance into her dominion offered a unique opportunity for Pocahontas to play a dramatic, central role in early American history. As a seemingly harmless young girl, she was uniquely placed to be a spy on behalf of her doting father. Unknowingly, she was also about to adopt the role of mediator, helping to preserve a tenuous peace between her own people and the foreigners.

In February, Wahunsenacawh sent word that he wanted to meet Captain Newport. The Englishmen took no risks, and when they sailed up the York River to Werowocomoco, they took both the *Discovery* and the shallop, which together could transport thirty or forty heavily armed men.

Smith was concerned that Wahunsenacawh might be trying to lure them into a trap, so he went ashore first to see the chief, accompanied by half the men. Smith's troupe waited as he was granted admittance to the great longhouse. Inside, the paramount chief greeted his new friend warmly. The chief was surrounded by about forty of his wives and countless bodyguards and advisers. Smith was impressed, and perhaps a little envious:

> This proude salvage, having his finest women, and the principall of his chiefe men assembled, sate in rankes as before is expressed, himselfe as upon a Throne at the upper ende of the house, with such a Majestie as I cannot expresse, nor yet have often seene, either in pagan or Christian.[26]

Smith presented Wahunsenacawh with gifts from his "father", Captain Newport: a suit of red cloth, a hat, and, most bizarrely, a greyhound dog. The chief's welcome continued to appear genuine, and so when he asked the whereabouts of Newport, Smith explained that he had stayed on board the pinnace, but would come the next day. Wahunsenacawh then asked about the guns he had been promised, again alluding to the tributes he expected. Smith replied that he had offered his messengers the guns, as agreed, "but they refused to take them; whereat with a lowed laughter, he desired [me] to give him some of lesse burthen, as for the other I gave him them, being sure that none could carrie them".[27] Wahunsenacawh fully understood the game Smith was playing.

The chief then invited Smith's armed guard to come in from outside. Always the soldier, Smith was wary; he knew they would be vulnerable to ambush inside the longhouse. He ordered his men to enter just two at a time. Each was presented with four or five pounds of bread, an act of greeting. Wahunsenacawh then said he expected these men to lay down their weapons when they entered his house, "as did his subjects". Smith quickly rebutted "that was a ceremonie our enemies desired, but never our friends".[28]

The two men continued to play their cat-and-mouse game, each testing the declared friendship of the other. But Smith was worried that if he did not make a gesture of solidarity to match the offering of bread, the day's meeting would end on a sour note, risking everything. He wanted Captain Newport to meet Wahunsenacawh in a convivial mood.

So Smith told the chief that when he deemed it convenient, they would attack the enemies of the Powhatan and "deliver [them] under his subjection". These adversaries were the Susquehannock in the north and the Monacan to the west. Wahunsenacawh was delighted, and "with a loud oration", he proclaimed Smith to be a *weroance*, and that the Englishmen could have free rein to his corn, his women and his country. Smith could not be more pleased. He had paved the way for a successful summit between Wahunsenacawh and Newport.

The next morning, Smith went down to the beach at Werowocomoco to meet Newport and the other colonists. It was to be a grand occasion, and Newport's party walked up through the town preceded by a trumpeter. The paramount chief welcomed his visitors and served them a breakfast. The men then sat down to discuss their collaboration, with Smith as interpreter. Newport presented a young lad of thirteen, who he said would come to live with the Powhatan and learn their language. In what might be a rare display of humour by the colonists, the chosen boy was called Thomas Savage. Wahunsenacawh reciprocated by offering Newport one of his own boys, whose name was Namontack.

With the formalities of the human exchange over, Wahunsenacawh continued to probe the Englishmen's intentions. Why had their party come to his house carrying weapons? Smith translated for Newport, but answered Wahunsenacawh directly, saying it was merely their custom. Newport, however, overruled Smith, and sent his men back to the beach to display his openness and civility. Smith felt humiliated, but, for now, he kept his feelings to himself.

The two leaders then moved on to discuss trading. Smith recalled that Wahunsenacawh took the initiative during this portion of their talks: "hee desired to see all our Hatchets and Copper together, for which he would give us corne; with that auncient tricke the Chickahomaniens had oft acquainted me."[29] Smith recognized this as the scam it was, but it was new to Newport, and Wahunsenacawh outmanoeuvred the senior captain. Instead of bartering laboriously, one piece at a time, as Smith knew must be done, Newport agreed to Wahunsenacawh's request for a bulk trade. The consequences were disastrous: instead of getting twenty hogsheads of corn from the deal (which Smith had hoped for), they came away with just four bushels, about one seventieth of what they were expecting.

Smith was furious but remained calm, toying with some blue beads in his hands. Wahunsenacawh noticed, and asked about them. Smith shrugged him off, saying they were "composed of a most rare substance of the coulour of the skyes, and not to be worne but by the greatest kings in the world".[30] The ruse had the desired effect, and made Wahunsenacawh "halfe madde to be the owner". A deal was struck, and Smith said the chief parted with two or three hundred bushels of corn in return for a handful of the beads.

Newport had not excelled in the art of bartering, but that was not his priority. He had backed himself into a corner with his paymasters in London by promising them quick profits. The very day he had landed in England in July 1607, he had written hastily to Lord Salisbury, one of the leading directors of the London Company: "The Contrie is excellent and verie Riche in gold and Copper."[31] Nothing was further from the truth, though Newport did not know that yet. The London Company made four tests on Newport's alleged gold samples, and all came out negative. Newport had loaded his hold with fools' gold, and he was now in a difficult position. Instead of acknowledging that he had made a mistake, Newport compounded his problem: he declared that he had accidently brought the wrong samples back with him. Now, he found himself back in Virginia, his reputation resting upon his ability to provide genuine gold.

Based on Newport's statements, the London Company's investors were expecting a bonanza. When the captain returned to Virginia, the company's leaders had sent two gold refiners with him, to purify the gold that he claimed to have found, as well as two goldsmiths, to create jewellery and other gold pieces on the spot. Both Ratcliffe and Martin shared Newport's confidence that gold *would* be found, and the colonists were ordered to spend valuable time swilling buckets of muddy water on the banks of the James, looking for the gleam from the tiny flakes of good fortune.

Smith was more pragmatic about their chances. He reasoned that if gold was to be found locally, the locals would already be mining it. He already knew the Powhatan did not have a local source of copper; the copper they did have was traded from a long way north. The American copper was also much inferior to that brought over by the settlers. Nevertheless, Smith was confident the region could provide a viable financial return for the company's shareholders – from more commonplace resources, such as fish and timber.

Once again Smith found himself at odds with the consensus, and he was exasperated. John Martin's manservant, Anas Todkill, overheard Smith and his master arguing:

> [Captain Smith] was not inamoured with their durty skill, breathing out these and many other passions, never any thing did more torment him, then to see all necessary busines neglected, to fraught such a drunken ship with so much gilded durt.[32]

Smith was not alone, however. Many of the other colonists shared his irritation. They were wasting their time on this fruitless search:

> But the worst was our guilded refiners with their golden promises made all men their slaves in hope of recompences; there was no talke, no hope, no worke, but dig gold, wash gold, refine gold, loade gold, such a bruit of gold, that one mad fellow desired to be buried in the sands least they should by there art make gold of his bones.[33]

During the early spring of 1608, while the colonists grew increasingly frustrated over the quest for gold, Pocahontas began to visit the fort regularly. Wahunsenacawh's daughter was naturally curious, and she was interested in these strange men from over the seas. Smith was keen to improve his Algonquian, and also wanted to keep his communications with Wahunsenacawh open, so the friendship suited them both.

Pocahontas often came to Jamestown carrying messages from her father and food for the men. Smith wrote: "for feature, countenance, and proportion, [she] much exceedeth any of the rest of his people, but for wit, and spirit, the only Nonpariel of his Country".[34] Her high spirits were a breath of fresh air in a settlement devoid of any female company, and soon the young English boys were copying her naked cartwheels through the fort's square.

As Captain Smith knew well, the journey from Werowocomoco to Jamestown involved crossing the York by canoe, and a day's hike through the wilderness. As a young girl, it was not something she would ever do unaccompanied. It is therefore reasonable to assume Wahunsenacawh was kept fully informed of his daughter's visits, by Pocahontas as well as the men who accompanied her.

On Sunday, April 10, 1608, Captain Newport finished loading the *John and Francis* with mined ore, not the planks of timber Smith wanted to send back to England. Newport also planned to take the young Powhatan boy Namontack with him. Wahunsenacawh knew Newport was about to depart, and he sent a leaving present of twenty turkeys, asking for twenty swords in return. He was aware this English captain was eager to please, and he was not disappointed. The chief of the Powhatan got his weapons.

Smith was not happy with the deal, but he was more focused on his relief at seeing the captain's ship disappear downriver. Of course, he was indebted to Newport for saving him from the noose, but the two men had clashed over the importance of searching for gold, and Smith was ready for Newport and his naïve bartering skills to be gone.

A mere ten days after Newport left for England, the alarm sounded at Jamestown. At the time, many of the men, including Smith, were out in the forest, cutting trees. They dropped their tools and picked up their weapons, expecting an attack. It turned out to be a signal that a ship had appeared around the bend in the river, and was approaching the fort. It was the *Phoenix*, a second supply ship that had left London at the same time as Newport, but which had gone missing, presumed lost. The *Phoenix* and her captain, Francis Nelson, brought more provisions and more settlers, a much-needed injection that so delighted Smith that he declared that:

> his so unexpected comming, did so ravish us with exceeding joy, that now we thought our selves as well fitted, as our harts could wish, both with a competent number of men, as also for all other needfull provisions, till a further supply should come unto us.[35]

However, the arrival of Captain Nelson and the *Phoenix* provoked yet another dispute between Smith and his fellow councillors. Ratcliffe and Martin were still preoccupied with finding gold and wanted to fill the *Phoenix* with more "gilded durt" for her return. In his capacity as president, Ratcliffe decided Smith should continue to reconnoitre further up the James River. Ratcliffe knew Smith was as keen as ever to explore, and this project would get the farmer's son out of his hair for several weeks at least.

Smith did not want to repeat the fiasco of his previous excursion up the Chickahominy River, so he spent a week putting about sixty-five volunteers through intensive training. He also appointed Matthew Scrivener to be his deputy on the scouting trip. Scrivener, who had arrived on Newport's supply ship and had been named a councillor, was the son of a Suffolk lawyer, and was the same age as Smith. He lacked leadership experience, but Smith found him dependable and practical, and he could help enforce discipline as they made their way into the interior.

Once Smith felt assured he had drilled his men into a disciplined force, he was ready to venture up the James, but he ran into an unexpected last-minute hitch: part of his volunteer force was recruited from the crew of the *Phoenix*, and Captain Nelson was impatient to leave for England. Nelson now demanded that if he was not allowed to sail, then the London Company must cover the cost of the ship's waiting time, plus the sailors' wages. It was an unrealistic claim, and Smith's expedition was aborted – much to Ratcliffe's embarrassment.

Worse, after Newport's departure, relations with the Powhatan began to deteriorate. Wahunsenacawh had been delighted with his "turkeys for swords" exchange, and he wanted to extract the same terms on a regular basis. He sent young Thomas Savage to the fort with a request for a similar deal, but Smith refused him. He saw no reason why he should arm his potential enemies for a few wildfowl. Smith packed Thomas back to Werowocomoco with a handful of gifts and a message for the chief that there was no deal.

Wahunsenacawh was not pleased by this show of defiance from his English *weroance*. The chief despatched some small groups of warriors to Jamestown to pilfer what they could not barter. The Powhatan made off with spades and other tools before the colonists realized what was happening. Inevitably several thieves were caught in the act. With the council's permission, Smith locked one of the offenders in the stocks as an example, while the others were sent packing.

Tensions with the Powhatan continued into May 1608. One afternoon the colonists detained a dozen more warriors, locking them up also for trying to steal from the fort. When Wahunsenacawh saw his men were not going to return, he sent envoys to Jamestown, asking for them to be released. Each time Smith replied with an uncompromising demand that all the stolen weapons and tools be returned, or the warriors would hang.

It was an unreasonable threat for Smith to make, with no justification under English law, and the situation rapidly escalated. Wahunsenacawh reported that he had taken two colonists hostage in response, and these men would be returned unharmed in exchange for the warriors.

Despite the risk to life involved, Smith remained resolute. With the approval of the council, he took an armed party upriver in the shallop, burning Powhatan villages and destroying canoes as they went, "that they might but know, what we durst to doe".[36] No locals were killed, but it was a swift and brutal assault on their property, and it had the desired effect. The two English prisoners were returned the next day, with no mention of the Powhatan detainees at Jamestown. Smith had stared down Wahunsenacawh, and Smith had won.

With the worst of the tensions between the Powhatan and the colonists now passed, Ratcliffe decided to release one of the warriors. The others would remain in custody, for he wanted to gain more intelligence from them. Smith was charged with interrogating them, as the colonist most familiar with the Algonquian language: "The Counsell concluded that I should terrifie them with some torture, to know if I could know their intent."[37] Smith tied one warrior to the main mast of the ship, and lined six colonists in front of him, their loaded muskets aimed at the terrified man. The man claimed he could not answer their questions, but said another prisoner called Macanoe, one of Wahunsenacawh's counsellors, knew more.

Under pressure, Macanoe quickly started talking. He explained that six tribes had been on a hunting expedition when they captured Smith and killed his men on the Chickahominy River back in December. Now the Paspahegh and the Chickahominy were planning a joint offensive on Jamestown, to steal more tools and weapons. He also confessed that Wahunsenacawh was planning an attack once Newport returned from England with the young Powhatan, Namontack. The chief intended to invite Newport, Smith and others to Werowocomoco, where they would be ambushed.

As if to confirm Smith's growing suspicions, around this time, Thomas Savage, who had been living with the Powhatan since January, was sent back to Jamestown with his chest and clothes. Thomas confirmed that Wahunsenacawh was having frequent secret meetings with his advisers, and that he detected unease in the longhouse in Werowocomoco. The chief said he was happy to have a replacement for the English lad – presumably somebody whose Algonquian was not as good as Thomas', and who would be less effective as a spy.

Intelligence and evidence was mounting against the Powhatan's "friendly intentions". The leaders of the colony had to decide how to handle the crisis. John Martin took up Newport's case for appeasement, saying that despite recent events, Wahunsenacawh should continue to be treated as a friend. Smith felt he needed more information to determine the best course of action. Without the backing of the council, he and Matthew Scrivener applied more psychological torture on their prisoners. The Englishmen separated the detainees, then fired shots into the air out of their sight, leaving the men to believe their companions had been executed. One by one, each of the Powhatan was given a chance to save his life by talking, and that they:

> all confirmed, that [the] Paspahegh, and Chickahammania did hate us, and intended some mischiefe, and who they were that tooke me, the names of them that stole our tooles, and swords, and that Powhatan received them, they all agreed.[38]

Smith now had confirmation that the Paspahegh and Chickahominy were the settlers' sworn enemies, and that Wahunsenacawh too was implicated in plotting against them. It was essential the rest of the council understand the dangerous position they were in. The tribes living nearest to Jamestown resented the presence of the strangers in their territory deeply, and were determined to do anything to get rid of them.

But Smith was wrong about one aspect of their perilous predicament. Wahunsenacawh took a slightly different position to the local tribes. From the broader perspective of the whole Powhatan empire, the paramount chief could see advantages in having the Englishmen as allies. He was probably facing stiff opposition to his own policy of appeasement, and he, more so than any of the Englishmen, could ill afford to be seen as a weak leader. To calm the situation, Wahunsenacawh desperately needed to get his warriors back from Jamestown.

Wahunsenacawh then played a masterstroke. He sent a delegation to Jamestown with a gift of venison and bread. His most trusted emissary, a man called Rawhunt, who was "of a subtill wit and crafty understanding", led the mission.[39] Rawhunt had full authority from Wahunsenacawh to negotiate with the Englishmen over the release of the warriors. And along with the fully armed Powhatan delegation came Pocahontas, who had obviously been sent with Wahunsenacawh's full approval.

It was a gamble by the chief – a show of diplomatic brinkmanship. Although Rawhunt did the talking, the presence of Pocahontas was an unspoken reminder to Smith of Wahunsenacawh's trust in him. The stratagem worked and the captives were freed. But Smith too could communicate in unspoken gestures, and the warriors were released not to Rawhunt, but to Pocahontas.

When Rawhunt's party left, Ratcliffe and Martin rounded on Smith, furious at his cruelty towards the prisoners. In the face of this antagonism, Smith retained the support of Scrivener and Anas Todkill, John Martin's manservant, who wrote that the council "would gladly have wrangled with Captaine Smith for his crueltie, yet none was slaine to any mans knowledge, but it brought them in such feare and obedience".[40]

Smith had certainly been ruthless towards the Powhatan, but, for the moment at least, they were no longer a threat.

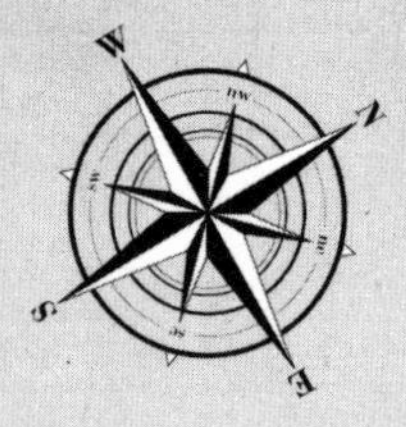

The map smuggled out of England by Spanish ambassador Pedro de Zúñiga. The map points up approximately west–northwest (courtesy of *Archivo General de Simancas*).

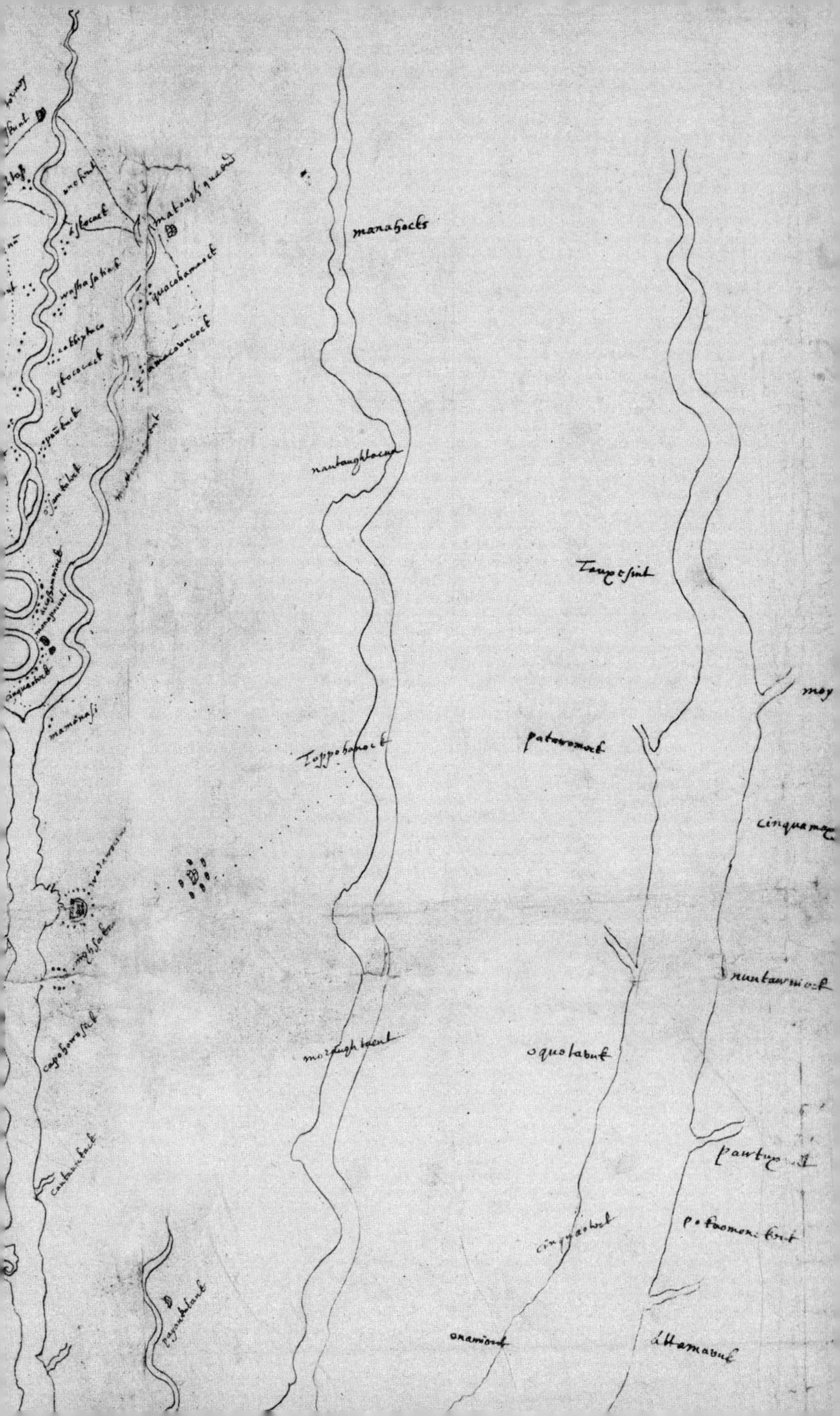

On June 2, 1608, the *Phoenix* cast off from her anchorage and drifted down the James River. Finally, Smith had won his case, and the vessel's hold was filled with cedar wood, not worthless ore. As the ship rounded up off Cape Henry, Smith, who followed the *Phoenix* this far in the shallop, handed over a package to Captain Nelson. It contained a sketch map of the region and a report covering more than forty tightly written pages. On board the ship was a single passenger, the ailing John Martin, whose poor health had been a constant problem. This released Anas Todkill for other duties, and he soon became one of Smith's most loyal acolytes.

Meanwhile, Newport had arrived in London, and his young Powhatan charge, Namontack, was paraded at the court of King James and myriad social functions in a transparent attempt to drum up publicity and investment for the Virginia venture. In a flagrant breach of royal protocol, he was presented as a "native prince" to enhance his public appeal. The wealthy investors in London might have been hoodwinked, but the Spanish ambassador, Pedro de Zúñiga, was not fooled so easily. He wrote to Philip III: "This Newport brought a lad who they say is the son of an emperor… [but] I hold it for surer that he must be a very ordinary person."[41]

The ever-resourceful Pedro de Zúñiga had well-placed spies in London. The original of Smith's map of the region north of the James River has not survived, but a copy of the map, obtained by the ambassador and passed on to his king, does. This chart has since become known as the Zúñiga Map. It remained hidden in the royal archives in Simancas, Spain, until the late nineteenth century.

On Smith's map, the most northerly river is the Patawomeck (Potomac), which Smith did not visit until the summer of 1608, so his outline of the waterway must have been conjecture. Next is the Rappahannock, which Smith visited briefly when he was held captive in December 1607. Below is the York River, with its two tributaries flowing into it from the left – the Mattaponi River to the north and the meandering Pamunkey River to the south. On the York's north shore, Werowocomoco is marked clearly. The most southerly river is the James (its local name was the Powhatan), with the Chickahominy tributary joining it from the north. Identified by a triangle with three circular bastions at each corner is Jamestown. These bastions feature in all three known descriptions of the early fort. The traditional "Indian Trail" from the peninsula to Werowocomoco is shown as a dashed line.

The package Smith sent back with Captain Nelson also contained Smith's forty-page report of everything that had happened to the colonists since they left London eighteen months previously. Nobody knows who the intended recipient was, but it was possibly Smith's confidant and adviser, Robert Bertie. Bertie had been a great help to Smith in London, assisting with introductions to people of influence, including the directors of the London Company. He was sure to be interested in news from his friend in Virginia. Regardless, within a few weeks of the *Phoenix*'s arrival in England, Smith's journal had been passed around London society.

One of the people who eventually got his hands on the manuscript was an editor and translator called John Healey, who worked for Thomas Thorpe, the publisher of Shakespeare's sonnets. Healey published Smith's document under the snappy title: *A True Relation of Such Occurences and Accidents of Note as Hath Hapned in Virginia Since the First Planting of that Colony, which is now resident in the South part thereof, til the last returne from thence.* The editing and printing of *A True Relation* proceeded without Smith's knowledge, and Healey had removed certain passages he considered "fit to be private". Indeed, three different title pages were printed. The first was ascribed to "a Gentleman of the said Collony"; the second attributed the work incorrectly to Thomas Watson. Only the third printing correctly named Smith as the author.

A coda was also added to the last published version of the work. The postscript contradicted much of the rest of Smith's work, and was seemingly added by Healey to furnish a more upbeat ending for his customers:

> wee now remaining being in good health, all our men wel contented, free from mutinies, in love one with another, and as we hope in a continuall peace with the Indians, where we doubt not but by Gods gracious assistance.[42]

If only it were true.

"Their Manner of Fishynge in Virginia", an engraving by Theodor de Bry after a watercolour by John White, from *A Briefe and True Report of the New Found Land of Virginia* (1597).

11
President

1608–1609

Presently from each side of the river came arrowes so fast as two or three hundred could shoot them
John Smith, The Generall Historie (1624)

Of the original seven councillors in Jamestown, only Smith and Ratcliffe now remained. The president still kept his double vote, but since the aborted expedition up the James River, Ratcliffe had lost the colonists' respect, and, with that, his authority. Matthew Scrivener was now a member of the governing body, and he and Smith were generally in agreement over how to run the colony. The balance of power in Jamestown had shifted in Smith's favour.

The threat of attack by the Powhatan had diminished, so Smith decided this was a convenient time to take off and explore the Chesapeake Bay. It was agreed Scrivener would stay behind to keep Ratcliffe in check, and most especially to curb his largesse when bartering with the locals. Smith chose his crew carefully, taking carpenters, a blacksmith, fishermen and labourers. He also chose his trusted friend Anas Todkill, and Walter Russell, a "doctor of physicke" to accompany the party.

The first Chesapeake expedition lasted seven weeks, from June 2 to July 21, 1608. Smith took the shallop across the bay to the eastern shore, and worked his way north, dipping into inlets and creeks, making copious notes as he went. As the days lengthened and the waters of the bay warmed, blue crabs and grass shrimp began their summer mating rituals, and fish were drawn into the warm bay by this rich supply of food. On shore, the wild rice marshes of the upper tidal rivers began to flourish, and the fields of corn grew tall and ripened slowly. The Powhatan were able to live well in this bountiful landscape, and there was no reason the Englishmen could not do the same – or, at the very least, survive.

Conditions in the Chesapeake region in the early seventeenth century were not quite the same as they are today. Over the centuries, deforestation has led to increased rainwater runoff, which has carried soil into the river system. This has led to more silt building up and reduced visibility in the water. During John Smith's time in the area, the saltwater tide came further up the rivers, allowing oysters and other marine creatures to flourish upstream. The water was also clearer, which encouraged plants and animals to thrive at lower depths.

The first tribe Smith encountered along the eastern shore of the bay was the Accomac (so-called because they lived "on the other side"), whom he found to be friendly and hospitable. Smith discovered numerous coves and creeks that might be suitable as harbours or settlements. As he worked his way north, he left the territory of the Powhatan empire and found the locals to be more wary of strangers.

By now, Smith's men were running short of drinking water, and things were becoming urgent. "We digged and searched in many places, but before two daies were expired, we would have refused two barricoes [kegs] of gold for one of that puddle water of Wighcocomoco", Smith recalled.[1] He found a spring of fresh water, but it was too hot to drink, and he worried about its safety. Smith called the area Point Ployer, in honour of the Comte de Ploüer, who had saved his life in Brittany.

Pressing on, the expedition entered the Nanticoke River (which Smith called the Kusharawaock). He led the shallop thirty miles upstream, as far as today's Maryland–Delaware state line, about 150 miles northeast of Jamestown by water. The Nanticoke tribe spoke a language related to Algonquian, but Smith did not yet know enough Algonquian to communicate easily with them. Like others, the Nanticoke were initially wary of the strangers. However, they later came down to the shore to trade, and he found them to be "the best Marchants of all other Salvages".[2]

After replenishing their water supplies, Smith turned the shallop to return downriver to the Chesapeake Bay. The party crossed to the western shore, making landfall near what is now Calvert Cliffs State Park in Lusby, Maryland. Smith named the headland Riccards Cliftes, after his mother's family. Here, Smith said the upper Chesapeake was devoid of settlements, with only dense woodland "much frequented with Wolves, Beares, Deere and other wilds beasts".[3] Drinking water was still scarce, what bread they had left was now mouldy, and the emptiness of the haunting primeval forest gnawed at the men's morale. Somehow, Smith kept his party motivated – probably with the assurance they would soon find food elsewhere.

They continued north along the western shore for another seventy miles. (Smith recorded the distance as thirty leagues – ninety miles – but he was, by necessity, sailing an indirect course.) After exploring the wide Patapsco River nearly as far as modern Baltimore, they continued briefly up the Gunpowder River to the north. However, the weather was poor, and several of his men became ill, so they finally headed back towards Jamestown.

Smith could not resist a detour, however, and veered into the Patawomeck River (the Potomac), thinking he might find a route over the mountains to the South Seas. Smith had been told about the river by the Powhatan further south, so he knew it was part of their empire. Immediately, he realized it was the biggest of the waterways he had found flowing into the Chesapeake Bay – seven miles wide at the mouth.

When he met the local tribe, the Patawomeck, they told him the paramount chief, Wahunsenacawh, had instructed them to attack the colonists. Worse still, Smith learned, the local *weroance* was aware of the mounting discontent in Jamestown. Smith was told there were rumours "our Captaine" – meaning Smith – "did cause them to stay in their country against their wills".[4] Evidently, the Powhatan knew the colonists were disgruntled, and that they would have left long ago were it not for Smith's pig-headedness. Perhaps Wahunsenacawh thought the colony would be abandoned quickly if a major attack was launched.

Undeterred, Smith pushed on up the great river, to find a good spot to begin their trek inland. He recruited a guide called Mosco, who was unusual in that he sported a thick, black beard. The Powhatan typically had little body hair, and Mosco's appearance suggested he had some European blood, perhaps from French explorers in the north. With

Mosco guiding the shallop, they continued up the Potomac River, beyond the present location of Washington, DC, which was then a muddy mosaic of creeks and forest indistinguishable from the surrounding area.

Smith was keen to follow up a report from a local villager, who claimed to have seen "glistering metal" in the upper reaches of the river. Rounding some low rocky cliffs, they found a stream with deposits of "a tinctured, spangled skurfe, that made many bare places seeme as gilded".[5] The *weroance* in the neighbouring village told Smith they would find similar deposits downstream in a nearby creek.

Despite his scepticism about their chances of discovering gold, Smith took the search seriously. It was, after all, the top priority for the leaders of the London Company. With the help of local guides, they located a mine that the Patawomeck had excavated using rudimentary tools – nothing more than shells and stone hatchets. The scouting party loaded samples of the ore into their bags for examination later in Jamestown. Predictably, once the refiners back on the James River examined the ore, it became clear they had found nothing of any value.

There were other riches to be had along the Potomac, of course. The area was abundant in wildlife: beaver, otters, bears, martens and mink, all of which had valuable furs. The river too was full of fish:

> lying so thicke with their heads above the water, as for want of nets (our boat driving amongst them) we attempted to catch them with a frying pan: but we found it a bad instrument to catch fish with.[6]

It is possible that during the summer months, water levels in the river had become particularly low, or the water had become de-oxygenated, thus forcing the fish to the surface to gasp for air. Unfortunately, the expedition was poorly prepared for this opportunity. Smith had brought a fisherman and a fishmonger with him, but they had no fishing equipment. They had no choice but to scoop the fish up as best they could with their frying pan.

It was time to turn around and head back to Jamestown. Again, Smith could not resist a detour, and he turned the shallop into the Rappahannock River, to revisit one of the spots Opechancanough had taken him to when he was in captivity. Smith and his men misjudged the tide, and ran aground in shallow water. The men were not unduly concerned, for they were short of food and Smith passed the time spearing fish with his sword while they waited for the tide to come in. Others copied him, and within an hour, they had more fish on board than they could eat.

Smith's last thrust into the water impaled a stingray. From his description, it was probably a cownose ray, *Rhinoptera bonasus*, which moves into shallow water to feed on soft-shell clams and small oysters. The fish typically grow to be three feet across, and can weigh thirty pounds or more. As Smith lifted the dying ray into the boat, it flicked the end of its tail, which is "bearded like a saw on each side" and coated with venom. Smith's wrist was slashed an inch and a half deep. He was in agony: "no bloud nor wound was seene, but a little blew spot, but the

Stingray Point, at the mouth of the Rappahannock River,
as it appears today (photo by Peter Firstbrook).

torment was instantly so extreame, that in foure houres had so swolen his hand, arme and shoulder."[7]

By the time the tide had turned, Smith's arm and shoulder were so swollen, he was convinced he was going to die. He identified a spot on the shore where he wanted his tortured body to be buried. Doctor Russell did what he could, bathing the wound with oil, which might have given a little relief to the agony. By nightfall, Smith's pain and swelling had subsided (which is typical for a sting from a ray), and the rising tide took the men ashore. That evening they lit a fire, and Smith had the satisfaction of eating his would-be killer: "his tormenting paine was so well asswaged that he eate of the fish to his supper, which gave no lesse joy and content to us then ease to himselfe."[8]

The crew solemnly named Smith's chosen burial place Stingray Isle, better known today as Stingray Point.

The party made one more stop on their return journey, at the Kecoughtan village at the mouth of the James River. The villagers noticed Smith was wounded, and that another man had been injured – apparently, he had tripped and accidently cut himself. The shallop was also piled high with furs. The Kecoughtan assumed the Englishmen were returning from a battle, loaded with booty. Smith rarely missed an opportunity to impress the locals, and he falsely confided that they had taken the furs from the Massawomeck, a tribe related to the Iroquois and hostile to the Powhatan.[9] Smith's boast had the intended result: "This rumor went faster up the river then [than] our Barge".[10]

When they got to the fort on July 21, 1608, it was obvious the colony had taken a turn for the worse in their absence. Many of the newly arrived colonists were sick. The men were also in open revolt against President Ratcliffe, according to Smith:

> There we found the last Supply were all sicke, the rest some lame, some bruised, all unable to doe any thing but complaine of the pride and unreasonable needlesse crueltie of the silly President.[11]

Ratcliffe, the men complained to Smith, "had riotously consumed the store: and to fulfil his follies about building him an unnecessary building for his pleasure in the woods, had brought them all to that misery".[12] Not only had Ratclifee claimed a president's share of the food, as Wingfield had done, but he had also started to build himself a presidential "palace".

With Ratcliffe's star on the wane, Smith was welcomed back by many as a hero. A call went out: depose Ratcliffe and appoint Smith as president. Constitutionally, this was an awkward situation. Ratcliffe had two votes on the council, and Smith and Scrivener had but one each. Ratcliffe also had two months remaining in office. It was a stalemate. Exactly what happened next was never made clear, but rather than force the issue, Ratcliffe elected to step down.

However, Smith was still recovering from the stingray attack, and said he was in no state to have this responsibility thrust upon him. He declined to take the presidential seat. It was agreed that Scrivener should govern, with the assistance of some "honest officers", for the remaining two months of Ratcliffe's rule. This freed Smith to continue with his great love – exploration – without entirely walking away from the chance of taking command of Jamestown in the future. It also allowed him to bide his time and avoid any accusation that he had deposed the incumbent president. Perhaps Smith was at last learning some political diplomacy.

A mere three days after returning to Jamestown, Smith felt strong enough to take off again, on July 24. This time he took a party of twelve men, including Nathanael Powell, who later wrote an account of the trip. Almost as soon as they set out, bad weather forced them to take refuge with the Kecoughtan. Smith again took the opportunity to amaze the locals, this time with his superior technology, and every night he fired off rockets, "which flying in the ayre so terrified the poore Salvages, they supposed [that] nothing [was] unpossible we attempted".[13]

Once the weather improved, they moved on, sailing to the most northerly part of the bay. By now, eight of his crew were sick, leaving Smith with only five able-bodied men, barely enough to row the shallop. As they crossed a large bay towards the Tockwogh River (now the Sassafras River), they met seven or eight canoes filled with warriors – members of the fearsome Massawomeck tribe.

Smith had to think quickly. With only six men well enough to fight, they were vastly outnumbered. His solution was as inventive as the multitude of glowing tapers he used to deceive the Turks during the siege of Olumpagh. First, he hid his eight sick men under a tarpaulin and took away their hats. These he placed on sticks that he wedged along the side of the shallop, to create the appearance of a larger crew. He then ordered the shallop to pursue the canoes, rather than retreat from them. The spectre of this "crowded" sailing boat bearing down on them sent the Massawomeck scurrying to shore. Smith followed the warriors into the shallows, then beckoned amiably for them to come over. It was the type of unexpected action that would have made Machiavelli proud.

Two of the more adventurous warriors paddled over to Smith. He presented each with a bell. Soon he was surrounded by the rest of the Massawomeck, all of them eager to trade. By the end of the day, his shallop was heaped with bear meat, venison and fish, as well as what proved to be very effective shields made from woven basketwork.

They had made a valuable new ally – but there were risks involved. The next day, the Englishmen found themselves challenged by the Tockwogh, sworn enemies of the Massawomeck. The Tockwogh spied the woven shields on board, and recognized them for the handiwork of their foes. Again thinking on his feet, Smith said they were the spoils of war. The warriors were impressed. These strangers must be very brave indeed.

The Tockwogh invited Smith and his party into their palisaded village. Smith noticed they had knives and hatchets made from iron and brass, something he had never seen with the Powhatan. An interpreter explained they came from the Susquehannock tribe, who were also sworn enemies of the Massawomeck.

Smith was keen to meet this new tribe, but they lived two days beyond the furthermost point where he could take the shallop. He set off on foot with an interpreter, reaching a waterfall about ten miles upstream from the mouth of the Susquehannock River. This would be the most northerly point of his travels on this trip, and he named the feature Smith's Falls (now the site of the Conowingo Dam), for himself and his father's family.

After a few days, about sixty warriors and five *weroances* arrived carrying gifts of venison and baskets, as well as huge ceremonial tobacco pipes. The Susquehannock were an Iroquoian-speaking people, but they had remained independent of the great Iroquois nation. Now it was Smith's turn to be impressed:

> Those are the most strange people of all those Countries, both in Language and attire; for their language it may well beseeme their proportions, sounding from them, as it were a great voice in a vault, or cave, as an Echo. Their attire is the skinnes of Beares, and Woolves, some have Cassacks made of Beares heads and skinnes that a mans necke goes through the skinnes neck, and the eares of the beare fastned to his shoulders behind, the nose and teeth hanging downe his breast.[14]

The Susquehannock returned with Smith to the Tockwogh village, where he quizzed them. He asked about the geography inland and was told of "a great water beyond the mountains" – presumably the Great Lakes. He learned about other tribes to the north and west, and he must have made copious notes, because his report listed the many tribes in great detail, including their approximate numbers and the language each spoke. He also confirmed that the tribes had received their metal weapons from the French in Canada, then called Nouvelle France. Smith had failed to find a promising route to the South Sea, but he had collected a vast amount of valuable intelligence. Now he had information about powerful tribes beyond the Powhatan empire – people who might be allies should the Powhatan turn against the Englishmen.

Before he left the Tockwogh village to return to Jamestown, Smith paid a debt of gratitude to his old friends and patrons from Lincolnshire. He named one hill Peregrine's Mount, and a river nearby Willoughby's River, names which are now lost. Then he set course south for Jamestown.

As the shallop made its way through the bay, Smith decided to turn into the Rappahannock River, which he had not yet visited. Thirty miles upstream they met their old guide, the bearded Mosco, and again took on his services. Mosco warned Smith there was trouble between the two Powhatan tribes living on the opposite banks of the river. The Moraughtacund to the north had kidnapped three Rappahannock women from the south. Mosco explained that anybody coming from the north into Rappahannock territory would be attacked. Smith thought Mosco was trying to prevent him from bartering with other tribes, so he ignored the advice.

When Smith and his men approached the south shore, a dozen or more Rappahannock warriors were waiting for them. Smith had learned that one defence against attack was to insist on exchanging hostages. The dependable Anas Todkill was sent ashore in return for a Rappahannock man. Thus far, all had gone to plan. But the colonists had fallen into a trap.

As he approached the woods from the river's beach, Todkill realized a large number of warriors were hiding behind the trees. He called out a warning to Smith, but Todkill's shout also alerted the Rappahannock hostage. The man leapt out of the shallop, but was shot dead in the water by one of the Englishmen. The Rappahannock then let fly a salvo of arrows; the Englishmen replied with gunfire; Todkill was caught between the two warring sides. He threw himself face down in the sand as a barrage of arrows and shot flew overhead, praying for the best.

The Massawomeck shields proved very effective against the arrows, giving the colonists protection as they fired and reloaded their muskets. The Rappahannock had let fly over a thousand arrows, by Smith's reckoning, before they retreated into the woods and a much-relieved Todkill was rescued. Smith acknowledged that Mosco's advice had been sincere after all. The guide was rewarded with spent arrows and abandoned canoes as spoils of war.

Now that the immediate threat had passed, Smith was left to consider his men's safety. Smith fastened the woven Massawomeck shields to the sides of the shallop, transforming the boat into an armoured gun ship. The very next morning, Smith's new system was tested when the Rappahannock attacked again from the shore. The arrows had little effect. The following day, the shallop was attacked for a third time. The shields again repelled the arrows, and this time the Englishmen also managed to capture a wounded warrior. Under interrogation, the captive said his name was Amoroleck, and that he was neither Moraughtacund nor Rappahannock, but from the Hassinunga tribe. His people, he said, lived near the headwaters of the Rappahannock River and were part of the Manahoac confederacy, not the Powhatan empire.[15]

Amoroleck said he had been told the colonists "were a people come from under the world, to take their world from them".[16] Smith understood just how serious this charge was. It meant the Powhatan were now spreading word beyond their territory that the English were not welcome. Smith knew they could fight off small attacks from the Powhatan, but if all the local tribes turned against them, they would be hopelessly outnumbered.

That night, the shallop came under renewed assault from warriors on the riverbank. Smith ordered the ship be moved to the middle of the river, out of range of their arrows. The next morning he tried to speak with the attackers, and Amoroleck called out that he had been well treated by the Englishmen. Two warriors swam out and presented a bow and arrows as a sign of peace. Smith was soon bartering with the tribe.

Emboldened by this success, Smith decided to return to Rappahannock territory. He realized his party would continue to be vulnerable for as long as the two Powhatan tribes were at war. He offered both a carrot and a stick as he sued for peace. First, he threatened to destroy the houses and corn of the Rappahannock unless they made peace with both the Moraughtacund across the river and the English. Then he invited the two *weroances* to sit together and negotiate a truce. The chiefs agreed to an armistice, but there was still the outstanding issue of the three kidnapped women. Smith gave the women beads and chains as compensation for their ordeal before turning to the *weroances* to decide the women's real fortunes. The Rappahannock chief got to choose his favourite of the three, then the Moraughtacund chief got to keep his favourite of the remaining two. Mosco, now laden with reward of arrows and canoes, was given the third. It seemed the women had no say in this settlement.

With the crisis neatly negotiated and the two Powhatan tribes at peace, it was time for Smith to head back to Jamestown. Once again they were caught at night in a squall, and "in crossing the bay in a faire calme, such a suddaine gust surprised us in the night with thunder and raine, as wee were halfe imployed in freeing out of water, never thinking to escape drowning".[17] After that fright, Smith had them stop at the Kecoughtan village for some much-needed rest and food. To be honest, he was in no rush to get back to the fort and the inevitable problems he expected were awaiting him. So the next day he sailed across the mouth of the James into the tributary that marked the start of Nansemond territory.

As they came up the Nansemond River, the Englishmen disturbed some men working on their fish traps. The fishermen immediately fled at the sight of the shallop. Smith left some "divers toys" on the shore, hoping to coax them back. The gesture worked and some of the fishermen came on board the shallop to negotiate. During their bartering, they invited the Englishmen to visit their village, then made excuses to go ashore to fetch their weapons. Smith's survival instincts were fully engaged by this turn in the conversation. Sure enough, seven or eight canoes of armed warriors soon appeared: "Presently from each side of the river came arrowes so fast as two or three hundred could shoot them."[18] Smith chased after the Nansemond, ordering his men to fire their muskets from behind the safety of the basket shields. The Nansemond ran for cover in the woods, abandoning their canoes.

Smith had clearly won the upper hand. The canoes were the Powhatan peoples' most valuable asset, and the Englishmen began to destroy them systematically. Seeing this, the Nansemond promptly returned and agreed to Smith's terms: four hundred bushels of corn as tribute. The colonists took all the corn they could carry, "and so departing good friends". Smith's expedition had been a great success. He – and by extension, the London Company – had gained a precious understanding of the local geography and of the many tribes that lived in the Tidewater region. But there was a heavy price to pay for Smith's absence.

It was the evening of September 7, 1608, when the shallop reached Jamestown. Though they had seen their share of troubles on the expedition, Smith had been right: more trouble was waiting for them. Ratcliffe had been arrested and charged with mutiny, presumably because he had attempted to regain control of the colony. Scrivener had done his best, organizing the collection of the harvest, such as it was, but most of their supplies had been spoilt by a leak in the storehouse. The settlers had never done well when food was scarce, and disputes had broken out.

There was an urgent need for a strong leader with a strategic vision and the authority to enforce discipline.

The men no longer wanted either Ratliffe or Scrivener as president. There was only one man cut out for the job.

On September 10, 1608, the Jamestown council invited John Smith to become their president. "Captain Smith received the letters patents, and took upon him the place of President: which till then by no means he would accept though hee were often importuned thereunto", he recounted.[19] The "poore tenant" farmer's son from Lincolnshire now had the chance to succeed where better-educated "gentlemen" had failed.

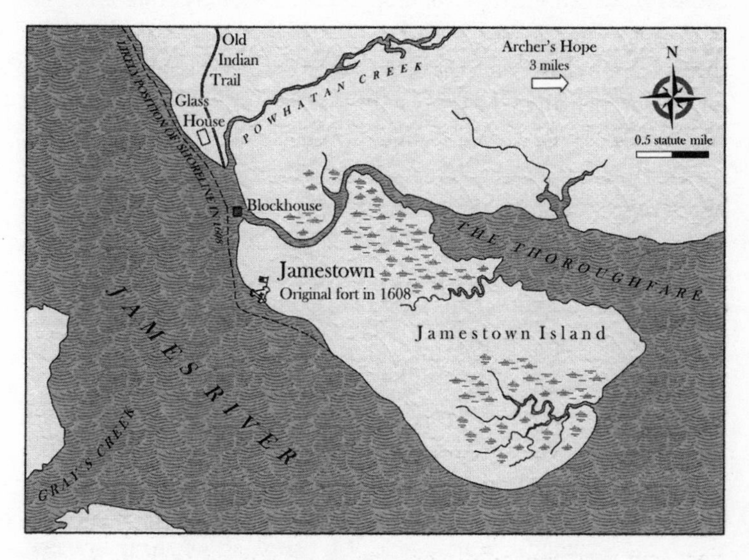

The vicinity of Jamestown, based on Philip L. Barbour, *The Three Worlds of Captain Smith*, (1964). The "Old Indian Trail" to Werowocomoco, the capital of the Powhatan empire, can be seen leading away to the north on the mainland. Part of the shoreline has eroded since 1608.

His selection was no trivial matter. Smith was still deeply unpopular with some of the settlers, and he had more than enough experience to know the position was a poisoned chalice. Indeed, he had identified several influential members of the colony who would do everything in their power to undermine him, and then blame him gleefully for his failures. Yet the majority of the men realized Smith was their best chance – perhaps their only chance – of putting Jamestown back on a solid footing.

Straight away, Smith got to work correcting what he considered to be the mistakes of Ratcliffe's regime. Work on his so-called presidential "palace" was halted; the storehouse and the church were repaired; the fort's defences strengthened, the order of the watch reviewed. Following Machiavelli's dictate that "few men are brave by nature, but good discipline and experience make many so", he drilled the men every Saturday, to the fascination of the watching Powhatan. Smith had seen the effectiveness of the well-trained janissaries during his time in Hungary and Transylvania, and he did what he could, under the conditions, to emulate their discipline.

Smith then looked at how they were collecting provisions. He asked the men to re-equip the boats, making them better suited for trading. At the end of the month, the aristocrat George Percy set off downstream to barter for the Powhatan's harvest. Before long, he encountered a ship coming upriver from the open ocean – it was Christopher Newport, back with the second supply.

The new supply had arrived several weeks earlier than expected, primarily because of the excitement generated back in London by the apparent "success" of the Virginia venture. Captain Newport had reported that Wahunsenacawh was offering information about a route west from the Chesapeake Bay to the Orient, and John Martin had waxed lyrical about the likelihood of finding gold. This news – although totally fanciful – was exactly what the investors wanted to hear, and they despatched the *Mary and Margaret,* loaded with more colonists and supplies, to Jamestown as swiftly as possible. Newport also brought fresh instructions from the London Company's directors for the Jamestown president. Smith was not pleased with what their letter had to say.

Firstly, the company admonished the colonists for their dissent and in-fighting. Secondly, the letter made clear that the president had to obey Newport's instructions. But there was worse still. The company had sent out two gentlemen, Richard Waldo and Peter Winne, both sea captains, who were to be members of the colony's governing council. Smith described them as "two ancient [experienced] and valiant gentlemen, but ignorant of the busines (being newly arrived)".[20] Newport, taking his prerogative to overrule the president, reinstated Ratcliffe to the council as well. Now, with the two new "valiant gentlemen", President Smith could be outvoted.

Newport had been given instructions "not to returne without a lumpe of gold, a certainty of the south sea or one of the lost company of Sir Walter Rawley [from the Roanoke Colony]".[21] He was also expected to bring back various goods to offset the cost of the venture. The colonists were to produce clapboard, pitch, tar, soap-ash (rendered animal fat mixed with wood ash) and glass to the value of two thousand pounds.

Smith was a realist, and he argued with Newport about how this could be done. Winter was fast approaching, and they had an extra seventy colonists, all inexperienced, to feed and house, including a "gentlewoman" called Mistress Forrest and her maid. The colonists urgently needed to build proper houses and trade food with the Powhatan.

Newport disagreed. He accused Smith of being uncooperative and for wanting to take all the credit for stockpiling food supplies. He also censured Smith for unnecessary cruelty towards the Powhatan – a potentially serious charge. It was also a fundamental issue dividing the two men in their management of Jamestown. Newport asserted "that the crueltie Smith had used to the Salvages, in his absence, might occasion them to hinder his designes".[22]

Most pressing was the issue of how to deal with the paramount chief, Wahunsenacawh. In a bid to bring the chief to agree to a long-term alliance with the English, Newport had brought gifts on behalf of the London Company: a bedstead and mattress, a washbasin and ewer (water jug), clothes and other "costly novelties". He had even brought a crown. In their deliberations about how to secure the settlement, the company's leaders had decided they would crown Wahunsenacawh as a king, ostensibly to show gratitude for his generosity and assistance, but more importantly, to make him subservient to King James. This was, of course, the same thinking that had inspired Wahunsenacawh to make Smith a *weroance*, so the paramount chief was unlikely to be fooled by this particular ploy. Smith quarrelled with Newport over the plan. He believed the way to gain the Powhatans' respect was to demonstrate power, not toady favours.

Perhaps in an attempt to defuse the situation, Smith offered to travel ahead to Werowocomoco with a small group. Recalling the warning given by the Patawomeck *weroance* about Wahunsenacawh's plans to ambush Newport, Smith approached the capital with circumspection. Newport had returned from London with the young Powhatan boy Namontack, and Smith asked that he be allowed to join the advance party. Maybe he thought this would help show the colonists' peaceful intentions, or perhaps Namontack could serve as an interpreter over complex negotiations.

Smith set out with Namontack and four fellow Englishmen for Werowocomoco. When they arrived, they were told the paramount chief was away hunting. The Powhatan offered to send a messenger for him, and, in the meantime, young women arrived to entertain them.

As the five colonists sat around a wood fire, they "heard such a hideous noise and shriking" that they feared they were being ambushed. To their relief, Pocahontas quickly appeared and reassured Smith that this was a welcoming ceremony. It was a greeting the Englishmen had never received before, and were unlikely to ever receive again. Thirty young women came running out from the woods, "only covered behind and before with a few greene leaves". Their otherwise naked bodies were painted from top to bottom in red, white, black and piebald dyes. The woman who seemed to be their leader stood out: she wore deer antlers on her head and otter skins around her waist and arm. Smith wrote:

> These feindes with the most hellish cries, and shouts rushing from amongst the trees, cast themselves in a ring about the fire, singing, and dauncing with excellent ill varietie, oft falling into their infernall passions, and then solemnely againe to sing, and daunce.[23]

As wild as this sounds, Smith said, the women sang and danced to a strict, unwavering rhythm.[24]

For the Powhatan people, music and dancing were central to village life, and used to promote friendships. After an hour, the women withdrew into the woods, only to reappear again and summon Smith into a longhouse. He did not say if the other men were also invited, and indeed he was somewhat cryptic about what occurred next: "but no sooner was hee within the house, but all these Nimphes more tormented him then ever, with crowding, and pressing, and hanging upon him, most tediously crying, love you not me?"[25] If Smith had been able to resist the allure of these native "Nimphes", he was a more virtuous man than most.

From what we know of Powhatan culture, women offered many forms of hospitality to important visitors, and considerable sexual freedom outside marriage was acceptable for both sexes. For example, the English writer and Virginia council member William Strachey later wrote that men and women were "most voluptuous", and consequentially were "full of their owne country-disease (the Pox) very young".[26]

Though the events of the longhouse remain lost to history, as a result of Smith's self-censorship, he was nonetheless ready to receive Wahunsenacawh when he returned to Werowocomoco the next day. Smith told the chief he was invited to Jamestown to receive presents. Powhatan was too shrewd to be taken in by this. According to Smith, he replied:

> If your king have sent me presents, I also am a king, and this my land, 8 daies I will stay to receave them. Your father [Newport] is to come to me, not I to him, nor yet to your fort, neither will I bite at such a baite.[27]

There is no denying Wahunsenacawh and Smith were well matched in this game of tit-for-tat diplomacy. Wahunsenacawh also made it clear he did not need the colonist's offer of help to deal with the threat from the Monacans. Finally, he quashed any suggestion the Englishmen might find a route over the mountains to the fictional South Sea: "But for any salt water beyond the mountaines, the relations [information] you have had from my people are false."[28]

Wahunsenacawh's stubbornness meant Newport had no option but to travel to Werowocomoco with the offerings from the London Company. He had the bulkier items loaded onto a ship, to be transported the eighty miles by water. Then, he and a guard of fifty men took the lighter items via the much shorter overland "Indian Trail", the quickest route between Jamestown and Werowocomoco. When all the gifts eventually made their way to the capital, they were presented to Powhatan with as much pomp and ceremony as Newport could muster from his men.

The first glitch involved the gift of a bright red cloak, which Wahunsenacawh feared would harm him. It took Namontack, now experienced in the ways of the English, to reassure the chief that the garment was safe to wear.

The second hitch involved the coronation, which rapidly deteriorated into a farce worthy of a Marx Brothers' movie. The crown was offered to Wahunsenacawh, who refused to kneel, or even to stoop, to have it placed on his head. The colonists tried "many perswasions, examples, and instructions", but to no avail. The chief understood that by doing so he would lower his status with respect to these men. He refused to bow before the English king.

Eventually a colonist leaned heavily on the chief's shoulders. As Wahunsenacawh bent under the strain, the crown was hurriedly popped on his head. Protocol triumphed, and to round off the event, a colonist fired a pistol – it was a signal for a musket salute from the ship anchored in the river: "the king start [jumped] up in a horrible feare, till he see all was well", Smith remembered.[29]

But Wahunsenacawh was not going to allow the foreigners to get the better of him. He returned the favour he had just received by presenting Newport with a mantle and an old pair of his shoes. This may be the Virginian native deerskin cloak embroidered with shells, reputed to be "Powhatan's mantle", which has been on display in the Ashmolean Museum in Oxford since at least 1638.

Now Newport could move on to getting the information the London Company wanted so desperately. Would the chief assist their expedition over the mountains into Monacan territory? Wahunsenacawh offered only very limited support. They could take Namontack as a guide and interpreter, together with seven or eight baskets of corn.

It was not a ringing endorsement of support from King James' latest vassal.

On his return to Jamestown, Captain Newport began to prepare for the expedition into Monacan territory. From the two hundred or so men in the colony, he hand-picked 120 of the strongest and most competent, including Scrivener, Percy and the two new councillors, Waldo and Winne. This left Smith with just eighty men to defend the fort, many of whom were either ill or otherwise unfit. He also needed able bodies to cut and load clapboard onto the *Mary and Margaret*.

Newport's large contingent headed upriver as far as the Richmond falls. They took a five-section barge to assemble above the rapids, to allow them to proceed further by water. Smith was not a fan of this new addition to the Jamestown fleet, and wrote a scathing critique of it to the London Company: "If he had burnt her to ashes, one might have carried her in a bag, but as she is, five hundred cannot, to navigable place above the Falles."[30]

Smith was right, and Newport's expedition was forced to leave the barge and walk into the Monacan lands. They found no route to the South Sea, nor any gold or silver. As if to rub salt into his own metaphoric wound, Newport kidnapped a local *weroance* and forced him to act as their guide. So much for his censure of Smith's bad treatment of the Powhatan. Newport returned to Jamestown without a single accomplishment to his credit.

One good thing came from Newport's return, however: Smith now had more able-bodied men available to meet the demands of the London Company to produce tar, glass, pitch and other items that might turn a sure profit. Smith set up workcamps in the woods downstream from Jamestown to harvest timber. Here at least some of the "gentlemen" did their best, but they were still unaccustomed to physical labour; their backs ached and their hands blistered, "that many times had a loud othe [oath] to drown the eccho". Such were the profanities unleashed in the camps, Smith instigated a coldwater dowsing for every offender, who "for every othe to have a Cann of water powred downe his sleeve". The penance had the desired effect, so that "a man should scarce heare an othe in a weeke."[31]

The colony also remained short of food for the coming winter, so Smith took the shallop up the Chickahominy River in the hope of making some trades. He was disappointed; the Powhatan were no longer interested. This has often been put down to a new policy dictacted by Wahunsenacawh to cut off food supplies to the English, but there is recent scientific evidence suggesting there might be another explanation for the Powhatan hoarding their harvest.

The bald cypress, *Taxodium distichum*, is a common deciduous conifer in the region, and it is particularly useful for determining historic climate conditions. This is partly because it lives for a very long time, often for more than a thousand years, and is proven to be an accurate indicator of the rainfall over its lifespan. From the annual growth rings of these trees, researchers have identified the period between 1606 and 1612 as being the worst drought in the area for 770 years.[32]

In these early years, the settlers made frequent reference to the fact that the annual crop yields of the Powhatan were only ever sufficient to carry them through to the next growing season. In 1608, Smith noted that "(their Corne being that yeare but bad) they complained extreamely of their owne wants".[33] The following year, Ratcliffe wrote that "the country people [natives] set no more than sufficeth each familye a yeare".[34] There is no documentation from the Powhatan themselves to support the theory that drought was the primary cause of a food crisis, as they had no written language. But they certainly seemed, according to tradition, to lead a hand-to-mouth existence, taking only what they needed from the land. When harvests were poor, they had little put away to get them through the lean times.

In any case, this period of low rainfall would also have contributed to the poor water quality in the James River during the summer months. The salty water of the Chesapeake Bay would have penetrated further up the river during a drought, resulting in a longer and deeper "salt wedge" running on the bottom of the James – more brackish water.

In retrospect, the London Company had chosen the worst possible time in nearly eight hundred years to try to establish a permanent settlement in Virginia.

John Smith had an answer to the colony's troubles, for he was the sort of man who, nearly always, had an answer for everything. When the Chickahominy refused to barter, Smith replied duplicitously that he had actually come upriver not to trade, but to punish them for their attack on him the previous winter. Smith ordered a task force of eighteen armed men to land on the shore, and the Chickahominy scattered. Soon, however, the villagers returned with a peace offering: one hundred bushels of corn, plus fish and birds. They could ill afford to give up this much food at this time of year, but it was exactly the outcome Smith wanted. His ships left filled with food for the winter. Unfortunately, in the process he had damaged relations further with his closest neighbours.

It would have been naïve for Smith to return to the fort expecting any gratitude, but he was not prepared for the reception awaiting him: there were calls he should be deposed as president. Some men argued that Smith left the fort without permission from the full governing council – a dereliction of his duties. Smith inevitably suggested the ringleaders of the movement against him were Newport and Ratcliffe. But in any case, the ridiculous accusation gives some indication of the resentment and even loathing Smith often provoked among the more well-connected settlers in Jamestown. Even with a handsome haul of corn, fish and fowl for the winter, he was subject to backbiting and complaint.

Out of desperation, some of the settlers had begun trading furs and woven baskets with the sailors on the supply ships, in return for home comforts like butter, cheese and beer. With the winter so bad, this "private trading" had become widespread during Smith's tenure as president. Smith claimed "ten-times more" supplies came into Jamestown through private deals than went into the colony's official storehouse. Such private trade was quite lucrative: one ship's master later sold his furs back in London for thirty pounds, which was more than he had been paid for making the return voyage. However, the furs were not the colonists' personal property; under the terms of the royal charter, they belonged to the London Company, and needed to be shipped back to England to help claw back the costs of mounting the expedition.

The problem, Smith said, had been exacerbated by Newport, who was himself guilty of personal trading: "And had not Captain Newport cryed Peccavi [guilty]" Smith wrote, "the President would have discharged the ship, and caused him to have stayed one yeare in Virginia."[35] It is unlikely Smith actually had the authority to detain Newport, but he was clearly very angry with the captain's poor example. The enmity between the two men was only growing.

But even more worrying, Smith learned that some colonists were bartering directly with the Powhatan, and getting furs in exchange for items Smith thought should be kept in English hands. Smith had always taken great care not to let the locals have metal tools of any sort, and he discovered not just farming implements, but pikeheads, knives, shot and gunpowder were going to the Powhatan behind his back.

To Smith's relief, Newport decided to return to London in December with whatever commercial goods the colony could muster. They managed "tryals of Pitch, Tarre, Glasse, Frankincense, Sope ashes; with that Clapboard and Waynscot that could be provided".[36] Before the ship set sail, Scrivener and Namontack went to Werowocomoco in the hope of trading for more supplies, but found the Powhatan "more readie to fight then trade". It took all their shrewdness and cunning to avoid a battle. They came away with only three or four hogsheads of corn, most of which was loaded on to the *Mary and Margaret* to feed the sailors on the return voyage.

Newport also took Ratcliffe back to London with him. Smith knew both men would report unfavourably about him to the London Company – after all, he had ongoing disputes with both men, and he could hardly stand the sight of Ratcliffe, whom he considered to be utterly incompetent. Smith also knew his only chance was to put forward his side of the story. So sometime in early December 1608, he wrote a letter addressed to the "Treasurer and Council of Virginia, London", which he asked to be carried back to the London Company.

Though it was ostensibly an update on the status of Jamestown, Smith penned a report that was partly a defensive justification of his own actions, and partly a personal attack on Ratcliffe and Newport. And Smith was furious; so much so, the tone of the letter won him few friends back in London. He called Ratcliffe "a poore counterfeited Imposture. I have sent you him home, least the company should cut his throat".[37] He begged the company to keep this type of person back in England in future, and send out only "Carpenters, husbandmen [farmers], gardiners, fisher men, blacksmiths, masons, and diggers up of trees, roots, well provided".[38] Smith was also disparaging about Newport's abortive expedition, claiming the captain's mission up the James "might as well have been done by one man, for the value of a pound of Copper".

At the same time, Smith tried to give an honest appraisal of the progress of the colony and the commercial viablity of the enterprise. He made it plain that the value of the goods on the return ship would not come close to the two thousand pounds the company had dictated. Nor would Virginia ever be able to compete commercially with Sweden and Russia for timber.

Honesty and candour might have been two of Captain Smith's virtues, but tact and discretion plainly were not. The London Company took offence. Who was this upstart throwing blatant criticisms at the very crux of their operation? The letter became widely known as "Smith's Rude Answer".

In mid-December 1608, Smith went downstream to collect the debt owed to him by the Nansemond, who had not forgotten (nor forgiven) his last visit. The president was responsible for the lives of two hundred people in Jamestown, and food was scarce. In the intervening weeks, Wahunsenacawh had apparently told the Nansemond not to trade with the English, so Smith decided to use force. He ordered a musket volley to be fired – it was the usual pattern of consequences. The Nansemond ran off into the woods. Smith went ashore and burned down a hut. Rather than see their whole village torched, the residents appeared reluctantly with a hundred bushels of corn. It was not enough to sustain Jamestown for very long in this harsh winter, but it was something.

Thus, relations between the colonists and the Powhatan had settled into a familiar pattern: refusal, reprisal and reckoning. From Smith's perspective, such a belligerent strategy was necessary if Jamestown had any chance to survive, but he was effectively robbing the locals, who were also suffering the harsh winter. Perhaps he was impervious to human suffering after witnessing the horrors of Transylvania; perhaps his only priority was the survival of the colony; or perhaps he cared little except for his own tenure as president of Jamestown.

In the midst of the bitter cold and shortages, the people of Jamestown at least found one thing to celebrate. John Laydon, one of the original 1607 settlers, married the maid who had come over on the second supply, Anne Burras. Theirs was the first English marriage in the New World. As soon as the celebrations were over, Smith renewed his search for food. Everywhere he went, the Powhatan were either in hiding or reluctant to barter. Smith knew the colonists were in a desperate position, and he was not prepared to accept this as their fate. So he proposed a reckless plan to attack the storehouses in Werowocomoco, the capital of the Powhatan empire.

Smith had to put the plan to the council. Richard Waldo favoured the idea and volunteered to be Smith's second-in-command. However, Matthew Scrivener (usually a supporter of Smith) spoke up against the proposal: Smith's plan was rash, he argued, and it could easily result in all-out war with the Powhatan. Scrivener was persuasive, and Smith lost the council vote. They were now at the mercy of the Powhatan.

Wahunsenacawh could see how desperate the colonists were for food, and he resolved to make them an offer, a proposition that could cement his status as the paramount leader of the whole Chesapeake region. He was prepared to trade a shipload of corn for having an English-style house built in Werowocomoco, and receiving a number of particularly desirable items, such as a grindstone, a breeding pair of chickens, copper, beads, muskets and fifty swords.

Smith was in a quandary. Most of the chief's requests were not a problem if it meant the colony survived the winter. But arming him with fifty swords and some muskets was out of the question. Nevertheless, he agreed to the terms in principle. At the very least, he knew he could generate some good will, maybe even secure some corn, before negotiations fell apart, which they inevitably would.

Smith's first step was to send an advance party to Werowocomoco to begin work on the English-style house. He recruited a "Dutchman" from the second supply ship who was trained as a glassmaker and whom he trusted as a perceptive spy. (Smith frequently referred to "Dutch" men when he probably meant German, a corruption from the designation *Deutsche.*) Smith feared the Powhatan were preparing for war, and that Wahunsenacawh's offer of trade was meant to lull them into a false sense of security. The bluff and double-bluff continued.

In late December, Smith set out for Werowocomoco to finalize the terms of the deal. He took three ships carrying more than seventy men. They spent the first night with the Warraskoyack tribe, in the lower reaches of the James River. Here their *weroance* cautioned Smith to be guarded around Wahunsenacawh – as if such a warning was necessary. The next day they encountered "extreame winde, rayne, frost and snow" and were forced to anchor off Kecoughtan, where the long-suffering villagers entertained the colonists yet again. It took them two weeks to sail to the Powhatan capital, during which time Smith celebrated his twenty-ninth birthday.

On their arrival at Werowocomoco, they found the river was frozen solid up to half a mile from the shore. They forced their way through on a rising tide, but when the tide went out, the ships were left beached on the "oosie shoules". Rather than stay on board, Smith made his men wade waist deep through the freezing mud.

The next day, Wahunsenacawh received them politely. He fed the colonists generously, but asked when they would be leaving, for he had not sent for them. He said he could manage forty baskets of corn in return for forty swords, if they wanted. Smith made clear he was there at the request of the chief's messenger, and that Wahunsenacawh must be forgetful. The chief laughed off the reproach. Undoubtedly, the chief of the Powhatan was playing another of his calculated games, but Smith had not yet worked out what the end of this game was likely to be, or mean.

The rest of the day passed with the two men pitching ruse and counter-ruse to each other. Smith said he had come out of goodwill to build the house for the chief. Wahunsenacawh tried to inveigle Smith into having his men leave their weapons on board the ships, "for here they are needless, we being all friends, and for ever Powhatans".[39] This was a pointed reminder to Smith that, as a *weroance*, he had made promises to the paramount chief, and he should fulfil his obligations. It was a long day's negotiation for both of them.

The next morning, Smith checked on the construction efforts of his advance party, and found very little had been accomplished. Most of the men sent ahead to Werowocomoco had come over on the second supply, and they were foreign – skilled German and Swiss labourers who had little allegiance to their English masters. Many seemed to have decided they were better off living with the Powhatan, letting either the chief or the winter finish off the Englishmen while they received food and shelter (and most likely some female company, too). Smith was far from impressed by this.

When Smith returned from his inspection, Wahunsenacawh was ready to again take up their game. The chief was doing everything he could to prise some weapons from Smith's unyielding grasp. He launched into a long speech about the danger of war between them, and the vulnerable position the colonists found themselves in:

> What can you get by warre, when we can hide our provisions and fly to the woods? whereby you must famish by wronging us your friends.[40]

It was a plea worthy of a leading Shakespearean player, but Smith would not be swayed. Still, the Powhatan chief kept wrangling with him.

As the back and forth continued, Smith began to fear that Wahunsenacawh was actually delaying while his warriors prepared to ambush him. He looked around and confirmed he only had John Russell with him in the longhouse. There was no way just the two of them could survive an attack. So he sent a signal to the men on the boats: come to the longhouse, immediately.

Instantly, the atmosphere inside the longhouse changed. Two or three women came in and focused their attentions on Smith and Russell. It was a distraction. Wahunsenacawh slipped outside while his warriors surrounded the house silently. Smith sensed something was wrong, and told Russell they had to make a run for it. It was a long way to the beach, and Smith knew it. As they ducked out of the house, Smith fired a warning shot to his ships. His men heard it, and met them on their way.

The arrival of reinforcements forced the Powhatan to change plans. They stopped and explained there had been a simple misunderstanding; their chief had left out of fear of Smith's guns, and the warriors had been assigned to guard the colonists' corn. Smith found the explanation ludicrous.

The sight of eighteen heavily armed Englishmen encouraged the Powhatan to help load the corn onto the colonists' ships. By now, however, the tide had ebbed, and the vessels were again left high and dry on the mud. It would be midnight before the ships could lift off, so the villagers invited the colonists back to the longhouse to rest and eat. Smith could have stayed the night on the ships in reasonable safety, but, surprisingly, he accepted the invitation.

After dark, a young girl slipped through the door of the longhouse, seeking Smith. "For Pocahontas his dearest jewell and daughter, in that darke night came through the irksome woods", was how Smith remembered it.[41] She told Smith her father would soon send them a feast, but the Powhatan had orders to kill the visitors as they ate. "Therefore if we would live shee wished us presently to bee gone", he reported.[42]

As she spoke these words, Pocahontas was clearly upset, according to Smith. He knew she was putting herself in great danger by doing him this favour, "for if [Chief] Powhatan should know it, she were but dead, and so shee ranne away by her selfe as she came", as he explained in *The Generall Historie*, published in 1624.[43] This version of the incident is nearly identical to the one Smith shared in his private letter to Queen Anne on Pocahontas' visit to London in 1616, when he wrote that:

> when her father with the utmost of his policie and power, sought to surprize mee, having but eighteene [men] with mee, the darke night could not affright her from comming through the irkesome woods, and with watered eies gave me intelligence, with her best advice to escape his furie; which had hee knowne, hee had surely slaine her.[44]

Smith was consistent in remembering this story, even so many years after the event.

Soon, as Pocahontas had predicted, "eight or ten lusty fellowes" with platters piled high with food came into the longhouse, and asked the colonists to extinguish the tapers used to fire their muskets, because the "smoake made them sicke". It was a peculiar request to make in a room already full of wood smoke. Smith grew ever more suspicious. He made the Powhatan taste every dish they served before he would eat from it. He even returned some of the food to Wahunsenacawh, saying he was ready for him, when the time came.

By midnight, the ships had lifted free of the mud. The Englishmen cautiously worked their way down to the beach, all the while maintaining the pretence of friendship with the Powhatan. It had been a close call, but at least Smith now understood Wahunsenacawh's real intentions.

The two men never met again.

Pocahontas had again saved Smith's life, or so he claimed. But in many ways, this second intervention is more difficult to explain than the first. Based on months of interactions, Smith would have been fully aware of the threat of an ambush. So Pocahontas' warning served no obvious purpose than to make him appear a less capable soldier and leader than he had made himself out to be.

Furthermore, if Smith's explanation in his letter to the Queen was accurate, then Pocahontas was not only distraught; her life was genuinely in danger. So why would she warn Smith of an imminent attack? Perhaps she was simply young and naïve, and did not realize that Smith fully understood that he might be ambushed. But why would she be prepared to risk her own life to give him a warning?

Worse still, it seemed her alarm fell on deaf ears. Smith certainly handled the situation badly. He said he treated Pocahontas as a child, brushing off her warning with a handful of beads: "Such things as shee delighted in, he would have given her", he said patronizingly.[45] This was not what an adolescent teenager wanted to hear. Pocahontas felt rejected, and "with teares running downe her cheekes, shee said shee durst not be seene to have any: for if Powhatan should know it, she were but dead, so she ranne away by her selfe as she came."[46]

Perhaps the answer to the dilemma is to view the situation from the perspective of a headstrong, impetuous pubescent girl, rather than of a guardian angel. Even as a daughter of the paramount chief, Pocahontas' existence was mundane, and her horizons in life limited – until these strange and curious men came and built a fort on that swampy, unusable peninsula. Then, every few weeks, she got to take off with her father's warriors to visit this extraordinary, entirely new world, where there were houses made of hewn wood, people wearing strange clothes and speaking in a peculiar tongue, and warriors who could create explosions at a whim. Her visits to Jamestown were exciting, and they made her feel special. Certainly none of the other children in the capital were allowed such a liberty – not even Wahunsenacawh's other favoured offspring.

All along, Smith assumed Pocahontas wanted to save his life. The reality might be much more prosaic: she most likely wanted simply to preserve her own privileged lifestyle.

John Smith wrestling with Opechancanough, the *weroance* of the Pamunkey tribe, from Smith's *The Generall Historie* (1624).

12

Dictator

1609

Master Russell brought us in news that we were all betraied: for at least 6. or 700. of well appointed Indians had invironed the house

John Smith, The Proceedings (1612)

John Smith and his men were lucky to get out of Werowocomoco alive. They had even obtained some supplies, though still insufficient to see the colonists through the winter ahead. And they now knew, beyond any doubt, they could no longer trust Wahunsenacawh.

In the circumstances, it would have been prudent for Smith to return to Jamestown with his men as soon as the ships slipped free of the mud. He needed to warn the colony about Wahunsenacawh's deception and treachery. Instead, Smith decided to go on bartering for food. It was a serious error of judgement for such an experienced soldier, and the consequences of this lapse would prove to be very serious.

Smith did not stay at Werowocomoco for further trading, however. From their anchorage in Purtan Bay, he ordered the ships to sail up the York River into Pamunkey territory, to Opechancanough's village. It was an audacious decision to leave the Powhatan capital and seek Wahunsenacawh's younger brother; perhaps even foolish in hindsight. Yet Smith had a few days to think over the move, so it was not a hasty one. They were delayed by bad weather for two or three days, and when they finally arrived at Opechancanough's village, there was another two or three days of "feasting and much mirth" with their hosts. Only after this had passed did they begin trading. The bartering went well at first, with Opechancanough promising the English more corn the next day.

Accompanied by fifteen of his men, Smith made his way to the *weroance*'s longhouse the following morning. Here they found four or five Pamunkey loaded with baskets of produce. Smith detected that Opechancanough was showing "strained cheerfulness", particularly as he explained "what paines he had taken to keepe his promise".[1] Soon enough, the *weroance*'s "paines" were apparent: one of Smith's men, John Russell, rushed into the longhouse clearly shocked and announced they were surrounded, "for at least 6. or 700. of well appointed [armed] Indians had invironed the house and beset the fields".[2] Smith had walked into yet another ambush, and this time the Englishmen were hopelessly outnumbered. Wahunsenacawh must have sent word to Opechancanough about the standoff in Werowocomoco, along with instructions to finish off Smith and his men once and for all.

The events that were about to unfold all seem to be part of Wahunsenacawh's grand strategy to deal with the colony. No sooner had Smith's ships left the Powhatan capital than the paramount chief had returned to his seat of power and put into effect a new plan to obtain his coveted metal weapons. The chief despatched two "Dutch" men, who were ostensibly still in Werowocomoco erecting the English-style house, back to Jamestown. (Smith names them Adam and Francis, but gave no surnames.) They were to inform Captain Winne that all was well, but Captain Smith had requisitioned their weapons. They needed replacements, together with more tools and clothing. In the absence of any news from Smith, it was a reasonable request, and Winne did as he was asked.

Next, Adam and Francis spoke secretly with several dissidents in the colony, trying to persuade them to defect. Before leaving the fort, these deserters pilfered various weapons, shot and gunpowder. These they passed to a group of Powhatan warriors waiting out of sight in the woods surrounding the fort. It was an act of treason by the defectors, and they must have known they were jeopardizing their fellow countrymen's lives. Their betrayal reveals the depth of desperation some of the residents of Jamestown had sunk to during that winter. And all the while, the one man who would have seen through this duplicity was twenty-five miles away, on the Pamunkey River, scrambling to find more supplies.

By now, Wahunsenacawh had assembled a considerable arsenal, including three hundred hatchets, fifty swords, eight muskets and eight pikes. It did not take long for the two Englishmen remaining in

Werowocomoco, Edward Brinton and Richard Savage, to realize what was happening, and they made a break for Jamestown. They did not get far. They were captured in the woods and brought back to the capital as prisoners. Surprisingly, Wahunsenacawh spared their lives – perhaps not wanting to have the conflict escalate into a full-scale war at this stage.

Meanwhile, Smith was focused on extracting himself and his men from Opechancanough's trap. He first did what any strong leader would do in the circumstances: he rallied his troops with a stirring speech: "we are now 16 and they but 700. at most, and assure your selves God wil so assist us...let us fight like men, and not die as sheep", he told them.[3]

Smith then turned his attention to assessing the situation. Instead of rushing into battle, which would surely have led to the indiscriminate slaughter of his men, Smith proposed to Opechancanough that they should fight each other, man-to-man, on a small island in the Pamunkey River. He named the stake for the combat: Indian corn for English copper, "and our game shalbe the conquerer take all."[4] Smith, of course, had faced adversaries in somewhat similar situations in Transylvania, but on this occasion it made no sense for Opechancanough to take up the challenge. More likely, Smith was buying some time and getting a sense of Opechancanough's style of leadership. It seemed the *weroance* lacked his older brother's guile and intellect, and Smith might have sensed this.

Opechancanough shrugged off the dare and instead tried to appease Smith by offering him a great present, to be presented just outside the door of the chief's longhouse. Smith was suspicious, and asked one of his men to check outside, but he was too terrified to do so – not even Smith's untested companions would fall for such an unsophisticated gambit. Smith was furious and worked himself into a rage, ordering George Percy, Francis West and several others to stand by their weapons in preparation for Smith leaving the relative security of the hut.

Perhaps recalling another lesson from *The Art of War*: "To know in war how to recognize an opportunity and seize it is better than anything else", Smith surprised everyone. He grabbed Opechancanough unexpectedly by his long hair and thrust a pistol against his chest. He then pushed the terrified *weroance* out through the longhouse's door to where his warriors were standing, their weapons at the ready. At this, the chief, "neare dead with feare", surrendered his bow and arrow, and "all his men were easily intreated to cast downe their armes".[5]

Triumphant, Smith let rip with another of his tirades, and reminded the Powhatan of "the promise I made you (before the God I serve) to be your friend, till you give me just cause to bee your enimie. If I keepe this vow, my God will keepe me, [and] you cannot hurt me".[6] The warriors, in shock, began trading hurriedly. Over the next hours they loaded the English ships with their precious corn.

Again, Smith's formidable resolve carried the day and he turned a potentially deadly confrontation to his advantage. It was a dramatic display of raw courage. Even making allowance for Smith's pompous script, it was quite an achievement. But did it really happen?

There were no other eyewitness accounts to confirm or contradict what Smith wrote about his daring exploits in Europe, so there we have to take him at his word; however, in Jamestown there were several. George Percy was part of Smith's trading party that day, yet the aristocrat – a prodigious diarist – never wrote about the encounter. But then Percy was no friend of Smith, so he may have chosen not to promote the captain's more heroic feats. Indeed in his published account of Jamestown, *True Relacyon*, Percy preferred to call Smith an "ambitious, unworthy and vainglorious fellowe".[7] There was no love lost between the Jacobean dandy, son of the Earl of Northumberland, and the mercenary soldier, son of a farmer from Lincolnshire. Yet it is also worth noting that Percy never publicly challenged Smith's version of these events, either.

There is, however, another record of the confrontation with Opechancanough. It appeared at the end of the third volume of *The Generall Historie*, in a verse written not by Smith, but by the brothers Michael and Wil Phettiplace, who were present that day – and by Richard Wiffin, who arrived at the Pamumkey village soon after the struggle:

> Pamaunkees King wee saw thee captive make
> Among seaven hundred of his stoutest men,
> To murther thee and us resolved; when
> Fast by the hayre thou ledst this Salvage grim,
> Thy Pistoll at his breast to governe him.[8]

The poem continued for another twenty-eight lines in much the same vein, and confirms many of Smith's details, including that there were sixteen Englishmen up against seven hundred Powhatan warriors.

Smith would have seen the verse before it was published, so he could have influenced the final wording. Even so, the poem, written by witnesses of the event, does confirm Smith's account of his showdown with Opechancanough.

Before Smith and the colonists finished loading their ships that evening, an unexpected visitor showed up at the village. It was Richard Wiffin, who appeared from the darkening woods with a confidential message for Smith. Wiffin had courageously come alone; nobody else was prepared to make the dangerous journey from Jamestown. And he was carrying some shocking news: nine days after Smith left Jamestown, Matthew Scrivener had taken a boat across the James River to the so-called Isle of Hogs, where the colonists kept a herd of pigs. With Scrivener were Richard Waldo, Anthony Gosnold (Bartholomew's surviving brother) and eight other men. It was meant to be a short trip, only a couple of miles downstream to get some fresh meat. But a vicious squall had swamped the boat, and all ten men had been lost. The only council member left remaining in the colony was Captain Peter Winne.

Smith decided to keep the tragic news from the rest of his party, and he swore Wiffin to secrecy. His priority was bartering for food, and nothing, not even a tragedy on this scale, was going to take precedence over that. Over the next few days, the Powhatan trudged to the village, braving the deep snow and bitter cold, to deliver corn-filled baskets "on their naked backs" to the Englishmen.

On the day appointed for the colonists to return to Jamestown, Opechancanough surprised them with a farewell feast. Smith's guard must have been down, for he allowed his men to eat the food without testing it. He and several other colonists became violently ill; they had been poisoned. Fortunately, the toxins were not deadly – the men vomited them out of their system and soon recovered. It was a chastening, if timely, reminder to Captain Smith that none of the local tribes could be trusted.

The next morning, Smith and his men dropped downriver. Smith wanted to surpise Wahunsenacawh. They arrived unannounced at the capital only to find the paramount chief had withdrawn, leaving Werowocomoco deserted. Smith's food expedition was over, and he sent messengers ahead on the Indian Trail to warn the colonists in Jamestown that he was returning and that relations with the Powhatan had reached an all-time low.

It had been a dangerous and eventful outing, but a successful one in Smith's view. He had secured 479 bushels of corn and two hundred pounds of deer suet as a result of his audacity. During their six weeks away, forty-six of his men had been fed by the native villagers. The total cost of this bounty was twenty-five pounds of copper and fifty pounds of iron and beads (although the defectors had also absconded with weapons, shot and gunpowder from the fort in Smith's absence). Smith had used aggressive, confrontational and bullying tactics to get what he wanted, and, in response, Opechancanough had handed over large quantities of corn he desperately needed for his own people. The food was just enough to get Jamestown through the rest of winter, and the president's "fear of starving was abandoned". He boasted (with some justification) that compared to the cruel raids of the Spaniards, his forays into Virginia achieved much with relatively little loss of life:

> tell me how many ever with such small meanes as a Barge of 2 tuns, sometimes with seaven, eight, or nine, or but at most twelve or sixteene men, did ever discover so many fayre and navigable Rivers, subject so many severall Kings, people, and Nations, to obedience, and contribution, with so little bloudshed.[9]

The Powhatan, of course, saw the situation very differently.

Even though Smith had secured food for the winter, he knew there were other pressing issues to resolve. The shareholders still expected a quick commercial return, and the settlers needed to be better prepared for spring planting than in previous years. As colony president, he ordered the men to split up into small working groups, each comprising ten to fifteen men.

Some groups began making tar, pitch and glass; some felled trees and cut clapboard; still others prepared the land for planting. Smith expected six hours of labour every day from each man, which, he said, would leave them some time "in pastime and merry exercises". Smith was serious about the need for hard work. He notoriously quoted from the Second Epistle of Paul the Apostle to the Thessalonians, 3:10: "If any will not work, neither should he eat." He also made clear that discipline was absolutely demanded. There would be no more gentleman shirkers under his management of Jamestown.

Another issue was the "Dutch" men who had defected to Wahunsenacawh's side. They were still living in Werowocomoco and Smith knew he could ill afford to allow a contingent of dissident Europeans to flourish across the York River. Relations with the Powhatan were bad enough without worrying who else among the settlers might turn against him.

One day, on his way back from the glass-making house on the narrow isthmus that connected the colony to the mainland, Smith encountered Wowinchopunck, chief of the Paspahegh. The *weroance*, who was "a most strong stout Salvage", raised his bow to shoot him. Smith was able to close in on the chief, and the two men wrestled until they fell into the James' freezing waters. Against the odds, Smith overpowered the warrior, who stood head and shoulders above him. Taking him by the throat, Smith threatened to behead him with his falchion. Wowinchopunck pleaded for his life. For better or for worse, Smith relented and took him back to Jamestown as a prisoner.

There is little reason to doubt this struggle took place, but in an early account from 1612, Smith said he was assisted by two other colonists, both Poles, who disappeared from later versions. Smith probably had help, as the likelihood of him getting the better of a much bigger, more powerful man without assistance stretches credibility.

The Paspahegh *weroance*'s family visited him daily, bringing food, which the chief might have used as a bribe to his guards to allow him to escape. Whatever the means, Wowinchopunck "finding his gard negligent (though fettered) yet escaped".[10] This was a failure by Smith to maintain proper discipline with the colonists and keep the upper hand with the Powhatan. He promptly ordered a search party of over fifty men to find the missing prisoner. Their methods were brutal: houses were burned, canoes taken, people were killed and others were taken prisoner.

This was only one of the symptoms of Smith's increasing problems with the Powhatan. On his return to the fort after searching for the *weroance*, he found stealing had become commonplace among the Chickahominy, who were close neighbours. Two Chickahominy brothers were being held as ransom because one of their associates had run off with a pistol. One brother was sent to recover the firearm, and Smith threatened to hang the other within twelve hours if the weapon was not brought back.

By the time the first brother returned with the pistol, the brother under detention was in a serious way. Smith claimed the young man had fallen unconscious in the smoke-filled hut, and had somehow rolled into the fire; from all appearances, he was dead. His brother was distraught. Smith took pity on him and promised to revive the comatose brother, providing they never stole again.

Apparently, the brother agreed to these terms, since Smith then gave the lifeless man a hefty slug of *aqua vitæ* mixed with vinegar. For the most part, the acerbic alcohol had the desired effect: the man was revived, but now he was drunk. This only served to confuse matters. His brother thought the man had been made crazy by Smith's "medicine". At this point, Smith promised he would perform a second miracle, and cure his brother's "madness". This he achieved simply by allowing the man to sleep off his hangover.

According to Smith, the episode restored his reputation of omnipotence across the Powhatan tribes. Within days, more stolen weapons were returned to Jamestown, together with gifts and pledges of peace. His cure had worked.

Dictator

Captain Peter Winne died early in 1609, leaving Smith as the only remaining member of Jamestown's governing council. The London Company had not foreseen this situation, and the office of the president had been given no authority to appoint new members. This left Smith in absolute control. With no council to challenge his opinions and check his decisions, the president became, for all practical purposes, a dictator.

Wielding a degree of autonomy he could only have dreamed of, Smith set about creating a colony that functioned with military efficiency, based on his experience and personal judgement. He was undoubtedly influenced by Machiavelli's counsel on the deployment of armed citizens, and his philosophy that when diplomacy fails, war serves as a form of political strategy.

Several projects needed urgent attention. The colonists were set to work preparing more goods for export. Forty or fifty barrels of tar, pitch and soap ash were produced, and glass samples were made. The security of their food and water supply was also addressed. A well was dug within the confines of the fort (although it still did not produce fresh water as hoped). Nets were woven and weirs constructed to improve fishing, and the care of livestock was made a priority. Smith also appreciated that it was time to think about sowing the fields for spring. Two Powhatan men were drafted to offer advice on planting thirty or forty acres of newly cultivated fields.

Security was also overhauled. A garrison was built on the Isle of Hogs to give warning of the approach of any traffic up the James River – whether Spanish galleons or canoes of enemy warriors. The fortification of Jamestown was improved. Twenty houses were built, together with a blockhouse to protect the narrow isthmus. Finally – perhaps remembering his days in eastern Europe – Smith ordered a fortified garrison be built at a high point across the river from Jamestown. It is possible this smaller fort was never finished, because another crisis struck that most definitely distracted the president.

Their cherished casks of stockpiled corn had started to rot, or had been eaten by the rats that had swarmed off the ships. (This was another self-inflicted problem, as rats were unknown in the New World before

European ships arrived.) Just when they thought they were through the worst of the winter, the inhabitants of Jamestown were again facing the prospect of starvation. Smith announced the colony had to be dispersed if it was going to survive the rest of the winter. After all the work to improve the fort, this was not a popular decision, but few of the men were prepared to question Captain Smith. True, it would be easier for them to forage in the woods for enough food to support the smaller groups of settlers. This is what the Powhatan often did during lean months. But at the same time, away from the fort, the colonists would be more vulnerable to attack. Smith had balanced the risks, and he believed this was the best option. He was running Jamestown as a quasi-military operation, and his judgement was to be taken as a command.

Smith sent sixty or seventy men downstream to live off oysters. Another twenty were led upstream by George Percy to live off fish (unfortunately, they caught nothing). A third party, led by Francis West, went up to the falls (but they too found little to eat). Some colonists were even sent to live with friendly Powhatan tribes, from whom they learned to make the most of wild plants and animals. There were sturgeon in the rivers, and nuts squirrelled away in the trees, and woodland roots that could be mashed and made into a type of bread.

However, many of the colonists were too apathetic to gather food, or were reluctant to experiment with the local produce. Before long, familiar demands could be heard around Jamestown. Some colonists wanted to trade their metal tools and weapons for food; others wanted to set sail for England. Smith maintained an iron rule over the colony throughout all these complaints. In particular, he punished the ringleaders for wanting to return home, and reminded the rest of the settlers of the consequences of disloyalty, that: "if I finde any more runners for Newfoundland with the Pinnace, let him assuredly look to arrive at the Gallows."[11] They were harsh words, but the president was deadly serious.

Smith was undoubtedly much tougher on the colonists than the previous presidents, and the heavy work and strict routine made some despise him. Yet, Smith also had a deeply embedded sense of justice, and he understood that a cooperative venture such as Jamestown would only survive if everybody did his share:

> The sick shall not starve, but equally share of all our labours; and he that gathereth not every day as much as I doe, the next day shall be set beyond the river, and be banished from the Fort as a drone, till he amend his conditions or starve.[12]

The results speak for themselves. Under Captain Smith's regime, only seven colonists died out of a population of two hundred, a fraction of the losses under previous administrations.

The breakaway faction of non-Englishmen who had come to Jamestown on the second supply was another worry. Smith desperately needed their labour back in Jamestown, and he understood that he could not allow these defectors to flourish with the Powhatan. He decided to send one of the Swiss colonists, William Volda, with the offer of a pardon to persuade the men to return. Volda went, but instead joined them. Smith had planted some informers with the defectors, "Thomas Douse, and Thomas Mallard (whose christian hearts relented at such an unchristian act)".[13] They reported back that the faction was planning an attack on Jamestown, seemingly with Wahunsenacawh's support.

Smith prepared his strategy for defending the colony. The spies should bring the defectors and the Powhatan warriors to a place in the woods where they could be ambushed, so "that not many of them should returne from our Peninsula".[14] The tactic made sense to a veteran of the brutal Ottoman war, but when Smith outlined his proposal to the other colonists, they objected to its ruthlessness. They argued that only the original two deserters should be punished, no more. Smith could see he would not win the support he needed for his plan to work, so he relented, and instead sent two trusted aides, Richard Wiffin and Jeffery Abbot, to assassinate the plot's ringleaders. In the event, both men pleaded for their lives, and Abbot spared them.

For his part, Wahunsenacawh denied any knowledge of the insurrection.

In mid-July, as the corn in Jamestown's fields began to ripen in the warm summer sunshine, an English ship sailed up the James River. The vessel was under the command of one Captain Samuel Argall, an agent of the London Company and a double cousin by marriage to Sir Thomas Smythe, the company's treasurer. He had brought food and wine to Jamestown, but had other, more important missions.

Argall had been sent to appraise a shorter transatlantic route to Virginia, via the Azores and Bermuda, which avoided the long detour south to the West Indies. His crossing had taken less than ten weeks, including two weeks becalmed. This was vastly quicker, saved on provisions and reduced the risk of running into a Spanish warship.

In fact, when Argall arrived in the Chesapeake Bay he had surprised a galleon sent by Philip III expressly to spy on the Jamestown settlement. Pedro de Zúñiga had at last convinced his king to do something about this English incursion. The captain of the Spanish ship, Francisco Fernández de Ecija, had been told by the Siouan-speaking Santee people, who lived more than three hundred miles to the southwest of Jamestown, that the English had built a wooden fort in the Chesapeake Bay.[15] When Argall's ship arrived, de Ecija had immediately turned his ship around and fled; if word of the encounter got back to London, the shareholders were sure to become ever more paranoid about the Spanish threat.

At Jamestown, Argall's prime task was fishing for sturgeon. The London Company's directors had decided they would try to bring Virginian roe to England before the European caviar arrived for the season. It was an expensive delicacy in England, and beating the market could make them substantial profits.

This initiative reflected a new, commercially minded mentality for the London Company. Although its objectives remained the same, the company had been granted a second royal charter, signed in May 1609, which provided "a further Enlargement and Explanation of the said [first] Grant, Privileges, and Liberties". The new charter extended the company's land rights and gave the investors greater control over determining their policies. Reports from John Smith and others had led the company's directors to conclude that their original plans had not been ambitious enough; what they needed was a large injection of workers who would be more difficult to dislodge, by either disease or attack, and with them the funds to support them. The second charter also conveniently distanced King James from the company; this was politically expedient for the English monarch, as the colony was becoming an increasing irritant to the Spanish crown.

The company hit on a new promotional strategy to raise funds and volunteers. For the first time, converting local peoples to Christianity would become more than just a token gesture, and clergymen were enlisted to promote the purchase of the company's stock for this mission. Sermons were given from parish pulpits, and pamphlets were printed. The first circular to drum up support for the conversion project appeared on the streets in February, with its imploring request for investment so that the Protestant English could "spread the kingdom of God, and the knowledge of the truth among so many millions of men and women, Savage and blind, that never yet saw the true light shine before their eyes".[16]

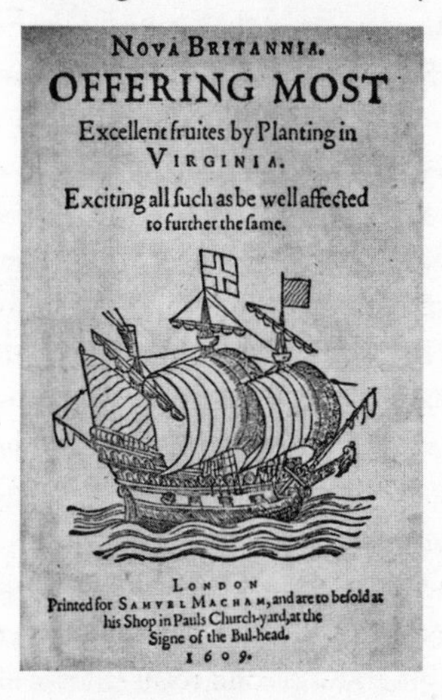

Robert Johnson's *Nova Britannia* was published on February 18, 1609. The pamphlet is dedicated to "the Right Worshipfull Sir Thomas Smith", Johnson's father-in-law, the treasurer of the London Company, and was intended to stimulate investments in the London Company and encourage emigration to Virginia (courtesy of the Virginia Historical Society).

This new initiative proved very popular with investors. Several city companies joined the scheme; 650 new individuals invested and more than 500 people volunteered to come out to Jamestown. (Coincidently, the ruinous Plymouth Company fell into disuse that same year, not to be revived until 1620, which may have helped boost the fortunes of its southern competitor.) This entrepreneurial coup was not lost on the ever-vigilant Spanish ambassador. On April 22 (NS), Pedro de Zúñiga wrote to King Philip III: "In this way a good sum of money is being collected, and they are making a great effort to take master-workmen and skilled artisans".[17]

Argall also brought a letter from the London Company's directors for John Smith, president of Jamestown. It was a full-throated and unforgiving evaluation of Smith's tenure. He was criticized for his harsh treatment of the Powhatan, and for failing to fully load the previous return ships with a profitable cargo. The letter also informed him that the structure of government in Jamestown would be changing.

The new royal charter allowed the company to replace the president and council with a Lord Governor and Captain General for South Virginia, appointed in London. The council would continue, but it would now be subordinate to the new governor, serving him more as an advisory group than as a privy council. According to the letter, Captain Smith would soon be out of power, though not until written authorization came from London. This official paperwork was still en route.

This time, the London Company really meant business. On May 15, 1609, a fleet of seven ships, plus two light boats towed astern, had left Woolwich on the River Thames for Virginia, funded by the success of the new charter. It was the biggest fleet ever to sail from England for the Americas. This was Jamestown's third supply, led by the Admiral of the Company himself, Sir George Somers. His ships carried livestock and provisions to last a year. Somers commanded the flagship *Sea Venture*; on board was Sir Thomas Gates, who would be put in charge until the named governor, Thomas West, Lord De La Warr, arrived the following year. Also on the *Sea Venture* was a copy of the authorization to change the governance of the colony, first to Gates and then to Lord De La Warr.

The company had been impatient to send off Somers' fleet. Unlike Argall, Somers chose to take the well-tested route across the Atlantic south, via the West Indies, even though it was already mid-summer. Predictably, it was a brutally hot crossing, and on just one ship thirty-two people died of "the calenture" (heat exhaustion), their bodies tossed unceremoniously overboard. Two babies were also born at sea, but neither survived.

Worse was to come. On July 14, the fleet ran into a storm in the mid-Atlantic, most likely a hurricane, for this was the beginning of the season for tropical storms. The ships of the fleet were separated and all were forced to jettison much of their cargo to stay afloat. The *Sea Venture* was newly built, and her timbers had not fully settled. She developed serious leaks and the pumps were overwhelmed; soon, water rose nine feet deep in the ship's hold. The crew and passengers alike were exhausted and demoralized.

After days of being tossed around in mountainous seas, a lookout on the *Sea Venture* spied the island of Bermuda on the horizon. Somers made a radical call to drive her onto the reef, in the process most likely saving the lives of everybody on board – 150 people and a dog. Among those who scrambled through the surf to safety were several company officials, including Captain Christopher Newport, Sir Thomas Gates, and secretary William Strachey, who had custody of the various documents from the London Company. All these papers survived. The crew and passengers were stranded on Bermuda for the next nine months, and the loss of the *Sea Venture* is believed to have inspired Shakespeare's play *The Tempest*.

Nearly a month had now passed since Argall had anchored in the James River, and the third supply fleet was overdue. Everybody was beginning to assume the ships had stopped over in the West Indies, or perhaps met a fate worse than that. On August 11, lookouts stationed on the Isle of Hogs sent word to the fort that four vessels had entered the James River. Smith instantly assumed it was a Spanish raid, and he put the colonists on high alert. However, these were the first ships of the supply fleet to limp into Jamestown. Whether that was good news for Smith was yet to be seen.

Two of the first men to come ashore were Gabriel Archer and John Martin, whom John Smith counted among his nemeses. Both men had joined John Ratcliffe and Captain Newport in mounting a smear campaign against Smith in London. On his return, Archer surveyed the state of the colony. He wrote to an unknown friend in England that the settlers "were found all in health", but he gave Smith no credit for their condition. He also complained that Smith was contemptuous towards him and Martin, and did not give "any due respect to many worthy Gentlemen, that came in our Ships".[18] Archer and Martin did not keep their opinions to themselves, either. Smith said they were "so railing and exclaiming against Captaine Smith, that they mortally hated him, ere ever they saw him".[19]

Archer, no doubt relishing the opportunity, announced to Smith that there was a new government for the colony, and that Smith was no longer president. Smith demanded to see the authorization himself. There was none. The London Company had prepared three copies of the detailed instructions for the change in command, intended for distribution among three different ships in case some encountered difficulties. However, the three guardians of the instructions all wanted the privilege (and the comfort) of sailing on Somers' flagship, so against the accepted practice of the period, all three copies ended up on the *Sea Venture*. No one had seen the *Sea Venture* in weeks, and it was now acknowledged that she and the other two ships and a small pinnace must have been lost with all hands.

Smith refused to yield the presidency without written orders. Among other things, he had no idea who he should be handing the presidency over to. Over the next couple of weeks, two more ships arrived, leaking badly and damaged, but neither was the *Sea Venture,* and neither had a copy of the authorization for the colony's new governor. On board one of the ships was none other than John Ratcliffe, who straight away threw his voice behind the others calling for Smith to be removed from his post, missing papers be damned.

By now, only the flagship of the fleet and the pinnace were unaccounted for, and it seemed the crucial documents of authority to abolish the presidency were gone forever with them. Still, Smith refused to step down. He appealed to the sailors for support (with Percy later insinuating that he bribed them). Smith argued he was the only legitimate president according to the original 1606 charter, which was, after all, the only authority the colonists had to follow.

In the face of Smith's obstinate stand, Ratcliffe and Martin nominated Francis West to be deputized as acting governor. They were not willing to let the governance of Jamestown remain in Smith's hands. They made one important proviso, so as not to provoke a full-on mutiny: they would "not disturbe the old President during his time [in office], but as [and when] his authority expired, then to take upon him the sole govenment".[20] Regardless, the "gentlemen" were forming a new, parallel government; although it was along the lines intended by the London Company, it had no official licence behind it. Despite this open challenge to his leadership, Smith retained the support of the ship captains and most of the other settlers.

As the weeks passed with still no word of the *Sea Venture*'s fate, Smith continued to manage the growing needs of the colony. There was an extra three hundred people to house, including several women and children. The corn was ready to harvest, and other foodstuffs had to be bartered with the Powhatan. And, of course, preparations had to be made for the next winter. But at every turn Ratcliffe, Martin and West criticized Smith's decisions, and fewer and fewer colonists wanted to stand up and fight for him.

Smith said he never gave up on Jamestown, but now the colony was giving up on him. He was weary from the backbiting, from the relentless opposition to his policies:

> Happy had we bin had they never arrived; and we for ever abandoned, and (as we were) left to our fortunes, for on earth was never more confusion, or miserie, then their factions occasioned.[21]

Uncharacteristically, he allowed himself the luxury of self-pity. It is rare to see Smith in such despair.

Eventually, he decided he had endured enough. With such strong opposition to his leadership, he could no longer function effectively as Jamestown's president. He would resign, and hand over the day-to-day governance to John Martin. At first, Martin accepted, but he changed his mind just three hours later, insisting that Smith take back control. By Smith's account, Martin, "knowing his own insufficiencie, and the companies scorne, and conceit of his unworthinesse, within 3 houres resigned it again to Captaine Smith".[22]

To survive the previous winter, Smith had broken up the colony into smaller, self-sustaining groups, as the Powhatan so often did. He was convinced that the survival of the colony depended on doing the same again this year. Now that the control of the colony's fortunes were back under his jurisdiction, Smith sent John Martin downstream to the Nansemond River, and Francis West upriver to the falls, to establish small winter settlements.

On his arrival at Nansemond, Martin sent couriers to the local *weroance*, asking to barter for his house, which stood on an island in the river. The couriers never returned. Later, George Percy revealed "they were sacrificed, and that their brains were cut and scraped out of their heads with mussel shells".[23] Their murder left Martin with few options. He took the *weroance* hostage and forcibly occupied his house. The Nansemond counter-attacked and rescued their chief, in the process killing two colonists and making off with one thousand bushels of much-needed corn. Martin called for reinforcements, which Smith sent, but they did little good.

Smith knew he still had the prospect of Francis West's settlement at the falls. He sailed upriver to see how this was faring. The site West had chosen was close to the river and liable to flooding. Smith looked around and decided the Powhatan village on a nearby small hill was better situated.

The Powhatan chose their sites well, and Smith negotiated with Parahunt, a younger brother of Wahunsenacawh, to buy the village. Parahunt agreed to the deal in return for copper. Alas, the 120 colonists assigned to move to the falls were less enthusiastic, and they refused to live there. Smith told them they had no choice if they wanted to survive the winter. They answered him with grumbles, then set about taking what they could from the local peoples – including hostages.

Part of the problem was that the London Company had given

the new intake of settlers an overly rosy portrait of life in Jamestown, and, consequently, excessively high expectations of the opportunities they could expect in Virginia. Smith encouraged the contingent at the falls to be more realistic about "their great gilded hopes of seas, mines, commodities, or victories they so madly conceived".[24] He also explained that they needed to be more accommodating towards the locals, and to refrain from "stealing their corne, robbing their gardens, beating them, breaking their houses, and keeping some prisoners".[25] These were fine words from Smith given some of his past behaviour. However, the colonists' prospects for the coming winter were not good, and Smith knew they could not go to war with the Powhatan on top of everything else.

After nine days at the falls, Smith gave up and returned to Jamestown. Parahunt's people had remained friendly while he was there, but as soon as he left they attacked. They rescued the Powhatan prisoners and "slew many" of the colonists.

Doubtless very displeased by now, Smith trekked back to the outlying settlement to enforce order. He arrested a handful of the main trouble-makers among the colonists, and made peace with Parahunt. He also insisted the colonists move to the village he had bought, as it boasted ready-made palisades, "sufficient to have defended them from all the Salvages in Virginia, dry houses for lodgings and neere two hundred acres of ground ready to be planted".[26] Perhaps in an attempt to make the village even more appealing, he named it Nonsuch, after Queen Elizabeth's favourite palace in Richmond, Surrey.

If Smith thought all was now settled, he was sadly mistaken. Francis West, who had been away at Jamestown, turned up at the falls to find that Smith had rejected his chosen site, and the colonists were in uproar about it. West and Smith had a furious row, according to George Percy, who wrote that "a great division did grow amongst them".[27]

For once, Captain Smith backed down. West moved his settlers back to "West's Fort" by the river, and Smith headed downriver. He was exhausted, frustrated and utterly disheartened.

On his cheerless return to Jamestown in his pinnace, Smith must have realized the power he had as president was ebbing away as surely as the falling tide on the James River. Exhaustion proved stronger than resentment, however, and he dozed off. He was awoken by the sudden noise of a loud detonation and an excruciating pain in his groin: the gunpowder bag which hung around his waist had exploded.

There is no knowing how much explosive Smith had in his pouch, but he had a reputation for carrying more than most. Whatever the quantity, the consequences were dreadful. Smith's wool and linen clothing caught fire, and, half crazed with pain and in shock, he threw himself over the side and into the river. His crew, still deafened and shaken by the explosion, reached out to bring him back into the boat, "where ere they could recover him he was neere drownd".[28] Once he was on board, the full extent of his injuries could be assessed, and the prognosis was bad.

Gunpowder only has the explosive power to propel a cannon ball or musket pellet when it is compressed into the barrel of a weapon. When the powder is loose, it is simply highly combustible and burns very quickly, with an intense red flame and a lot of white smoke. Gunpowder burns at about 5,000 degrees Fahrenheit (2,800 degrees Celsius)[29] for an instant, and the effect on Smith's body was catastrophic.

All the images of Smith suggest he was right-handed, and therefore he would have carried his powder pouch around his midriff on that side of his body. The flame, which he described as a "tormenting fire, frying him in his cloaths",[30] stripped away the flesh from his waist and thigh, nine or ten inches square. The heat of the flame would have instantly given him a third-degree burn, deep into the subcutaneous tissue. Away from the centre of the burn, over a large part of his body, he would have experienced lesser second- and first-degree burns.

Even today, with analgesics, sterile dressings and skin grafts, a gunpowder explosion next to the body creates a very serious injury, with no guarantee the patient will even survive. Accidents in Chinese firework factories suggest that mortality rates are very high, with half of all deaths occurring within a week of the injury.[31] The most common cause of death is septicaemia (blood poisoning), followed by hypovolemic shock, where severe blood and fluid loss leave the heart unable to pump enough blood to the rest of the body.

Smith was extremely fortunate to survive, which is a testament to his physical resilience. However, he would have been badly scarred for life, with severe burn damage and scarring to his groin in particular. He lived to the old age of fifty-one, yet he never married – which was unusual for the period. This terrible injury might explain why.

There was no medication available at Jamestown to alleviate his pain or prevent infection. Smith claimed that while he was suffering these agonies, some in the colony considered murdering him: "seeing the President unable to stand, and neare bereft of his senses by reason of his torment, they had plotted to have murdered him in his bed".[32] He certainly had enemies, and there were several who would have relished the chance to get rid of him. A more charitable interpretation is that the colonists might have considered his condition so hopeless that a mercy killing was in his best interest.

There have also been suggestions that the explosion on the boat was an attempt on Smith's life,[33] but this seems far-fetched, for the potential assassin would just as likely have blown himself up in the boat. If anybody was serious about murdering Smith, a musket ball in the back of the head on a deserted forest path would have been a much more reliable solution; or even better, a borrowed bow and arrow would have shifted the blame to the Powhatan. Smith's gunpowder pouch was most likely ignited by accident, either from a careless ember from a tobacco pipe, or his own burning taper, which all musketeers carry with them to fire their weapon at short notice.

In any case, Jamestown was not the place to recover from such a serious injury. A ship was scheduled to leave the next day for England, and Smith decided that his best chance of survival meant returning to London on her. He tried again to renounce his presidency, but nobody would accept the role. Eventually, George Percy, who was also due to leave for England, was persuaded to stay and take over the position.

Alas, there was no swift departure for Smith, nor much sympathy either. Smith's ship was held at Jamestown for another three weeks, prolonging his nightmare. The reason? The "gentlemen" of the colony wanted to draw up complaints and charges against him, to be sent back to the directors of the London Company.

Smith must have felt totally dejected and humiliated to leave the colony in this manner. Yet his departure had one ironic aspect, worthy of a Shakespearean tragedy. Smith was totally unaware of the contents of the instructions from the London Company now presumed missing on board the *Sea Venture*, save that he was to be replaced as president by a newly appointed governor. Either his detractors in Jamestown knew nothing of the detailed contents either, or they elected not to tell Smith about them: in fact, the instructions had specified an important role for Smith in Jamestown's management. He had been nominated to be a high-ranking member of the new governor's council, preceded in seniority only by Sir George Somers, the deputy governor himself. Furthermore, in appreciation for his acumen as a soldier, Smith had been appointed "Chief of Colonial Defense". The instructions were explicit about what this entailed: "To this commaunde wee desire Captaine Smith may be allotted [appointed] aswell for his earnest desire as the greate confidence & trust we have in his care & diligence."[34]

On October 4, the sixth ship of the supply fleet, the pinnace *Virginia*, arrived at Jamestown carrying sixteen more settlers. This was the small ship built in the Popham Colony the previous year, and she had now completed a double Atlantic crossing. The crew reported that they had no news of the *Sea Venture*. The return fleet was ready to drop down the James and sail out into the Chesapeake Bay, despite the state of limbo in which the colony was now left.

The responsibility for this did not lie with Smith. His time in Jamestown had been short, only thirty months, but he had mapped every mile of the shoreline of the bay for hundreds of miles to the north, and he was leaving the colony better prepared to face the harsh winter than at any time since it was founded. During his time at Jamestown, he had become a passionate advocate for the colonization of North America. Were it not for Smith's stubbornness, determination and guile, Jamestown most surely would have been lost, like Sir Walter Raleigh's Roanoke Colony twenty-two years before.

There must surely have been several smug "Gentlemen" who stood on the shoreline that day watching John Smith's ship disappear around the bend by the Isle of Hogs. Yet, despite the animosity of these self-important colonists, there were many who lamented Smith's departure. Wil Phettiplace (Fettiplace) wrote that:

> in all our proceedings, [Smith] made Justice his first guide, and experience his second...never allowed more for himselfe, then his souldiers with him; that upon no danger would send them where he would not lead them himselfe...that loved action more than words, and hated falsehood and covetousnesse worse than death.[35]

Smith took his last glance back at Jamestown, and the ships were away.

The only known contemporary portrait of John Smith, from Smith's *A Map of New England* (1616).

13
Admiral

1609–1615

Now we all found the losse of Captaine Smith, yea his greatest maligners could now curse his losse
Unknown contributor, The Generall Historie (1624)

On October 4, 1609, or very soon after, the fleet of five ships dropped down the James River on their return to London. John Smith probably sailed on the *Falcon*, under the command of his friend Captain Francis Nelson. The ex-president lay in his bunk for the next seven weeks as the ship ambled across the ocean at the speed of a gentle stroll. He was still weak and each lurch of the vessel must have tossed him into agony. Although the nerves immediately around his groin would most likely have been destroyed or cauterized in the explosion, the second- and first-degree burns over much of the rest of his body would have made every movement painful.

The weather in the North Atlantic is often bad late in the season, and this year was no exception. In mid-November the fleet was struck by a violent storm in the Western Approaches. Two ships were driven ashore on the coast of Brittany with huge loss of life. The remaining three vessels survived and disembarked in London at the end of the month, bringing word of the disappearance of the *Sea Venture* with them. The news brought the London Company close to panic – Sir Thomas Gates, Captain Newport and the secretary William Strachey were all assumed dead, together with over 140 colonists. The Jamestown settlement had lost its leaders, countless vital supplies, and a large portion of the influx of recruits who were supposed to help turn the venture into profit.

Winter soon descended upon the capital, but without quite the deadly impact it had in Jamestown. Snow covered the filth of the streets, thankfully masking some of the stench; but it also drifted into alleyways and piled high in doorways and yards, making it difficult to move around the city. The houses were so draughty and poorly heated that Londoners wore almost as many clothes inside as they did out.

Smith certainly needed plenty of clothes and a complete new wardrobe to replace his threadbare garments. Wearing his new attire in the latest fashion and sporting a freshly trimmed beard, he presented himself at the offices of the London Company on Philpot Lane. He would have been wise to prepare himself for a frosty reception. His "rude letter" had been the talk of the company over the past year. Everybody there was now well aware of his criticisms, and many would have found them ill-mannered and impertinent. The returning fleet had also brought a letter from John Ratcliffe addressed to Lord Salisbury, criticizing Smith: "This man is sent home to answere some misdeamenors whereof I perswade me he can scarc[e]ly clear him selfe from great imputation of blame."[1] Henry Spelman, one of the colonists who was part of the detachment sent up the James to live by the falls, claimed Smith had "conspired with the Powhatan to kill Capt weste".[2] Still more complaints were lodged against Smith by colonists who had been granted passage back to England in exchange for testifying against him. They were relieved to be home safely, and willing to make any claim to ensure their wellbeing.

The situation must have presented a dilemma for the senior members of the London Company. Under their revised instructions sent out on the *Sea Venture*, Smith would have been placed in a powerful position on the new council and given responsibility for the Jamestown's defence; now reports were coming back accusing him of incompetence, even treason.

Smith knew he might be facing quite serious charges, and he was prepared to defend himself resolutely. Had he tried to poison the "Dutch" settlers who took up work in Werowocomoco? No, but that did not alter the fact that they were traitors anyway. Had he planned to marry Pocahontas and make himself king of Jamestown? Pure nonsense! Had he forced colonists out of the fort to live downstream on oysters? Yes, that was true, but it was also necessary to disperse the colony to give them any chance of surviving the winter. Did he conspire with the natives to kill Francis West? Poppycock! Had he disrespected the many "worthy gentlemen" who returned to Jamestown with the most recent supply? Well, that might have been a difficult one for him to answer honestly.

The records of the London Company prior to 1619 have been lost, so there is no record of whether Smith actually faced a formal trial or an informal cross-examination. But there can be little doubt he would have been challenged about his actions in Virginia, and any inquest involving the London Company's directors versus the farmer's son from Lincolnshire would surely have been a spirited affair. And the odds would have been stacked against Captain Smith.

In the early seventeenth century, there was little notion of being innocent until proven guilty. Any tribunal, whether public or private, was therefore heavily weighted against the accused, and evidence was kept from the defendant until presented at the inquiry. The defendant would not have been allowed any counsel to assist in his defence, nor was he allowed access to documents or witnesses. Nevertheless, Smith was familiar with the arguments of his accusers; he also knew their aim was to tarnish his record as president and cover up their own failures of leadership.

However, Smith was not the London Company's only concern. Its shareholders had many other things to worry about: the *Sea Venture* was missing, presumed lost; two other ships had foundered on the return voyage; the three vessels that had returned safely carried a cargo whose value was simply not enough to maintain the colony. Nor was there any sign of the promised gold, nor a route to the South Sea. It was a very different picture to the one presented from the pulpits of England less than a year before, and investors were pulling out in droves.

The inquest into Smith's conduct in Jamestown was thus far from being the most troublesome issue facing the company. With all the papers lost, there is no surviving document declaring a verdict of sentence for Smith's alleged acts. Two years later, the charges against him were still being disseminated, which suggests he was neither cleared nor condemned. The company was preoccupied with other business, including preparations to send a new supply fleet with a new governor to Virginia.

It seems likely that Smith's inquest was simply swept aside and his reputation remained tarnished.[3]

At much the same time Smith was answering the charges against him in London, his main accuser, John Ratcliffe, was suffering worse punishment in Virginia. That winter, Ratcliffe went upriver in the colony's shallop to trade for food with the Powhatan, but he was ambushed. He was tied naked to a tree, then a group of Indian women used mussel shells to scrape the flesh from his body. They threw the bloody pulp into a fire before his eyes for as long as he lived, which mercifully was not for long. George Percy wrote pithily: "and so for want of circumspection [he] miserably perished".[4]

The Powhatan followed up Ratcliffe's murder with an attack on his boat. Only sixteen of the crew of fifty escaped, and the shallop returned to Jamestown without corn, without Ratcliffe and without two-thirds of its crew. This skirmish marked the beginning of the first Anglo-Powhatan War, 1609–1614.

Things were becoming ever more desperate. Most urgent of all, the colonists needed food. President George Percy sent Francis West to trade with the Patawomeck, a tribe living in the northern Chesapeake region along the Potomac River. Smith had encountered them the previous summer when searching for gold (they had taken him to the open mine on the riverbank). Percy hoped that as the Patawomeck had seen nothing of the English since then, they might be more open to trading than the southern Powhatan tribes now seemed to be. Regardless, West and his men chose to confront the Patawomeck with gratuitous force. Percy later admitted that the Englishmen had "used some harsh and cruel dealing by cutting off two of the savages' heads and other extremities".[5]

West succeeded in obtaining a boatload of corn from the beleaguered Patawomeck, but instead of returning to Jamestown with this essential cargo, he headed out of the Chesapeake Bay and sailed for England. By normal standards, such duplicity was inexcusable, but West was the younger brother of Lord De La Warr, the man named as the first governor of Virginia. Instead of being disciplined when he arrived in London, West was given a new command and sent back to Jamestown.

When Percy realized West was not returning from his trip up the Potomac, there was no doubting the seriousness of their situation.

Wahunsenacawh, the paramount chief, had ordered an end to trading with the English. Open hostilities with the Powhatan meant Jamestown's food supply was effectively shut down. The subsequent deaths during the winter of 1609/10 – the first without Smith around to lead the settlers – were the worst in the young colony's history. These months became known as the "Starving Time", as hundreds perished. The problems Smith had faced in earlier years returned with a vengeance: the ships of the third supply had jettisoned much of their vital cargo in the great storm; trade withered; drought left the fields barren; the winter was bitterly cold. The settlers were also living in terror. Wahunsenacawh had ordered that any settler who left the security of the fort should be attacked. One contributor to *The Generall Historie* observed:

> Now we all found the losse of Captaine Smith, yea his greatest maligners could now curse his losse: as for corne, provision and contribution from the Salvages, we had nothing but mortall wounds, with clubs and arrowes.[6]

Food was in such short supply that weapons and metal tools were now willingly traded for a pittance of corn. The colonists were so fearful of leaving the fort, they demolished their houses in Jamestown to feed their fires. Smith's one-time archenemy George Percy shared the most complete account of the catastrophe he was facing, noting at one point: "Then having fed upon horses and other beasts as long as they lasted, we were glad to make shift with vermin, as dogs, cats, rats, and mice."[7] Later excavations at Jamestown confirm the colonists resorted to eating many objectionable foods, including poisonous snakes.[8]

Even the greatest taboo of all – the consumption of human flesh – was broken, according to forensic archaeologists. One presumed victim was a fourteen-year-old girl (the researchers called her "Jane") who arrived in 1609 and whose remains were uncovered in 2012. Detailed analysis of markings on her skull and tibia indicate that she was dismembered by two people; one appeared to be an experienced butcher, the other an amateur.[9] It is unlikely the girl was killed for food; she most probably died from starvation, with her body carved up and shared to save the living. Even so, her bones corroborate the contemporary accounts of cannibalism in the colony, including those from George Percy.

A less fortunate casualty was the wife of another of the newcomers. Henry Collins took a knife to his pregnant wife and murdered her as she slept. He first removed his unborn child from her womb, slipping the foetus into the freezing James River. Then he chopped up his wife's remains and salted down her body parts for the winter. One report even claimed that Collins had eaten everything except his wife's head before his crime was discovered. George Percy's response was to hang Collins by his thumbs until he confessed; he was later executed. One witness recalled with black humour: "now whether shee was better roasted, boyled or carbonado'd [grilled], I know not, but of such a dish as powdered [salted] wife I never heard of."[10]

This murder was the exception, but Percy admitted that cannibalism of the recently departed became common in these dark days, and that:

> nothing was spared to maintain life and to do those things which seem incredible, as to dig up dead corpse out of graves and to eat them, and some have licked up the blood which hath fallen from their weak fellows.[11]

The London Company had no knowledge of the horrors unfolding in Jamestown, but they were keen to fund and victual another supply. Their goal was not to end the starving time, but to install the colony's leadership. Sir Thomas Gates, presumed lost on the *Sea Venture*, had been sent out only as an interim governor, and it was imperative that Lord De La Warr and his fleet get to Virginia as soon as possible.

Smith was busy defending his reputation, but the company's distractions also afforded him time to recuperate from his burns. The most Smith could expect from the physicians of the day was a warm, comfortable bed, a daily bowl of soup, and perhaps soothing oils to help speed his healing. He would have been badly burned across much of his lower body, and the scar tissues would most likely have given him pain for the rest of his life. He lived for another twenty-two years with the injury, yet he never again referred to it in any of his published writings.

Despite his struggles with the company, Smith emerged as one of the most passionate champions for the opportunities offered to England by colonizing the Americas. He had copious notes and survey logs from his expeditions, and from 1610 onwards Smith set about drawing the first proper chart of the Chesapeake region, even though he had no formal training in map-making. Smith had probably learned simple triangulation and range-finding techniques from artillery officers during his time in eastern Europe, but he must have picked up some of his cartographic skills while in London.

During his stay in the capital between 1605 and 1606, Smith most likely met Thomas Harriot, the famous astronomer and mathematician. Harriot was on the 1585 expedition to Roanoke, and later hired by Sir Walter Raleigh to run a school for navigators.[12] The astronomer was also a proficient linguist, and he published the first English-Algonquian dictionary and book of grammar (now lost). When Smith was helping Bartholomew Gosnold set up the logistics for the Jamestown expedition, Harriot was in the employment of Henry Percy, the Duke of Northumberland and older brother of George Percy. Thus, Harriot was almost certainly involved in the London Company's early planning in some way. So it is quite likely Smith received valuable tuition from Harriot in both Algonquian and map-making before he left for Virginia.

Once Smith drafted his *Map of Virginia*, he would have needed to find an engraver and printer for it. His first call would have been to the area surrounding St Paul's Cathedral, where narrow alleyways were crammed with more than one hundred publishers and countless booksellers. Alas, Smith said he could find no printer anywhere in London prepared to take on his manuscript. The reason almost certainly lay just a hundred yards from the main entrance to St Paul's, in Abergavenny House in Ave Maria Lane, the new headquarters of the Stationers' Company.

The Stationers' Company controlled all the printing presses in London, and no work could be published without first being submitted to Stationers' Hall for approval. The merchants of London were a close-knit community, and they frequently invested in each other's ventures.

Several members of the Stationers' Company had made substantial investments in the Virginia colony, and the Stationers' Company itself had paid £125 into the joint-stock company. Anything Smith made public would be a vindication of his vital role in the colony and would help clear his name; but any revelations would most likely also come at the expense of the reputation of various "gentlemen". Consequently, it seems he was forced to look farther afield. This might explain why, in 1612, Smith chose to publish his work with the only printer based in Oxford, two days' journey from London.

Joseph Barnes was the university printer in Oxford, where the Stationers' Company of London had no influence. Barnes usually kept his business to printing religious and academic treatises, but he was not against elbowing in on the competition from London.

A typical printer's premises in the seventeenth century, from an engraving by Abraham van Weerdt (Archiv für Buchgewerbe und Graphik).

Smith's book was edited by the Reverend William Symonds, an Oxford graduate and acquaintance of Robert Bertie, now the 14th Lord Willoughby. Smith dedicated his book to Sir Edward Seymour, 1st Earl of Hertford and 1st Baron Beauchamp, who also had links with Lord Willoughby. Bertie quite possibly introduced Smith to important contacts in Oxford, and Seymour's name in this position of honour suggests he too might have helped in bringing the book to press, possibly by underwriting the costs. Smith made no money from his first book, *A True Relation,* which had been published in 1608 without his knowledge; he is unlikely to have made very much from his second one either. He may not have cared. This publication was more about establishing himself as an explorer, ready for hire, and making public his version of the events for which he had been censured.

Smith's book was presented in two parts. The first, *A Map of Virginia, With a Description of the Countrey,* included a finely engraved chart based on his explorations of the Chesapeake Bay, the finest map of Virginia for nearly two hundred years, and one of Smith's most enduring legacies. The map was accompanied with thirty-nine pages of text describing the geography, resources, animals, plant life and people of Virginia – the first detailed record of the life and customs of the native peoples of North America during this period. The quarto volume was written factually, without endorsement or condemnation, and it ranks as one of the finest early colonial ethnographic chronicles.

The second part of the book, entitled *The Proceedings of the English Colonie,* was less of a sensation. A rambling, vague account of Jamestown's early years, incorporating writing from several other authors, it nonetheless stands as the only comprehensive narrative of life in Virginia from April 1606 to mid-1609.

When John Smith left Jamestown in October 1609, there were five hundred colonists. Six months later, only sixty remained. In the words of George Percy (who was president at the time), "the reste beinge either sterved throwe famin or cut of by the Salvages".[13] If Smith ever wanted

Smith's *Map of Virginia* (1612) remained in active use for seven decades and helped open up this part of North America to European exploration, settlement and trade.

As recently as 1909, his map was cited in a legal dispute over the boundary between the states of Maryland and West Virginia.[14]

exoneration for his handful of sins in Virginia, then this was his judge: the heavy toll of that winter was not inevitable.

In March 1610, after the worst of the winter had passed, George Percy dropped downriver to visit the men whom Smith had stationed in a small settlement at a place called Point Comfort, close to the Kecoughtan village. Smith had sent them there, hoping the area would have enough resources to make them self-sufficient. Percy found the men to be fit and healthy, having survived on crabs, oysters and a few pigs. Smith's policy of winter dispersal worked. If his strategy had been applied more widely, there is every chance more colonists would have survived the scourge of that cruel season.

On May 22, 1610, one of the settlers at Point Comfort called out – two ships were coming across the Chesapeake Bay. It was the *Deliverance* and *Patience* – in the circumstances, very appropriately named. The two ships had sailed from Bermuda and they carried the survivors of the wrecked *Sea Venture*.

The vessels had been built on the island, partly from timbers and equipment salvaged from the wrecked flagship. The forty-foot *Deliverance* had received most of the *Sea Venture*'s usable materials. In the case of the twenty-nine-foot *Patience*, only one bolt had been used from the flagship, everything else having been fabricated from local trees. It was a remarkable feat of ingenuity, hard work and leadership. One hundred and fifty people had left Woolwich on the *Sea Venture* the year before, and all but six of them completed the passage to Virginia.

Sir Thomas Gates, Captain Newport and the other *Sea Venture* survivors moored at Jamestown two days later. They were totally unprepared for what they found. The colony was a ghost town, with no sign of life: houses were torn down, weeds grew across pathways, and the gates to the fort were hanging off their hinges. Governor Gates ordered the church bell to be rung, rousing the colonists from their stupor. They staggered, blinking, into the daylight, near-skeletons "crying out we are starved! We are starved!"[14]

The newcomers from the *Sea Venture* were traumatized, for they had been led to believe they were sailing to a fully functioning colony, not a community of the living dead. They had already survived what they thought was the worst of hells; now they were stranded in another. Gates had only brought scant rations from Bermuda for the trip to Jamestown. They had a small surplus, but only enough to feed the settlers for a couple of weeks. He looked around and saw there was nothing to eat at the colony. Anything remotely edible had long been consumed, and nothing had been planted.

Gates saw only one way forward. He had four small ships at his disposal. They would strip the fort, load the ships, sail north to Newfoundland, and hope they could catch fish on the voyage to keep them alive. The colony's heavy cannon were buried outside the gate to keep them from the hands of the Powhatan. Some of the colonists urged Gates to set fire to Jamestown as a final act of defiance. Gates was more temperate and opposed the idea on the grounds that others may one day arrive from England expecting shelter. "We know not but that as honest men as ourselves may come and inhabit here", he reportedly told them.[16]

On June 7, 1610, a lone drummer beat a solemn cadence as the remnants of the Jamestown colony boarded the ships, the *Patience* and the *Deliverance,* together with the *Virginia* and the *Discovery*. The refugees from Bermuda were still in shock, the survivors from Jamestown barely able to stagger up the gangplanks. At midday, musketeers fired a ceremonial round as the desperate fleet dropped from its moorings.

They had a slow start, drifting a short distance downriver before anchoring for the night off the Isle of Hogs. That evening, they watched the sun set over Jamestown, just two miles away, a wretched reminder of their failed experiment. They were yet another Roanoke – proof the English could not make a permanent settlement in America.

The following day, the ships had barely set off down the James when a lookout spotted a small boat approaching them from further downstream. A messenger, one Captain Edward Brewster, clambered on board Gates' ship, pressing a letter into the hand of the astonished acting governor. It was from Lord De La Warr, and it explained that he had sailed from London on April 1 with three ships. He had another 150 recruits with him, as well as enough supplies to keep Jamestown going for a year. His fleet had anchored at Point Comfort just two days previously, and the men there had told him about Gates' planned evacuation. He ordered Gates to turn around immediately.

De La Warr[17] had now assumed his position as governor and captain-general of Virginia. Gates was no doubt relieved he had prevented the torching of the fort, and he gave the order to return. With a following breeze, the four ships were moored off Jamestown before nightfall, little more than twenty-four hours after their departure.

De La Warr finally arrived at Jamestown proper on Sunday, June 10. He was appalled at the condition of the fort and the idleness of the colonists. If they had thought John Smith's regime was tough, they had not counted on De La Warr. He demanded the area be cleared of filth and rubbish at once.

He then turned his attention to relations with the Powhatan. The company's directors had suggested converting the "savages" to Christianity, as they preferred to have the colonists live peacefully alongside their neighbours. At least this seemed a suitable scheme from the distance of London. But these laudable ambitions were soon set aside. His Lordship demanded that Wahunsenacawh, the paramount chief, return their stolen weapons and tools. Wahunsenacawh replied with "proud and disdainful answers", and suggested that next time the English messengers should return with a gift of a coach and three horses! De La Warr recognized this as the humiliating snub the Powhatan chief had intended.

The new governor's response was swift and brutal. He sent a punitive force under George Percy to the Paspahegh village: the *weroance* and several warriors were killed, the village burnt down, and the chief's wife and her children taken hostage. On his way downstream, Percy decided to dispose of the children "by throwing them overboard and shooting out their brains in the water".[18] On arrival at Jamestown, De La Warr said he wanted the queen "dispatched (the best way he thought to burn her)".[19] Percy chose to take her ashore and "put her to the sword".

De La Warr did not limit his brutality to the Powhatan people. He revised the laws in Jamestown, introducing the death penalty for adultery, theft and unauthorized trade with the locals. Those who did "the necessaries of nature" within a quarter mile of the fort, who were late for work, or who questioned his authority, received a lighter punishment – they were merely whipped.

Smith wrote little about his life in the capital after his return from Jamestown, instead concentrating on the publication of his maps and accounts of Virginia. He still had a farm in Lincolnshire, which provided him with a modest income, and he might have gone north to check on his tenants, and visit his family and friends. However, London was where everything of importance happened, and where anyone of importance lived. So he is unlikely to have stayed away from the capital for long.

His sometime mentor, Peregrine Bertie, 13th Baron Willoughby de Eresby, had died in 1601, while Smith was away fighting the Turks. Since inheriting his father's title, Robert Bertie had become a very influential man. The 14th Baron Willoughby was certainly in London during the summer of 1610, because the King had sent him to Gravesend to welcome Lewis Frederick, Prince of Wirtemberg, and escort him up the Thames to Westminster. Bertie's younger brother Peregrine, now twenty-five, had recently married, and was a Member of Parliament for Lincolnshire, so he too spent much of his time in London. Given John Smith's penchant for networking, there is little doubt he would have made calls on both brothers and shared tales of his adventures in Virginia.

Smith also met the Reverend Samuel Purchas, vicar of Eastwood parish church in Essex. Purchas was a few years older than Smith and destined to become successor to Richard Hakluyt as England's most respected compiler of travellers' voyages. By 1610 or 1611, Purchas was in London working on a major tome with a fittingly immodest title: *Purchas His Pilgrimage: or Relations of the World and the Religions observed in all Ages and Places discovered, from the Creation unto this Present.* (It is interesting to note that Purchas had no problem finding a publisher in London; his manuscript was sold by William Stansby at a shop in St Paul's churchyard.) Smith must have met Purchas around this time, because Purchas' section on Virginia borrowed heavily from Smith's knowledge of the region and events at Jamestown – so much so, it was biased in Smith's favour. The book's popularity must have gone some way towards rehabilitating Smith's name; it was reprinted four times between its publication in 1613 and Purchas' death in 1626, and it was said the King had read it seven times.[20]

Purchas' book may have been partial towards Smith, but it was not the only respected publication to support his version of the Jamestown story. William Strachey, who had been among those marooned on Bermuda when the *Sea Venture* was wrecked, had taken on the role of colony secretary when he finally arrived in Jamestown. In late 1611, he returned to England, where he completed *The History of Travel into Virginia Britannia*. Strachey arranged for George Percy (also recently returned from Jamestown) to present a copy to his brother, the Duke of Northumberland, in 1612.[21] In his *History*, Strachey complimented Smith's management of the colony:

> Sure I am there will not return from thence in haste anyone who hath been more industrious [than Captain John Smith], or who hath had – Captain George Percy excepted – greater experience amongest them, however misconstruction may transduce him here at home.[22]

As an independent witness to the events in question, Strachey's reverence must also have helped Smith recover his good character.

On November 6, 1612, the eighteen-year-old Henry Stuart, the Prince of Wales, died – most likely of typhoid fever. Henry was widely seen as a promising heir to his father's thrones. He was also a great supporter of colonization and had been actively involved in the London Company, despite his youth. His body lay in state for a month while the country went into mourning. His funeral was held on December 7, and the elaborate procession surpassed even that for Queen Elizabeth. Two of the chariots carried musicians dressed as "Virginian priests", while others in the parade dressed as "Indian slaves", in tribute to the prince's interests. His father detested funerals and refused to attend any of the proceedings. His younger brother, Charles, who was twelve at the time, succeeded Henry as heir apparent.

Henry's death came as a blow to those trying to establish permanent English settlements in North America. Smith, for his part, was undeterred. He could not return to Jamestown, but he continued to glean everything he could from ships returning. He was prepared to do anything he could to regain his standing and get back to America.

Finally, in early 1614, he won his chance. A group of London merchants agreed to fund a fishing expedition to what was then called Northern Virginia (today's Maine). Smith was given command of two whaling ships, with the captains Michael Cooper and Thomas Hunt under his authority. Sailing with the fleet was the Patuxet warrior called Squanto, who had "volunteered" to come to England with Captain George Weymouth back in 1605. (Some claim he was kidnapped.) Now Smith was taking Squanto back to his homeland, near the modern town of Plymouth, Massachusetts.

On March 3, the two ships left the Kent Downs with a favourable wind and headed down the English Channel for the Atlantic. This was pure elixir for Captain Smith. The weight of the years of defending his name and of struggling to get sponsorship fell away and disappeared into the ship's wake.

The ships were heading for the fishing station of Monhegan Island, a craggy lump of rock scarcely a square mile in area, jutting out of the Atlantic ten miles off the Maine coast. They made landfall sometime in April 1614 after an uneventful crossing. The island was already a familiar haunt of English sailors, and there were up to two hundred fishing boats at anchor in the harbour at any one time.

This was strictly a financial venture for the London merchants, and Smith was instructed to hunt for "jubartes" – a general term for rorqual or finback whales. These cetaceans are fast swimmers, making them difficult to hunt. When it became clear he would not be able to fill his holds with jubartes, Smith told his men to turn to fishing and trading furs, aiming to bring in some sort of profit for the fleet's investors.

While his men kept busy trading and fishing, Smith took a crew of eight in a small boat to explore the northeastern coastline of America, scouting suitable sites for a permanent English settlement. Indeed, he was always more interested in exploring than fishing and had brought six or seven charts of the area with him for this clandestine side mission. Unfortunately, he found these maps to be:

> so unlike each to other, and most so differing from any true proportion, or resemblance of the Countrey, as they did mee no more good, then so much waste paper, though they cost me more.[23]

There was nothing for it but to make his own.

For the next few weeks, Smith and his crew surveyed "from Point to Point, Ile to Ile, and Harbour to Harbour, with the Soundings, Sands, Rocks, and Land-marks as I passed close aboard the Shore in a little Boat",[24] travelling as far south as Cape Cod. The result was the most accurate chart so far of the coastline of northern Virginia. Smith had been taken with the French name for Canada, "Nouvelle France", and he called the area "New England". (Perhaps secretly, he also hoped for a knighthood to match Drake's award for naming "New Albion".)

On his map, Smith identified a variety of "Land-marks". There was Cape Tragabigzanda, named after his paramour in Constantinople (now called Cape Anne). He called the three islands off Cape Tragabigzanda's headland the Turk's Heads, from his coat of arms (now Milk Island, Thacher Island and Straitsmouth Island). He named a small island archipelago six miles off the coast of New Hampshire and Maine the Smith Islands (now the Isles of Shoals). Smith also marked a site he claimed had "an excellent good harbour, good land; and no want of any thing, but industrious people".[25] It was this endorsement that led a group of colonists to choose the spot for a landing six years later. Smith called it Accomack; it is now known as Plymouth.

When Smith returned from Monhegan Island on July 18, 1614, he arranged for Captain Hunt to load a cargo of dried fish into his ship. The plan was to take the shipment to Spain, where there was always a high demand for Friday fish among observant Catholics. Before he set out, Hunt decided to indulge in some unauthorized trading for personal profit: he lured twenty or so locals on board his ship with the intention of selling them as slaves in Spain. Among the men was Squanto, who Smith had only just returned to his people. Smith was disgusted by this treachery.

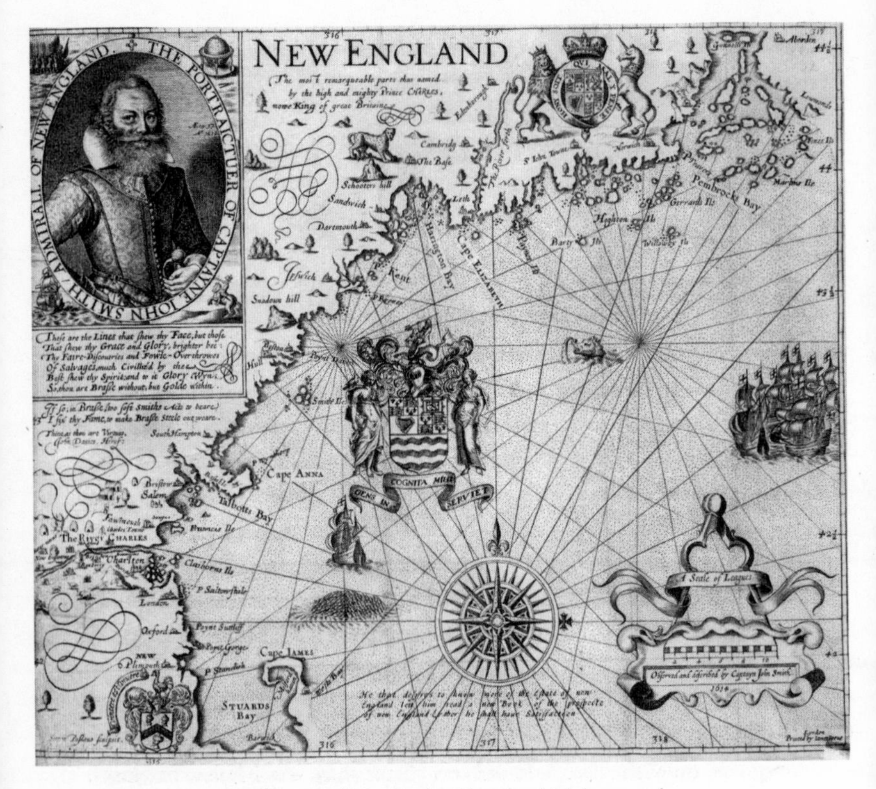

Smith's map of *New England* (1616), which he named.

This was not the end of Hunt's betrayal, in Smith's view. In 1616, he went on to accuse Hunt of trying to steal his charts of New England to present as his own in London. To ensure the success of the scheme, Smith said, Hunt planned to strand him on an uninhabited island. As Smith recounted Hunt's acts, he seethed with rage:

> Though I have had many discouragements by the ingratitude of some, the malicious slanders of others, the falsenesse of friendes, the trechery of cowards, and slowness of adventurers; but chiefly by one Hunt, who was Master of the ship, with whom oft arguing these projects.[26]

It was a rant against the lifetime of injustices Smith had suffered, with Hunt named as the vilest of his many antagonists. Smith always claimed he was the victim of a social system that allowed others far less competent than him to flourish, purely because of their superior status and connections. In his mind, such injustices would no longer exist in the egalitarian society he hoped would be established across the seas in America.

Smith's return from New England was uneventful, and on August 5 he made landfall at Plymouth, England. The Mount Batten peninsula there had long offered a perfect natural harbour at Cattewater, and as early as the fourteenth century, Plymouth had been used as a base for England's naval operations against France. When Smith was a boy, Sir Francis Drake had famously waited at Plymouth to launch his attack on the Spanish Armada, and the city was still at the heart of the nation's maritime defences. Plymouth's open access to the Atlantic had made the harbour the departure point of choice for transatlantic voyages, and it was the first port of call for many ships on their return. That was partly why the second royal charter James established for exploration of the New World went to Plymouth as the base for its operations.

Fired up with a vision for starting his own colony in New England, Smith called on "his honourable friend" Sir Ferdinando Gorges, who was a major shareholder in the Plymouth Company. Gorges had helped fund the disastrous Popham Colony in 1607, but his enthusiasm for sponsoring settlements in America had not dimmed. There was more money to be found in London, but Plymouth sailors were expert fishermen, so Smith opted to stay and raise investors from the West Country.

In comparison with the capital, Plymouth was a small city, tightly contained within its defensive walls.[27] Only eight thousand or so people called it home, making it thirty times smaller than London. Even so, Plymouth had one big advantage for a stranger like John Smith: the whole town was devoted to the maritime trade, yet it was small enough for him to make the acquaintance of anyone important within a very short time.

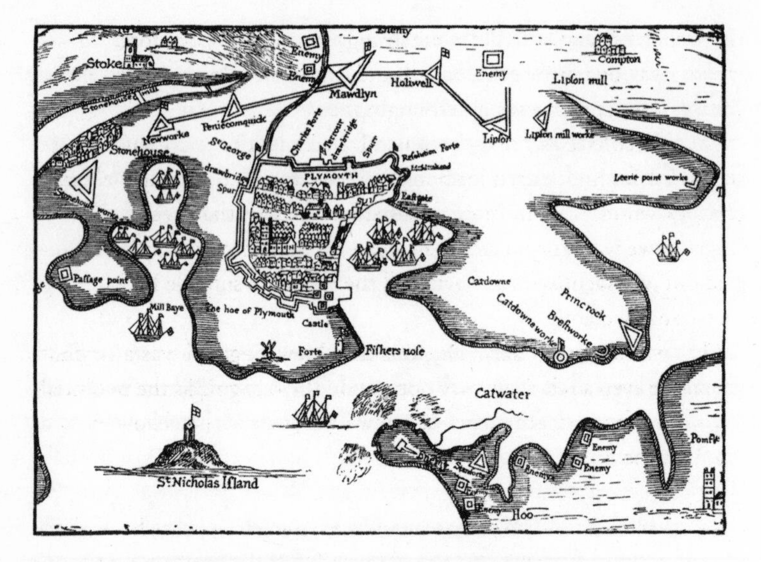

Part of "A True Mapp and Description of the Towne of Plymouth and the Fortifications thereof at the last siege, 1643." From a 17th century map reproduced in Bracken, C.W. 1931. *A History of Plymouth and her Neighbours*, Underhill, opp. p. 126.

Within a matter of weeks, Smith was promised four ships to be ready by Christmas for a transatlantic journey. Happy news in hand, he set out for London with his most valuable assets, the survey notes and records from his recent excursion. Once again, he needed a publisher, but this time he found one in London without a problem. This suggests the embargo on his writings had been lifted and his rehabilitation was complete.

Smith's new book, entitled *A Description of New England*, was first printed by Humfrey Lownes, and sold by Robert Clerke from his shop in Chancery Lane in June 1616. *A Description* included a valuable inventory of the economic resources on offer in the region; no mention here of gold, or a route to the South Sea, but instead a comprehensive list of the timber, fish and furs that would bring real profits to investors. Smith's writing was, by now, accomplished, and demonstrated his expertise and authority as an explorer and ethnographer.

However, *A Description* was also far more ambitious than its title suggested, for Smith used the book as a platform for outlining his vision of a new world. "Heer nature and liberty affords us that freely, which in England we want, or it costeth us dearely", he wrote grandly.[28] He singled out Massachusetts as having all the elements suitable for building a sustainable colony.

He was under no naïve illusions that New England was a verdant utopia, or even a relatively easy option. But he recognized the potential of this newfound country, and he knew how to entice his fellow men to join him there:

> If a man worke but three dayes in seaven, he may get more then hee can spend, unless he will be excessive…[or] fish but an houre in a day, to take more then they eate in a weeke.[29]

Smith also promoted his dream of how to create a new form of society, free from the shackles of old England: "here are no hard Landlords to racke us with high rents", he said, for "here every man may be master and owner of his owne labour and land."[30] These were the ideals on which the United States of America would be founded some 160 years later. From the crucible of his struggles and adventures, John Smith was fired up to become one of the first pioneers in this new land – and its first blazing promoter.

Smith returned to Plymouth in January 1615 with two hundred pounds from London investors and six willing colonists, but he found not a single ship was actually available to them. The indefatigable Sir Ferdinando Gorges managed to attract more sponsors, and eventually two ships were placed under Smith's command – now supported by the majestic title of "Admiral of New England". One of the ships was sizeable, weighing two hundred tons and therefore considerably larger than the *Susan Constant*. The smaller ship was fifty tons, perhaps a little bigger than the *Godspeed*. The ships were adequate for the purpose in hand.

The fleet left Plymouth in March with a plan to set up a small colony of sixteen men, and send the ships home to England loaded with whatever dried fish and whale oil they could collect before the winter. However, Smith's sailing jinx returned, and the ships were struck by a storm during the crossing. Nothing was ever heard again of the smaller ship. Smith's flagship lost her masts and nearly foundered, with each watch pumping five or six thousand strokes to keep the ship afloat. The crew limped back to Plymouth under jury rig.

Undeterred, Smith left again on June 24 in what he called "a small bark of sixty tons", a relatively small ship, perhaps eighty feet long. On board were fourteen sailors, plus his sixteen prospective colonists. His luck was no better on this second voyage: shortly after land dipped below the horizon, another vessel spotted them and pursued them for the next two days.

Eventually, they were caught. It was glaringly obvious to Smith that these were pirates, and when they came alongside, he bizarrely took offence and locked himself in his cabin, refusing to leave. Some of the buccaneers came aboard and Smith wrote that they called down to announce they were his former colleagues. Who knows from where? Perhaps from the Mediterranean, or from one of the Jamestown voyages. If he joined them, they claimed, they would make him their captain. This was probably a trick to get Smith out of his cabin. If so, it failed. Smith refused, and, he said, the pirates gave up and sailed off. In the circumstances, it is a difficult story to believe, but Smith had nothing to lose or to gain by its telling, except perhaps to reinforce his stubbornness.

This period in the early decades of the seventeenth century was a great age for piracy, mainly as a result of international reconciliations. In 1604, England and Spain had officially made peace. Five years later, the Netherlands and Spain agreed their own truce. These treaties left hundreds of ships and thousands of sailors without a means to earn a living in their nations' navies. Still, there were rich prizes to be had – gold and silver from the Americas, and silks and spices from the Orient. Any hapless merchantman on the high seas was now fair game.

Having escaped this threat once, Smith chose to sail to New England via the Azores, hoping the strong presence of well-armed Spanish ships in those waters might offer some deterrence to pirates. But as he approached the island of Flores, he found himself pursued again, this time by two pirate ships. Smith's crew feared they were Turks (they were in fact French), and they argued for a prompt surrender, rather than risk being killed in a fight or being taken as slaves. Smith declared he would rather "fire the powder and split the ship, if they would not stand to their defence".[31] They were fired upon, but managed to sail clear and escape once again.

Smith should have realized there was a strong likelihood of an attack. The Azores were a Spanish base, set up to resupply galleons en route from Mexico and Peru with their precious treasure for Philip III. Consequently, the surrounding seas were infested with pirates. Within a day, four more ships – again French – closed in on Smith's vessel. Again Smith wanted to engage in battle, but his ship was hopelessly out-gunned and his sailing master and other officers wisely advised against it. They reminded their admiral they were there to fish, not to fight.

Smith went on board the pirates' flagship to negotiate. The sailors claimed they were Protestants from La Rochelle and were carrying *lettres de marque* from the French government, authorizing them to attack and rob ships from Catholic nations, or those dedicated to piracy. Under the rules of the day, this meant they were strictly not pirates, but privateers. But when they attacked Protestant ships, including English ones like Smith's, it was illegal under maritime law – an act of piracy. This legal nuance did not stop them from arresting Smith, taking his ship, and dividing his crew among their own fleet. Over the next five or six days, the enlarged squadron of five ships chased every vessel they sighted, capturing some and plundering others.

At this point, the Frenchmen decided to return Smith's ship to his command. Smith scrambled from ship to ship of the pirate fleet, gathering his equipment and weapons, including "powder, match, hookes, instruments, his sword and dagger, bedding, aqua vitæ, his commission, apparell, and many other things".[32] As he conducted his search, another sail was sighted, and the fleet gave chase. Now Smith was marooned on board the flagship, the *Don de Dieu* (Gift of God), where he was obliged to spend the night.

Here, events become confused. The next morning, Smith said, his ship's master, Edmund Chambers, brought his vessel close to the French flagship, calling on Smith to come aboard. Smith ordered Chambers to send a boat to pick him up, to which Chambers replied that the longboat was damaged, and Smith should come over in a French boat. (In a court case heard several months later, six witnesses testified that Chambers was lying about the state of the boat.) When Chambers approached, he accidentally split his ship's mainsail on the cross-spars of the French vessel. With the mainsail torn, Chambers' ship would have lost speed and she fell astern. Before long, Smith had lost sight of his flagship over the horizon.

He was now trapped on the *Don de Dieu* with nothing more than the clothes on his back. For days, the French flotilla cruised the area looking for prizes. On several occasions they stopped English ships, and Smith was locked away below decks in the gunroom, lest he try to escape. Eventually, the French spied what they wanted – heavily armed Spanish galleons heading east from the Americas.

As a child dazzled by the Armada, and as a veteran of the war in the Low Countries, Smith had no love of the Spanish, and he agreed to fight them alongside his captors. For several hours the two fleets exchanged fire, until the sails of the Spanish ships were shredded. Still the Spaniards would not submit. The French commander dared not board the galleons with their lethal guns primed ready for a broadside. It was a stalemate, and the two fleets separated.

Smith's life as a privateer continued for the next several months, which proved to be a very promising career move. Thirty thousand "pieces of eight" were taken from one Spanish ship alone; another yielded fourteen chests of silver and eight thousand rialls of gold, "besides the good pillage and rich coffers of many rich passengers".[33] The French commander had assured Smith a share of the spoils when they got to France. With so many failed ventures trailing behind him, Smith needed the income.

In October, Smith was transferred to a French caravel taking sugar

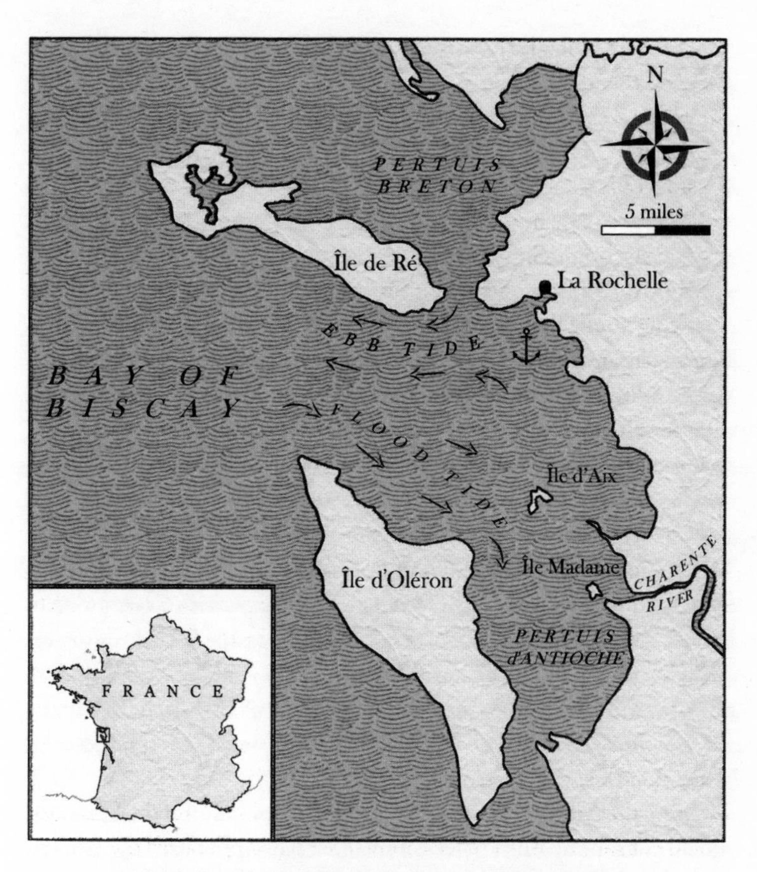

La Rochelle and surrounding islands. Smith escaped from the *Don de Dieu* at anchor, hoping to get to the Île de Ré. However, the strong ebb tide first swept him out to sea, and when the flood tide brought him back, he landed further south, on Île Madame.

to La Rochelle. He knew this was the first step towards his freedom and his fortune. The commander of the privateering fleet decided to accompany the caravel as far as the city port, where he anchored in one of the many small bays. This was part of a manoeuvre to cheat Smith out of his share of the plunder. On their arrival, the Frenchman threatened to turn Smith over to the authorities on a trumped-up charge.

That night a fierce storm blew up. While the crew of the *Don de Dieu* sheltered below decks, Smith crept out, slipped over the side and took the ship's longboat, casting the boat off in the rising gale. Unfortunately, there were no oars on board and he did not have the means to row himself. He intended to land on "Rat Isle" – the Île de Ré – which is now connected to the mainland by a two-mile-long bridge. With only a half pike (a long-handled spear) to steer with, he was carried out to sea by the tide, the waves threatening to swamp his boat at any moment. After more than twelve hours bobbing around in the storm, the wind and tide conspiring to drive him well off-course, he crawled ashore on another island, an "oazie [muddy] Ile", where wild fowlers "found mee neere drowned, and halfe dead, with water, colde, and hunger".[34] Smith pawned the longboat and used the proceeds to buy passage to La Rochelle. Here he learned that during the night's storm, the *Don de Dieu* had dragged her anchor and was wrecked, with half her crew drowned.

This saga has all the hallmarks of one of Smith's tall tales, but he provided enough details in his account to test his veracity. Contemporary French records confirm much of the story about the French privateers attacking the Spanish galleons, and their subsequent attacks on English ships.[35] Smith claimed the longboat was swept out to sea and back again, and this is exactly how he would have floated on an ebb tide followed by the flood.

Smith also claimed he was cast ashore on an island "by Charowne", which in all probability referred to the Charente River; this muddy, sluggish river enters the Bay of Biscay six miles south of La Rochelle. This is precisely the spot where the tidal currents would naturally have carried Smith's boat, especially with the benefit of a strong on-shore gale.

It has been argued that Smith may have washed up on the Île d'Aix,[36] a few miles south of La Rochelle, but this small rocky island does not fit Smith's account. A more likely spot is further south, in the mouth of the Charente River itself – the Île Madame. This low-lying island of oozy mud and sand matches Smith's description perfectly, even centuries later.

As soon as he got to La Rochelle, Smith reported to the Admiralty Office to complain about his treatment by the French sailors and claim compensation. Some of the survivors from the *Don de Dieu* substantiated

The "oazie" Île Madame at the mouth of the Charente River, where Smith's longboat eventually ran aground after drifting for twelve hours (photo by Peter Firstbrook).

his statement, and Smith was granted a share of whatever valuables might be recovered from the wreckage. Promises, however, would not pay his passage home.

Once again, Smith was destitute in a foreign country, and once again a lady of high standing came to his rescue, "Madam Chanoyes at Rotchell".[37] She was most likely a member of a prestigious family of lawyers, the Chaurroys, but other than her name, and an enigmatic reference to her generous assistance, he revealed no more.

The salvage teams were at work on the wreck of the *Don de Dieu,* and they swiftly recovered coins and other valuables worth 3,600 crowns (equivalent to about four years' wages for a craftsman).[38] The French Admiralty court told Smith he would receive his share in good time. With this hollow promise and Madam Chanoyes' help, he decided it was time to return home to England.

John Smith's coat of arms, which he presented to the Royal College of Heraldry for their endorsement in 1625. He chose the motto "Vincere est vivere" – "To conquer is to live".

14
Grandee

1615–1631

I know I shall bee taxed for writing so
much of my selfe, but I care not much
John Smith, The Generall Historie (1624)

By early December 1615, John Smith was back in Plymouth. It was rumoured he had drowned with the *Don de Dieu*, and had been buried in France along with the rest of the lost crew. Not for the first time, he reappeared suddenly as proof he had beaten the odds. However, Smith had given up his flagship, which did not thrill his investors. They expected an explanation from the admiral. He complained they had "not onely buried mee, but with so much infamy, as such trecherous cowards could suggest to excuse their villanies".[1] Fortunately, Smith was able to muster support to his side at his inquiry. On December 8, the steward on Smith's ship presented a deposition, confirmed by six others, that his commander had been left on the French pirate ship against his will. This exonerated Smith of blame and pointed the finger at the ship's master, Edmund Chambers, for being the real villain. Smith must also have met up with Sir Ferdinando Gorges during his stay in Plymouth, for Gorges repeated Smith's story in his own memoirs, *A Briefe Relation of the Discovery & Plantation of New England*.

With his good character restored once again, Smith travelled on to London, where he began work on *A Description of New England*. This relatively brief, sixty-four-page book was entered at Stationers' Hall, and seemed headed for a typical publication. But at the eleventh hour, Smith pulled off a masterstroke. As the *Description* was literally going through the presses, he used a contact – almost certainly Robert Bertie – to finagle an audience with the heir apparent to the throne. Smith asked the fifteen-year-old Prince Charles to bestow names to the coastline he had explored in Northern Virginia.

Charles changed Cape Tragabigzanda to Cape Anne (after his mother); and Accomack became "Plimouth" (four years before the Pilgrims established their colony). Other points of interest were also named: the prince called the river that flowed out into the Atlantic at Boston after himself. Several names were marked on Smith's map, including Aberdeen, Barnstable, Boston, Cambridge, Dartmouth, Ipswich, Oxford and South Hampton, although most of these towns are no longer where Charles originally placed them. Finally, the Prince agreed with Smith that the region should be known as New England.

With the place names agreed, Smith arranged for one of the leading engravers of the day, the Dutchman Simon van de Passe, to complete his map of the area. In the top left-hand corner de Passe included a portrait of the Admiral of New England – the only picture of John Smith made during his lifetime.

Because of the last-minute nature of these changes, the names on the map no longer matched the names used in the text of the book. Smith got around this problem by adding a table, which listed the old and new names alongside each other.

Nearly seven years had passed since John Smith's ignominious departure from Jamestown. In his absence, the colony had grown considerably, and he would no longer have recognized it. Little from Smith's tenure remained. When Lord De La Warr arrived from Bermuda in May 1609, he had ordered the colonists to rebuild the main fort. Yet, Smith's influence was still felt at Jamestown and his publications were generating more and more interest in the colonization of Virginia.

When Smith left Jamestown, Pocahontas had been told the captain had died, probably because his death seemed imminent when he boarded the ship for London. According to Powhatan oral histories she soon married an Indian warrior called Kocoum. This was probably in 1610, when she was around fifteen. Again according to oral history, they had one child.[2]

A man called John Rolfe, one of the survivors from the *Sea Venture*, began exporting Jamestown's first crop of tobacco in 1612. He seemed to throw himself into the work, perhaps still mourning the recent death of his wife and infant daughter. Sale of the leaf became a real money-spinner, and the colony began to expand.

In April 1613, during the First Anglo-Powhatan War, Captain Samuel Argall kidnapped Pocahontas. She was taken to the newly established English settlement of Henricus (Henrico) on the James River, about nine miles downriver from present-day Richmond. Her husband, Kocoum, was reportedly killed in a skirmish with the colonists sometime after her abduction. At Henricus, Pocahontas converted to Christianity and took the Christian name Rebecca. When the opportunity arose for her to return to her own people, she chose to remain with the English.

By then, Rolfe was a wealthy man with no wife or family. He took notice of the young "Indian princess" who lived across the river from his plantation, Varina Falls. A strong physical attraction began to torture this serious and pious man, who fretted about his "many passions and sufferings which I have daily, *hourly* – yea".[3] He claimed he had fallen in love with Pocahontas, but at the same time worried that her "education hath been rude, her manners barbarous, her generation accursed".[4]

They were married most likely on April 5, 1614. Their union was welcomed in Jamestown, with Deputy-Governor Thomas Dale declaring the event "another knot to bind the peace" with the Powhatan. Pocahontas' father, Wahunsenacawh, also gave the couple his blessing, and, more importantly, a piece of Powhatan land on the James River. John and Rebecca Rolfe lived at Varina Farms for the next two years, and on January 30, 1615, Pocahontas gave birth to their son. He was christened Thomas, after Sir Thomas Dale. Despite the well wishes, back in London there was a heated debate over the legitimacy of the union, and some thought Rolfe might be committing treason by marrying Powhatan royalty.

Jamestown was now well established – the very definition of a permanent English settlement – and satellite communities were springing up all along the James River. The London Company was always eager to capitalize on good news, and in 1616 it was decided the Rolfes should sail to England for a promotional tour. The public relations exercise was meant to show that the "heathen savages" could indeed be civilized. The message was clear: the Virginia colony was not just a sound investment, but also a secure one.

The Rolfes' ship, the *Treasurer*, landed in Plymouth on June 12, 1616, after a quick and uneventful passage. On board were Sir Thomas Dale, a cargo of John Rolfe's tobacco leaf, and an escort of eleven Powhatan men and women, including Pocahontas' half-sister Matachanna, who came as Thomas' nurse. Matachanna's husband, Tomocomo (also known as Uttamatomakkin), was a priest-counsellor to Wahunsenacawh; he accompanied Pocahontas, wearing full body paint and traditional skins.[5] Wahunsenacawh had given Tomocomo a stick with instructions to put a notch in it for every English person he saw. Smith wryly remarked "he was quickly wearie of that taske".[6]

The entourage made the long journey by coach to the capital, more than two hundred miles away. Until Pocahontas set foot in England, she had not seen a settlement that housed more than a few hundred people, let alone a coach, bridge or cobbled road. The cross-country journey was gruelling, taking over a week, including stops every night in overcrowded, flea-ridden inns. At the end of the ordeal she arrived in a city with a population of over a quarter of a million people. It was all a far cry from the dense forests and broad rivers of her homeland.

Her visit to London caused some anxiety over proper etiquette among the Court of King James, as well as the directors of the London Company. Smith had been clear in his letter to Queen Anne that Pocahontas should be treated as a royal princess, yet she had married a commoner. And the King himself considered Rolfe's involvement with her to be just short of subversion. To complicate matters, Pocahontas was now baptized a Christian, yet she was born a heathen and was therefore an "Indian Savage" in the eyes of the English. If her reception was handled well, it could lead to a lasting peace in Virginia and provide a stimulus to colonization. If handled badly, the consequences could be dire.

Pocahontas and her entourage stayed in a house in Brentford, then a small village ten miles west of the capital. A mile upriver from Brentford was Syon House, the country residence of the Earl of Northumberland, a home so magnificent that the body of Henry VIII lay overnight there in 1547 on its passage upriver for burial at Windsor. The London Company had sponsored the Rolfes' visit, but ever mindful of the bottom line, only allowed a miserly four pounds a week to accommodate the whole group. By comparison, in 1611, when Sir Robert Shirley arrived in London, acting as a special envoy from the Shah Abbas of Persia, he received four pounds a day for food, plus twenty pounds a month for rent, from the joint-stock Levant Company.[7]

When she landed at Plymouth, Pocahontas received the news that Smith was still alive. Her old friend was engaged busily in publishing *A Description of New England*, and so did not visit her immediately. He did, however, find time to write to the Queen and share the story of how Pocahontas had saved his life. The original letter does not survive, but Smith claimed he reproduced an abstract of "a little booke" in his *Generall Historie*, which suggests the original document was longer than the 906 words included there.[8]

Despite Smith's entreaties to Queen Anne, there is no record of Pocahontas ever being given a formal audience with the King at his court. She was undeniably received by "divers particular persons of Honour", including John King, the Lord Bishop of London, who "entertained her with festival state and pomp beyond what I have seen in his greate hospitalitie afforded to other ladies".[9] Lady De La Warr also introduced the Powhatan "princess" to Queen Anne.

On January 5, 1617, Pocahontas attended a Twelfth Night Masque Ball held at the old Banqueting House in the Palace of Whitehall, where she met both the King and Queen. She was accompanied by Tomocomo, but there is no evidence her husband joined them for the evening. It might simply have been that, as a commoner, he was not invited, especially since King James disapproved of the marriage. There might have been another diplomatic motivation for his absence, however. Rolfe was the chief promoter of Virginia's growing tobacco trade. The King was revolted by the smoking habit, which he argued was "a custome loathsome to the eye, hateful to the nose, harmefull to the braine, [and] dangerous to the lungs".[10] In the circumstances, it was probably prudent for everyone involved if John Rolfe kept a low profile.

The custom of the masquerade ball had been copied from the French court, and was an important part of the winter social season in London. Guests wore sumptuous costumes and were treated to an evening of elaborate theatre – singing, dancing and surreal performances, scripted on this occasion by none other than Ben Jonson. High-born ladies acted parts in the plays, and based on contemporary sketches, they often wore scandalous outfits, sometimes even baring a breast. On this particular evening, the Queen caused tongues to wag and fans to flutter when she danced with her husband's supposed lover, the handsome George Villiers, who had only the day before been created the new Earl of Buckingham.

Quite what Pocahontas and Tomocomo made of the spectacle is not known, but dressing in elaborate costumes, wearing masks, and singing and dancing were normal features of Powhatan entertainment. The reaction to the Queen dancing with Buckingham was perhaps the only portion of the evening they might have found bewildering.

During her visit, Pocahontas also had her portrait painted, and then engraved by Simon van de Passe, the same Dutch artisan who caught Smith's likeness for the *Map of Virginia*. The painting now hangs in the National Portrait Gallery in Washington, DC. Her Powhatan heritage is captured in her high cheekbones, golden skin and large dark eyes, while her tall hat, starched ruff and ostrich-plume fan – a typical European symbol for royalty – seem incongruous. A quizzical gaze hints at a dignified resignation over her predicament. She was a stranger here and a long way from home.

Surprisingly, Smith appeared in no hurry to visit Pocahontas. Clearly he wanted to help her as best he could, because he had tried to smooth her visit by writing to the Queen. But Pocahontas had been in London for several months before they met. There seems to be no valid reason for his delay, and he may have been needlessly postponing their inevitable meeting.

Portrait of Pocahontas, then going by her English name, Rebecca Rolfe, in an engraving by Simon van de Passe, circa 1616 (courtesy of the British Museum).

When they eventually did meet, it was an awkward reunion. Smith had never been at ease with women, and here before him was a fine-looking young lady, whom he fondly remembered as a girl turning naked cartwheels in the fort at Jamestown. Perhaps he was also embarrassed because his status in England was far below the commanding figure he cut in Virginia. In any case, when Smith finally made the trip to Brentford, he did not go alone:

> but hearing shee was at Branford [Brentford] with divers of my friends, I went to see her: After a modest salutation, without any word, she turned about, obscured her face, as not seeming well contented.[11]

It was not a promising start. Smith decided to give Pocahontas some time to herself, hoping she would warm to him. After two or three hours, he rejoined her, and then the recriminations started, and:

> she began to talke, and remembred mee well what courtesies [help] she had done: saying, You did promise Powhatan what was yours should bee his, and he the like to you; you called him father being in his land a stranger, and by the same reason so must I doe you.[12]

Pocahontas was angry. She reminded Smith of his obligations towards her father, and by extension to herself. When Smith was made a *weroance*, he had accepted certain responsibilities: "what was yours should bee his". Smith had been initiated into her tribe and he had not lived up to what was expected of him. Her father had given Smith land, a village, power, yet the Englishman had not returned this great favour. Smith had entirely misinterpreted the importance of the ritual he had endured at Werowocomoco ten years earlier.

But Pocahontas was not finished with her rebukes:

> They did tell us alwaies you were dead, and I knew no other till I came to Plimoth; yet Powhatan did command Uttamatomakkin [Tomocomo] to seeke you, and know the truth, because your Countriemen will lie much.[13]

Smith also spent time with Tomocomo, who asked him to "shew him our God, the King, Queene, and Prince". Smith explained about God as best he could, and told Tomocomo that he had already met the King. Tomocomo could not believe the shambling figure he had seen – with spindly legs and rolling eyes, his fingers constantly fiddling with his codpiece – was the ruler of the English. He was used to leaders who commanded respect. In comparison to Powhatan, James cut a comical figure.

In March, John Rolfe, his wife, his son and some of the other Powhatan visitors boarded the *George*. The master of the ship was Samuel Argall, who had kidnapped Pocahontas from the Patawomeck village. Now he was in charge of returning her to Virginia. But after Pocahontas boarded the ship, she was taken ill. As the ship dropped downriver from the Pool, her condition deteriorated quickly. The ship anchored off Gravesend, where she died soon after being taken ashore. According to her husband, her last words were, "all must die, but tis enough that her childe liveth".[14] She was twenty-two years old.

Pocahontas' death could have been caused by any of the many illnesses that plagued the citizens of the capital. However, she had been well just ten days previously, so her infection was most likely a fast-acting pathogen like smallpox, plague or typhoid, rather than a bronchial condition like pneumonia or tuberculosis. According to their oral history, the Powhatan believed she was poisoned,[15] although it is difficult to understand what the English stood to gain from her death. She was buried on March 21, 1617, in the parish church of St George's, in Gravesend. Her grave was said to be under the chancel, but the church was destroyed by fire in 1727, and the exact position today is not known.

John Rolfe felt he had to continue on to Virginia, though young Thomas was also visibly unwell. When the ship arrived in Plymouth, Rolfe left his two-year-old son in the care of Sir Lewis Stewkley, a cousin of Sir Walter Raleigh. Little Thomas stayed with Stewley's family until he could be turned over to his uncle, Henry Rolfe.

John Rolfe would not live to see his son again.

The *George* arrived in Jamestown in the early summer of 1617, during a period of expansion and prosperity. Rolfe's tobacco plantation had shown that a valuable cash crop could be raised in Virginia, and others were following his example. Estates were growing up on both sides of the James, using land seized from the Powhatan. Soon the colony numbered more than a thousand people. The make-up of the settlement also changed, with young families replacing all-male encampments. The English were clearly here to stay, and the Powhatan viewed this development with increasing concern.

The following year, Wahunsenacawh died. He was probably in his seventies or eighties, and with him went his moderating influence. He was initially succeeded by one brother, and soon after by another,

Opechancanough – John Smith's old adversary. The new chief changed his name to Mangopeesomon, which had a significance lost on the English colonists. When a Powhatan chief changed his name, it traditionally marked a new direction for the tribe; in this case, it was move away from their relatively peaceful accommodation of the colonists.[16]

In 1619, the colony established a general assembly, with members elected by Virginia's male landowners. This became the model for representative government in later colonies. In the same year, about twenty Africans arrived at the settlement on a slave ship captured from the Portuguese. The Africans stayed on at Jamestown as indentured servants, put to work picking tobacco. They became the first African slaves to work on an English plantation in North America.

The Powhatan became increasingly enraged by the colonists' insatiable appetite for land, and on the morning of Friday, March 22, 1622, Mangopeesomon ordered his warriors to attack all the English settlements along the James River. Nearly four hundred men, women and children were killed or injured. The death toll would have been much higher if not for a last-minute warning from some friendly Powhatan, which saved Jamestown. John Rolfe's plantation was one of those destroyed, and around this time Rolfe died, although it is unclear if he was killed in an attack or died as a result of illness or injury. He had remarried on his return to Virginia, and left a young widow, Jane, and their two-year-old daughter, Elizabeth.

Mangopeesomon hoped the assault would frighten the colonists into abandoning their settlements, but he misjudged their determination. When news of the attacks reached London in July, the consensus was for revenge; the wholesale slaughter of the "barbarians" was endorsed heartily. This started what became known as the Second Anglo-Powhatan War, which raged for the next ten years.

In 1623 Mangopeesomon sued for peace, and asked for a meeting with the colonists to discuss how they might live side by side. The English agreed to get together, but then laid an ambush and killed as many Powhatan as they could to revenge the massacre. They went on to raid several villages, burning the cornfields and buildings, before accepting a truce with the Powhatan.

The March 1622 massacre of the English colonists by the Powhatan, from a 1628 woodcut by Matthäus Merian (courtesy of the Colonial Williamsburg Foundation).

Despite the end of hostilities, the Virginia venture was in financial crisis. From the beginning, the London Company had been a losing proposition; by 1612 its debts had risen, and there was no cash to pay dividends to the original investors. In 1619 the company offered fifty-acre parcels of land in payment instead. The next year, the company introduced a new scheme to attract more colonists to Jamestown, allowing investors and existing residents to acquire land by paying for the passage of new settlers. In most cases, newcomers worked a period of servitude in exchange for the company's help. This initiative fuelled the land-grab in Virginia and triggered the Powhatan insurrection of 1622.

In May 1623, a Crown commission was established to investigate the company's alleged mismanagement of Virginia. Within a few months the commission concluded the settlement was in a "weak and miserable" condition: thousands had died; attempts to create a diversified economy had failed; and the company itself was bankrupt. On July 31, the attorney general reported to the King, advising that the letters patent of the company should be revoked.[17] In an attempt to take control of the situation, James dissolved the company on May 24, 1624, and declared Virginia to be the first official Crown colony, administered by a governor appointed by the King. In effect, the colony returned to something close to the original plan of 1606. And so ended the London Company, but not the English expansion into America.

Throughout the Second Anglo-Powhatan War, the English had built new communities along both sides of the James River, as well as south of the York River. Then, in 1633, the settlers palisaded off the whole peninsula between the York and the James, around the present site of Williamsburg. This encroachment into the most fertile land in the area stoked simmering resentments among the Powhatan. In 1644, Mangopeesomon, now in his early nineties, led another rebellion against the English – the start of the Third Anglo-Powhatan War.

This time, the Powhatan would not be able to make peace. In 1645 the paramount chief was captured and taken to Jamestown, where he was shot in the back by an English guard. His death effectively led to the disintegration of the Powhatan empire. The new chief, Necotowance, was forced to sign a treaty that ceded most of his land to the English, who also forced him to pay an annual tribute to the colonial governor.

During these years of change and turmoil in Virginia, John Smith was active behind the scenes. After the publication of *A Description of New England* in 1616, he tried to organize a new expedition. He was promised a fleet of twenty ships by the Plymouth Company, but the finances were as shaky as ever and his great fleet shrank to just three ships and a handful of prospective colonists. Undaunted, he prepared to sail for New England, but endless southwesterly gales pinned his fleet in Plymouth for three months during the spring of 1617. By the time they relented, it was too late in the year to make the crossing. The ships were sent fishing to earn their keep and Smith returned to London, where he tried to find another way to return to America.

First, he wrote an extended letter to Sir Francis Bacon, the new Lord Chancellor, making a strong business case for the settlement of New

England. It was an honest and realistic assessment of the potential for the region, promising no "mines of gold", but fish, furs and good timber for shipbuilding. Tactlessly, Bacon did not even give Smith the honour of a negative reply. But there was interest from other quarters for setting up another colony in the Americas.

King James had never been very tolerant of religious nonconformists, and the more radical groups, collectively called the Separatists, had moved to the Netherlands, where they hoped to find greater religious freedom. The Separatists considered their differences with the Church of England to be irreconcilable, as they wanted their worship to be independent of the traditions and organization of any central church. However, life was not perfect in the Netherlands either. The Separatists found the Dutch, if anything, too liberal. The language and culture were different, and their children were becoming more integrated into local customs as each year passed. In time, they feared their group, and therefore their beliefs, would be diminished in numbers, and in God's eyes.

In 1619, the London Company decided to grant the Separatists land at the far northern end of their chartered territory, near the mouth of the Hudson River. The prospective colonists knew they would need an expert navigator for the voyage, and John Smith offered his services. His experience in New England was second to none, but the Separatists had their doubts – Smith came with his reputation as a difficult and truculent man. They chose instead to enlist Captain Myles Standish, who had military experience in the Dutch wars, but who was unfamiliar with both the Atlantic and New England.

The so-called Pilgrims knew they needed Smith's expertise, so they bought his charts and navigational notes as they planned their journey. Two ships were procured. The sixty-ton *Speedwell* was a little larger than Smith's *Godspeed*, at about eighty feet long, and was used to bring colonists over from their exile in Leiden to the English port of Southampton. In Southampton the *Speedwell* rendezvoused with the much larger, 180-ton *Mayflower*.

No sooner were the Pilgrim ships at sea than the crew reported the *Speedwell* was taking in water. She was an old ship, built in 1577, and had seen action against the Spanish Armada; they had bought her cheaply, so her failure should not have come as a surprise. But it was an unfortunate setback. The ships put into Dartmouth for repairs; and almost as soon as they sailed, they had to put into Plymouth for the same reason. The leaks in the *Speedwell* could not be stopped, and she was deemed unsuitable for the crossing. If they wanted to make it to Virginia before the winter, they had to offload the *Speedwell* to a willing buyer in Plymouth harbour. A portion of the *Speedwell*'s crew was transferred to the *Mayflower*.

Then the Atlantic crossing itself did not go well. Through a combination of bad weather and poor navigation, the *Mayflower* veered from her intended course, and the Pilgrims landed on Cape Cod, two hundred miles north of the Hudson River. The Pilgrims had inadvertently made landfall in the wrong part of Virginia; instead of landing in the northern part of the London Company's sector, they found themselves in the southern part of Virginia originally awarded to the Plymouth Company.

After scouting along the coast for a good spot to build a settlement, the Pilgrims chose Plymouth – the site Smith had so heartily endorsed in his *Description of New England*. Unfortunately, their choice did not give Smith a last opportunity to find passage back to New England; instead he spent the rest of his life writing and promoting colonization.

In December 1620, Smith entered *New England Trialls* at Stationers' Hall for publication. This booklet was based on the letter he wrote to Sir Francis Bacon in 1618, and included both his Virginia and New England maps. A second, enlarged edition was printed in 1622, which included Smith's first public mention of his rescue by Pocahontas, albeit only briefly:

> It is true in our greatest extremitie they shot me, slue three of my men, and by the folly of them that fled tooke me prisoner; yet God made Pocahontas the Kings daughter the means to deliver me: and thereby taught me to know their treacheries to preserve the rest.[18]

With each passing month, Smith grew more frustrated at not being able to return to New England. In 1623, he published a four-page circular announcing the publication the following year of *A Generall Historie of Virginia, New-England, and the Summer Isles*, which would surely demonstrate his authority on all things related to the New World. Printing the work would be expensive, and Smith estimated the cost to be one hundred pounds, "which summe I cannot disburse". He needed a patron; thus, the circular. The pamphlet brought Smith's plans to the attention of Frances Stewart (née Howard), the Duchess of Richmond, and Lennox and Countess of Hertford.

Frances Howard was in her early forties when she was introduced to Smith. In her youth she had been a celebrated beauty, and she had married well. Her first husband, an investor in the London Company, died when she was just twenty-one, making her a very wealthy widow. Her second husband was Sir Edward Seymour, 1st Earl of Hertford, to whom Smith had dedicated his 1612 book, *A Map of Virginia*. Seymour had died in April 1621, and within months of his death, Frances took on her third husband, Ludovic Stewart, 2nd Duke of Lennox and 1st Duke of Richmond, and a cousin of King James.

Popularly known as the "Double Duchess", Frances Howard was the perfect benefactor for an impoverished and ambitious explorer like John Smith. She was one of the richest women in England and had negotiated shrewdly and maintained her position in society. She was also the last in the long line of high-ranking ladies who helped Smith in his time of need. To show his gratitude, Smith had the duchess' portrait engraved for *The Generall Historie* and added a map called *Oulde Virginia*, which he peppered with flattering references to her, including Herfords Ile, Howard's Mountaynes, Lennox rocks, Richmonds steps and Stuards reach.

The Double Duchess' patronage allowed Smith to publish *The Generall Historie* in 1624 with quite a splash. Fine engravings of Queen Elizabeth, King James and Prince Charles were to adorn the front cover, along with vignettes from the Americas and four coats of arms, one of which Smith was undoubtedly claiming for himself, with its depiction of three turbaned heads and its motto, *Vincere est vivere* – "To conquer is to live". This was of course a depiction of the coat of arms Smith had received from Sigismund Báthory, Prince of Transylvania. It made a handsome package, and Smith was keen to get copies into the bookshops quickly, perhaps anticipating a boon to sales after King James revoked the royal charter of the London Company in May.

The "Illustreous Princesse" Frances Howard, known as the Double Duchess, as engraved by Simon van de Passe for inclusion in John Smith's *General Historie* (1624).

Whatever the reason for the rush, Smith split the manuscript between two printers. This meant he had to guess at the number of pages for each half, with an eye to the fact that books were printed in folios of sixteen pages. He guessed wrongly, and word came back from the printer of the first half that he had ten blank pages at the end – right in the middle of the book. Smith managed to fill two of the pages with poems and prose, "as my worthy Friends bestowed upon New England", but all copies of *The Generall Historie* were sold with pages 97 to 104 entirely empty.

The rush to press could also be seen in the volume's text. *The Generall Historie* comprised nearly 200,000 words, but was a poorly organized compilation of writings from many sources about the early English exploration of Virginia, Bermuda and New England. Smith himself admitted, "for my owne part I rather feare the unpartiall Reader wil thinke this rather more tedious then necessary".[19] It was not his finest work, but he had to take his opportunities when they were presented to him.

Smith was now starting to move in some very influential circles, and he knew he should curry favour with more well-connected men. In *Ould Virginia*, he inserted a place name, "Segars grove", just inland from Cape Henry, in honour of one of his targets, Sir William Segar. Underneath

THE
GENERALL HISTORIE
OF
Virginia, New-England, and the Summer
Isles: with the names of the Adventurers,
Planters, and Governours from their
first beginning An: 1584. to this
present 1624.
With the Proceedings of those Severall Colonies
and the Accidents that befell them in all their
Journyes and Discoveries.
Also the Maps and Descriptions of all those
Countryes, their Commodities, people,
Government, Customes, and Religion
yet knowne.
DIVIDED INTO SIXE BOOKES.
By Captaine JOHN SMITH sometymes Governour
in those Countryes & Admirall
of New England.
LONDON.
Printed by I.D. and
I.H. for Michael
Sparkes.
1624.

The title page of John Smith's *The Generall Historie* (1624). The portraits at the top are of Queen Elizabeth, King James and Prince Charles. The coat of arms at the bottom right is Smith's three "Turks' heads".

Segars grove, in the bottom corner of the map, Smith had also asked the engraver to include the coat of arms displaying the three Turks' heads. How convenient it must have been when showing Sir William his name immortalized for prosperity on the map, for Smith also to mention his coat of arms. The following year, Smith would present his coat of arms to the Royal College of Heraldry, where Sir William was Garter Principal Kings of Arms. The inscription was surely no coincidence.

Ever since the fifteenth century, the Kings of Arms has had the authority from the monarch to confirm heraldic arms that might be claimed from an ancestor, or to grant new arms to those who qualify. Smith's petition to the Royal College in Derby Place, just south of St Paul's Cathedral, stated that his award from Sigismund Báthory was legitimate, given for heroic military service to the Prince of Transylvania during the war against the Ottoman Turks. He wanted his heraldic arms and his chosen motto to be affirmed by the Kings of Arms and recognized by English society.

As proof of his claim, Smith offered a letter of commendation from Sigismund Báthory. The letter, dated December 9, 1603, had apparently been sealed in Leipzig and was written in Latin. Although Smith had been awarded his coat of arms in the summer of 1602, he had been taken prisoner and sold into slavery, and he must surely have lost all his papers around that time. It was only when he escaped, and traced the prince to Germany in late 1603, that he could get these important papers re-issued.

However, there were critical mistakes in Báthory's letter, which a sceptical eye might notice. The prince had begun:

> Sigismundus Bathori, Dei gratia Dux Transilvaniæ, Wallachiæ, et Vandalorum; Comes Anchard, Salford, Growenda; Cunctis his literis significamus qui eas lecturi aut audituri sunt, concessam licentiam aut facultatem Iohanni Smith, natione Anglo Generoso, 250. militum Capitaneo...[20]

This passage was translated as:

> Sigismundus Bathor, by the Grace of God, Duke of Transylvania, Wallachia, and Moldavia, Earle of Anchard, Salford, and Growenda; to whom this Writing may come or appeare. Know that We have given leave and licence to John Smith an English Gentleman, Captaine of 250. Souldiers...

This commendation was almost laughable. Firstly, Báthory could not be "Earl of Anchard, Salford, and Growenda"; these titles did not exist, and the prince could not have actually been referring to the English town of Salford (which happened to be close to where Smith's father was born).

But most damning of all was Báthory's title, "Duke of Transylvania, Wallachia, and Moldavia". Báthory was *Prince* of Transylvania, not a mere duke, and neither Báthory nor anyone associated with him would have issued a document with such a gross error. Báthory would have been expected to use terminology along the lines of:

> Sigismundus Dei gratia Transsilvaniæ et Sacri Romani Imperii Princeps, Partium regni Hungariae dominus, Aurei velleris Eques ac Siculorum Comes ecc.[21]

This translates as:

> Sigismund Transylvania, the grace of God and the Holy Roman Empire Prince, lord of the kingdom of Hungary, Knight of the Golden Fleece and the Sicilian Count etc.

It is impossible to be absolutely certain what had actually happened. What could have motivated John Smith to risk presenting a forgery to the Royal College of Heraldry? There is little reason to doubt Báthory had awarded Smith heraldic arms, and every reason to believe the original papers were taken from him when he was a slave. Smith himself even asserted that the prince had reissued these papers in late 1603. Over the subsequent twelve years Smith had lived a turbulent life, and Báthory had died in Prague in 1613. Smith could easily have lost the new papers at any time, and he could no longer appeal to the prince for another replacement. It seems that at some time after 1603, but before 1625, Smith tried to recreate the letter from memory, and he clearly did not do a very good job of it.

Despite the letter's inaccuracies, Sir William Segar accepted it as authentic. John Smith was awarded his armorial bearings on August 19, 1625. He had finally "arrived".

In the early seventeenth century, the average life expectancy of an Englishman was about forty years.[22] At forty-five years old Smith was now considered an old man, and had to acknowledge his exploration days were over.

In 1626, Smith's friend Samuel Purchas died at the age of forty-eight. The death must have focused Smith's mind on his own mortality. There is some evidence that Purchas was heavily in debt when he died, in large part because of the expense of publishing his extensive volumes on English explorers – *Purchas His Pilgrimage, Purchas his Pilgrim or Mirocosmus* and, most recently, *Hakluytus Posthumus,* which aspired to take up the work of Richard Hakluyt. This too must have served as a salutary warning to Smith.

For the next five years, Smith devoted himself to writing and publishing. He observed in *The Generall Historie* that he had "writ too much of some, too little of others", and he may have felt compelled to set the record straight on several matters. However, his next projects were dedicated to the knowledge he had gained during his many years at sea.

First, in 1626, came a dictionary of ship terminology entitled *An Accidence, or the Pathway to Experience Necessary for all Young Seamen.* The following year, a larger and more comprehensive version, called *A Sea Grammar,* was published. These are generally considered to be the first works on seamanship published in the English language – no mean achievement for a man who was, by training, a cavalry captain, not a sailing master. Because of their practical nature, both books were probably a commercial success.

Despite its prosaic nature, *A Sea Grammar* offers a hint to where and how Smith might have been living in his later years. The son of a wealthy Lord Mayor of London, Sir Samuel Saltonstall, financed the publication of the book. In his will, Smith mentioned a "trunk standing in my chamber at Sir Samuel Saltonstall's house in St. Sepulchre's Parish",[23] so it seemed Saltonstall's patronage extended beyond the printer's bills.

Then, in 1630, Smith's writing became even more ambitious. He published *The True Travels, Adventures and Observations of Captain John Smith*, a proper attempt to write his personal life story. The book can be frustratingly vague and chaotic, but it gives a rare glimpse into the cruelty and misery inflicted by war in Europe at the beginning of the seventeenth century. It was also one of the first examples of a secular autobiography.

Smith lived at a time when the autobiography was only just emerging as a distinct literary style. Professor Paul Delany of Simon Fraser University argued, "the development of the autobiography came from the interest aroused by the extraordinary political disturbances of the seventeenth-century, which created in many men an urge to record their own participation in important events".[24] This was certainly the case with John Smith, and we can see him struggling with the new form, as he penned the chronicle of his life in the third person. "The seventeenth-century autobiographer tends to claim individual significance by virtue of some specific quality or accomplishment", Delany said, "or because he has been a witness to the affairs of the great."[25]

The True Travels clearly stood out as a rare, early example of this new genre, not least because it shared fantastic stories of the Ottoman Empire and the New World. Smith had always wanted to count himself among the great men of the day who had witnessed and participated in the unfolding of historic events. This was his epitaph.

Smith's last book, *Advertisements for the Unexperienced Planters of New England, or Anywhere*, was published on March 25, 1631, just three months before he died. The book summarized everything he had learnt from the colonization of America. *Advertisements* was written more freely than many of his previous works, and as a result it is an easier read today. Though Smith was more circumspect about his accomplishments in it, he could not help but reflect on his life with obvious pride. Nor did he hold back from launching criticism at those he felt were wrecking all his dreams for America. The "purses and lives" of the colonists in Virginia, he complained:

> were subject to some few here in London who were never there...every yeere trying new conclusions [experiments], altering every thing yearely as they altered opinions, till they had consumed more than two hundred thousand pounds, and neere eight thousand lives.[26]

He also seemed to realize that his extraordinary exploits were a thing of the past, pondering:

> Have I not much reason both privately and publikely to acknowledge it and give God thankes, whose omnipotent power onely delivered me to doe the utmost of my best to make his name knowne in those remote parts of the world, and his loving mercy to such a miserable sinner.[27]

Smith was in the end a pious man, shaped by the Reverend Marbury's lessons at the petty school in Alford and by the principles of the Puritans. He was well known as a brave, ingenious, tenacious soldier and a swashbuckling advocate of colonization, whose actions had been marked by a sense of danger, intrigue and controversy. Yet he was not only a man of action. During the course of his lifetime, and without the benefit of a university education, he wrote a dozen books totalling some 400,000 words, and published several maps of enduring importance. With them he left a lasting intellectual legacy.

In the spring of 1631, Smith could tell his constitution was failing him. London was a crowded, dirty, disease-ridden place, and death often arrived suddenly and mysteriously. The plague was always present in the capital, but he had somehow survived the epidemic of 1625, when one in eight of the population had died – about 35,000 people. A "Bill of Mortality" from a typical week in June listed Londoners' most common causes of death: consumption (63), fever (43), plague (43), convulsion (31), griping in the guts (27), and "teeth" (25).[28] Tuberculosis, pneumonia, smallpox, typhoid or perhaps even plague might have been the end of him.

No matter, he knew the end was close. On June 21, 1631, he dictated his will. The major beneficiary was Thomas Packer, a clerk with the King's Privy Seal, and presumably a friend. He was bequeathed Smith's farm in Lincolnshire, ten pounds and Smith's cherished "Coate of Armes". Sir Samuel Saltonstall and a "Mistris Tredway" received five pounds each, and one Steven Smith and his sister (who were possibly blood relatives but remain unidentified) got six pounds and thirteen shillings. Smith's widowed sister-in-law received ten pounds. A generous twenty pounds was set aside to ensure a good send-off for him.

A review of the will itself suggests Smith made every effort to sign his name, but his first attempt resulted in a messy blot of ink. He tried a second time, but the man who had wrestled Powhatan chiefs along the James River no longer had the strength to hold his quill, and the ink splattered again. Whoever assisted him added "the marke of the sayd Iohn", and "Smithe" below the illegible scrawl.[29]

Smith died later that day. A large jug of wine would have stood by his coffin, as refreshment for his friends who came to pay their last respects. On the day of his internment, his friends carried his body to his local church, St Sepulchre-without-Newgate,[30] so named because in medieval times it stood outside the city walls. Traditionally, a bell was rung for the dead or dying: nine rings for a man, followed by one for each year of his life. Today, a stained glass window of John Smith is set in the south wall of the church, casting its bright colours into the dim twelfth-century interior.

Smith was aware that history might judge him to be a contentious figure, self-important and self-mythologizing. As he wrote in *The Generall Historie*:

> I know I shall bee taxed for writing so much of my selfe, but I care not much, because the judiciall know there are few such Souldiers as are my examples, have writ their owne actions, nor know I who will or can tell my intents better than my selfe.[31]

The frontispiece to David Lloyd's satirical poem *Legend of Captain Jones* (1631).

Epilogue

I believe that it is possible for one to praise, without concern, any man after he is dead since every reason and supervision for adulation is lacking.
Niccolò Machiavelli, The Art of War (1521)

It is probably fair to assume John Smith left behind more detractors than he did friends. He had been controversial in life, and he remained so in the grave.

His headstone, inside the parish church of St. Sepulchre-without-Newgate, carried the epitaph:

To the Living Memory of his
deceased Friend, Captaine JOHN
SMITH, who departed this mortall
life on the 21. Day of June 1631.
With his Armes, and this Motto,
Accordamus, vincere est vivere.

Here lies one conquer'd,
that hath conquer'd Kings,
Subdu'd large Territories,
and done things
Which to the World
impossible would seeme,
But that the truth
is held in more esteeme.[1]

The tribute soon came back to haunt him.

Before the year was out, a little-known Welsh clergyman called David Lloyd published a bawdy satire ridiculing Smith's autobiography. *The Legend of Captaine Jones* pulled no punches in mocking Smith's life story. The very first page began:

> The Legend of Captaine Jones: relating His adventure to Sea: His first landing, and strange Combat with a mighty Bear. His furious Battel, with his six and thirty men, against the Army of eleven Kings, with their overthrow and deaths. His relieving of Kemper Castle. His strange and admirable Sea-fight with six huge Gallies of Spain, and nine thousand Souldiers. His being taken Prisoner, and hard Usage. Lastly, His setting at Liberty by the Kings command, and return for England.[2]

It was a cheap attack on a man who could no longer defend himself. *The Legend* proved so popular it was reprinted several times over the next forty years, making it arguably more popular than Smith's own works. Lloyd capitalized on its success and penned a sequel in 1648, which suggests Smith's notoriety lingered on:

> The legend of Captaine Jones continued from his fiurst part to his end, wherein is delivered his incredible advantures and atchievements by sea and land: particularly, his miraculous deliverance from a wrack at sea by the support of a dolphin, his severall desperate duels, his combate with Bahader Cham, a gyant of the race of Og, his loves, his deep imployments and happy successe in businesse of state: all which and more is but the title of his own relation, which he continued until he grew speechlesse, and died.[3]

The English historian Catherine Armstrong believes Smith subjected himself to such derision because he subverted the traditional notion of chivalry when he claimed he was saved from death by a young "Indian" girl. A "true" knight would surely have played the hero and saved her.[4] This could explain why Smith was initially reluctant to share the story

"Captain Smith and Pocahontas", one of nineteen scenes in the *Frieze of American History,* Capitol Rotunda, Washington, DC.

of his "rescue" by Pocahontas. Unfortunately, we will never know for certain the truth behind this foundational story of the colonization of America – and of Smith's role in it.

In America, early chroniclers were more generous towards Smith than David Lloyd. At first, most accepted his romanticized story as untainted fact. In 1791, lexicographer and spelling reformer Noah Webster noted with breathless admiration: "What a hero was Captain Smith! How many Turks and Indians did he slay!"[5] This Founding Father[6] of the United States may even have seen the democratic ideals of the new Constitution in Smith's upstart adventures.

Over the next fifty years the legend of John Smith as the saviour of the Virginia colony – and of Pocahontas as his rescuer – was accepted as a predominant part of America's origin story. When the young republic recovered from the battering War of 1812 against the British, it was time to rebuild the Capitol. The architect commissioned a "Frieze of American History" depicting significant events to be painted around the rotunda, and a *trompe l'oeil* fresco of Smith and Pocahontas made the final selection.[7]

However, Smith's legacy in the United States attracted dissent soon enough. As the political divisions between North and South opened, and civil war grew increasingly inevitable, Smith became something of a political football. Northern historians began to challenge the veracity of this "pin-up boy" of Confederate Virginia. In his 1858 book, the *History of New England*, Massachusetts Representative John Gorham Palfrey started debunking the John Smith myth in earnest. "I presume I am not the first reader who has been haunted by incredulity respecting some of the adventures of Smith", Palfrey wrote.[8] He reminded his readers that "hack-writers abounded in London" at this time, and warned that Smith could easily have fallen into their devious hands. Later, the Boston historian Charles Deane pointed out that Smith had changed the story of his first meeting with the paramount chief dramatically, and that "Smith, with his strong love of the marvellous, was disposed to garnish the stories of his early adventures." In other words, Deane was calling Smith a liar and a braggart.[9]

The Civil War put a temporary halt to the demolition of Smith's reputation; there was no time for writing counter-histories during such awful bloodshed. But in the post-war years, the bitter attacks on Smith were renewed north of the Mason–Dixon Line. In 1867, another respected historian from Boston, Henry Adams, wrote an article in the *North American Review*, in which he argued Smith's Pocahontas tale was bogus, the product of an incorrigibly vain and inept mind.[10] Nevertheless, Smith still had his defenders. The *Southern Review* rebutted the attacks on the Pocahontas legend coming from the North, saying, "Her critics wield their most deadly blades, dipped in poison", and arguing that Deanes' writings showed "great cold-heartedness and unfairness".[11]

The squabble went global in 1890, when the Hungarian historian Lewis L. Kropf challenged Smith's account of his activities in Hungary and Transylvania.[12] This only added fuel to the simmering flames devouring Smith's reputation as a chronicler of his own life and the early years of American colonial history. However, according to Laura Polanyi Striker, a later Hungarian historian, Kropf did not dig deep enough into this confused period of eastern European history, and his criticisms were not justified.[13]

Throughout all this debate, the fundamental question has remained: can John Smith be relied on to be an honest writer and historian, or is his record so fraught with uncertainties that he cannot – and should not – be trusted?

There are a few facts that are entirely undisputed. Smith was born in 1580, the son of a "poore tenant" farmer. He had a good schooling until the age of fifteen, but he never benefited from a university education; nor, from all accounts, was he a particularly diligent student. Although Smith's writing style and spelling leaves much to be desired, it is remarkable that somebody with such limited education left such a body of literary work, including one of the earliest autobiographies and the first English-language guidebook to seamanship.

However, none of these achievements establish his integrity as an historian. To test his record, we must always return to a line-by-line reading of his writings – both those that can be verified against his contemporaries (mainly from his years at Jamestown) and those where there are no other eyewitness accounts (as with his time fighting and sailing around Eastern Europe, the Mediterranean and the Atlantic).

Smith's activities at Jamestown were well documented by several other colonists, including George Percy, Gabriel Archer, Edward Wingfield and John Ratcliffe. The style of the period was romantic, and each of these men wrote from their own perspective, so their accounts inevitably differ in the details. Often each man was keen to justify his own behaviour, and to deflect criticism onto others. There is no doubt Smith was unpopular with most of these other writers, and he receives little credit from them for the successes he might have achieved.

Yet despite more than two years of records from others at Jamestown, there are few significant challenges to Smith's version of events. For example, when Smith wrote about his encounter in early 1609 with Opechancanough on the Pamunkey River, George Percy wrote nothing about Smith negotiating their way out of the ambush, but nor did he contest Smith's account when it became public. It was left to the little-known colonists Michael and Wil Phettiplace to write the verse that substantiates Smith's memory of the events.

Smith's earlier writings about his time in eastern Europe and Russia are more difficult to validate. There are certainly inconsistencies in his accounts; for example, his explanation of his defeat at the battle of "Rottenton" does not fit the established histories of the period, and instead seems to be a hazy amalgamation of two different battlefield experiences. Yet most of the rest of Smith's recollections from Hungary and Transylvania correspond very well with the confused and rapidly changing diplomatic and military situation in the region. Indeed, that is an understatement. Smith's writings show a remarkable understanding of this very complex and complicated period in the region.

The other test of the veracity of Smith's writings comes from challenging his accounts against the physical terrain of the places he visited, as well as his descriptions of the people he met, and their customs. While the location of "Regall" cannot be confirmed with any certainty, Smith's report of the siege of "Olumpagh" describes the geography around Lendava accurately. When he escaped from the French ship during the storm off La Rochelle, his tale of running ashore on an oozy island matches Île Madame perfectly. Even his story of being thrown overboard by Catholic pilgrims at Nice can be explained, once it is understood that the mysterious Isle St Mary may no longer be an island. Elsewhere, whether it is Smith's journey through the Black Sea to the Russian steppe, or his description of Marrakech in the early seventeenth century, his accounts accord with others.

At the same time, some sections of Smith's writings are undeniably inaccurate. The brief opening chapter of *The True Travels* covers Smith's life to the age of nineteen and, as the historian Philip Barbour declared,[14] it was "a masterpiece of disorganized writing". Smith got his chronology completely mixed up at first, claiming that both his parents died when he was thirteen; in fact only his father died, but not until he was sixteen, and his mother lived on. For somebody who might expect to be challenged on his accuracy, this was not an encouraging start.

Yet Brooke Conti, an associate professor of English at the State University of New York, maintains that this vagueness is not unusual for the period:

> Sixteenth- and seventeenth-century autobiographies do not look much like later ones; autobiographical moments occur in a variety of genres and are likely to be fragmentary and fugitive, frustrating those who seek such things as background detail, motivation, and sometimes even just a clear sense of chronological progression.[15]

The claim that Smith made about becoming orphaned when he was "about thirteen" might have been a crude attempt to win the reader's compassion. In his defence, *The True Travels* was not written and published until 1630, a year before his death, and more than thirty-five years after the event. This distant past may have seemed inconsequential in light of everything that had happened to him since childhood.

With more than four hundred years separating Smith's writing from today, it is unreasonable to expect everything Smith said about his exploits can be completely verified. There are certainly unexplained gaps in his record, and whole periods of his life that are covered in a fleeting paragraph. Occasionally, his poor writing invites misinterpretation; at other times, his *braggadocio* is so over the top it can make even the most sympathetic reader question a story.

Yet where Smith's testimony can be challenged in the details, his writing mostly stands up to intensive scrutiny. It is therefore reasonable to say he was generally accurate, candid and reliable, and that his writings are a vital firsthand history of his period.

Captain John Smith would probably claim there should be more to the assessment of his life than just his writings. He was a tough, fit, resilient man who survived and even thrived on privation, hardship and arduous conditions. He endured illnesses, injuries and accidents that would have killed most men several times over. If he were alive today, he might claim that his greatest contribution to history came not from his writings, but from his performance as a soldier and leader – an equal (so he would like to believe) to Elizabeth's favourite, Sir Walter Raleigh, and the rest of the men who had helped England emerge as the foremost power of the age.

Smith saw action in several military campaigns: the war in the Low Countries, perhaps also in Ireland, certainly in Eastern Europe, at sea in the Mediterranean and the Atlantic, and of course in North America. He gained mettle on the battlefield and at the council table, but he was not without fault. Indeed, he made several tactical mistakes during his time in Jamestown, not least by sailing up the Pamunkey River during the drought-stricken winter of 1608 in search of food, instead of warning the settlers back in Jamestown of the duplicity of Wahunsenacawh and the danger this posed to the colony. He was also undoubtedly arrogant, testy and difficult.

Yet he was more competent and better experienced than most, if not all, of his contemporaries in Virginia. Good leadership was severely lacking in those early years of the colony, and Smith's tenure as a dissident rebel and later as an authoritarian president most likely saved the settlement. Had it not been for Smith's vision, bloody-minded determination and guile, Jamestown would almost certainly have been added to the list of abandoned English colonies, along with Roanoke (1590), Cuttyhunk Island (1602) and Popham (1608).

In *The Art of War*, Machiavelli wrote, "Nothing is of greater importance in time of war than in knowing how to make the best use of a fair opportunity when it is offered", and it seems Smith took this lesson to heart. He was the one Englishman the paramount chief of the Powhatan seemed to genuinely respect. The regime Smith established as colony president was uncompromising, but he never expected anything from his men that he was not prepared to experience himself. Unlike others, such as Wingfield and Ratcliffe, Smith did not award himself privileges while denying them to others.

Smith also seemed to realize that the long-term interests of the English colonists in Virginia depended on the neighbours they made. He was often guilty of gratuitous brutality towards the Powhatan, but by the standards of the period he was relatively restrained. The London Company was keen to maintain amicable relations with the locals, and Smith was censured by his London paymasters for his failures in this area. However, when others assumed positions of leadership, their treatment of the Powhatan was often far more reprehensible. Less than a year after Smith's departure from Jamestown, George Percy led his raid on the Paspahegh, killing the *weroance* and as many as seventy of his people, burning their village, then kidnapping and murdering the chief's wife and children – all on the direct orders of Governor De La Warr. This brutality was a disproportionate response to the theft of weapons, and triggered the First Anglo-Powhatan War.

As a diplomat, however, Smith was rather less accomplished – particularly when dealing with the "gentlemen" investors in the London Company. He resented the rigid class system of Elizabethan and Jacobean England, and believed he never received full credit for his accomplishments because of his lowly social status. This life-long grievance did him no credit, as again and again he antagonized and alienated his social superiors. Almost without exception, Jamestown's senior men despised Smith with a vengeance, and his "rude letter" gained him few friends back in London. Somehow, he managed to temper himself in his later years, successfully wooing wealthy benefactors to back his expensive publications. It was quite an accomplishment; either he learned to moderate his social outrage, or he matured and became more temperate with age.

There was also a vulnerable side to John Smith, especially with respect to women. Like his contemporaries, Smith grew up in a world dominated by men. His two schools were for boys, his apprenticeship in King's Lynn was an exclusively male environment, and his time in the army kept him away from women, except perhaps prostitutes and camp followers. The Jamestown colonists for the first sixteen months of settlement were all men, and Smith's time spent in New England and at sea completely excluded women. This was not unusual in this day. Yet from what we can glean from Smith's writings, his relationship with the opposite sex was anything but normal. This has led some writers to suggest Smith might have been homosexual, citing the evening when he claimed half-naked Powhatan maidens "tormented him" in a longhouse in Werowocomoco".[16] However, his description of that incident probably had more to do with his natural reticence to write about a provocative approach by nubile young women, rather than an indication of his sexual predilections. The *real* story is probably much more complicated – and much more interesting.

The first woman about whom Smith wrote in any detail was Charatza, who wielded the absolute power that a mistress has over a slave, though he hinted that their relationship became much more than that. After Charatza, there was "the good Lady Callamata, [who] largely supplied all his wants" in Russia; then his pre-teen saviour, Pocahontas, in Virginia; Madam Chanoyes, who bailed him out of penury in La Rochelle, and his wealthy patron, the "Double Duchess", who adopted him and his writing in London. All these women held positions of influence and power. The only other woman who appeared in his writing was his mother, who, he believed, had abandoned him when she remarried. Oddly, all these women – with the exception of his mother – stepped in to save Smith when he needed it most.

His relationships with women were never spelled out on the page, which was normal for the period – this was not the age for "kiss and tell" stories. Smith had also aspired to be a chivalric knight since his days studying in the woods around Willoughby. The abstemious and virtuous nature demanded of such an icon would therefore have given Smith the perfect excuse to develop close relationships with women, yet keep those relationships unsullied by a sexual liaison – the very sort of thing that had led to his mother betraying him. Of course, the grisly injuries from the gunpowder explosion on the James River might also explain why he did not marry later in life, once his adventuring days were over. In any case, Smith died a bachelor, and with no record of any progeny. His name would only live on through his writing and map-making.

From the day in 1607 when John Smith came ashore in Virginia, he strode into American folklore. In those early years he was fired up with the eagerness of exploring a new continent, with all it had to offer. Even though he was more circumspect than most about getting rich quickly, he did initially get carried away and allowed himself some unrealistically high expectations. Within the first few weeks in Virginia, he enthused: "the rockes being of a gravelly nature, [are] interlaced with many vains of glistring spangles".[17]

Smith soon became more pragmatic about what the new world had to offer, and realized gold was not the answer: "So doating of Mines of gold, and the South Sea, that all the world could not have devised better courses to bring us to ruine."[18] Smith's few summer months in New England in 1614 only confirmed what he had come to understand in Jamestown. Minerals were not the key to unlocking the door to a successful colony; trading marketable goods and creating a functioning community were. "In doing so, a servant that will labour, within foure or five yeares may live as well there as his master did here: for where there is so much land lie waste", he wrote.[19]

Smith's turbulent years in Jamestown have cast his achievements in New England in the shade. Although he spent only a short summer surveying the coast from Monhegan Island to Cape Cod, his charts and writings laid a foundation for a different style of settlement in the Americas for decades to come. In New England, Smith saw the opportunity for an individual to create a new life through determination and hard work, in a union of equals. Here a man could be free from the social shackles that had constrained him from birth.

After his voyage to New England, Smith became single-minded in his promotion of the colonization of the Americas. Six years later, using his charts and sailing directions, the Pilgrims settled in Plymouth, and put into practice his vision for a new society in the New World. Over the next four centuries, millions of people followed in their footsteps.

If John Smith has one enduring legacy, it is that he was the first Englishman to understand the great American Dream.

Appendix 1
Timeline of key events

c. 1545	Wahunsenacawh, the paramount chief of the Powhatan from before 1607 until 1618, is born in Virginia.
January 9, 1580	John Smith is baptized at Willoughby parish church, Lincolnshire. His father, George Smith, is a tenant farmer and rents his farm from Lord Willoughby, 13th Baron Willoughby de Eresby (1555–1601).
c. 1588	Smith attends the Reverend Marbury's "petty school", Alford.
July 29, 1588	Spanish Armada is sighted off southwest England.

In 1588, both the Julian and Gregorian calendars were being used. The Protestant states (including England) were still using the Julian calendar, whereas most Catholic states had adopted the Gregorian system.

August 7–8, 1588	Battle of Gravelines; Spanish Armada defeated.
c. 1592–5	Smith attends King Edward VI Grammar School, Louth.
1593	For unexplained reasons, John tries to run away from school, but his father "stayed him".
1595	Smith is made an apprentice under merchant Thomas Sendall, King's Lynn.
c. 1595–6	Pocahontas is born in Virginia, daughter of Wahunsenacawh.

Late March 1596	George Smith dies; he is buried April 3. His wife, Alice, remarries within a year and moves out of the village.
Late 1596 or early 1597	Smith leaves England for the Low Countries. He fights under the command of Captain Joseph Duxbury in support of the Dutch during "Eighty Years' War" or "Dutch Revolt" (1568–1648).
Before June 1599	Smith returns to England.
After June 26, 1599	Smith travels to France with Peregrine Bertie, younger son of Lord Willoughby.
Late 1599	Smith returns from France and sails for Scotland but his ship is wrecked off Lindisfarne. He continues to Edinburgh but his ambition to join the Court of King James VI of Scotland comes to nothing.
Spring and summer 1600	Smith returns to Willoughby and lives alone in the woods, reading and riding. Late in the summer he moves to Tattershall Castle, where he is tutored in horsemanship.
Late summer 1600	Smith sails for the Low Countries and then to France, where his belongings are stolen by four "Gallants". He makes his way to Marseilles, where he boards a ship for Rome.
Winter 1600/1	Anchored in a bay near Nice, Smith is thrown overboard by superstitious pilgrims. He boards a French ship sailing for Alexandria in Egypt.
Early 1601	Smith sails around the eastern Mediterranean. His ship encounters a Venetian "argosy" which is plundered. Smith disembarks at Antibes in France and is awarded his share of the loot, then travels on to Rome.
Easter, April 12, 1601	In Rome Smith makes contact with the Jesuit priest Father Robert Parsons. He then travels south to Naples before heading to Venice.

Summer 1601	Smith arrives in Graz, Austria, where he enrols in the Habsburg Imperial Army to fight the Ottoman Turks in the "Long War". In late summer he sees action at the siege of "Olumpagh" and is promoted to captain, commanding 250 cavalrymen. In September his regiment lays siege to the city of Alba Regalis (in today's Hungary).
Winter 1601/2	Smith and his regiment are sent to Transylvania.
Summer 1602	At the siege of "Regall", Smith kills and beheads three enemy commanders in hand-to-hand duels, for which he is given a pension and a coat of arms by the Transylvanian prince Sigismund Báthory.
Late 1602	Smith is injured at the Battle of Rottenton and left for dead. He is saved by scavengers and sold as a slave to a Turk.
Early 1603	Smith's master sends him to Constantinople (Istanbul) where he works as a manservant. Smith claims that his mistress, "Charatza Tragabigzanda", falls in love with him.
March 24, 1603	James VI of Scotland succeeds the last Tudor monarch, Elizabeth I. As James I he reigns in all three kingdoms for the next twenty-two years, often using the title "King of Great Britain and Ireland", until his death in 1625.
Early summer 1603	Smith is sent to work for Charatza's brother, who is a minor official in a remote Turkish outpost on the Russian steppe. Smith kills his new master and escapes.
Late 1603	Smith finds his way back to his company in Transylvania, then travels on to Leipzig where he collects his pension from Prince Báthory.
Late 1603 into 1604	Smith takes a sightseeing tour through Germany, France and Spain before going on to Morocco. He becomes a crew member to a French privateer.
c. December 9, 1604	Smith returns to London.
1605	Smith possibly travels to Ireland; if so, it was not for long.
1605–6	Smith becomes involved with plans to colonize Virginia for profit.

April 10, 1606	King James I signs the first charter of the Virginia Company, thereby creating two separate stock-holding companies, the London Company and the Plymouth Company. In return, the King receives a twenty percent share of any precious minerals found.
December 19, 1606	The London Company expedition sets sail from London in three small ships, the *Susan Constant*, the *Discovery* and the *Godspeed*, under the command of Captain Christopher Newport.
January 1607	The fleet is stormbound off the Kent coast, delaying arrival in Virginia.
February 17, 1607	Probable date of arrival of the fleet at Gran Canaria, Canary Islands.
February 21–2, 1607	The most likely date the fleet leaves Gran Canaria; Smith is restrained as a prisoner on charges of treason.
March 23, 1607	The fleet sights the island of Martinique, having sailed across the Atlantic.
March 27, 1607	The fleet lands in Nevis and a gallows is built for Smith. His life is spared but he remains under arrest.
April 21, 1607	The fleet is forced to lie "a hull" during a storm off the coast of Virginia.
April 26, 1607	Virginia is sighted around 4 a.m.; later that day, the colonists search for a suitable site for a settlement and have their first skirmish with the Powhatan.
May 1–3, 1607	Some colonists are entertained at the Kecoughtan village while Smith remains in custody.
May 8, 1607	The fleet sails up the James (Powhatan) River.
May 13, 1607	A low-lying marshy peninsula is chosen as the site for the colony to be called Jamestown.
May 14, 1607	The men land at Jamestown and stores and equipment are unloaded. The London Company's governing council is revealed to the colonists and Edward Maria Wingfield is elected president by the council members excluding Smith, who is still under arrest.

May 21, 1607	Newport takes a party up the James River and makes contact with several Powhatan tribes.
May 26, 1607	The Paspahegh attack Jamestown with 200 men.
June 10, 1607	John Smith is belatedly sworn in as a councillor.
June 15, 1607	The fortified triangular fort at Jamestown is completed.
June 22, 1607	Newport sails for England. He is expected back in November with the "first supply".
August 6, 1607	The failings of the Jamestown site become apparent. John Asbie dies of the "bloodie Flixe" and he is followed by dozens more over the next few weeks. Most of the colonists become ill from disease, infection or poor water.
August 22, 1607	Captain Gosnold, one of the main instigators of the London Company, dies.
September 10, 1607	John Ratcliffe, John Martin and John Smith constitute a majority vote on the council and depose President Wingfield. Ratcliffe is made president.
September 17, 1607	Wingfield is found guilty of withholding food and for "wronging" Smith; he is ordered to pay £200 in compensation.
November 9, 1607	Smith makes the first of several successful trading expeditions up the Chickahominy River.
December 12, 1607	Smith is captured by a Powhatan hunting party led by Opechancanough, Wahunsenacawh's younger brother. For the next two weeks Smith is moved from one village to another and witnesses several Powhatan rites.
December 30, 1607	Smith is taken to Werowocomoco, Wahunsenacawh's capital, where he thinks he is about to be executed. The chief's daughter, Pocahontas, steps forward and Smith believes she saves his life. He is subjected to an initiation rite, becoming a *weroance*.
January 2, 1608	Powhatan warriors return Smith to Jamestown, where he is arrested by Ratcliffe and sentenced to hanging for the death of two companions on his December trip. Newport returns with the first supply and reprieves Smith.
January 7, 1608	Fire destroys "all the houses at the fort" in Jamestown.

February(?), 1608	Newport meets Wahunsenacawh.
Spring 1608	Pocahontas becomes a regular visitor to Jamestown.
April 10, 1608	Newport sails for England with a load of ore thought to be gold; it is worthless.
April 20, 1608	Captain Francis Nelson arrives in the *Phoenix,* the missing ship from the first supply.
June 2, 1608	Smith sends a long letter, now known as *A True Relation,* back to England on the *Phoenix,* probably with the original Smith/Zúñiga map. He then starts his first exploration of the Chesapeake Bay.
Mid-July 1608	While exploring the Chesapeake Bay, Smith is stung by a stingray and is convinced he is going to die.
July 21, 1608	Smith returns to the fort and finds an open revolt against President Ratcliffe. Newly arrived colonist Matthew Schrivener becomes president.
July 24, 1608	Smith takes his second expedition up the Chesapeake Bay. He makes contact with new tribes in the northern Chesapeake region, including the Massawomeck, the Tockwogh and the Iroquian-speaking Susquehannock.
Summer 1608	*A True Relation* is published in London without Smith's knowledge.
September 7, 1608	Smith returns to Jamestown to find Ratcliffe has been arrested and food is in short supply.
September 10, 1608	Smith is made president of Jamestown.
Late September, 1608	Newport returns early with the second supply in the *Mary and Margaret*. On board are seventy new colonists, including two woman.
October 1608	Newport visits Wahunsenacawh with gifts from the London Company and attempts to crown him "king" under the jurisdiction of James.
Early December, 1608	Newport returns to England with Smith's "Rude Letter".

Late December 1608	Smith travels to Werowocomoco to organize construction of an English-style house for Wahunsenacawh and to trade for food. Pocahontas warns him of the threat of ambush. Smith never sees Wahunsenacawh again.
Late December 1608	Smith visits the Pamunkey village to trade for food and is ambushed by Opechancanough. Smith leaves with food, but learns that dissidents in Jamestown meanwhile have stolen weapons and defected to Werowocomoco.
Early 1609	Captain Peter Winne dies, leaving Smith as the only remaining member of the council. Smith decides to disperse colonists for the winter because of food shortages and establishes strict rules for security and provisions.
Spring 1609	Stealing of guns, swords and tools by the Powhatan becomes commonplace. Smith inflicts reprisals.
May 23, 1609	The second charter of the London Company is signed, granting it more land and extra powers.
July 13, 1609	Captain Samuel Argall arrives with further supplies and news that the third supply is on its way with revised directives for Jamestown's governance.
August 11–18, 1609	The surviving ships of the third supply reach Jamestown, but no copy of the directives replacing Smith as president; they seem to be on the *Sea Venture,* which is presumed lost at sea. There is stalemate over the colony's governance.
Late September 1609	Smith tries to establish a smaller settlement near the falls at Richmond, but is fiercely resisted. On returning down the James River, he sustains serious burns from a gunpowder explosion.
Early October 1609	Smith returns to England, most likely on the *Falcon,* because of his injuries; the fleet also carries charges against Smith to be delivered to the London Company. George Percy becomes president of Jamestown.
November 30 1609	Smith arrives in London some time before this date.

c. December 1609	In Smith's absence, Ratcliffe attempts to trade with the Powhatan but is killed along with thirty colonists, marking the beginning of the first Anglo-Powhatan war, 1609–14.
Winter 1609/10	The "Starving Time", when all but about sixty colonists die.
Early 1610	In London, Smith faces an inquiry into his governance in Jamestown; his reputation remains in limbo.
May 21, 1610	The survivors of the wrecked *Sea Venture,* carrying the new directives for the colony's governance, arrive off Point Comfort at the mouth of the James River. Deputy Governor Sir Thomas Gates decides to abandon Jamestown.
June 7, 1610	As the colonists leave Jamestown they meet Governor Lord De La Warr's fleet. De La Warr orders everyone to return to Jamestown.
June 10, 1610	Lord De La Warr arrives in Jamestown.
March 12, 1612	The third charter for the London Company is signed.
Late 1612	*A Map of Virginia* and *The Proceedings* are published.
April 1613	Pocahontas is kidnapped by Samuel Argall. She converts to Christianity and takes the name Rebecca.
March 3, 1614	Smith sails for Monhegan Island in Maine and surveys the coast south as far as Cape Cod, marking the region as "New England" in his initial charts. He returns to England by late August.
April 5(?), 1614	John Rolfe and Pocahontas are married by the Rev Richard Bucke.
January 30, 1615	Pocahontas has a son, whom she and her husband name Thomas.
March 1615	Smith sails from Plymouth, England, with two ships to found a new colony in Virginia, but the fleet is hit by a storm and Smith returns with his ship dismasted.
June 24, 1615	Smith makes a final attempt to return to America but is captured by French pirates off the coast of the Azores. He escapes after several months.

Early December 1615	Smith returns to Plymouth to face charges over the loss of his ship.
c. April 12, 1616	The Rolfe family sails for England.
June 12, 1616	The Rolfe family arrives in England. Between this date and the end of the year, Smith writes a letter to Queen Anne about Pocahontas.
June 18, 1616	Smith publishes *A Description of New England.*
January 1617	Smith is promised a large fleet out of Plymouth to establish a colony in "New England", but only three ships become available.
January 5, 1617	Pocahontas attends Ben Jonson's Twelfth Night masque ball, *The Vision of Delight*; King James I and Queen Anne are present.
Mid-March 1617	Pocahontas is taken ill and boards a ship for Virginia.
March 21, 1617	Pocahontas is taken ashore at Gravesend, where she dies.
March 1617	Smith's fleet is held up in Plymouth due to bad weather; Smith eventually abandons his plans to sail for New England.
April 1618	Wahunsenacawh dies in Virginia.
September 6, 1620	The *Mayflower* leaves Plymouth for the Hudson River, but is diverted from its course by bad weather and poor navigation. On November 9 they sight Cape Cod, two hundred miles north of their intended route.
March 21, 1621	The surviving passengers disembark from the *Mayflower* at Plymouth, in New England, having spent the winter on board.
March 22, 1622	Opechancanough leads an uprising during which approximately a third of the Virginia colonists are killed, marking the beginning of the second Anglo-Powhatan war, 1622–6.
Spring 1622	John Rolfe dies, either from attack or from illness.
October 1622	Smith advertises himself as an "Indian expert" in an expanded edition of *New Englands Trialls.*

May 24, 1624	The London Company's third charter is dissolved and Virginia is declared a Crown Colony.
July 12, 1624	*The Generall Historie* is entered into the Stationer's Register.
March 27, 1625	King James I dies. He is buried on May 7 and is widely mourned. Charles I succeeds his father as King of England until his execution on January 20, 1649.
August 29, 1629	*The True Travels* is entered into the Stationer's Register and published the following year.
June 21, 1631	John Smith dies at the age of fifty-one and is buried in the church of St Sepulchre-without-Newgate.
1633	The English settlers on the James River construct a palisade across the whole peninsula between the York and James Rivers
April 18, 1644	Opechancanough leads another uprising (the third Anglo-Powhatan war, 1644–6). In 1646, he is captured; while a prisoner, he is shot in the back by an English guard.

Appendix 2
John Smith's writings

John Smith wrote a dozen books about his experiences and ideas between 1608 and 1631, the year of his death. Together, they comprise more than 400,000 words, which was no mean feat for somebody who was only educated up to the age of fifteen. There is little consistency of style in his writings, and they vary from being confused and disorganized, to focused and erudite. This can be attributed partly to heavy-handed changes by an editor; on other occasions Smith borrowed from other writers and incorporated their words into his own. Despite their variability, his books offer a rare and insightful look into the world of the early seventeenth century, both at home and abroad.

A True Relation of Such Occurrences and Accidents of Noate as Hath Hapned in Virginia (1608)
Originally written in Jamestown in 1608 as a letter to an associate in England, this work represents the first account of the first year of the Jamestown Colony. Smith's letter probably filled up to forty sheets of foolscap paper and folded once to resemble an unbound book. On arrival in London, his letter was edited ruthlessly, printed badly and published hastily – all without his knowledge or permission. In the rush to publish the pamphlet, John Smith's name was originally omitted from the front page.

Smith's account was awaited eagerly in London, and much of its contents were optimistic. Yet is seems likely it also contained episodes deemed unsuitable for widespread distribution, and these might have been cut from the published version so as not to discourage potential investors.

A Map of Virginia, With a Description of the Country, the Commodities, People, Government and Religion (1612)
The first part of this publication, referred to by the title *Map of Virginia*, comprised an engraved map of the region, together with a detailed description of Virginia's location, geography, resources and people. At the beginning of the seventeenth century, it was by far the best account of the region's flora, fauna and cultures.

The Proceedings of the English Colony in Virginia (1612)
This account was written after Smith returned from Virginia with severe burns. It is a hazy and vague description of what happened in the early years of Jamestown. However, it remains the only comprehensive narrative of the period from April 1606 to the summer of 1610.

A Description of New England (1616)
Written after his return from New England in the summer of 1614, this book represents a clear progression in Smith's writing style. This is a more accomplished account, in which we see his true personality as a narrator, explorer and ethnographer emerge. This publication also includes some practical descriptions of survival, soldiering and seamanship skills.

New Englands Trialls (1620 and 1622)
This short book is based primarily on a letter Smith wrote to Sir Francis Bacon in 1618. (Bacon had been the attorney general, and by then was a privy councillor.) Both Smith's letter and the subsequent *Trialls* provide a geographical description of New England and detailed inventory of the resources available, and the profits to be made from their exploitation. The second edition of *Trialls*, published in 1622, is better written and has an expanded scope.

The Generall Historie of Virginia, New-England, and the Summer Isles (1623)
This short publication is essentially a prospectus or circular to announce the publication of the full *The Generall Historie* the following year.

The Generall Historie of Virginia, New-England, and the Summer Isles (1624)
This substantial work was probably written in response to the need for a history of Virginia. It is divided into six books, and represents a compilation of writings from many sources about the early years in Virginia, Bermuda and New England. It is not well organized, and Smith himself admitted that he had "writ too much of some [persons or actions], too little of others".

An Accidence, or the Pathway to Experience Necessary for all Young Seamen (1626)
In Smith's day, a handy compendium of the names of the equipment and people that make up a ship and her crew did not exist. This publication was written to meet this need. There is some evidence Smith might not have written the final text, but dictated it from hastily scribbled notes. Indeed, the publication of *An Accidence* seems to have been made with some urgency.

A Sea Grammar (1627)
This is a more comprehensive version of *An Accidence*, and is generally considered to be the first work on seamanship published in the English language.

The True Travels, Adventures and Observations of Captain John Smith (1630)
This is the only comprehensive attempt by Smith to write an autobiography. In the first half of the seventeenth century, this was a novel literary form, especially in English. The book contains twenty chapters recounting Smith's exploits to the age of twenty-four. It is frustratingly disorganized, but nevertheless offers a rare glimpse into the cruelty and misery created by warfare in Europe in the period. *The True Travels* was published just a year before his death.

Advertisements for the Unexperienced Planters of New England, or Anywhere (1631)
A summary of all that Smith had to say about the colonization of Virginia and New England, published in the year he died. This work is written with a freer hand, and in many respects it reads more easily than any of his other works. Smith is less petulant and boastful, and he looks back on his lifetime's accomplishments with obvious pride.

Appendix 3

John Smith's letter to Queen Anne (1616)

Most admired Queene,

The love I bear my God, my King and Countrie, hath so oft emboldened mee in the worst of extreme dangers, that now honestie doth constraine mee to presume thus farre beyond my selfe, to present your Majestie this short discourse: if ingratitude be a deadly poyson to all honest vertues, I must bee guiltie of that crime if I should omit any meanes to be thankfull. So it is,

That some ten yeeres agoe being in Virginia, and taken prisoner by the power of Powhatan their chiefe King, I received from this great Salvage exceeding great courtesie, especially from his sonne Nantaquaus, the most manliest, comeliest, boldest spirit, I ever saw in a Salvage, and his sister Pocahontas, the Kings most deare and wel-beloved daughter, being but a childe of twelve or thirteene yeers of age, whose compassionate pitifull heart, of my desperate estate, gave me much cause to respect her: I being the first Christian this proud King and his grim attendants ever saw: and thus inthralled in their barbarous power, I cannot say I felt the least occasion of want that was in the power of those my mortall foes to prevent, notwithstanding al their threats. After some six weeks [sic] fatting amongst those Salvage Courtiers, at the minute of my execution, she hazarded the beating out of her owne braines to save mine, and not onely that, but so prevailed with her father, that I was safely conducted to James towne, where I found about eight and thirtie miserable poore and sicke creatures, to keepe possession of all those large territories of

Virginia, such was the weaknesse of this poore Common-wealth, as had the Salvages not fed us, we directly had starved.

And this reliefe, most gracious Queene, was commonly brought us by this Lady Pocahontas, notwithstanding all these passages, when inconstant Fortune turned our peace to warre, this tender Virgin would still not spare to dare to visit us, and by her our jarres have beene oft appeased, and our wants still supplyed; were it the policie of her father thus to imploy her, or the ordinance of God thus to make her his instrument, or her extraordinarie affection to our Nation, I know not: but of this I am sure; when her father with the utmost of his policie and power, sought to surprize mee, having but eighteene with mee, the darke night could not affright her from coming through the irksome woods, and with watered eies gave me intelligence, with her best advice to escape his furie; which had hee knowne, hee had surely slaine her. James towne with her wild traine she as freely frequented, as her fathers habitation; and during the time of two or three yeers, she next under God, was still the instrument to preserve this Colonie from death, famine and utter confusion, which if in those times, had once beene dissolved, Virginia might have line [lain] as it was at our first arrivall to this day. Since then, this businesse having beene turned and varied by many accidents from that I left it at: it is most certaine, after a long and troublesome warre after my departure, betwixt her father and our Colonie; all which time shee was not heard of, about two yeeres after shee her selfe was taken prisoner, being so detained neere two yeeres longer, the Colonie by that meanes was relieved, peace concluded, and at last rejecting her barbarous condition, [she] was maried to an English Gentleman, with whom at this present she is in England; the first Christian ever of that Nation, the first Virginian ever spake English, or had a childe in marriage by an Englishman, a matter surely, if my meaning be truly considered and well understood, worthy [of] a Princes understanding.

Thus, most gracious Lady, I have related to your Majestie, what at your best leisure our approved Histories will account you at large, and done in the time of your Majesties life, and however this might bee presented you from a more worthy pen, it cannot from a more honest heart, as yet I never begged anything of the state, or any, and it is my want of abilitie and her exceeding desert; your birth, meanes and authoritie, hir birth, vertue, want and simplicitie, doth make mee thus bold, humbly to beseech your Majestie to take this knowledge of her, though it be from one so unworthy to be the reporter, as my selfe, her husbands estate not being able to make her fit to attend your Majestie: the most and least I can doe, is to tell you this, because none so oft hath tried it as my selfe, and the rather being of so great a spirit, how ever her stature: if she should not be well received, seeing this Kingdome may rightly have a Kingdome by her meanes; her present love to us and Christianitie, might turne to such scorne and furie, as to divert all this good to the worst of evill, where finding so great a Queene should doe her some honour more than she can imagine, for being so kinde to your servants and subjects, would so ravish her with content, as endeare her dearest bloud to effect that, your Majestie and all the Kings honest subjects most earnestly desire: And so I humbly kisse your gracious hands,

Captain John Smith, 1616

Acknowledgements

When writing a book you incur many debts of gratitude, and it is often the spontaneous kindness of strangers that makes research and writing such a pleasure.

In Willoughby, Chris and Christine Sykes, the Reverend Daffyd Robinson and Ian Evans, chairman of the Willoughby History Group, opened their doors to me both figuratively and literally.

Research in Jamestown was made all the more satisfying and insightful for the help of Dr Bill Kelso and Merry Outlaw at the Preservation Virginia Jamestown Rediscovery project, together with their many colleagues who patiently answered my questions and emails. At the site of Werowocomoco, Bob and Lynn Ripley were very generous with their time and their hospitality, as they took me through their personal journey of discovering such a fascinating place.

Also in Virginia, the writer and historian Aleck Loker shares my passion for John Smith's story. He has been unstinting in his time and support, constructively challenging my ideas at times, but always positive and encouraging.

Eastern Europe, and especially Transylvania, brought its own challenges. Tudor Sălăgean, director of the Ethnographic Museum of Transylvania in Cluj-Napoca, and Florin Ardelean were very patient in guiding me through this complicated period in central European history.

In London, my agent, Sheila Ableman, has always been persistent and patient on my behalf. And at Oneworld, Robin Dennis and Fiona Slater have, as editors, always been encouraging, understanding and helpful in getting the book from computer to page.

Finally, my wife, Paula, as always, has been especially supportive. As a professor of psychology, she has been particularly useful in helping me to understand John Smith as a real human being; ever patient, she has endured rather more evenings and weekends alone than she ought.

I thank them all.

Finally, despite every care taken over checking the manuscript, my biggest concern is that mistakes might have crept in. If so, the responsibility is all mine. I trust they are not so serious that they detract from what I hope you will find to be an extraordinary story.

Notes

For full titles of John Smith's works, please refer to Appendix 2. Quotes from Niccolò Machiavelli's The Art of War *come from the the edition translated, edited and with a commentary by Christopher Lynch (University of Chicago Press, 2003).*

Prologue

1 Smith, John. 1624. *The Generall Historie,* in Philip L. Barbour. 1986. *The Complete Works of Captain John Smith (1580–1631),* vol. 2. University of North Carolina Press, p. 127.
2 Smith, John. 1608. *A True Relation,* in Philip L. Barbour. 1986. *The Complete Works of Captain John Smith (1580–1631),* vol. 1. University of North Carolina Press, p. 53.
3 Smith, *The Generall Historie,* in *The Complete Works of Captain John Smith,* vol. 2, p. 259.
4 Percy, George. 1612. *A True Relation,* in Edward Wright Haile (ed.). 1998. *Jamestown Narratives: Eyewitness Accounts of the Virginia Colony – The First Decade: 1607–1617.* RoundHouse, p. 502.

1. Apprentice

1 July 26, 1588, using the Julian calendar. After 1582, most Catholic countries used the "New Style" Gregorian calendar. "Old Style" is used throughout unless indicated "(NS)", which runs ten days later than the Julian calendar.
2 Tincey, John. 1988. *The Armada Campaign 1588.* Osprey, p. 32.
3 Several different commemorative Armada medals were struck, with slightly different inscriptions. Queen Elizabeth is believed to have awarded the medals to her admirals. Some used the phrase *Flavit Deus et Dissipati Sunt,* while others used the Hebrew name for God, *Flavit Jehovah et Dissipati Sunt.*
4 The records in Willoughby are remarkably intact. The village priest who baptized John Smith was called Libeus Sadler, and he had lived in the village since 1576.

5 The inventory of contents of George Smith's home was recorded on his death and is now stored as item INV/87/250 in the Lincolnshire Archives. The manuscript goes into great detail about the Smiths' personal effects, yielding valuable insights into the life of this farming family.

6 Around £8,000 in today's prices; see http://www.nationalarchives.gov.uk/currency/.

7 Lincolnshire Archive. Court Rolls Anc. 26/5–8.

8 Cummins, John. 1996. *Francis Drake: The Lives of a Hero*. Palgrave Macmillan, p. 5.

9 From the 1576 charter granted by Queen Elizabeth.

10 Monroe, Paul. 1911. *A Cyclopedia of Education*, vol. 1. Macmillan, p. 6.

11 Brook, Benjamin. 1813. *The Lives of the Puritans*. James Black, p. 226.

12 LaPlante, Eve. *American Jezebel: The Uncommon Life of Anne Hutchinson, the Woman Who Defied the Puritans*. Harper, 2004, p. 26.

13 Ibid, p. 33.

14 Ibid, p. 2.

15 Smith, John. 1630. *The True Travels*, in Philip L. Barbour. 1986. *The Complete Works of Captain John Smith (1580–1631)*, vol. 3. University of North Carolina Press, pp. 153–4.

16 Defoe, Daniel. 1928. *A Tour Thro' the Whole Island of Great Britain*, vol. 2. J.M. Dent, p. 95.

17 Smith. *The True Travels*, in *The Complete Works of Captain John Smith*, vol. 3, p. 154.

18 Arber, Edward (ed.). 1884. *Captain John Smith: Works, 1608–1631*. English Scholar's Library Edition, no. 16, and "Last Will of George Smith" in *The Complete Works of Captain John Smith*, vol. 3, pp. 377–8.

19 Smith. *The True Travels*, in *The Complete Works of Captain John Smith*, vol. 3, p. 154.

20 Wernham, R.B. 1994. *The Return of the Armadas: The Last Years of the Elizabethan War against Spain 1595–1603*. Oxford University Press, p. 132.

21 Smith. *The True Travels*, in *The Complete Works of Captain John Smith*, vol. 3, p. 155.

22 Mousnier, Roland. 1973. *The Assassination of Henry IV* (trans. by Joan Spencer). Faber and Faber, p. 114.

23 Papazia, Mary Arshagouni (ed.). 1972. *Jonne Donne and the Protestant Reformation: New Perspectives*. Wayne State University Press, p. 179.

24 Lee, Sidney (ed.). 1889. *Dictionary of National Biography*, vol. 58. Smith Elder, p. 232.

25 Smith. *The True Travels*, in *The Complete Works of Captain John Smith*, vol. 3, p. 157.

26 Lodge, Edmund. 1835. *Portraits of Illustrious Personages of Great Britain*, vol. 5. Harding and Leopard, p. 2.

27 Barbour, Philip L. 1965. *The Three Worlds of Captain John Smith: Adventurer, Colonist, Promoter*. Houghton Mifflin, p. 11.

28 Howard, Clare. 1914. *English Travellers of the Renaissance*. John Lane, p. 86.

29 Smith. *The True Travels*, in *The Complete Works of Captain John Smith*, vol. 3, pp. 154–5.
30 Ibid, p. 155.
31 Ibid, p. 155.
32 Ibid, p. 155.
33 Ibid, pp. 155–6.

2. Pirate

1 Smith, John. 1630. *The True Travels*, in Philip L. Barbour. 1986. *The Complete Works of Captain John Smith (1580–1631)*, vol. 3. University of North Carolina Press, pp. 155–6.
2 Wright, Louis Booker. 1980. *Middle-Class Culture in Elizabethan England*. Octagon, p. 122.
3 Hallam, Henry. 1837. *Introduction to the Literature of Europe in the Fifteenth, Sixteenth and Seventeenth Centuries*, vol. 1. Crapelet, p. 313.
4 Russell, P.E. (ed.). 1973. *Spain: A Companion to Spanish Studies*. Taylor & Francis, p. 59.
5 Smith. *The True Travels*, in *The Complete Works of Captain John Smith*, vol. 3, p. 156.
6 Cole, Mary Hill (ed.). 1999. *The Portable Queen: Elizabeth I and the Politics of Ceremony*. University of Massachusetts Press, p. 93.
7 Pettifer, Adrian. 2000. *English Castles: A Guide by Counties*. Boydell & Brewer, pp. 145–7.
8 Smith. *The True Travels*, in *The Complete Works of Captain John Smith*, vol. 3, pp. 156–7.
9 Ibid, p. 157.
10 Ibid, p. 157.
11 Ibid, p. 157.
12 Ibid, p. 158.
13 Ibid, p. 158.
14 Ibid, p. 159.
15 Ibid, p. 159.
16 Ibid, p. 159.
17 Ibid, p. 159.
18 Barbour, Philip L. 1965. *The Three Worlds of Captain John Smith: Adventurer, Colonist, Promoter*. Houghton Mifflin, p. 22.
19 Smith. *The True Travels*, in *The Complete Works of Captain John Smith*, vol. 3, p. 159.
20 Cawthorn, George. 1798. *Observations on the Expedition of General Buonaparte to the East*. George Cawthorn, p. 22.

21 Teonge, Henry. 1825. *The Diary of Henry Teonge, Chaplain on Board His Majesty's Ships Assistance, Bristol, and Royal Oak, Anno 1675 to 1679*. Charles Knight, p. 91.

22 Smith. *The True Travels*, in *The Complete Works of Captain John Smith*, vol. 3, p. 160.

23 Ibid, p. 161.

24 Ibid, p. 161.

25 Ibid, p. 161.

26 Ibid, p. 161.

27 Carrafiello, Michael L. 1998. *Robert Parsons & English Catholicism, 1580–1610*. Susquehanna University Press, p. 11.

28 Barbour. 1965. *The Three Worlds of Captain John Smith: Adventurer, Colonist, Promoter*. p. 26.

29 Smith. *The True Travels*, in *The Complete Works of Captain John Smith*, vol. 3, p. 162.

3. Mercenary

1 Barbour, Philip L. 1965. *The Three Worlds of Captain John Smith: Adventurer, Colonist, Promoter*. Houghton Mifflin, p. 26.

2 Smith, John. 1630. *The True Travels*, in Philip L. Barbour. 1986. *The Complete Works of Captain John Smith (1580–1631)*, vol. 3. University of North Carolina Press, p. 163.

3 Bourne, William. 1578. *Inventions or Devices, Very Necessary for All Generalles and Captaines, or Leaders of Man, as wel by Sea as by Land*. Thos. Woodcocke, p. 61.

4 Smith. *The True Travels*, in *The Complete Works of Captain John Smith*, vol. 3, p. 163.

5 Ibid, p. 164.

6 Smith, Bradford. 1953. *Captain John Smith: His Life & Legend*. Lippincott, p. 45.

7 Barbour. 1965. *The Three Worlds of Captain John Smith: Adventurer, Colonist, Promoter*. p. 27.

8 Striker, Laura Polanyi. 1953. "Captain John Smith's Hungary and Transylvania", in Bradford Smith. 1953. *Captain John Smith: His Life & Legend*. Lippincott, p. 312.

9 Smith. *The True Travels*, in *The Complete Works of Captain John Smith*, vol. 3, p. 165.

10 Ibid, p. 165.

11 Ibid, p. 166.

12 Ibid, p. 167.

13 Forster, Edward Seymour (trans.). 2005. *The Turkish Letters of Ogier Ghislain de Busbecq: Imperial Ambassador at Constantinople, 1554–1562*. Louisiana State University Press, p. 150.

14 Smith. *The True Travels*, in *The Complete Works of Captain John Smith*, vol. 3, p. 168.

15 Ibid, p. 168.

16 Ibid, p. 168.

17 Barbour, Philip L. 1986. *The Complete Works of Captain John Smith (1580–1631)*, vol. 3. University of North Carolina Press, p. 168.

18 Barbour, *The Three Worlds of Captain John Smith: Adventurer, Colonist, Promoter*. p. 36.

19 Ibid, pp. 408–9.

20 Smith. *The True Travels*, in *The Complete Works of Captain John Smith*, vol. 3, p. 169.

21 De Bethune duc de Sully, Maximilien. 1817. *The Memoirs of the Duke of Sully*, vol. 2. Edward Earle, p. 534.

4. Knight-Errant

1 Smith, John. 1630. *The True Travels*, in Philip L. Barbour. 1986. *The Complete Works of Captain John Smith (1580–1631)*, vol. 3. University of North Carolina Press, p. 170.

2 McCoy, F.W., and G. Heiken (eds.). 2000. "Volcanic Hazards and Disasters in Human Antiquity". *Geological Society of America Special Paper*, no. 345, p. 18.

3 Witze, Alexandra. 2008. "The Volcano That Changed the World". *Nature*, April 11, doi:10.1038/news.2008.747.

4 Smith. *The True Travels*, in *The Complete Works of Captain John Smith*, vol. 3, p. 171.

5 Ibid, p. 170.

6 Ibid, p. 710.

7 Ibid, p. 171.

8 Ibid, p. 171.

9 Ibid, p. 171.

10 Ibid, p. 171.

11 Ibid, p. 171.

12 Eltis, David. 1998. *The Military Revolution in Sixteenth-Century Europe*. I.B. Tauris, p. 82.

13 Smith. *The True Travels*, in *The Complete Works of Captain John Smith*, vol. 3, p. 172.

14 Ibid, p. 172.

15 Ibid, p. 172.

16 Ibid, p. 172.

17 Ibid, p. 172.

18 Ibid, p. 173.

19 Ibid, p. 173.

20 Ibid, p. 173.

21 Ibid, p. 173.

22 Ibid, p. 174.

23 Ibid, p. 175.

24 Ibid, p. 175.

25 Sălăgean, Tudor. Director, *Muzeul Etnografic al Transilvaniei*. Personal communication, October 2013.
26 Smith. *The True Travels*, in *The Complete Works of Captain John Smith*, vol. 3, p. 175.
27 Ford, Emanuel. 1680. *Of the Famous and Pleasant History of Parismus, The Valiant and Renowned Prince of Bohemia*, part 1, ed. 8. Henry Woodgate and Samuel Brook, p. 24.
28 Sălăgean. Personal communication, April 2014.
29 Striker, Laura Polanyi. 1953. "Captain John Smith's Hungary and Transylvania", in Bradford Smith. 1953. *Captain Smith: His Life & Legend*. Lippincott, p. 327.
30 Ibid, p. 328.
31 *Theatrum Orbis Terrarum* ("Theatre of the World") is considered to be the first true modern atlas. It was created by Abraham Ortelius and first printed on May 20, 1570, in Antwerp.
32 Fumee, Martin. 1600. *Historie of the Troubles of Hungarie*. Felix Kyngston, p. 215.
33 Ibid, p. 215.
34 Smith. *The True Travels*, in *The Complete Works of Captain John Smith*, vol. 3, p. 172.
35 Ibid, p. 180.
36 Ibid, p. 180.
37 Ibid, p. 179.
38 Ibid, p. 181.
39 Ibid, p. 181.
40 Ibid, p. 182.
41 Ibid, p. 182.
42 Ibid, p. 183.
43 Ibid, p. 184.
44 Ibid, p. 185.
45 Ibid, p. 184.
46 Ibid, p. 184.
47 Ibid, p. 185.
48 Ibid, p. 185.
49 Ibid, p. 186.

5. Slave

1 Veress, Andrew. 1934. *Fundaţiunea Regele Ferdinand I, Documente Privitoare la Istoria Ardealului, Moldovei şi Tarii-Romaneşti*, vol. 7 *(1602–1606)*, Cartea Românească, p. 15.
2 Lithgow, William. 1632. *The Totall Discourse of The Rare Adventures Painefull Peregrinations of Long Nineteene Yeares Travayles from Scotland to the Most famous Kingdomes in Europe, Asia and Affrica*. MacLehose, p. 122.

3 Smith, John. 1630. *The True Travels*, in Philip L. Barbour. 1986. *The Complete Works of Captain John Smith (1580–1631)*, vol. 3. University of North Carolina Press, p. 186.
4 Barbour, Philip L. 1957. "Captain John Smith's Route through Turkey and Russia". *William and Mary Quarterly*, series 3, vol. 14, no. 3, p. 360.
5 Smith. *The True Travels*, in *The Complete Works of Captain John Smith*, vol. 3, p. 186.
6 Schweigger, Salomon. 1608. *Eine newe Reyssbeschreibung auss Teutschland nach Constantinopel und Jerusalem*. Nachdruck der Ausgabe Nürnberg (reprinted 1964), pp. 125–7.
7 Smith. *The True Travels*, in *The Complete Works of Captain John Smith*, vol. 3, p. 187.
8 Ibid, p. 187.
9 Ibid, p. 188.
10 Ibid, p. 188.
11 Ibid, p. 188.
12 Barbour. "Captain John Smith's Route through Turkey and Russia". *William and Mary Quarterly*, series 3, vol. 14, no. 3, p. 364.
13 Smith. *The True Travels*, in *The Complete Works of Captain John Smith*, vol. 3, p. 188.
14 Ibid, pp. 189.
15 Ibid, p. 188.
16 Ibid, p. 189.
17 Ibid, p. 200.
18 Ibid, p. 200.
19 Ibid, p. 200.
20 Ibid, p. 200.
21 Lewin, Moshe. 1985. *The Making of the Soviet System*. Menthuen, p. 53.
22 Smith. *The True Travels*, in *The Complete Works of Captain John Smith*, vol. 3, p. 200.
23 Ibid, p. 201.
24 Barbour. "Captain John Smith's Route through Turkey and Russia". *William and Mary Quarterly*, series 3, vol. 14, no. 3, p. 365.
25 Smith. *The True Travels*, in *The Complete Works of Captain John Smith*, vol. 3, p. 202.
26 Ibid, p. 203.
27 Ibid, p. 203.
28 Ibid, p. 204.
29 Ibid, p. 206.
30 Ibid, p. 211.
31 Ibid, pp. 211–12.
32 Ibid, p. 212.
33 Ibid, p. 212.
34 Ibid, p. 212.

35 Ibid, p. 212.

36 Ibid, p. 212.

37 Ibid, p. 213.

38 Ibid, p. 213.

6. Entrepreneur

1 Purchas, Samuel. 1613. *Purchas His Pilgrimage: Or Relations of the World and the Religions Observed in all Ages and Places Discovered, from the Creation unto This Present*, vol. 2. William Stansby, p. 1370.

2 Bruce, John (ed.). 1868. *Diary of John Manningham, of the Middle Temple, and of Bradbourne, Kent, Barrister-at-law, 1602–1603*. J.B. Nichols, p. 146.

3 Fisher, F.J. (ed.). 1936. *The State of England Anno Domo. 1600 by Thomas Wilson*. Camden Society, p. 5.

4 Pevsner, Nikolaus. 1957. *The Buildings of England: Cities of London and Westminster*, vol. 1. Pevsner Architectural Guides, p. 48.

5 Platter, Thomas. 1599. *A Swiss Tourist in London* (translated from his diary, originally written in German), in Leonard R.N. Ashley. 2004. *Elizabethan Popular Culture*. Bowling Green University Popular Press, p. 8.

6 Wheatley, Henry Benjamin, and Peter Cunningham. 2011. *London Past and Present: Its History, Associations, and Traditions*. Cambridge University Press, p. 210.

7 Barbour, Philip L. 1964. *The Three Worlds of Captain John Smith: Adventurer, Colonist, Promoter*. Houghton Mifflin, p. 85.

8 Smith, John. 1612. *A Map of Virginia*, in Philip L. Barbour. 1986. *The Complete Works of Captain John Smith (1580–1631)*, vol. 1. University of North Carolina Press, pp. 160–1.

9 Barbour, Philip L. (ed.). 1969. *The Jamestown Voyages under the First Charter, 1606–1609*, vol. 1. Hakluyt Society, p. 231.

10 "Charles Leigh (d. 1605)" in *Dictionary of National Biography*, 1885–1900, vol. 32. Smith, Elder, p. 431.

11 Kupperman, Karen Ordahl. 2007. *The Jamestown Project*. Harvard University Press, p. 184.

12 Smith, John. 1630. *The True Travels, Adventures and Observations of Captain John Smith*, in Philip L. Barbour. 1986. *The Complete Works of Captain John Smith (1580–1631)*, vol. 3, University of North Carolina Press, p. 224.

13 Rose, J. Holland, A.P. Newton and E.A. Benians (eds.). 1929. *The Cambridge History of the British Empire*, vol. 1. Cambridge University Press, p. 86.

14 Hermann Schomburgk, Robert. 2010. *The History of Barbados*. Cambridge University Press, p. 258.

15 Rose. *The Cambridge History of the British Empire*, vol. 1, no. 74. p. 86.

16 Firstbrook, Peter. 1997. *The Voyage of the Matthew*. BBC Books, pp. 130–45.

17 Wilson, Ian. 1996. *John Cabot and the Matthew*. Breakwater Books, p.32.

18 Ruddock, A.A. 1974. "The Reputation of Sebastian Cabot", *Bulletin of the Institute of Historical Research*, vol. 42, pp. 95–9.

19 Smith, Bradford. 1953. *Captain John Smith: His Life & Legend*. Lippincott, p. 82.

20 http://www.nationalarchives.gov.uk/currency/.

21 Smith, John. 1624. *The Generall Historie*, in Philip L. Barbour. 1986. *The Complete Works of Captain John Smith (1580–1631)*, vol. 2. University of North Carolina Press, p. 137.

22 The First Charter of Virginia, April 10, 1606.

23 *Eastward Hoe* was first published 1605 and was written, at least in part, in response to an earlier satire entitled *Westward Ho* by Thomas Dekker and John Webster.

24 Woolley, Benjamin. 2007. *Savage Kingdom: Virginia and the Founding of English America*. HarperPress, pp. 16–17.

25 The First Charter of Virginia, April 10, 1606.

26 Jonson, Ben. John Marston and George Chapman. 1999. *Eastward Hoe*. Manchester University Press, pp. 138–40.

27 Barbour, Philip L. 1969. *The Jamestown Voyages Under the First Charter, 1606–1609*. Cambridge University Press, pp. 55–6.

28 Purchas, Samuel. 1625. *Hakluytus Posthumus: Or Purchas His Pilgrimes, Contayning a History of the World in Sea Voyages and Lande Travells, by Englishmen and Others*, in Barbour, Philip L. 1964. *The Three Worlds of Captain John Smith: Adventurer, Colonist, Promoter*. Houghton Mifflin, p. 113.

7. Colonist

1 RMS Special Report. 2007. *1607 Bristol Channel Floods: 400-Year Retrospective*. Risk Management Solutions, pp. 1–4.

2 I[aggard] W[illiam]. 1607. *From a booklet, printed at London for Edward White, to be solde at the signe of the Gunne at the north doore of Paules.*

3 Percy, George. 1608? [before April 12, 1612]. *Discourse*, in Philip L. Barbour. 1986. *The Jamestown Voyages Under the First Charter, 1606–1609*, vol. 1. Cambridge University Press, p. 129.

4 Smith, John. 1624. *The Generall Historie*, in Philip L. Barbour. 1986. *The Complete Works of Captain John Smith (1580–1631)*, vol. 2. University of North Carolina Press, p. 137. Smith refers to December 19, 1606, the actual date of departure, whereas Percy's account quoted above refers to the following day, December 20, when the fleet dropped downriver.

5 Smith, *The Generall Historie*, in *The Complete Works of Captain John Smith* vol. 2, p. 137.
6 Percy. *Discourse*, in *The Jamestown Voyages Under the First Charter, 1606–1609*, vol. 1, p. 129.
7 Barbour, Philip L. 1986. *The Complete Works of Captain John Smith (1580–1631)*, vol. 1. University of North Carolina Press, p. 16.
8 Knox-Johnston, Robin. 2013. "Practical Assessment of the Accuracy of the Astrolabe". *The Mariner's Mirror*, vol. 99, no. 1, p. 71.
9 Smith. *The Generall Historie*, in *The Complete Works of Captain John Smith* vol. 2, p. 139.
10 Purchas, Samuel. 1625. *Hakluytus Posthumus or Purchas his Pilgrimes, contayning a History of the World in Sea Voyages and Lande Travells, by Englishmen and others* (originally published in 4 vols, reprinted 1905–7, vol. 18). James MacLehose, p. 404.
11 Brown, Alexander. 1890. *The Genesis of the United States: A Narrative of the Movement in England, 1605–1616*. Houghton, Miffin, p. 964.
12 Bell, James Elton, and Frances Jean Bell. 2007. *Sir Robert Bell and His Early Virginia Colony Descendants*. Wheatmark, p. 12.
13 Percy. *Discourse*, in *The Jamestown Voyages Under the First Charter, 1606–1609*, vol. 1, pp. 129–30.
14 Ibid, p. 130.
15 Ibid, p. 130.
16 Ibid, p. 130.
17 Smith, John. 1630. *The True Travels*, in Philip L. Barbour. 1986. *The Complete Works of Captain John Smith (1580–1631)*, vol. 3. University of North Carolina Press, p. 236.
18 Ibid, p. 235.
19 Ibid, p. 235.
20 Percy. *Discourse*, in *The Jamestown Voyages Under the First Charter, 1606–1609*, vol. 1, p. 131.
21 Ibid, p. 132.
22 Ibid, p. 133.
23 Ibid, p. 133.
24 Smith, John. 1624. *A Map of Virginia*, in Philip L. Barbour. 1986. *The Complete Works of Captain John Smith (1580–1631)*, vol. 1. University of North Carolina Press, p. 144.
25 Rountree, Helen C. 1990. *Pocahontas's People: The Powhatan Indians of Virginia Through Four Centuries*. University of Oklahoma Press, p. 18.
26 Barbour, Philip L. 1964. *The Three Worlds of Captain John Smith: Adventurer, Colonist, Promoter*. Houghton Mifflin, p. 121.
27 Percy. *Discourse*, in *The Jamestown Voyages Under the First Charter, 1606–1609*, vol. 1, pp. 133–4.

28 Kupperman, Karen Ordahl. 2007. *The Jamestown Project.* Harvard University Press, p. 7.

29 Sometimes Wahunsenacawh is spelled Wahunsenaca (see Linwood "Little Bear" Custalow in *The True Story of Pocahontas*) or Wahunsonacock (see Philip L. Barbour in *The Complete Works of Captain John Smith*); I have chosen to follow the spelling used by renowned anthropologist of the Powhatan peoples Helen C. Rountree in *Pocahontas's People.* Similarly, Powhatan is sometimes spelled Powatan or Powhaten.

30 Lewis, Clifford M., and Albert J. Loomie. 1953. *The Spanish Jesuit Mission in Virginia, 1570–1572.* University of North Carolina Press, p. 45.

31 Rountree, Helen C. 1990. *Pocahontas's People: The Powhatan Indians of Virginia Through Four Centuries.* University of Oklahoma Press, p. 27.

32 There were three identical boxes, containing identical instructions, one for each ship. This way, if one or two of the ships was lost on the crossing, the surviving colonists would still know the wishes of the London Company's directors.

33 *Instructions from the Virginia Company of London to the First Settlers.* 1606. Thomas Jefferson Papers, series 8. US Library of Congress Manuscript Division, p. 3.

8. Survivor

1 Percy, George. 1608? [before April 12, 1612]. *Discourse,* in Philip L. Barbour. 1986. *The Jamestown Voyages Under the First Charter, 1606–1609,* vol. 1. Cambridge University Press, p. 134.

2 Ibid, p. 134.

3 Ibid, p. 135.

4 Smith, John. 1612. *A Map of Virginia,* in Philip L. Barbour. 1986. *The Complete Works of Captain John Smith (1580–1631),* vol. 1. University of North Carolina Press, p. 160.

5 Percy. *Discourse,* in *The Jamestown Voyages Under the First Charter, 1606–1609,* vol. 1, p. 135.

6 Ibid, p. 136.

7 Archaeologists found the remains of the house of the *weroance,* other village houses, mortuary structures, and items including ceramics and copper. See Mary Ellen Hodges and Charles Hodges (eds.). 1994. *Paspahegh Archaeology: Data Recovery Investigations of Site 44JC308 at the Governor's Land at Two Rivers, James City County, Virginia.* James River Institute for Archaeology.

8 Percy. *Discourse,* in *The Jamestown Voyages Under the First Charter, 1606–1609,* vol. 1, p. 136.

9 Ibid, p. 137.

10 Ibid, p. 138.

11 Smith, John. 1608. *A True Relation*, in Philip L. Barbour. 1986. *The Complete Works of Captain John Smith (1580–1631)*, vol. 1. University of North Carolina Press, p. 29.
12 De Castro, Marcia Caldas, and Burton H. Singer. 2005. "Was Malaria Present in the Amazon before the European Conquest?" *Journal of Archaeological Science*, vol. 32, no. 3, pp. 337–40.
13 Virginia Company of London. 1606. "Instructions from the Virginia Company of London to the First Settlers". p. 1.
14 Smith, John. 1612. *The Proceedings of an English Colonie*, in Philip L. Barbour. 1986. *The Complete Works of Captain John Smith (1580–1631)*, vol. 1. University of North Carolina Press, p. 205.
15 Ibid, pp. 205–6.
16 Percy. *Discourse*, in *The Jamestown Voyages Under the First Charter, 1606–1609*, vol. 1, p. 138.
17 Virginia Company of London. 1606. "Instructions from the Virginia Company of London to the First Settlers". p. 3.
18 Smith, John. 1624. *The Generall Historie*, in Philip L. Barbour. 1986. *The Complete Works of Captain John Smith (1580–1631)*, vol. 1. University of North Carolina Press, p. 138.
19 Virginia Company of London. 1606. "Instructions from the Virginia Company of London to the First Settlers", p. 2.
20 Ibid.
21 Archer, Gabriel? [written by a gentleman of the colony]. 1607. *A Relatyon*, in Philip L. Barbour. 1986. *The Jamestown Voyages Under the First Charter, 1606–1609*, vol. 1. Cambridge University Press, p. 82.
22 Ibid, pp. 82–3.
23 Smith. *The Generall Historie*, in *The Complete Works of Captain John Smith*, vol. 2, p. 138.
24 Smith. *A Map of Virginia*, in *The Complete Works of Captain John Smith*, vol. 1, p. 156.
25 Smith. *The Generall Historie*, in *The Complete Works of Captain John Smith*, vol. 2, p. 138.
26 Virginia Company of London. "Instructions from the Virginia Company of London to the First Settlers", p. 3.
27 Smith. *The Generall Historie*, in *The Complete Works of Captain John Smith*, vol. 2, p. 139.
28 Ibid, p. 139.
29 Archer. *A Relatyon* in *The Jamestown Voyages Under the First Charter, 1606–1609*, vol. 1, p. 97.

30 Ibid.

31 Ibid.

32 "Joint Letter from the Council of Virginia to the London Company", June 22, 1607, in Philip L. Barbour. 1986. *The Jamestown Voyages Under the First Charter, 1606–1609*, vol. 1. Cambridge University Press, pp. 78–9.

33 Archer. *A Relatyon* in *The Jamestown Voyages Under the First Charter, 1606–1609*, vol. 1, p. 143.

34 Wingfield, Edward Maria. 1608 [after May 21]. *Discourse*, in Barbour, Philip L. 1986. *The Jamestown Voyages Under the First Charter, 1606–1609*, vol. 1. Cambridge University Press, pp. 214–15.

35 Smith. *The Generall Historie*, in *The Complete Works of Captain John Smith*, vol. 2, p. 143.

36 Ibid, p. 143.

37 Percy, *Discourse*, in *The Jamestown Voyages Under the First Charter, 1606–1609*, vol. 1, p. 144.

38 Ibid, p. 143.

39 Kelso, William M. 2006. *Jamestown: The Buried Truth*. University of Virginia Press, p. 142.

40 The skeletal remains are now on public display in historic Jamestown.

41 Wingfield. *Discourse*, vol. 1, p. 215.

9. Prisoner

1 Percy, George. 1608? [before April 12, 1612]. *Discourse*, in Philip L. Barbour. 1986. *The Jamestown Voyages Under the First Charter, 1606–1609*, vol. 1. Cambridge University Press, p. 145.

2 Wingfield, Edward Maria. 1608 [after May 21]. *Discourse*, in Philip L. Barbour. 1986. *The Jamestown Voyages Under the First Charter, 1606–1609*, vol. 1. Cambridge University Press, p. 216.

3 Ibid, p. 219.

4 Ibid, p. 222.

5 Ibid, p. 222.

6 Smith, John. 1624. *The Generall Historie*, in Philip L. Barbour. 1986. *The Complete Works of Captain John Smith (1580–1631)*, vol. 2. University of North Carolina Press, p. 143.

7 De Zúñiga, Pedro. 1607. "Letter from Don Pedro de Zúñiga to King Philip III", Sept. 22 (NS), in Philip L. Barbour. 1986. *The Jamestown Voyages Under the First Charter, 1606–1609*, vol. 1. Cambridge University Press, pp. 114–15.

8 Ibid, p. 118.

9 Ibid, pp. 119–20.

10 Smith, John. 1608. *A True Relation,* in Philip L. Barbour. 1986. *The Complete Works of Captain John Smith (1580–1631),* vol. 1. University of North Carolina Press, p. 35.

11 Ibid, p. 35.

12 Ibid, p. 35.

13 Ibid, p. 37.

14 In his 1858 *History of New England,* John Gorham Palfrey was "haunted by incredulity" over some of Smith's adventures. Charles Deane, Boston merchant and historian, claimed that Smith was a notorious liar and braggart. In 1867, the respected Boston historian Henry Adams declared in the *North American Review* that Smith was incorrigibly vain and inept.

15 Smith. *A True Relation,* in *The Complete Works of Captain John Smith,* vol. 1, p. 39.

16 Ibid, p. 41.

17 Ibid, p. 45.

18 Beverley, Robert. 1705. In Louis B. Wright (ed.). 1947. *The History and Present State of Virginia.* University of North Carolina Press, p. 61.

19 Smith. *A True Relation,* in *The Complete Works of Captain John Smith,* vol. 1, p. 47.

20 Ibid, p. 47.

21 Smith. *The Generall Historie,* in *The Complete Works of Captain John Smith,* vol. 2, p. 147.

22 Ibid, p. 147.

23 Smith. *A True Relation,* in *The Complete Works of Captain John Smith,* vol. 1, p. 47.

24 Ibid, p. 47.

25 Smith. *The Generall Historie,* in *The Complete Works of Captain John Smith,* vol. 2, pp. 147–8.

26 Smith. *A True Relation,* in *The Complete Works of Captain John Smith,* vol. 1, p. 49.

27 Ibid, p. 49.

28 Smith. *The Generall Historie,* in *The Complete Works of Captain John Smith,* vol. 2, p. 149

10. Trader

1 Smith, John. 1624. *The Generall Historie,* in Philip L. Barbour. 1986. *The Complete Works of Captain John Smith (1580–1631),* vol. 2. University of North Carolina Press, p. 150.

2 Ibid, p. 127.

3 Smith, John. 1608. *A True Relation,* in Philip L. Barbour. 1986. *The Complete Works of Captain John Smith (1580–1631),* vol. 1. University of North Carolina Press, p. 55.

4 Smith. *The Generall Historie,* in *The Complete Works of Captain John Smith,* vol. 2, p. 151.

5 Ibid, p. 151.

6 Smith, John. 1616. "Letter to Queen Anne of England", in Philip L. Barbour. 1986. *The Complete Works of Captain John Smith (1580–1631)*, vol. 2. University of North Carolina Press, pp. 258–62.

7 Smith, John. 1612. *The Proceedings*, in Philip L. Barbour. 1986. *The Complete Works of Captain John Smith (1580–1631)*, vol. 1. University of North Carolina Press, p. 207. Some of the theories as to Smith's motivations were previously put forward by Bradford Smith, among other Smith biographers.

8 Smith. *A True Relation*, in *The Complete Works of Captain John Smith*, vol. 1, p. 53.

9 Ibid, p. 53.

10 Smith. *The Proceedings*, in *The Complete Works of Captain John Smith*, vol. 1, p. 213.

11 The earliest and most vocal sceptics of John Smith and the Pocahontas story were American historians from the North, including Massachusetts Representative John Gorham Palfrey and the Boston antiquarian Charles Deane. Later, after the Civil War, Henry Adams resumed the attack on Smith. See the epilogue for an exposition of this debate.

12 It is not clear exactly when John Smith wrote to Queen Anne. Pocahontas arrived in Plymouth on June 12, 1616. She then travelled by coach to London and should have arrived before the end of June. It is therefore reasonable to assume that Smith wrote to the Queen before Pocahontas arrived in the capital.

13 Smith. *The Generall Historie*, in *The Complete Works of Captain John Smith*, vol. 2, p. 259.

14 Rountree, Helen C. 1990. *Pocahontas's People: The Powhatan Indians of Virginia through Four Centuries*. University of Oklahoma Press, p. 36.

15 Smith. *The Generall Historie*, in *The Complete Works of Captain John Smith*, vol. 2, p. 151.

16 Ibid, p. 151.

17 Ibid, p. 152.

18 Ibid, p. 152.

19 Ibid, p. 153.

20 Wingfield, Edward Maria. 1608 [after May 21]. *Discourse*, in Philip L. Barbour. 1986. *The Jamestown Voyages Under the First Charter, 1606–1609*, vol. 1. Cambridge University Press, p. 227.

21 Smith. *A True Relation*, in *The Complete Works of Captain John Smith*, vol. 1, p. 61.

22 Perkins, Francis. 1608. "Letter to a Friend" (March 28), in Philip L. Barbour. 1986. *The Jamestown Voyages Under the First Charter, 1606–1609*, vol. 1. Cambridge University Press, p. 160.

23 Smith. *The Generall Historie*, in *The Complete Works of Captain John Smith*, vol. 2, p. 154.

24 Perkins. "Letter to a Friend", in *The Jamestown Voyages Under the First Charter, 1606–1609*, vol. 1, p. 160.

25 Custalow, Linwood "Little Bear", and Angela "Silver Star" Daniel. 2007. *The True Story of Pocahontas: The Other Side of History*. Fulcrum, pp. 6–9.

26 Smith. *A True Relation*, in *The Complete Works of Captain John Smith*, vol. 1, p. 65.

27 Ibid, p. 65.

28 Ibid, pp. 65–6.

29 Ibid, p. 71.

30 Smith. *The Generall Historie*, in *The Complete Works of Captain John Smith*, vol. 2, p. 156.

31 Barbour, Philip L. 1986. *The Jamestown Voyages Under the First Charter, 1606–1609*, vol. 1. Cambridge University Press, p. 76.

32 Smith. *The Generall Historie*, in *The Complete Works of Captain John Smith*, vol. 2, p. 156.

33 Ibid, p. 157.

34 Smith. *A True Relation*, in *The Complete Works of Captain John Smith*, vol. 1, p. 93.

35 Ibid, p. 85.

36 Ibid, p. 89.

37 Ibid, p. 89.

38 Ibid, p. 93.

39 Ibid, p. 93.

40 Smith. *The Generall Historie*, in *The Complete Works of Captain John Smith*, vol. 2, p. 160.

41 De Zúñiga, Pedro. 1608. "Letter from Don Pedro de Zúñiga to King Philip III", June 26 (NS), in Philip L. Barbour. 1986. *The Jamestown Voyages Under the First Charter, 1606–1609*, vol. 1. Cambridge University Press, p. 227.

42 Smith. *A True Relation*, in *The Complete Works of Captain John Smith*, vol. 1, p. 97.

11. President

1 Smith, John. 1624. *The Generall Historie*, in Philip L. Barbour. 1986. *The Complete Works of Captain John Smith (1580–1631)*, vol. 2. University of North Carolina Press, p. 164.

2 Ibid, p. 165.

3 Ibid, p. 165.

4 Ibid, p. 167.

5 Ibid, p. 167.

6 Ibid, p. 168.
7 Ibid, p. 168.
8 Ibid, p. 169.
9 Pendergast, James F. 1991. "The Massawomeck: Raiders and Traders into the Chesapeake Bay in the Seventeenth Century". *Transactions of the American Philosophical Society*, vol. 81, no. 2, p. 6.
10 Smith. *The Generall Historie*, in *The Complete Works of Captain John Smith*, vol. 2, p. 169.
11 Ibid, p. 169.
12 Ibid, p. 169.
13 Ibid, p. 170.
14 Smith, John. 1624. *A Map of Virginia*, in Philip L. Barbour. 1986. *The Complete Works of Captain John Smith (1580–1631)*, vol. 1. University of North Carolina Press, p. 149.
15 Santoro, Nicholas J. 2009. *Atlas of the Indian Tribes of North America and the Clash of Cultures*. iUniverse, p. 156.
16 Smith. *The Generall Historie*, in *The Complete Works of Captain John Smith*, vol. 2, p. 175.
17 Smith, John. 1624. *The Proceedings*, in Philip L. Barbour. 1986. *The Complete Works of Captain John Smith (1580–1631)*, vol. 1. University of North Carolina Press, pp. 232–3.
18 Smith. *The Generall Historie*, in *The Complete Works of Captain John Smith*, vol. 2, p. 179.
19 Smith. *The Proceedings*, in *The Complete Works of Captain John Smith*, vol. 1, p. 233.
20 Ibid, p. 235.
21 Ibid, p. 234.
22 Ibid, p. 235.
23 Ibid, p. 236.
24 Rountree, Helen C. 1992. *The Powhatan Indians of Virginia: Their Traditional Culture*. University of Oklahoma Press, pp. 98–9.
25 Smith. *The Proceedings*, in *The Complete Works of Captain John Smith*, vol. 1, p. 236.
26 Rountree. *The Powhatan Indians of Virginia: Their Traditional Culture*, p. 91.
27 Smith. *The Proceedings*, in *The Complete Works of Captain John Smith*, vol. 1, p. 236.
28 Ibid, p. 236.
29 Ibid, p. 237.
30 Smith, John. 1608. "Letter to the Treasurer and Council of Virginia, London", in Philip L. Barbour. 1986. *The Jamestown Voyages Under the First Charter, 1606–1609*, vol. 1. Cambridge University Press, p. 242.

31 Smith. *The Generall Historie*, in *The Complete Works of Captain John Smith*, vol. 2, p. 185.
32 Blanton, Dennis B. 2000. "Drought as a Factor in the Jamestown Colony, 1607–1612". *Historical Archaeology*, vol. 34, no. 4, pp. 74–81.
33 Smith. *The Generall Historie*, in *The Complete Works of Captain John Smith*, vol. 2, p. 186.
34 Ratcliffe, John. 1609. "Letter to the Earl of Salisbury" (4 October), in Alexander Brown. 1890. *The Genesis of the United States: A Narrative of the Movement in England, 1605–1616*. Houghton Mifflin, pp. 334–5.
35 Smith. *The Generall Historie*, in *The Complete Works of Captain John Smith*, vol. 2, p. 187.
36 Ibid, p. 187.
37 Smith. "Letter to the Treasurer and Council of Virginia, London", in *The Jamestown Voyages Under the First Charter, 1606–1609*, vol. 1, p. 244.
38 Ibid, p. 244.
39 Smith. *The Generall Historie*, in *The Complete Works of Captain John Smith*, vol. 2, p. 195.
40 Ibid, p. 196.
41 Ibid, p. 198.
42 Ibid, p. 199.
43 Ibid, p. 199.
44 Smith, John. 1624. "Letter to Queen Anne" (dated 1616), in *The Generall Historie*, in Philip L. Barbour. 1986. *The Complete Works of Captain John Smith (1580–1631)*, vol. 2. University of North Carolina Press, p. 259.
45 Smith. *The Generall Historie*, in *The Complete Works of Captain John Smith*, vol. 2, p. 199.
46 Ibid, p. 199.

12. Dictator

1 Smith, John. 1624. *The Proceedings*, in Philip L. Barbour. 1986. *The Complete Works of Captain John Smith (1580–1631)*, vol. 1. University of North Carolina Press, p. 251.
2 Ibid, p. 251.
3 Ibid, p. 252.
4 Ibid, p. 252.
5 Ibid, p. 253.
6 Ibid, p. 253.
7 Percy, George. 1624. *A True Relation of the Proceedings and Occurrents of Moment Which Have Hap'ned in Virginia*, in Edward Wright Haile. 1998. *Jamestown*

Narratives: Eyewitness Accounts of the Virginia Colony – The First Decade: 1607–1617. RoundHouse, p. 502.

8 Smith, John. 1624. *The Generall Historie*, in Philip L. Barbour. 1986. *The Complete Works of Captain John Smith (1580–1631)*, vol. 2. University of North Carolina Press, p. 229.

9 Ibid, p. 207.

10 Smith, John. 1624. *The Proceedings of the English Colonie*, in Philip L. Barbour. 1986. *The Complete Works of Captain John Smith (1580–1631)*, vol. 1. University of North Carolina Press, p. 260.

11 Smith. *The Generall Historie*, in *The Complete Works of Captain John Smith*, vol. 2, p. 213.

12 Ibid, p. 214.

13 Ibid, p. 216.

14 Ibid, p. 216.

15 Smith, Bradford. 1953. *Captain John Smith: His Life & Legend*. Lippincott, p. 153.

16 Johnson, Robert. 1609. *Nova Britannia: Offering Most Excellent Fruites by Planting in Virginia*. Samuel Macham, p. 6.

17 Zúñiga, Pedro de. 1609. "Letter to King Philip III" (12 April [NS]), in Philip L. Barbour. 1986. *The Jamestown Voyages Under the First Charter, 1606–1609*, vol. 2. Cambridge University Press, pp. 259–260.

18 Archer, Gabriel. 1609. "Letter to an Unknown Friend" (31 August), in Philip L. Barbour. 1986. *The Jamestown Voyages Under the First Charter, 1606–1609*, vol. 2. Cambridge University Press, p. 282.

19 Smith. *The Proceedings*, in *The Complete Works of Captain John Smith*, vol. 1, pp. 268–9.

20 Archer. "Letter to an Unknown Friend", in *The Jamestown Voyages Under the First Charter, 1606–1609*, vol. 2, pp. 282–3.

21 Smith. *The Proceedings*, in *The Complete Works of Captain John Smith*, vol. 1, p. 269.

22 Ibid, p. 269.

23 Percy. *A True Relation of the Proceedings and Occurrents of Moment Which Have Hap'ned in Virginia*, p. 501.

24 Smith. *The Proceedings*, in *The Complete Works of Captain John Smith*, vol. 1, p. 271.

25 Ibid, p. 271.

26 Smith. *The Generall Historie*, in *The Complete Works of Captain John Smith*, vol. 2, p. 223.

27 Percy. *A True Relation of the Proceedings and Occurrents of Moment Which Have Hap'ned in Virginia*, p. 502.

28 Smith. *The Proceedings*, in *The Complete Works of Captain John Smith*, vol. 1, p. 272.

29 Russell, Michael S. 2009. *The Chemistry of Fireworks*, 2nd ed. Royal Society of Chemistry, p. 41.

30 Smith. *The Proceedings*, in *The Complete Works of Captain John Smith*, vol. 1, p. 272.

31 Chen, X.L., Y.J. Wang, C.R. Wang and S.S. Li. 2002. "Gunpowder Explosion Burns in Fireworks Factory: Causes of Death and Management". *Burns*, vol. 28, no. 7, pp. 655–8.

32 Smith. *The Proceedings*, in *The Complete Works of Captain John Smith*, vol. 1, p. 272.

33 Ivor Noël Hume, among others, makes the case that this was attempted murder. As supporting evidence, he points to the second plot in Jamestown to kill Smith as he lay injured, see: Hume, Ivor Noël. 1996. *The Virginia Adventure: Roanoke to James Towne, an Archaeological and Historical Odyssey*. Knopf, p. 251.

34 Bemiss, Samuel M. (ed.). 1967. *The Three Charters of the Virginia Company of London: With Seven Related Documents, 1606–1621*. Clearfield, p. 62.

35 Smith. *The Generall Historie*, in *The Complete Works of Captain John Smith*, vol. 2, pp. 224–5.

13. Admiral

1 Ratcliffe, John. 1609. "Letter to Lord Salisbury" (October 4), in Philip L. Barbour. 1986. *The Jamestown Voyages Under the First Charter, 1606–1609*, vol. 2. Cambridge University Press, p. 284.

2 Spelman, Henry. 1609. *Relations of Virginea*, in Edward Arber (ed.). 1910. *Travels and Works of Captain John Smith*, vol. 1. John Grant, p. cii.

3 Smith, Bradford. 1953. *Captain John Smith: His Life & Legend*. Lippincott, p. 174.

4 Percy, George. 1624. *A True Relation*, in Edward Wright Haile. 1998. *Jamestown Narratives: Eyewitness Accounts of the Virginia Colony – The First Decade: 1607–1617*. RoundHouse. p. 504.

5 Ibid, pp. 504–5.

6 Smith, John. 1624. *The Generall Historie*, in Philip L. Barbour. 1986. *The Complete Works of Captain John Smith (1580–1631)*, vol. 2. University of North Carolina Press, p. 232.

7 Percy. *A True Relation*, in *Jamestown Narratives: Eyewitness Accounts of the Virginia Colony – The First Decade: 1607–1617*, p. 505.

8 Kelso, William M. 2006. *Jamestown: The Buried Truth*. University of Virginia, p. 92.

9 Horn, James, et al. 2013. *Jane: Starvation, Cannibalism, and Endurance at Jamestown*. Colonial Williamsburg Foundation and Preservation Virginia.

10 Smith. *The Generall Historie*, in *The Complete Works of Captain John Smith*, vol. 2, pp. 232–3.

11 Percy. *A True Relation*, in *Jamestown Narratives: Eyewitness Accounts of the Virginia Colony – The First Decade: 1607–1617*, p. 505.

12 Loker, Aleck. 2008. *Profiles in Colonial History*. Solitude Press, p. 12.

13 Percy. *A True Relation*, in *Jamestown Narratives: Eyewitness Accounts of the Virginia Colony – The First Decade: 1607–1617*, p. 507.

14 State of Maryland, Complainant, v. State of West Virginia, 217 U.S. 1 (1910), 217 U.S. 1. Argued November 2, 3, 4, 1909. Decided February 21, 1910.

15 Percy. *A True Relation*, in *Jamestown Narratives: Eyewitness Accounts of the Virginia Colony – The First Decade: 1607–1617*, p. 507.

16 Ibid, p. 508.

17 The state of Delaware was later named by the English in honour of Lord De La Warr.

18 Percy. *A True Relation*, in *Jamestown Narratives: Eyewitness Accounts of the Virginia Colony – The First Decade: 1607–1617*, p. 510.

19 Ibid, p. 510.

20 Aune, M.G. 2012. "Samuel Purchas", in Garrett A. Sullivan Jr, Alan Stewart, Rebecca Lemon, Nicholas McDowell and Jennifer Richards (eds.). 2012. *The Encyclopedia of English Renaissance Literature*, vol. 1. Wiley, p. 805.

21 Pritcharrd, R.E. 2008. *Captain John Smith & His Brave Adventures*. Haus. p. 165.

22 Strachey, William. 1612. *The History of Travel*, in Edward Wright Haile. 1998. *Jamestown Narratives: Eyewitness Accounts of the Virginia Colony – The First Decade: 1607–1617*. RoundHouse, pp. 608–9.

23 Smith, John. 1616. *A Description of New England*, in Philip L. Barbour. 1986. *The Complete Works of Captain John Smith (1580–1631)*, vol. 1. University of North Carolina Press, p. 326.

24 Ibid, p. 326.

25 Ibid, p. 340.

26 Ibid, p. 352.

27 Wrigley, E.A. 2010. "English City Population Ranking, 1600–1851", in E.A. Wrigley (ed.). 2010. *Energy and the English Industrial Revolution*. Cambridge University Press, pp. 62–3.

28 Smith. *A Description of New England*, in *The Complete Works of Captain John Smith*, vol. 1, p. 347.

29 Ibid, p. 347.

30 Ibid, p. 332.

31 Ibid, p. 355.

32 Ibid, p. 356.

33 Ibid, p. 358.

34 Ibid, p. 358.

35 Barbour, Philip L. 1964. "A French Account of Captain John Smith's Adventures in the Azores, 1615". *Virginia Magazine of History and Biography*, no. 72, pp. 293–303.

36 Barbour, Philip L. 1964. *The Three Worlds of Captain John Smith: Adventurer, Colonist, Promoter.* Houghton Mifflin, p. 322.

37 Smith. *The Generall Historie*, in *The Complete Works of Captain John Smith*, vol. 2, p. 435.

38 The silver crown was one of several coins in common circulation throughout Europe, and worth five shillings. It was equivalent to a Venetian ducat, a Flemish gelder or a French êcu.

14. Grandee

1 Smith, John. 1616. *A Description of New England*, in Philip L. Barbour. 1986. *The Complete Works of Captain John Smith (1580–1631)*, vol. 1. University of North Carolina Press, p. 359.

2 Custalow, Linwood "Little Bear", and Angela L. "Silver Star" Daniel. 2007. *The True Story of Pocahontas: The Other Side of History*. Fulcrum, p. 43.

3 Rolfe, John. 1614. "Letter to Sir Thomas Dale" (probably written in June), in Edward Wright Haile. 1998. *Jamestown Narratives: Eyewitness Accounts of the Virginia Colony – The First Decade: 1607–1617*. RoundHouse, p. 853.

4 Ibid, p. 853.

5 Woodward, Grace Steele. 1969. *Pocahontas*. University of Oklahoma Press, pp. 174–5.

6 Smith. *The Generall Historie*, in *The Complete Works of Captain John Smith*, vol. 2, p. 261.

7 Lee, Sidney (ed.). 1897. *Dictionary of National Biography*, vol. 52. Macmillan, p. 136.

8 Smith. *The Generall Historie*, in *The Complete Works of Captain John Smith*, vol. 2, pp. 258–60.

9 Purchas, Samuel. 1625. *Hakluytus Posthumus, or, Purchas his Pilgrimes*, vol. 19. Henrie Fetherston, p. 118.

10 King James. 1672. "His Counterblast to Tobacco". Hancock. Accession GT3020, J35 1672a, Special Collections, Library of Virginia, Richmond, Virginia.

11 Smith. *The Generall Historie*, in *The Complete Works of Captain John Smith*, vol. 2, pp. 260–1.

12 Ibid, p. 261.

13 Ibid, p. 261.

14 Rolfe, John. 1617. "Letter to Edwin Sandys" (June 8), in Susan Myra Kingsbury (ed.). 1933. *Records of the Virginia Company, 1606–26*, vol. 3. US Government Printing Office, p. 71.

15 Custalow, Linwood "Little Bear", and Angela L. "Silver Stair" Daniel. 2007. *The True Story of Pocahontas: The Other Side of History*. Fulcrum, p. 85.

16 Rountree, Helen C. 1990. *Pocahontas's People: The Powhatan Indians of Virginia Through Four Centuries.* University of Oklahoma Press, p. 73.
17 Neill, Edward D. 1869. *History of the Virginia Company of London.* Joel Munsell, p. 413.
18 Smith, John. 1622. *New England Trialls,* in Philip L. Barbour. 1986. *The Complete Works of Captain John Smith (1580–1631),* vol. 1. University of North Carolina Press, p. 432.
19 Smith. *The Generall Historie,* in *The Complete Works of Captain John Smith,* vol. 2, p. 474.
20 Smith, John. 1630. *The True Travels,* in Philip L. Barbour. 1986. *The Complete Works of Captain John Smith (1580–1631),* vol. 2. University of North Carolina Press, p. 176.
21 Sălăgean, Tudor, 2013. Personal communication, director, *Muzeul etnografic al Transilvaniei, Cluj-Napoca.*
22 This young age is partly determined by the high rate of infant mortality in this period, as about one in every three children died before their fifth birthday.
23 Smith, John. 1624. "Last Will", in Philip L. Barbour. 1986. *The Complete Works of Captain John Smith (1580–1631),* vol. 3. University of North Carolina Press, p. 383.
24 Delany, Paul. 1969. *British Autobiography in the Seventeenth Century.* Routledge, p. 10.
25 Ibid, p.108.
26 Smith, John. 1624. *Advertisments,* in Philip L. Barbour. 1986. *The Complete Works of Captain John Smith (1580–1631),* vol. 3. University of North Carolina Press, p. 270.
27 Ibid, p. 285.
28 Bell, John. 1665. *London's Dreadful Visitation: or, A Collection of All the Bills of Mortality for this Present Year: Beginning the 20th of December 1664 and Ending the 19th of December Following.* Cotes, June 6–13.
29 Barbour, Philip L. 1969. "A Note on the Discovery of the Original Will of Captain John Smith: With a Verbatim Transcription". *William and Mary Quarterly,* vol. 26, no. 4, pp. 625–8.
30 The church was named after the Holy Sepulchre in Jerusalem, and was first mentioned in 1137. It was rebuilt in 1450, but badly damaged in the Great Fire of 1666. The burnt-out shell was rebuilt by Wren's masons in 1670–1 and St Sepulchre's now stands as the largest church in the city of London.
31 Smith. *The Generall Historie,* in *The Complete Works of Captain John Smith,* vol. 2, p. 317.

Epilogue

1 Herbert, George and John Cotton, 1867. "Epitaph to Captain John Smith" in *Proceedings of the Massachusetts Historical Society,* vol. 9, 1866–7, p. 455.

2 Lloyd, David. 1631. *The Legend of Captain Iones*, pt. 1. Humphrey Moseley, frontispiece.
3 Lloyd, David. 1648. *The Legend of Captain Iones*, pt. 2. Richard Marriot frontispiece.
4 Armstrong, Catherine. 2007. *Writing North America in the Seventeenth Century: English Representation in Print and Manuscript*. Ashgate, p. 186.
5 Webster, Noah. 1791. *The Little Reader's Assistant*. William Butler, p. 12.
6 Kendall, Joshua. 2011. *The Forgotten Founding Father: Noah Webster's Obsession and the Creation of an American Culture*. Putnam.
7 The *trompe l'oeil* was designed by the Italian artist Constantino Brumidi, who created the original sketch in 1859. However, the actual painting of the frieze on the Rotunda was not authorized until 1877. Two other artists were involved, Filippo Costaggini and Allyn Cox.
8 Palfrey, John Gorham. 1858. *History of New England*, vol. 1. Little, Brown, p. 89.
9 Deane, Charles (ed.). 1860. "Edward Maria Wingfield's *A Discourse of Virginia*". *Archaeologica Americana*, p. 33.
10 Adams, Henry. 1867. "Captain John Smith". *North American Review*, January, pp. 1–30.
11 n.a. 1869. "Review of *A Discourse of Virginia* by Edward Maria Wingfield and *A True Relation of Virginia by Capt. John Smith*". *Southern Review*, July, pp. 160–81.
12 Kropf, Lewis L. 189. "Captain John Smith of Virginia," *Notes and Queries*, ser. 7. no. 9, (January 4, 18, February 8, March 1, 22, April 12, 1890), 1–2, 41–43, 102–104, 161–62, 223–24, 281–82.
13 Striker, Laura Polanyi. 1953. "Captain John Smith's Hungary and Transylvania", in Bradford Smith. 1953. *Captain John Smith: His Life & Legend*. Lippincott, pp. 311–42.
14 Barbour, Philip L. 1986. *The Complete Works of Captain John Smith (1580–1631)*, vol. 3. University of North Carolina Press, p. 125.
15 Conti, Brooke. 2014. *Confessions of Faith in Early Modern England*. University of Pennsylvania Press, p. 9.
16 Hoobler, Dorothy, and Thomas Hoobler. 2006. *Captain John Smith: Jamestown and the Birth of the American Dream*. Wiley, pp. 173–4.
17 Smith, John. 1608. *A True Relation*, in Philip L. Barbour. 1986. *The Complete Works of Captain John Smith (1580–1631)*, vol. 1. University of North Carolina Press, p. 31.
18 Smith, John. 1631. *Advertisements*, in Philip L. Barbour. 1986. *The Complete Works of Captain John Smith (1580–1631)*, vol. 3. University of North Carolina Press, p. 272.
19 Ibid, p. 287.

Index

References to illustrations are in *italics*.

About the Author

Peter Firstbrook is author of *The Voyage of Matthew* (about the explorer John Cabot), *Lost on Everest* (about George Mallory), and *The Obamas: The Untold Story of an African Family*. For twenty-five years, he worked for the BBC as a television producer, director and executive producer specializing in historical documentaries. He has won over thirty international awards, including the Royal Television Society award for best documentary, twice. He lives in West London.